Volume 4 / Issue 25-26
April-May 2016

THE SPRING SPECIAL

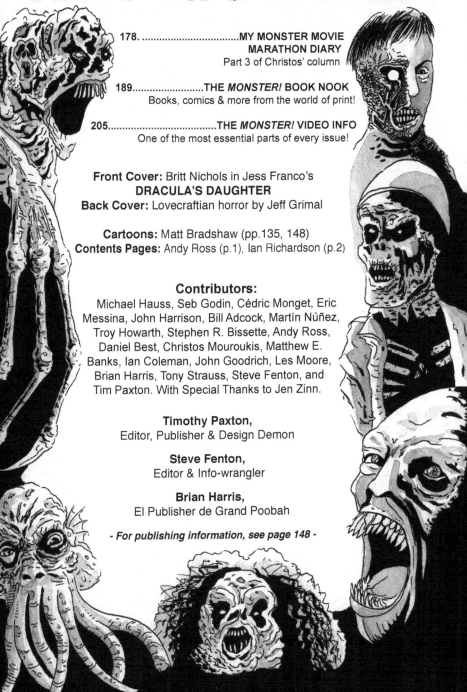

MONSTER!

Front Cover: Britt Nichols in Jess Franco's
DRACULA'S DAUGHTER
Back Cover: Lovecraftian horror by Jeff Grimal

Cartoons: Matt Bradshaw (pp.135, 148)
Contents Pages: Andy Ross (p.1), Ian Richardson (p.2)

Contributors:

Michael Hauss, Seb Godin, Cédric Monget, Eric Messina, John Harrison, Bill Adcock, Martín Núñez, Troy Howarth, Stephen R. Bissette, Andy Ross, Daniel Best, Christos Mouroukis, Matthew E. Banks, Ian Coleman, John Goodrich, Les Moore, Brian Harris, Tony Strauss, Steve Fenton, and Tim Paxton. With Special Thanks to Jen Zinn.

Timothy Paxton,
Editor, Publisher & Design Demon

Steve Fenton,
Editor & Info-wrangler

Brian Harris,
El Publisher de Grand Poobah

- For publishing information, see page 148 -

Welcome to the first ever *Monster!* Spring Combo Special. And I am hoping it will be the last. Honestly, we want to keep this zine on track as a monthly publication, but due to a number of unforeseen events, that just didn't happen. Issue #28 was going to be our Lovecraftian Horrors Vol. 2, and that was shaping up nicely with reviews and article lined-up for inclusion. Issue #29 was scheduled to be a good ol'-fashioned mix of the usual lovely monsterific material, with much of it focusing on an assortment of vampire-related flicks. But that didn't happen, so you hold in your hands the *Monster!* Spring Combo Special. With *two* cover variants, yet!

Now, as a preview for next issue I would like to welcome Cédric Monget to our staff. I have included in this editorial the first of many reviews that we are in the process of translating from their original French into English. I had hoped to have two reviews and an article from Monget, however the translation process has taken a lot longer than I had anticipated. There is more than just plugging a review or article into Google Translate or Babelfish and expect something worthwhile in return. There's a big difference between translating and transliteration. The review below is Cédric's first in a series on HPL-related short films (of which there are legion), and by *Monster!* #30 we should also have his article "Japanese Cinema and its Lovecraftian Elements" *[sic]* ready, too. ~**Tim Paxton**

Nyarlathotep

Reviewed by Cédric Monget

USA, 2001. D: Christian Matzke

"Nyarlarhotep" by Christian Matzke is a near-perfect example of how a whole lot of money is not needed for producing excellent cinema, horror films included. "Nyarlarhotep" is 13 minutes of subtle terror which cost to complete, all in all, only $800. Of course, it is necessary to add that this is partly explained by the fact that the participants were all volunteers, and the time it took for Matzke to shoot the short *was* two years! With the little funds allocated to him, Christian Matzke succeeded on a level that many other directors were never able to achieve, even with budgets thousands of times higher.

Technically, what Matzke utilized to make the short was also comparably modest: a Sony Camcorder digital 8 and, as a means of aging the images, a computer program called "After Effects", which added graininess, changed the image to black-and-white, and thus eliminating the neatness of modern video. These were all the methods and means at Matzke's disposal, and the end result is more than suitable! Here we have the first pre-war-set film made in imitation of Lovecraft's style. "Nyarlathotep" was produced four years before "The Call of Cthulhu", the famous silent short feature made by the H.P. Lovecraft Historical society and directed by Andrew Leman, which was another period piece. Despite "Nyarlathotep" not being a silent film, as there is a voice heard on the audio track, the characters do not "talk", but the musical score is omnipresent. Add to this several decorated sets and period costumes, and Christian Matzke

Shot from the film *Nyarlathotep*. Nyarlathotep is one of Lovecraft's most well-known and more frequently-cited entities (possibly second only to Cthulhu). According to Leslie S. Klinger (The New Annotated H.P.Lovecraft, 2014), Nyarlathotep appears as a character in six of HPL's tales (cited in *https://lovecraftian-science.wordpress.com/2014/11/23/nyarlatho-tep-lovecrafts-dual-prespective-on-the-won-der-and-fear-of-science*)

has proven that it is not hard to recreate Lovecraft in his time (which was the 1920s and 30s), and everything works quite well.

This short was inspired by the short story "Nyarlathotep", one of Lovecraft's earlier works (first published in the November 1920 issue *of The United Amateur*). This choice of source material was perhaps a little strange to base a film on. It is often said that the writings of Lovecraft are impossible to film, and in this case is not even really a story, properly speaking, but a fragment from his "dream cycle". Lovecraft himself said that it was a dream he wrote down before he was even truly awake. Thus, there is practically no real action as the narrator/protagonist just passively communicates

3

what is occurring around him, and unfortunately what happens is never even clearly-defined. This correlates perfectly to the tradition of a "poem in prose" as it is used to transmit an emotion, a sentiment, a perception, of course. But how would you translate this into a *cinematographic* format? In the case of his film, Matzke uses a very simple method of storytelling by reviving the ancient origins of cinema, as seen during the era of "prehistoric cinema". Before the advent of moving pictures there were the magical lanterns, which were the spectacles of fantastic optical theatre. This makes for a short film, more destined to simply *tell* a story rather than actually *show* it. What is the true subject of Nyarlathotep? It is about a man who is a monster, but of human appearance. Truthfully, this precisely lends itself to this type of phantasmagorical spectacle.

In the film, our heroic narrator is Dr. Burke (played by Christian Matzke himself), who tells the tale of witnessing one of these magical lantern shows provided by the mysterious Egyptian, Nyarlathotep (Dan Harrod). Playing the postmodern pedantic, Matzke beautifully places himself in that void made by a film's director casting himself in a small film within his own film! And *what* does this film-within-a-film show us? Little is clearly-defined for us, although a lot is suggested. We must go back

a little in history… The world in which this story was created is not quite the 1920s in America, the date for which the text is noted. The social and political contexts of the story are very tense—more tense than historically existed, without doubt. There are soldiers in the streets, announcements of traitors on the walls of buildings, without defining precisely what are these so-called traitors' acts of treason. Therefore, the people are restless, troubled, and sick; to which is shown, for their entertainment, a spectacle presented by the sulfurous presence of Nyarlathotep, a showman who seems to be a construct of the Frères Lumières, the oddball Italian adventurer Alessandro Cagliostro, and the brilliant-but-mysterious Serbian scientist of the era, Nikola Tesla.

But the spectacle presents nothing entertaining: it includes disconcerting images of horror—electrical phenomena, plus footage of a nuclear test (without a doubt images from the atomic tests conducted at Desert Rock, Nevada between 1951-57). The public are terrified by what they see, and flee. In the chaos that follows, Dr. Burke loses his glasses, as we see him searching for them practically prone on the ground. At the moment he finds them, we see a giant crustaceous *pincer* grabbing at him. He screams—albeit silently—his reaction completely conveyed by Derek C.F. Pegritz's excellent, strident music.

Finally, everyone is reunited on the outside and are trying to comfort one another. In fact, everyone decides to return to their homes, but will the city still be the same? Not quite. Henceforth, the new world appears almost dead, sterilized, powerless. An inexplicable snow covers everything and reflects the light from a gibbous moon. All of these details are from Lovecraft's text, but Christian Matzke adds an extra pinch of salt. In showing a silhouette on the ocean and the narrator's hat floating at the edge of the clouds, he suggests his suicide. Beyond what the film recounts, just as in the film of "Nyarlathotep" itself, the archives of images reflect WWII, or possibly the world immediately after the war, and natural catastrophes (volcanic or solar eruptions, etc). This paradox—the narrator's death before the end of the narration—is used by Matzke to show the inherent limits of adapting a prose poem to cinema, but also demonstrates Matzke's talents in doing so.

In summation, this first attempt is the attempt of a master, and Christian Matzke makes a formidable Lovecraft cinematographer indeed! He revealed all the correct measures of his talent later in his 2005 short, "Experiment 17". Hopefully someday he will have at his disposal a sufficient budget to truly showcase his talent!

WANTED! More Readers Like Colin & Alexander "Sasha" Theodore Daigoro Geddes (born April 5, 2016)

Slimetime! One of The Deep Ones gives us the fisheye in **DAGON**

DAGON
(*Dagon, la secta del mar*)

Reviewed by Brian Harris

Spain, 2001. D: Stuart Gordon

Five Lovecraft films: Gordon sure loves his HPL adaptations, doesn't he?! You can't deny his passion for the source material, that's for sure. I do believe he holds the unique distinction of being the director with the most feature-length Lovecraft films under his belt. He's undoubtedly given us some of the most memorable adaptations available. It's rare to not hear **RE-ANIMATOR** mentioned when someone rattles off their favorite horror films.

Much like his Full Moon production **CASTLE FREAK** (1995, USA [see *Monster!* #27, p.28]), 2001's **DAGON** receives far less adoration from the fans than his first two adaptations (**RE-ANIMATOR** [1985], **FROM BEYOND** [1986]),

or even his last (the *Masters of Horror* episode "Dreams in the Witch-House" [2005, all USA]). Honestly, I can't imagine why. Outside of a small misstep or two, **DAGON** is exactly the kind of bleak, gruesome horror that fans have come to expect from Gordon.

A beautiful day spent sailing off the coast of Spain turns to disaster for Paul Marsh (Ezra Godden, "Dreams in the Witch-House"), his girlfriend Barbara (Raquel Meroño, **BENEATH STILL WATERS** [*Bajo aguas tranquilas*, 2005, Spain/ USA, D: Brian Yuzna]) and their friends Howard (Brendan Price, **THE NAMELESS** [*Los sin nombre*, 1999, Spain, D: Jaume Balagueró]) and Vicki (Birgit Bofarull), when a freak storm rolls in, dashing their boat against some rocks. Caught off-guard by the collision, Vicki ends up pinned to the floor of the cabin by the pierced hull. With the water rising fast and Vicki desperately in need of medical attention, Paul and Barbara volunteer to go ashore to seek help, leaving Howard to comfort his wife.

Top: Australian/New Zealand DVD cover.
Center: One of **DAGON**'s Deep Ones goes even deeper. **Above:** Weirdly alluring "mermaid" Uxía (Macarena Gómez) spews up some cheesy CG tentacles in the same film

The dilapidated coastal village—here named Imboca instead of Innsmouth ("Imboca" being its loose Spanish translation)—appears to be abandoned, but they're able to find a priest (Ferran Lahoz, **THE MACHINIST** [*El maquinista*, 2004, Spain/USA, D: Brad Anderson]) in the local church ("Esoterica Orde De Dagon") willing to help. He arranges for a fishing boat to take Paul out to help Howard and Vicki, while Barbara is directed to the local hotel to get a room. It doesn't take long for Paul to discover that his friends are no longer on the boat, or anywhere to be seen. Assuming they're dad, he heads back to shore, where the priest informs him that Barbara has gone to find the police in the next village and he's to wait at the hotel.

Upon reaching the hotel, Paul has a rather awkward one-sided conversation with the odd owner and spies Barbara's lighter lying on the front desk. As if things couldn't get any more suspicious, he notices what appear to be *gills* on the hotelier's neck! Unsure of what he's just seen, he makes his way to the room: a filthy, unkempt hovel that looks as if it hasn't been occupied in years. Despite the squalor, he passes out, only to be startled awake soon after by a nightmare featuring a beautiful young woman he's been having reoccurring dreams about. Upon heading to the window to get some air, he sees dozens of villagers, limping and staggering about in the rain. His curiosity turns to panic, though, when they spot him and make their way into the hotel. Unable to keep them from entering his room, Paul leaps through a window, crashing through the skylight of a building below. Instead of safety, he finds the skin of his friend Howard, and the mob discovers him. He narrowly escapes their clutches by setting a fire in the building and running for it.

As Paul slips away into the night, he runs into an old drunk named Ezequiel (respected Spanish thespian Francisco Rabal, of **NIGHTMARE CITY** [*Incubo sulla città contaminata*, 1980, Italy/Spain/Mexico, D: Umberto Lenzi], in his final film; he died the year it was produced) and forces the indigent to share Imboca's horrifying secret: a past filled with strange pagan rites and human sacrifice, all in the service of a watery god named... Dagon.

Armed with the truth, including Ezequiel's assurance that Barbara is dead, Paul decides to unsuccessfully steal the only vehicle in town and flee. Instead he's forced into the estate of the car's owner, where he discovers the owner's daughter Uxía (Macarena Gómez, **SEXYKILLER** [*Sexykiller, morirás por ella*, 2008, Spain, D: Miguel Martí])—none other than the very woman he's been seeing in his dreams! Though she assures him that he's safe, and that she's also dreamed of him, he's too revolted by her hideous secret and, once again, does a runner. His final attempt to escape lands him right into the hands of the priest and his unholy minions, whereupon he learns that Barbara, Vicki and Ezequiel are all alive and well, and captives as well. The disciples of Dagon need human sacrifices to call forth their god, and Uxía has a special plan for Paul and friends...

DAGON really never lets up, so don't expect any cheap scare gags or comedic moments to let things simmer down. The tension just continues mounting, as Paul plays cat-and-mouse with his pursuers. I'm always on the edge of my seat when watching it, though I must admit that one of the issues I have with this film is the tedious "run, Paul, run" formula. It gets old, but that's just me. When you take it all in—the rain, the mind-blowingly cool location (shot in Galicia, Spain), the darkness, the chase and the monstrous villagers—you really get a sense of the alien world that Gordon was attempting to create. Imboca is a place out of time, caught in the clutches of an ancient, interdimensional monster just biding its time, waiting for the right moment to return to the surface.

If pagan religion, murder, monster rape, mutations, mutilations and incest sound like something you wouldn't mind checking out, you are one sick puppy! Who am I kidding: you're gonna *love* it! In one particular sequence—the gorehounds have *gotta* appreciate this—we get a shocking "facelift" that's quite impressive, considering the movie's 15 years old. The FX work, done by a crew of Spanish effects artists, was really on point. Outside of a few "wobbly" B-movie tentacles, this looked damn *cool.* The same cannot be said for the visual effects though, as the CGI was atrocious. I understand the budget was a little under $5 million and low-budget productions could only get so much from CGI back in 2000/2001, but ugly is ugly. Don't let it get you down though, as there's really not that much, so that's a plus.

Now, here's where I get mean. The acting was quite good, campy when needed but always more than adequate. However, Ezra Godden was, in my opinion, the low-point of this film. Imagine an amalgamation of Jerry Lewis, Robert Carradine's Lewis Skolnick (from **REVENGE OF THE NERDS** [1984, USA, D: Jeff Kanew]) and Joe Pantoliano, now yank out any charisma there, and—yep—that's Paul. He's hard to sympathize with, and perhaps that was Gordon's intention, to not have us get to know or like him; who knows. Whatever the case may be, he's not a likable

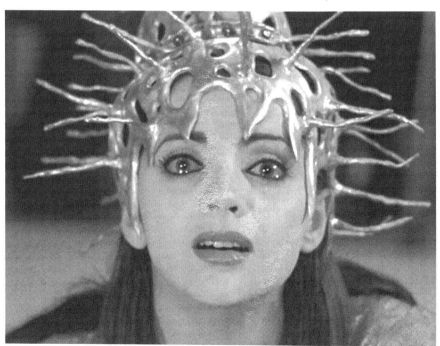

Do The Macarena? "You are my brother. You will be my lover... *forever!*' – In **DAGON**, *señorita* Gómez as sexy, sea-dwelling siren Uxía expresses the love that dare not speak its name to her incestuous romantic interest, the landlubber Paul (Ezra Godden)

H.P. LOVECRAFT'S
THE **COLOR**
OUT OF **SPACE**

character, and considering he's the lead, it sort of makes it hard to emotionally invest. That's all me, though; you all may find him far more tolerable.

In the end, I'm sure **DAGON** could be improved upon, but then what film couldn't? Still, I think it kicks all kind of ass (mutated or not) and it really does a great job of merging Lovecraft's "Dagon" with "The Shadow Over Innsmouth". If you're a fan of both Stuart Gordon's and Lovecraft's work, you're going to need to own this gem. Sadly, it's not available here in the States on Blu-ray, so no HD goodness yet. We may well see the return of Dagon himself before we ever see Lionsgate remastering this one, but you never know...

THE COLOR
OUT OF SPACE
(*Die Farbe*)

Reviewed by Tony Strauss

Germany, 2010. D: Huan Vu

There's just *something* about the unique atmosphere and enigmatic dread of H.P. Lovecraft's work that captures the imagination, and begs for it to be realized in a visual medium (amusingly ironic, when one considers the frequency with which the author himself labeled his horrors as "too horrible to describe" in the very narratives that

presented them). His tales were bursting with monsters and terrors of both terrestrial and cosmic origins, unheard of and unimagined by any other mythologies referenced or created by his peers, and it's a testament to his skills as a storyteller that he is not only remembered today, but his work is still the source of many a nightmare for readers from every generation since his death. It's no surprise, then, that there've been so many attempts at adapting his stories to the screen over the years, in varying degrees of quality, success, and faithfulness to source material. Indeed, the fact that most casual readers have even heard of Lovecraft today can be attributed to the resurgence in popularity his work has experienced due to the success of successful cinematic adaptations of his stories leading to enough demand to justify his bibliography remaining in-print.

Though the most well-remembered and culturally-referenced Lovecraft stories by far are those involving the Cthulhu Mythos and the tales of the Great Old Ones, in the realm of cinema most people are most familiar with the adaptations from the Stuart Gordon/Brian Yuzna camp (the *Re-Animator* films, **FROM BEYOND** [1986], **DAGON** [2001; see p.5 this ish], etc.), perhaps the most well-regarded and successful tale he ever penned was "The Colour out of Space", a short story which was originally published in the September 1927 issue of *Amazing Stories*. A chilling story of an alien force's insidious infestation of a remote valley, it was born out of Lovecraft's frustration with the sci-fi stories of his time's uninspired and lazy insistence on presenting all-too-humanesque alien life-forms; so he decided to bring to earth a terror of a *truly* alien nature. Lovecraft himself famously named it as his personal favorite of all his stories, and many a reader, literary critic, and HPL scholar seems to feel the same.

Despite the fact that the story has been declared "unfilmable" more than a few times, there have been a fair number of attempts made at bringing "The Colour out of Space" to the screen. The 1965 Daniel Haller-helmed/Karloff-headlined **DIE, MONSTER, DIE!** (a.k.a. **MONSTER OF TERROR**) was based on it, though it's a fairly "free" adaptation of the material, and—despite the fact that it's not a terrible little B-picture in and of itself—if truth be told, it completely misses the mark in terms of the atmosphere of paranoia, dread, and otherworldly nature of the threat which was intended with the original story. In 1987, actor-*cum*-director David Keith took a shot at it with **THE CURSE**[1], starring Will Wheaton, which was a bit more faithful to the story than Haller's attempt,

1   See *Monster!* #27, p.31 and *Weng's Chop* #6, p.55.

and did a better job at capturing the paranoid atmosphere, but again, despite it being a decent B-horror, it kind of derailed at the end and didn't quite capture that Lovecraftian magic that makes the original tale so effective and memorable. The Italian indie film **COLOUR FROM THE DARK** (2008), directed by Ivan Zuccon, took another go, but was a disappointing example of ambition being bigger than ability, both in technique and budget.[2]

Then, in 2010, along comes a group of German university students with an adaptation which started out as a student film project and ballooned into a full-length feature—and things get *really* interesting...

By far the most faithful cinematic presentation of the story to date (though a fair number of embellishments are added), the German film, written and directed by Huan Vu, transplants the story from late-19th Century Arkham, Massachusetts to rural pre- and post-WWII Germany, with a (somewhat superfluous) framing story taking place in the 1970s. It at least begins in Arkham, with an American man named Jonathan Davis (Ingo Heise) being informed that his apparently mentally frail father has suddenly flown to Frankfurt for reasons unknown. Jonathan, confused and concerned for his dad's well-being, follows, and tracks his trail to a remote village which, due to the planned flooding of the nearby valley, is only accessible via a bumpy, overgrown backwoods "road". Arriving to find the village eerily quiet, he visits a tavern to show around photos of his missing father. Nobody recognizes the most recent photo, but one man, a particularly morose local by the name of Armin Pierske (Michael Kausch), startles Jonathan by claiming to recognize a wartime photo of the elder Davis, saying he met him when Armin (played in flashback by Marco Liebnitz) returned from the war to find American soldiers—Jonathan's then-field medic father (Ralph Lichtenberg) among them—investigating the Pierske farm as a possible temporary housing for refugees. They asked him if anyone lived down in the nearby valley, and young Pierske immediately panicked, urging them not to go down there. Suspicious of his behavior, they arrested him and forced him to accompany them while they investigated the valley.

Pierske's tale then jumps back to just before the war, back when the village was relatively normal, and not the macabre version of its former self that it later became. The trouble all started one night

What color is that?

Top: Lancer Books' late '60s paperback edition (art by Virgil Finlay). **Above & Center:** Even the brainiacs of science can't figure out what the hell the "colour" is

---

2   There was also a French TV adaptation in 1983 called *La couleur de l'abîme*, but despite the fact that what I've seen of it didn't look too impressive in terms of atmosphere and mood, I can't knowledgeably comment on it, as I was unable to find a version with English subtitles.

when a meteor fell out of the sky and landed on the valley farmland of Nahun Gärtener (Erik Ratstetter) and his family. When scientists arrived to investigate, they found at the bottom of the impact crater a large rock with some extremely unusual properties. Being made of a substance they could not identify or classify, the rock was radiating heat with no indication of ever cooling, and was rapidly shrinking. The samples they took back to the lab for study yielded little discovery, and continued shrinking until they had completely disappeared by the next day. When the investigators returned to the site for more samples, they cracked open the ever-shrinking meteorite to discover a glowing sphere inside of an unusual color…a color never seen on earth and impossible to describe. The additional samples taken by the science team again yielded no useful results, but that night, there was a great storm in the valley, with the lightning focused directly into the crater, as if the meteor was drawing it into itself. The next morning, the lab samples had again evaporated into nothingness, and when the scientists returned to the crater, the meteor itself was also gone, with only charred earth left to mark its place.

Things soon returned more-or-less to a state of normalcy in the village, the strange incident seemingly forgotten…until months later when, at harvest time, Gärtener revealed to his friend Pierske that his crops had grown to enormous size. Pierske eagerly accepted the offer of a football-sized pear and took a big bite, but he immediately spat it out—it had a foul taste to it. It didn't take long to verify that seemingly every bit of this strangely enormous-sized crop was inedible. Gärtener was devastated; he still had good crops from the hillside land, but everything he grew in the valley where the meteor struck—which made up the bulk of his farmable land—was ruined, and that represented a huge financial loss for his family.

Over the next few weeks, the village saw less and less of the Gärtener family, and on the rare occasions that any members of the family did visit the town, they were ignored and shunned by the townsfolk, who seemed to sense that something wasn't right with them, although not knowing exactly what. Pierske still maintained occasional friendly contact with Nahun, helping him with his in-town errands and so forth, and witnessed with his own eyes

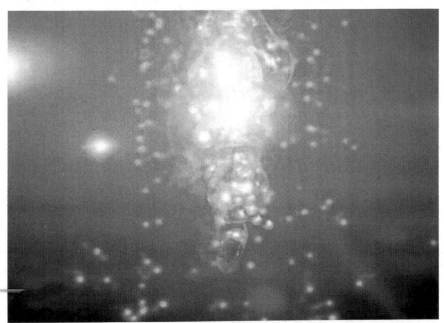

Digital effects are used judiciously in **THE COLOR** [sic!] **OUT OF SPACE**, and their very sparseness works well within the context to convincingly convey some of the eerie otherworldliness found in HPL's original 1927 short story: *"Then without warning the hideous thing shot vertically up toward the sky like a rocket or meteor, leaving behind no trail and disappearing through a round and curiously regular hole in the clouds before any man could gasp or cry out. No watcher can ever forget that sight, and Ammi stared blankly at the stars of Cygnus, Deneb twinkling above the others, where the unknown colour had melted into the Milky Way"*

some ominous things. First, Mrs. Gärtener (Marah Schneider) had gone near-catatonic, always just staring off at nothing, completely unresponsive to outside stimulus. Then, young Thaddäus Gärtener (Jonas Zumdohme) began hallucinating, forcing Nahun to lock up his wife and son in their own house for safety. And then there were the strange lights glowing at night out in the field—lights of that otherworldly, indescribable color from inside the meteor.

After going two full weeks without hearing from Nahun, Pierske decided to visit the Gärtener farm to check up on his friend, and what he discovered there was far more horrifying than any spoiled crop or strange lights in the fields. He witnessed true horror that day—a horror not born of this Earth...

For a film that is not only a blown-up low-budget student film, but one that tells its story in a flashback-within-a-flashback framework, this movie handles its narrative surprisingly well, and is for the most part quite easy to keep up with as it jumps to and fro between timeframes. That alone is impressive, but then add to that the fact that this movie so skillfully pulled off what so many bigger and more experienced productions have for the most part universally failed to do—actually capturing and conveying the absolutely essential atmosphere of confusion, paranoia and terror that is required to do this or pretty much any Lovecraft story proper justice—and what you've got here is a pretty damned solid home-run of a movie.

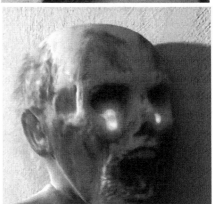

Presented in black-and-white with exception to "the color" itself[3], the directing is confident and skilled, and does an excellent job both constructing and servicing the thick and gloomy atmosphere that just oozes from every corner of this picture. The acting, although occasionally uneven (and suffering from a bit of linguistic awkwardness when characters converse in English, being that it's an all-German cast), is generally quite good, and Vu shows that he knows how to utilize his talent and play to their skills, never asking more than they can handle, so even what one would consider the worst of the acting is never really too bad at all. The budgetary restraints might cause OCD historians to notice the occasional anachronisms here and there, but I myself had no problem suspending disbelief when it came to the period settings. Nitpicky Nellies might also scoff at some of the less-than-perfect CGI effects, but they really are just "less-than-perfect" rather than actually bad,

Ever-so-slowly, odd things begin happening to a poor family of farm folk, the Gärteners. A bizarre blight has infected their crops, strangely oversized insects seem to exert control over them, and eventually they themselves begin to be consumed by the inexplicable alien force in their midst

---

3   For this ever-important effect, the film wisely chose to not use the color green—as might well have been an easy goto for the "indescribable" color—but instead used a multifaceted shade of pinkish purple, which really goes a long way toward lending the color an "otherworldly" effect.

and the rough edges are generally smoothed over by the B&W presentation. Given the admittedly limited conditions under which this was made, Vu and his team really show adept skills at finding ways to make their weaknesses into strengths, and end up delivering a genuinely topnotch adaptation of one of Lovecraft's most-beloved stories.

As I mentioned previously, there are some embellishments added to the material, most of which work well, though the film does tack-on one additional "twist" that I felt was unnecessary, but it by no means detracted from my enjoyment of the film, and after having watched and thoroughly enjoyed this film three times through now, I believe I can comfortably name it as my all-time favorite screen adaptation of Lovecraft. Even if you don't agree with me on that particular qualification, you'll find yourself having a difficult time denying the film's entertainment value and unquestionable

merit as part of the cinematic Lovecraft canon. For serious HPL fans, this one warrants an outright purchase, and will end up being a cherished entry in your Lovecraft movie library.

THE PROJECTED MAN

Reviewed by Steve Fenton

UK, 1966. Ds: Ian Curteis, John Croydon

Narration from stateside distributor Universal Pictures' US trailer: *"A brilliant scientist submits himself to a machine to prove his theory... with disastrous results! ...Suspense! ...Shock! Science runs amuck when human beings tamper with unknown forces! ...Explosive scenes, as Nature's forces demonstrate their superior power against Man's efforts to interfere with the normal order of mind and matter. A shattering suspense film to rivet your attention, from its dramatic opening to its devastating climax. Be sure you see this terrific film!"*

Another rarely-screened—at least until recent years, that is—slice of '60s British mediocrity, co-

presented by the moderately prolific Tony Tenser (who also had his hand in **THE BLOOD BEAST TERROR** [see p.25] and numerous other British films, especially those of the "psychotronic" kind; **TBBT** was scripted by Peter Bryan, who also had his pen-hand in the screenplay of the present title under review). While he only produced just over 30 films between 1961 and '74, Tenser (1920-2007)'s lasting filmic legacy includes a goodly number of prime horror and/or exploitation titles. Debatably his "finest hours" came via working in a producer's capacity on both Roman Polanski's **REPULSION** (1965) and **CUL-DE-SAC** (1966, both UK); although in the minds of many more horror-oriented movie buffs, he is likely equally—if not more-so—remembered for his producing chores on cult icon Michael Reeves' **THE SORCERERS** (1967) and **WITCHFINDER GENERAL** (1968, both UK). Speaking of Reeves, it has been reported that he derived some inspiration for that former film—a mod/psychedelic psychological shocker set in Swinging 'Sixties London, starring an aged Boris Karloff—from **THE PROJECTED MAN** (presumably its "futuristic" projection equipment alone, because there really aren't any similarities of plot or theme that I could detect).

Prof. Paul Steiner (the pock-faced, weak-chinned if nonetheless still strangely photogenic/charismatic Bryant Haliday, best-known to many as seedily sinister ventriloquist "The Great Vorelli" from **DEVIL DOLL** [1964, UK, D: Lindsay Shonteff]) toils diligently on top secret experimentation in the lab of the prestigious if underfunded Farber Research Foundation. "I'm working on the conversion of solid objects into pure energy," comes the familiar scientific explanation. "(Energy, which can be) projected over long distances and then turned back into the object again." Five minutes into the tale, the script wastes no time in laying bare its roots: yes, with the previous year's **CURSE OF THE FLY** (1965, UK, D: Don Sharp) still fresh in their memories, another Limey production team came up with still another derivative by-product of Brit author George Langelaan's "The Fly" (first published in *Playboy*, June 1957 and first adapted to the silver screen by James Clavell under Kurt Neumann's direction the following year as **THE FLY**).

After his first "successful" experiment subject, a guinea pig (of the literal rather than figurative human variety) suddenly up and croaks shortly following being zapped through the zapper then reconstituted afterwards, Steiner calls in pathologist Dr. Patricia Hill (portrayed by prim, pointy-featured blonde Mary Peach, who received top billing) to study the effects of his

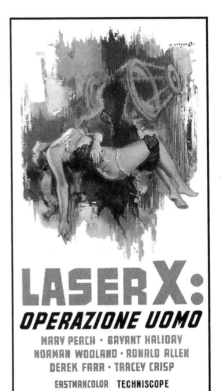

Italian *locandina* for **THE PROJECTED MAN**
(art by A. Cesselon)

laser-powered ray transmitter machine on the physiologies of potential human lifeforms rather than simple rodents. Rounding out the topnotch team of boffins on the project is Dr. Chris Mitchel (pompadoured, sleepy-eyed, square-jawed Ronald Allen, who looks like he might bust out a skiffle tune at any moment), also providing mandatory potential love interest for the peachy keen Ms. Peach. While not really known for much fantastic filmic fare other than our present title, the year following its production this popular South African-born actress co-starred opposite Patrick Troughton as the title character in the *Doctor Who* serial "The Enemy of the World" (1967-68, UK). **TPM** amounts to her sole bona fide creature feature. Like his co-star Peach and many another British-based actor before and since, the film's male protagonist Allen is likewise a *Who* alumnus, appearing opposite both Troughton in 1968's "The Dominators" serial and subsequently opposite "new" doc Jon Pertwee in the 1970 *DW* serial "The Ambassadors of Death").

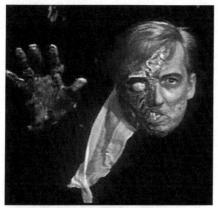

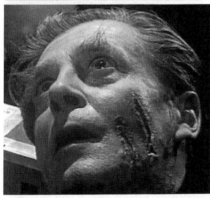

Top: The projected man, in all his grisly glory!
Center: Haliday prepares to put the shock-lock on the deserving Norman Woodland.
Above: Character actor Derrick De Marney (1906-1978) makes his final appearance in his final film

proverbial rug out from under Steiner's lifelong studies but literally pulling the plug on them too. As the bushy-bearded, bastardly Blanchard, Norman Woodland (who at times vaguely evokes a much more unctuous, unpleasant and untrustworthy version of Andrew Keir in his Prof. Quatermass characterization) perfectly conveys his smarmily smiley-faced if backstabbing bureaucrat character, who can go from being civilly condescending to an out-and-out authoritarian asshole without skipping a beat. Needless to say, nobody in his employ can stand the sight of this dickie-bow-tied dickhead… any more than we can the sight of Haliday in his post-transformative state, if for different reasons.

Hardly coming as much of a surprise, in order to retest his gear after a malfunction occurs during his demonstration due to sabotage by an unknown if strongly-suspected party, Steiner decides to go against the governing scientific body's official ruling and use himself as a human guinea pig to prove his theories ("If *only* I could do the same thing with a live creature!"). Lo and behold, after recklessly having the untrained, ditzy lab secretary operate the buttons while he lies on the transmission table under the zap-gun, he comes out the other end of the projector with the greater part of his face reduced to a grotty mess of tangled tissues: muscle, veins, nerve-endings and gristle all left painfully exposed; this with the added bonus of horribly-scorched hands possessing a lethal touch that enables him to emit deadly jolts of electricity at will (shades of Lon Chaney, Jr. as **MAN-MADE MONSTER** [a.k.a. **THE ELECTRIC MAN**, 1941, USA, D: George Waggner] or that same actor as **INDESTRUCTIBLE MAN** [1956, USA, D: Jack Pollexfen]).

The present film amounts to a quite tolerable effort, product of a less-jaded time when B-grade sci-fi wasn't yet afraid to utilize time-worn 1950s dramatic devices in a serious manner (rather than the trendy "spoof" or "camp" later fashion seen in prefab "cult" movies). Hell, there's even a played-straight scene in which the projected man lugs around a scantily-clad girl in his arms, this in the shapely form of Tracey Crisp, playing Sheila, the science project's perky secretary, who is interrupted while changing her clothes (*natch!*) and thereafter spends a good deal of her screen-time wearing nothing but her bra and panties (or "knickers", to use the vernacular). The smokin' hot Miss Crisp very nearly gets her shapely goose cooked but good after Steiner—his mean streak having been greatly accentuated and aggravated by his monstrous mutation/mutilation—locks her in her one-room bedsit flat with only a burning settee for company after he impulsively sets it afire with

Dr. Blanchard, the head of the institute, along with another jealous party seeking to discredit Steiner's research, sabotages the matter-transmission hardware during a crucial demonstration put on for the bigwigs. This has the desired result of the all-powerful "committee" pulling not only the

his electric clutch during a sudden flash of rage (it's far too late for him to take an anger management course at this stage, though).

Almost immediately following his botched molecular reconstitution, having been dematerialized in the lab then improperly rematerialized by the beam projector in a different part of town, the horribly-disfigured, electrically-charged Steiner proceeds to prowl London's darkened streets, offing anybody he encounters simply by touching them. Veteran Irish actors Derrick De Marney (1906-1978)—**TPM** was his final screen credit—and the super-prolific Sam Kydd (1915-1982), who was also seen in Val Guest's exemplary **THE QUA-TERMASS XPERIMENT** (a.k.a. **THE CREEP-ING UNKNOWN**, 1955, UK), play two of the man-monster's numerous victims. In fact, some elements of that first theatrical *Quatermass* franchise entry even come into play here, most especially in the scenes wherein Haliday as Steiner in his newly-mutated form prowls the city streets, pitiably horrific in appearance and in an understandable state of disorientation as a result of the traumatic rearrangement and "modification" his scrambled molecules have undergone.

With his unflattering newfound complexion and deadly electro-buzz handshake, Steiner and his accentuated (well-founded) paranoid feelings toward his treacherous colleagues go on a soul-purging, flesh-frazzling rampage. Remainder of

the movie depicts Steiner's mutated vendetta, as he brings down shocking electrical retribution on those whom he perceives have wronged him and, either wittingly or unintentionally, contributed to making him the monster he has become, largely as a result of his own overeager recklessness. While "The Projected Man" is indeed quite the sight to see—although he gets into the habit of concealing the mangled (right) side of his face behind bandages in-between kills, prior to which he "unveils" himself, for shock value—his method of murdering his victims isn't exactly very visually dynamic; all he does is barely come into contact with them using just one hand (after first slipping off its insulating rubber glove for the purpose). We then hear a slight, short sizzling sound, then the recipients of his first and last caress promptly keel over stone dead with little in the way of histrionics beforehand. Compounding matters, most of the murders are either lazily-framed or directed in such an offhanded manner that they don't register anywhere near as effectively as they should.

Stuntman-actor Alf Joint (1927-2005), whose many credits include episodes of such TV series as *Doctor Who* and *Space: 1999*, as well as the outrageous Hammer monster-fantasy **THE LOST CONTINENT** (1968, UK, Ds: Michael Carreras, Leslie Norman), plays a night-watchman who has a run-in with the electrified killer. Unaffected even by a hail of police gunfire—which only causes him to give off showers of sparks at each hit—Steiner repeatedly

Italian *fotobusta* for **THE PROJECTED MAN** (art by A. Cesselon)

eludes capture. However, the more energy his body discharges without the means of replenishing it, the more he weakens, like a battery gradually running down. The grand finale amidst zapping laser-blasts and explosive pyrotechnics seems to be striving for some sort of poetic poignancy. But for all its sound and fury, it registers rather too weakly for the closing act to make much of a lasting impression. (*SPOILER ALERT!*) Haliday's suicidal subhuman monstrosity simply fades away to nothingness in time for the final fade-out, and that's that.

Kenneth V. Jones' orchestral score largely sticks to standard horror motifs, with some obligatory Hammeresque strains periodically worked into the mix. Frankly, for the most part, his music, while competent enough, seems more suited to a period piece rather than a contemporaneous one with "hi-tech" elements such as this (I think perhaps some sort of *avant-garde* electronic soundtrack might have better fit the circumstances). The main strengths of **TPM** lie in the reliably professional sheen of the players' performances—the savior of many a low budget nonentity from the realm of absolute unwatchability. The unpolished, sub-Hammer look is quite well-suited to the material, while pretty gruesome (for the time) makeup adequately conveys a sense of "body horror" and stands up very well when compared to more latter-day prosthetic/CGI overindulgence. While pretty much of a similar grade as the same year's **THE BLOOD BEAST TERROR** quality-wise—if probably made on a slightly lesser budget, as it's not a period piece—**THE PROJECTED MAN** is every bit as modestly enjoyable, with some unspectacularly decent moments that stick in your memory.

This film was originally issued in the USA by Universal Pictures on a double-bill with Terence Fisher's **ISLAND OF TERROR** (1966, UK), which also featured the aforementioned Sam Kydd in a supporting part. Both John Croydon and Richard Gordon, veterans of several '50s B-monster classics (e.g., Arthur Crabtree's **FIEND WITHOUT A FACE** [1958] and Robert Day's **FIRST MAN INTO SPACE** [1959, both UK], each starring stodgy genre stalwart Marshall Thompson), were also involved in the project, the former actually functioning in an uncredited capacity as co-director, the latter also going without screen credit as a co-producer. Although he only mentions **TPM** twice in passing without going into any details about the film, Gordon does allude to his involvement on the project in an interview with him entitled "The Producer", which ran in issue #8 of the American fanzine *Bits & Pieces* (Summer 1993).

Whilst its title character most certainly looks like chopped liver (and then some!), the rest of

the production doesn't, thanks to adequate if economical set design and art direction. FX work is kept simple and works all the better for it, while the super-scientific hardware mandatory to such material appears a good deal more believably functional than usual (although they do sometimes overdo the spacey "sci-fi" sound effects and "futuristic" flashing lights from time to time).

Even while strictly going through the motions in a mostly rigidly formulaic manner without ever once deviating from its pre-set path and hitting all the usual stops along the way, **THE PROJECTED MAN** nevertheless emerges as entertaining enough and, like the **THE BLOOD BEAST TERROR**, appears that much better when viewed at its proper aspect ratio in a decent print on DVD.

NOTE: The original British version runs 86 minutes, which is substantially longer than that of Universal's stateside release, which only clocked-in at 77m.

CTHULHU MANSION
(*La mansión de los Cthulhu*)

Reviewed by Les Moore

Spain/UK, 1990. D: Juan Piquer Simón

Republic Pictures' Home Video VHS/Beta box hype: *"A magician's fascination with the forces of the dark side unleashes an ancient evil in CTHULHU MANSION, a supernatural thriller inspired by the writings of H.P. Lovecraft (THE RE-ANIMATOR, THE DUNWICH HORROR)."*

Yes indeed, that same facile and difficult-to-disprove claim "inspired by the writings of H.P. Lovecraft" also actually appears onscreen, so the producers were making no bones about attempting to pass this off (like the title wasn't obvious enough) as being in at least some way connected to his oeuvre.

Okay, okay, I know that any even remotely-devout HPL fans who might have actually bothered reading this far are likely turning up their noses and curling their lips in disgust merely from seeing the title alone, as it is generally regarded (or rather, reviled) as one of *the*—if not *THE*—crappiest, most pathetic (etc.) nominal adaptations of Lovecraft ever made. So if your nose is already beginning to get out of joint and turning up towards the ceiling, don't even bother reading any further, because this "objective" (but possibly also *sub*jective) appraisal from a non-purist, more casual Lovecraft fan is guaranteed not to appeal to that snobbish elitist kind who balks at the mere mention of **CTHULHU MANSION** and gets a look on their face like they just stepped into something nasty without any shoes on and nothing to wipe their foot off with. Because, do you wanna know what? Even though this is the second of *Monster!*'s primarily HPL-themed issues, rather than review this particular title through a would-be "Lovecraftian" (there goes *that* word again!) lens—which seems a fruitless cause anyway, as even an HPL novice like me can tell—I've instead elected to appraise it completely independently of the Mythos instead, to see how well (or not) it fares as a stand-alone item disconnected from Lovecraft's canon, rather than being lumped in with it simply by any associations of its unfortunate choice of title, which is purely nominal at best and ill-advised at worst. And just for the record, this makes the first time I've ever seen **CM** (it wasn't at the top of my viewing list, let's say), so I had neither any prior knowledge nor a single advance misconception about it other than knowing what low esteem in which it is generally held, not only by HPL buffs but by horror movie fans in general.

But first a bit of backstory about its woefully unsung director (who I've always kinda thought of in some ways as a loose Spanish equivalent of Italian hack director Alfonso Brescia, alias "Al Bradley")... All either Spanish or Spanish/American co-productions, J.P. Simón (1935-2011) helmed a number of cheapjack, often mercilessly-lambasted exploitative efforts within the horror/fantasy fields: firstly the daft, dino/giant ape-at-the-Earth's core opus **WHERE TIME BEGAN** (*Viaje al centro de la Tierra*, 1977); the even dafter, dopier superhero spoof (?) **SUPERSONIC MAN** (1979); the indescribably wacked-out pseudo-creature feature **MYSTERY ON MONSTER ISLAND** (*Misterio en la isla de los monstrous*, 1981); the trashy, splashy, splattery slasher schlocker **PIECES** (*Mil gritos tiene la noche*, 1982); the slimy, slithery ghastly Gastropoda gorefest **SLUGS: THE MOVIE** (*Slugs, muerte viscosa*, 1988); and, last but by no means least, the soggy aquatic monster mash **THE RIFT** (*La grieta*, a.k.a. **ENDLESS DESCENT**, 1990). *[Both those lattermost titles were reviewed, respectively, in* Monster! *#4 (p.26) and #15 (p.79) – ed.]*

Having previously seen every last one of JPS' other humble above-listed efforts and—call me easy to please!—enjoyed them all to varying degrees, I

Top: Brazilian VHS jacket for **CTHULHU MANSION** (art unsigned). **Center:** Frank "Chandu" Finlay communes with Cthulhu (*not!*)

17

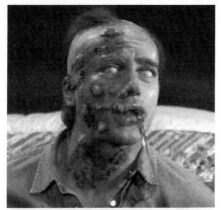

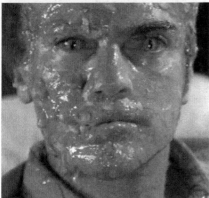

HPL Goes All To Heck: Luis Fernando Alvés *[top]* and Brad Fisher *[above]* in **CTHULHU MANSION**. If nothing else, at least the film's special makeup FX are real moist and squishy!

see absolutely no reason why (sight as yet unseen) I won't find at least some entertainment value here, whether it be a brainless bastardization which takes Lovecraft's hallowed name in vain or not. So, even though I'm approaching it from a "skewed" angle, I suppose you could say it fits the non-rigidly-structured guidelines for our second HPL special anyway. Since my *Monster!* mentor Steve F. has a bit of a soft spot for Simón's *canón del crud* himself *[Right smackdab in the center of my squudgy Velveeta® brain – SF]*, he was all for me giving my personal take on the current title, as, coincidentally enough, he just happens to have seen all those aforementioned JPS films but **CM**, too. So, feeling that the cosmic karmaic biorhythms (or whatever the fuck you wanna call 'em) were right, I figured why the hell not. So, for better or worse, here goes…

Rather than even bother coming up with any plot breakdown of my own this time out, I figured I'd

just transcribe the back cover copy to Republic's 1991 videocassette release verbatim instead (howzat for a time-saver!):

"When a gang of fugitive teenagers looking for a hide-out break into the forbidding estate of a carnival illusionist (Frank Finlay, LIFEFORCE), they unwittingly set free a long-buried demonic spirit from deep within the aging mansion. Feeding on fear, the satanic, primal forces of Cthulhu, the Devil's footsoldiers, now stalk the hallways in search of vengeance… As the inhabitants of the house begin to disappear in a series of gruesome attacks, the terror escalates to a frenzied pitch until the survivors are left begging—not for their lives—but for their deaths!"

That's it in a nutshell, and it looks pretty good on paper; at least, no worse than any thousand other direct-to-video releases that were around back in the day when this first hit the shelves.

Things kick off in promisingly sub-William Castlesque style with rumbling thunder and a way-over-exaggerated sound effect of a creaking door superimposed atop the main title (which is presented in a plain, stark white font on a black background, as are the rest of the credits). Sounds of whistling wind, frantic footsteps running up (or down) stone steps, a howling cat and shrieking woman then play behind the opening credits, with still no actual visuals being shown yet other than for the titles. More swooshing wind and other less-readily-identifiable sounds (some sort of gurgling?) are followed by—campiest of all—some hilariously overdone "spooky" laughter to do ol' master showman Wm. C. proud (that ghostly guffaw couldn't help but remind me of Castle's camp creepy old mansion classic **HOUSE ON HAUNTED HILL** [1959, USA], which may well have been JPS' express intention). At last the visuals proper begin, attended by the sinisterly ominous organ strains of Bach's "Toccata and Fugue in D minor", a singular piece of music which has likely been heard in more horror movies than just about any other classical composition (it is probably most famous to the average psychotronic movie geek as the main title theme to Norman Jewison's dystopian futuristic SF epic **ROLLERBALL** [1975, USA]).

Actually playing a character named Chandu decked-out in full *faux* "Eastern" get-up (white turban inclusive!), distinguished Brit star Frank Finlay (1926-2016)—who at times here resembles his countryman colleague, the late Pete Postlethwaite (1946-2011) both facially and vocally—enters from stage-right to stand in front of a diabolic pentagram and intone, "We are now on a long journey, a journey of no return, a journey into the shadows of the unknown: the dark side of life, into unknown dimensions..." However, it is shortly revealed to all only be part of his stage show, whose shtick includes Chandu levitating his beauteous female assistant-*cum*-lover, the psychically adept Leonor (lithe, lanky, leggy blonde Marcia Layton) into midair above the altar upon which she is lying while he reads aloud a Latin incantation from an ancient-looking text loudly marked "CTHULHU". During the magician's reading, not just the goat-headed pentagram bursts into flame, but poor altar-girl Leonor does as well. After this cheesy if promising opener, which is followed by some nicely-shot B&W flashbacks to Chandu and Leonor in happier days (i.e., when she was still living rather than getting roasted alive during a diabolic ceremony), we then proceed to the start of the plot proper—at which things suddenly take a sharp turn for the worst, and it looks like it might well be all downhill from there on in, judging by the procession of unlikable characters we are shortly introduced to. These leather-jacketed pseudo-punks/punkettes—more like wannabe "new wave" preppy poseurs—enter the picture with all the subtlety of a herd of bulls in a china shop after the comparatively classy introductory sequence. Rightly described as "little riffraff hoodlums" (by a lowlife cocaine dealer, of all people!), their ringleader Hawk (Brad Fisher) starts off their night of partying on a high note by shanking said dealer and making off with his quarter-kilo of blow.

Evidently not much of a griever, Finlay as Chandu has since the prologue hastily gotten himself a new assistant in the form of his daughter Lisa, who is the dead-spit of her late mother Leonor (and played by same actress Layton, natch). Hawk and gang, trapped in the amusement park by authorities following the dealer's murder and having nowhere to run to, commandeer Chandu's car, which now contains not just he and his assistant Felix (Francisco "Frank" Braña), but Lisa and no less than a half-dozen or so gang members, too; which is quite the load, even for a spacious American station-wagon (*circa* late-1970s model)! After forcing their hostages to help them at gunpoint, the entire party drives out to Chandu's isolated mansion ("It's like a goddamn museum!"), which does indeed say "Cthulhu" right on its front gate. Once inside this manse, the narrative settles into standard "old dark house" groove.

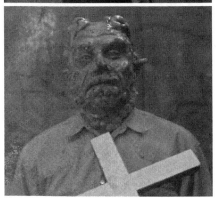

Cruz Control: As the intrepid magic-man Chandu, Finlay is right in his element dealing with lumpy-headed things from beyond

With Finlay billed on the top line to satisfy the British side of the production deal, even though there was apparently no Yank money sunk into this venture, we also get a number of American actors, including

Melanie Shatner (you-know-whose daughter; playing Hawk's boyishly bowlcut-haired #1 moll Eva) in the principal cast, all reading their lines in undubbed English; this was obviously a tactical ploy by the producers to ensure they secured a stateside deal (which they did, of sorts, if only on the home video market). Incidentally, **CM**'s casting director was no less than Viennese actor Werner Pochath

(1939-1993), who is likely best-known to many a Euro horror buff as the serial killer of Marijan Vajda's Swiss-made sickie **BLOODLUST** (*Mosquito der Schänder*, 1977), but who also appeared in plenty other Continental exploitation fare, including "Anthony Ascot"/Giuliano Carnimeo's ratty-ass mutant rodent creepy-cheapie **RAT MAN** (*Quella villa in fondo al parco*, 1988, Italy). As for **CM**, it also features frequent Simón employee Braña, who had appeared in all the director's other downscale horror/sci-fi cheapies. Looking beefy (and hairy!) in a black muscle-shirt, Braña helps out with Finlay's chintzy Chandu performances, including one wherein Layton—sealed inside a coffin—is seemingly impaled by a row of apparently telekinetically-controlled sabers which drop from above. Not only is this unconvincing bit of prestidigitation presented methodically and without any "magic" whatsoever, but the corny, too-emphatic and stereotypical "circus oompah" music heard in the background to this scene sounds distinctly out of place. Too much time is spent dwelling on Finlay's lame stage act, which comes across as all the lamer considering he is billed on his poster as "The Greatest Magician in the World".

It isn't until past the 50-minute point that any real supernatural shenanigans start up, typically "poltergeist activity" with objects being dragged or dangled on invisible wires and lots of loose sheets of newspaper being whipped about by wind machines to add to the terrifying effect (sarcasm alert!). During what for me was about the best scene in the film (by this point, just about *anything* would look good, simply by contrast), tertiary female lead Kaethe Cherney goes down to the kitchen for a midnight snack, whereupon—whilst observed impassively by a nearby black cat—she gets dragged inside the refrigerator by an otherwise unseen thing with giant knobby-knuckled claws. I was really hoping we'd get to see what was on the other end of those formidable talons at some point in the action, but… no such luck (☹); presumably all they did was make a pair of monster mitts, and that was that. Actually, I'd be willing to bet that said mitts were recycled leftovers from Simón's own aforementioned **THE RIFT**. In an earlier scene while a pair of obnoxious assholes are on a funfair haunted house ride, they pass by what appears to be a "refitted" leftover animatronic monster puppet from that same film (JPS' frequent SFX man Colin Arthur also worked on this one, so it seems perfectly plausible that some cost-cutting recycling was done on a cheapie such as this).

Nothing quite says "ominous old house" better than flaming front gates! (**CM**'s final image, which sums it up just perfectly. Roll end-credits!)

CM was executive-produced by paella exploitation cinema veteran José Gutiérrez Maesso, whose Eurotrash cinema credits are legion, most notably co-scripting or producing a number of key '60s spaghetti westerns, including Sergio Corbucci's seminal **DJANGO** (1966, Italy/Spain). While not generally known for producing horror fare, he did receive a credit in that capacity on **THE HOUSE OF EXORCISM** (known as *El diablo se lleva a los muertos* in Spain), the trashier 1975 reedit/alternate version of Mario Bava's eloquent occult thriller **LISA AND THE DEVIL** (*Lisa e il diavolo*, 1973, Italy/West Germany/Spain). For this reviewer, one of J.G. Maesso's most over-the-top and entertaining exploitationers— on which he served solely as its co-writer—is the consummately-grungy/gruesome Eurocrime actioner **RICCO** (*Un tipo con una faccia strana ti cerca per ucciderti*, a.k.a. **THE MEAN MACHINE** or **CAULDRON OF DEATH**, 1973, Spain/Italy, D: Tulio Demicheli), starring Chris Mitchum in the title role, which amounts to one of the absolute bloodiest, grimiest crimeslimers of the '70s (indeed, about the only genre entry to top it for splattering the red stuff all over the screen was Lucio Fulci's kickass **CONTRABAND** [*Luca il contrabbandiere*] in 1980).

Except for a rather ear-pleasingly delicate if derivative tinkling music-box piece heard a few times throughout, composer Tim Souster's score quite frankly mostly didn't fit the proceedings worth beans. Another thing I couldn't help noticing was that, while all the other hair on both Braña's head and the rest of his visible body parts (chest, arms and back included) is silvery grey, his "trademark" big bushy eyebrows and the "grampa"-style shoebrush 'stache he took to wearing in his later years are brunette, evidently having been dyed that color. Yes indeed, in formulaic, flabbily-paced flicks such as this, one often finds one's attention wandering to such trivial peripheral details as these when there's nothing more interesting onscreen to hold it. The scene where an unmanned manual typewriter begins automatically clacking out the name "Leonor" over and over again was clearly inspired by Nicholson's iconic "All work and no play makes Jack a dull boy" bit in Kubrick's **THE SHINING** (1980, USA), but only serves to remind us of how infinitely superior that film is to this one. In another scene (late into the 31st minute), the boom mike's shadow is clearly visible thrown on a wall above the actors' heads. Later still, Paul Birchard's pudgy, loud-mouthed Billy character goes to take a post-coital shower. Having only just supposedly doffed his boxers just outside the edge of the frame, as he steps into the stall we fleetingly glimpse the waistband of said garment,

UK VHS cover. ("From the Imagination of H.P. Lovecraft" indeed!)

still in place; not that I was in any way interested in seeing him actually *drop* 'em, you understand (I just wanted to make that clear. Oh, and just for the record for them who like that sort of thing, we do get a couple quick shots of his exposed male unit while he is drowning inside the stall, which fills up with blood-red water after the door "mysteriously" jams shut, trapping him inside). As if those other "Ed Woodisms" I mentioned above aren't enough, like he's channeling Wood's **PLAN 9 FROM OUTER SPACE** (1959, USA), in another scene the apparently highly self-destructive cokehead/dickhead Hawk scratches himself on the side of the skull with the muzzle of his revolver… with his finger on the trigger and the safety off, yet! A real comedian, not only does this same character unflatteringly call his brassy bitch secondary moll Candy (Cherney) "Miss Piggy" and a "little coke-whore", but he also takes to addressing Layton's fair-haired Lisa as "Goldilocks", Finlay's magician as "Mr. Magic" or "Chan-dude" and Braña's Felix character as "Popeye", evidently unimpressed by how much of a badass Braña—who looks like he could snap him in half easier than a stale Twiglet—had been as an actor-stuntman in umpteen spaghetti/paella westerns. As the stoic mute Felix herein, his character's inability to speak was clearly written into the script just so the Spanish-born actor wouldn't have to deliver any dialogue in the vernacular (he had done so on prior occasions, but his natural Castilian accent was so thick as to render his delivery of English lines at times difficult to understand; so, rather than bother dubbing him, they simply gave him none). Certain incidental bit-players are obviously English-dubbed Spaniards, although the vast bulk of the footage was to all appearances shot with live sound.

Here making his screen debut, Fisher—who at times rather resembles a sneerier, nastier version of new millennial tele-heartthrob Jared "*Supernatural*" Padalecki—admittedly gives a decent enough performance as the thoroughly despicable punk leader Hawk ("It's nothin' but 'hocus-pocus' shit!"), and he clearly had some natural acting ability, so it's rather surprising he only made a handful more appearances after this before evidently calling it quits for keeps in 2002 (though possibly he may have continued working on the stage?). Other than for Spanish-born player Luis Fernando Alvés, none of the rest of the supporting cast of Yankee youngsters barring Birchard worked much either before or after appearing in **CM**, so evidently having it on their CVs (assuming they even listed it on them!) didn't do anything for their careers. Even Ms. Shatner's career bottomed-out before she hit 20 credits. With all her pops' connections in the entertainment biz, you'd think she would have been able to forge some sort of a name for herself, if only on TV, but maybe she decided she simply wasn't cut out for the actor's life.

While it's most certainly no (to misquote HPL, from his *The Whisperer in Darkness*) "fantastic piece of bizarrery", as cheap, schlocky '80s horrors go, **CTHULHU MANSION** is not without its entertaining moments, although even as fake Lovecraft goes it rings far falser than most tenuous adaptations of his works, and that's sure saying something. But then, since it did have the audacity to take his name in vain (one can easily imagine the much-laureled author spinning in his grave like a top, going 78 rpm at least), when the wrought iron letters spelling out "C T H U L H U" atop the mansion's gate suddenly and inexplicably caught fire at the end—branding the movie's closing image on our brains—it was tempting to think of it as Lovecraft's angry spirit expressing his posthumous opinion of the filmmakers' efforts.

Come to think of it, that might make an interesting plotline for a movie in which, thanks to The Old Ones, HPL is returned to the world of the living in order to wreak monstrous retribution on a hack film crew making yet another cruddy horror movie allegedly "based on" or "inspired by" his writings and the Cthulhu Mythos. If anyone's interested in producing it, I'll gladly lend an assist with the script…

NOTES: Finlay's Chandu (usual pronunciation: Shandu) character was obviously intended to recall one of the same name (based on a famous

Beyond Horror's modern wallpaper design for **HOUSE** poses as an '80s US lobby card

real-life prestidigitator/radio personality) who had initially been played on film (i.e., **CHANDU THE MAGICIAN** [1932, USA, Ds: William Cameron Menzies, Marcel Varnel]) by Edmund Lowe, whereafter the heroic role was assumed by no less than Bela Lugosi—who had ironically enough played the villain in the preceding feature—in a spinoff serial, **THE RETURN OF CHANDU** (1934, USA, D: Ray Taylor). In the present film, the spelling of Ms. Layton's initial character's name is all over the place. Not only is it seen repeatedly spelled as "Leonor" during the course of the narrative, but Chandu repeatedly refers to her as "Leonora" (though, to give the continuity person [if any!] the benefit of the doubt, this might feasibly have been his pet name for her; or then again, maybe Finlay was just pronouncing it wrong and nobody bothered to correct him). However, both the cast list during the end credits and also the IMDb give its spelling as "Lenore" (after Poe?).

HOUSE

Reviewed by Eric Messina

USA, 1986. D: Steve Miner

Norwegian ad-line (a literal translation of the Anglo one): *"Ding Dong. Du Er Død!"*

This is one of the best films made by the usually hacky Steve Miner, who launched his career on the back of Jason Voorhees. Just before he made this film, he brought one of the most offensive '80s minstrel shows, **SOUL MAN** (1986, USA) to the world. I previously mentioned that terrible flick—which is a crime in certain corners of the world!—in my review of **WARLOCK** (1989, USA; see *Monster!* #21 [p.51]). The extremely talented Fred Dekker wrote this haunted house movie, co-starring William Katt and Richard Moll. Moll looks suspiciously—or, to my enjoyment, anyway—*exactly* like the army zombie in the cover artwork of Texas hardcore thrash act Dirty Rotten Imbeciles (D.R.I.)'s *Dirty Rotten EP/LP.*I had no idea at the time that, in-between his residential status on the TV sitcom *Night Court*, he acted in tons of B-movies, like **EVILSPEAK** (1981, USA, D: Eric Weston) and **CATACLYSM** (a.k.a. **THE NIGHTMARE NEVER ENDS**, 1980, USA, Ds: Phillip Marshak, Tom McGowan, Gregg Tallas)...with a full head of hair, yet! As for Katt, after nearly *[A miss is as good as a mile, as they say! – SF]* becoming immortalized as Luke Skywalker and bumbling his way through the comedic superhero teleseries *The Greatest American Hero* (1981-86, USA), he here plays 'Nam vet and horror

author Roger Cobb. The premise of Katt's Cobb character returning to the exact same house where his late loony aunt (played by Susan French) committed suicide and his son disappeared—possibly into another dimension, of all places—is what we've got here for this cryptic horror comedy.

This movie makes being an author look pretty exciting, with Katt as Cobb shown signing books for his adoring fans, including cute punk girls. He's divorced from his onscreen wife Sandy, played by Kay Lenz—who they would have us believe is this giant celebrity soap opera star with much greater success in her career than her former husband has had in his. Frankly, having Katt as a Vietnam War combat survivor/writer sorting out his personal demons and possibly losing his mind after being bitten by a few monsters that now reside in the family mansion is piss-poor casting, it must be said. The subject of PTSD is handled in an extremely flimsy and goofy way. Had they attempted to reinforce this message in a more serious manner, then it would've elevated the film to an ahead-of-its-time level; but perhaps the subject matter was just too "heavy" for them to convey in this comedic context. Another reason it doesn't work in a serious tone is because Katt is too yuppified by half, and I didn't find him very believable in this role as a traumatized Veteran. Because I like this film a lot, I let it slide, but to enjoy it, you have to suspend a *ton* of disbelief. Incidentally, I used to have a slightly embarrassing preteen obsession with this particular horror comedy where

Top: Richard Moll as wisecracking KIA grunt "Big" Ben. **Center:** William Katt meets the monster in the closet! **Above:** Dirty Rotten Imbeciles' 1987 record sleeve design for their *Dirty Rotten* LP post-dates **HOUSE**. However, the back cover to their 1984 7" 5-song *Violent Pacification* "EP" (< note quotes) ain't called "speedcore" for nothing!) actually boasts a different B&W line rendering of the same basic "zombie soldier" design, so it did officially predate the movie ~SF

I would tape-record snippets of its dialogue then edit them together. I'm not ashamed (well, maybe a *little* that I taped parts from this movie!); I used to do the same thing with Coppola's **APOCALYPSE NOW** (1979, USA) in high school. This was back in the day when I'd rent a movie from a video store and keep scenes I liked in audio form before I had to bring the tape back. Jason "Skunkape" Cook and I discussed this a few months ago, about how he once tried to get so much mileage out of a tape before he had to return it; as in the case of **REPOSSESSED** (1990, USA, D: Bob Logan), which if you revisit nowadays is pretty unfunny, at least to me.

The makeup by Brian Wade and Barney Burman for **HOUSE** is really cool. One of my favorite creatures is the ghastly, bloated, shrieking witch version of Sandy, Roger's ex-wife. She has sunken-in eyes, matted, stringy hair and sharp, gummy fangs/ tusks. Our hero blasts her away with a shotgun; she later gets her own back by taunting and shrieking at Roger while aiming said gun at his head. All of these creature sightings might be interpreted as Roger simply having hallucinations or flashbacks, but the clean-cut, lucid way in which Katt comes off doesn't give license to that notion, at least not for me. Now, if they'd had an actor adept at playing unhinged, psychotic types—such as Michael Shannon or Brad Dourif, for example—cast in his place, it could've worked on a more psychological level, but doesn't. It's still a solid horror comedy, though, that plays it subtler with the laughs than scares. Comic actor George Wendt from *Cheers* is pretty amusing as Harold the nosey neighbor, and in the same period he even played a Stephen King/ Garth Marengi-style horror in **DREAMSCAPE** (1984, USA, D: Joseph Ruben).

One black comedy device that *half* works shows Roger dismembering his mutant ex-wife's corpse and burying the parts in the backyard, even while the chopped-up limbs continue to move around by themselves. That gnarled, cadaverous severed hand shown ringing the doorbell on the poster art (tagline: *"Ding Dong, You're Dead"*) is presumably supposed to represent Roger's dead spouse's appendage, although the actual one in the movie is lots fatter and bluer and has long red fingernails. It ends up being dug up by a dog *[Prompting one of numerous shock sight-gags in horror cinema that reference a similar "dog-with-hand-in-mouth" scene from Kurosawa's* **YOJIMBO** *(用心棒 / Yōjinbō, 1961, Japan) – SF]*, then later gets flushed down the toilet. Elsewhere, there's this "Lovecraftian"-style beast that has a long skeletal tail and human faces bursting from the sides of its head. I wanted to see more of this creature, but sadly its existence is never explained. Our heroes set up a bunch of cameras to try and capture it in motion as it bursts out from behind a closet door. It sticks its face into the camera and drags Roger off on one of his periodic Nam flashbacks, where Richard Moll's character is waiting for him. Shades of the little girl who got swallowed up by a TV set by dark forces in Hooper/Spielberg's **POLTERGEIST** (1982, USA), Roger's son had disappeared into an interdimensional vortex beneath the garden pool years ago before his grieving father moved away, and through his Aunt's artwork he somehow discovers how to get the boy back. Apparently the son has been suspended in a state of "arrested development" while he was gone, because when Dad finally tracks his son down, the kid hasn't aged a day since he last saw him (this idea seems reminiscent of two *Twilight Zones:* "The Bewitching Pool" and "Little Girl Lost" episodes). Another one of my favorite monsters is a skull with bat wings that twirls a shotgun around in its talon lickety-split and almost shoots Roger in the foot. This winged skull looks a lot like the mascot of East Coast thrash band Overkill; maybe that's one of the reasons why I like this film so much, because it contains a number of creatures connected to my favorite hardcore and metal bands.

Richard Moll as Big Ben, the wisecrackin' "D.R.I. army zombie" lookalike, shows up to deliver all the bad one-liners you can stomach (he's so corny, they should've given him a brick wall and blazer to go with his half-assed standup comedy act!). As an adult you might well interpret all of the monsters featured here as "metaphorical" or "metaphysical", but that flew way over my head as a 10-year-old. Then again, as for whose body parts were being hacked-up and buried in the background, they can't be his ex's, because she makes a reappearance towards the end. But even with all its plot-holes and other flaws and inconstancies, this film is still a lot of fun. Too bad I can't say the same for the fucking atrocious sequels that followed, including **HOUSE II: THE SECOND STORY** (1987, USA, D: Ethan Wiley), which features a cameo by none other than Bill Maher; avoid that one like the plague![4]

4 Just for the record, the other two sequels were: thirdly, **THE HORROR SHOW** (a.k.a. **HOUSE III**, 1989, USA, Ds: James Isaac, David Blyth), starring Lance Henriksen and Brion James; and, fourthly and finally—er, *kinda*—**HOUSE IV** (1992, USA, D: Lewis Abernathy), for which William Katt belatedly reprised his Roger Cobb character. It was the "official" Pt.3 rather than the unconnected, in-name-only entry that preceded it, which has its adherents but totally doesn't fit into the series. Hell, even **H4** gets its fair share of positive user reviews on the IMDb. A fifth non-entry (in more ways than one) was "Clyde Anderson"/Claudio Fragasso's **BEYOND DARKNESS** (*La casa 5*, Italy), which was released in some quarters as **HOUSE 5**—well, it does indeed have a house in it, so… In typical Italian exploitation fashion, in its country of origin, it was even at some time alternately known as **EVIL DEAD 5!** – ed.

However, this the first film in the *House* franchise is fun to revisit, warts and all, and the gruesome makeup FX help smooth-over any gaping gaps in logic and plot.

THE BLOOD BEAST TERROR
(a.k.a. THE VAMPIRE-BEAST CRAVES BLOOD)

Reviewed by Steve Fenton

UK, 1967. D: Vernon Sewell

Poster tagline: *"The Blood Lust of a FRENZIED VAMPIRE!"*

Trailer narration: *"From this old house some evil thing was spawned, to bring terror to the surrounding countryside! What was Professor Mallinger's gruesome secret, and how was his beautiful daughter involved?...What kind of*

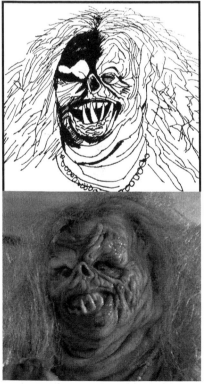

Top: Eric M's pen-and-ink impression of **HOUSE**'s hideous hagbag from hell

monster *lived in this prison? What kind of creature brought terror to a whole community?"*

Hysterical eyewitness, to the police inspector on the case: *"It was a 'orrible creature, sir! With 'uge eyes, sir! ...And the wings, the wings, sir...! Yes, I saw* wings*, sir. 'Orrible wings, sir...!"*

While this Tony Tenser/Tigon British horror period piece was also variously released as both **BLOOD BEAST FROM HELL** and **THE DEATHSHEAD VAMPIRE**, the version I am reviewing here bore the original British title **THE BLOOD BEAST TERROR**, which has no connection whatsoever with either **REVENGE OF THE BLOOD BEAST** (UK title for **THE SHE BEAST** [*La sorella di Satana*, 1966, UK/Italy, D: Michael Reeves]), **NIGHT OF THE BLOOD BEAST** (1958, USA, D: Bernard L. Kowalski [see *Monster!* #17, p.33]) or **BLOOD BEAST FROM OUTER SPACE** (US title for **THE NIGHT CALLER** [1965, UK, D: John Gilling]) Got that? Then let's proceed, shall we...

Amusingly enough, dating it considerably, **TBBT** opens with a brief pre-credits sequence, set in "Africa" (note quotes)—or rather, an artificial if passable enough simulacrum thereof. Clad in a spotlessly-white pith helmet and matching tropical bush fatigues, a British colonial adventurer name of Britewell (William Wilde), a naturalist in the field, is shown being ferried downriver— allegedly the Limpopo in southern Africa, but undoubtedly actually somewhere much closer to home; like along the River Thames somewhere in rural Middlesex, say—by a pair of African men. These natives' primitive "dug-out" canoe is clearly actually a modern aluminum one that, in a half-hearted attempt at verisimilitude (*not!*), has merely been given a coat of "wood"-brown paint (they painted the outside of the hull, but neglected to do the inside as well, so the silvery metallic surface is highly apparent; something which that carven tribal juju idol mounted as figurehead on the prow fails to distract our attention from). And not only that, but the footage was obviously canned back home in merrie olde England rather than anywhere even close to the Dark Continent. In hopes of bringing some superficial semblance of geographical authenticity to the scene, a cacophonous assortment of "exotic" animal noises are heard dubbed onto the audio track, and the odd stock documentary shot of African wildlife (e.g., a monkey and parrot, etc.) is inserted, plus

Pacemaker Pictures' US half-sheet poster (art unsigned) for **THE BLOOD BEAST TERROR**, here double-billed with **CURSE OF THE BLOOD-GHOULS** (*La strage dei vampiri*, a.k.a. **SLAUGHTER OF THE VAMPIRES**, 1964, Italy, D: Roberto Mauri)

26

the film stock does match-up better than usual for this sort of thing. That said, while the rural scenery is plainly British through and through, it does look especially verdant, lush and lovely in widescreen on Redemption Films' unexpected 2012 Blu-ray edition, which flew in from right out of nowhere. Having originally viewed the film in far-from-optimal form (i.e., a murky full-frame pan-and-scan print) on a long-defunct Canadian cable channel in about 1987-88 or so, getting to finally view it in such a sumptuous version all these years later came as quite the eye-opening (and mind-broadening) revelation to me. Which is why I am not only here dutifully revising/updating a much more negative review I wrote of the film which originally ran in my long-dead Toronto-based zine *Killbaby* (#4, June 1990), but shall also be modifying my opinion of it accordingly, where necessary, for what it's worth all these years later.

After traipsing through the aforesaid "jungle" for not much upwards of a minute, said explorer Britewell comes across a pair of strange bluish chrysalises inside a rotten tree-stump. Cue credits, followed by the narrative proper...

Much in the spirit of that endearingly featherbrained Limey/Canuck terror turkey **THE VULTURE** (1966, D: Lawrence Huntington), starring Robert Hutton and Akim Tamiroff, the present film commences with some dimly-glimpsed, wing-flapping *whatsit* offing an expendable Brit bit-player in a benighted woodland region on a common somewhere outside London.

Scotland Yard assigns the intrepid Inspector Quennell (Peter Cushing) to the case of the recent spate of grisly murders, after which the victims (six to date, all of the male persuasion) are left drained of blood and in a shocking state ("...severe injury to the cranium region, thorax severely damaged, and ribcage subject to extreme pressures"). The sole survivor who's borne witness to the killer—a coachman named Joe (Leslie Anderson) who unwittingly happened along at the scene of the latest murder, interrupting the perpetrator in its commission—has predictably been rendered a gibbering lunatic (i.e., "mad as a hatter") by the sheer shock of the encounter. Strewn all over the heath at the scene of the latest murder, a number of strange, scale-like objects have been discovered by investigating bobbies from the Yard (including imposing, baritone-voiced, Malayan-born British [Welsh?] actor Glynn Edwards as Sgt. Allan, sporting an impressive sideburns-and-mustache combo fitting to his rank. Edwards would go on to play the latter eponymous character in same director Sewell's history-based horror drama

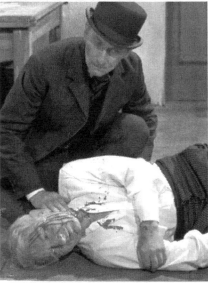

Dr. Hichcock Meets Baron Frankenstein! Flemyng and Cushing regard a taxidermized eagle in **THE BLOOD BEAST TERROR**; it isn't called the blood beast for nothing; and stonefaced butler Granger (Kevin Stoney) bears the scars of a run-in with *something* bearing claws

BURKE & HARE [1972, UK], for which Derren Nesbitt played his partner-in-crime Burke).

Commanding Liverpudlian actor Robert Flemyng—yes, it's no less than Riccardo Freda's former horrible Dr. Hichcock himself!—portrays an outwardly prim-and-proper Viennese insect expert named Professor Mallinger, F.R.E.S. ("Fellow of the Royal Entomological Society"), whose area of specialization happens to be *Lepidoptera*: moths. Seeking his professional scientific opinion as to what might be the origin of those aforementioned "scales", Quennell gives one to entomologist Mallinger for analysis. Seeing seasoned old thesping pros Cushing (1913-1994) and Flemyng (1912-1995) playing in scenes together is a real treat, and the two actors exhibit some convincing interaction, genuinely appearing to enjoy sharing the screen and not seeming in any way eager to upstage or steal scenes from each other; a sure sign of true professionals secure about their abilities. Not only were they of almost identical age at the time, but also of similar height, build and in the general "aristocratic" structure of their facial features, so they are evenly-matched, both physically and, as their respective characters, intellectually too. They even shared topmost billing on the film, albeit with Cushing getting billed first (natch). In one scene, Flemyng, acting his shiftiest best, deftly snuffs-out a still-barely-alive young male victim of the monster right under the very noses of police, who fail to spot his sudden shiftily sinister facial expression and sleight of hand while committing the deadly deed. Cushing bats nary an eyelash in suspicion after Flemyng then casually and authoritatively announces that the poor fellow has died (with a little help from him!).

Requisite to the film is its would-be Hammer look—as with much of their fare, it is likewise set during the Victorian era—along with the familiar stable of competent British character actors, who try their best to salvage what they can from the overall derivative, rather unimaginative, if far from unwatchable proceedings. Pleasantly scenic English country locations and good period detail,

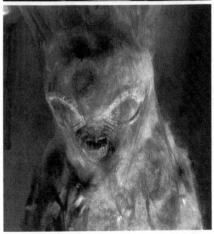

Left, Top to Bottom: A scene from **THE BLOOD BEAST TERROR**'s cool "live theatre" sequence; moth-woman Wanda Ventham next to her "daddy's" newest insectoid creation; no, it's *not* a shot of Flemyng as Freda's Dr. Hichcock, but of the actor as the similarly obsessed and driven Prof. Mallinger in **TBBT**; unfortunately, we never do get to see what comes out of this human-sized chrysalis, because it gets burned to crisp before that ever happens

all captured by DP Stanley Long's appealingly composed cinematography, are the major (if far from only) plusses, other than for the presences of the "name" stars; though, while Cushing gives his usual professionally-polished performance on the surface, it at times seems that his heart wasn't entirely in the material. However, rather than wearing that all-too-familiar "just-gimme-my-damn-paycheck-and-lemme-get-the-hell-outta-here" expression common to actors while slumming it in material which they believe to be beneath their station, he instead gives it his best shot; as do the rest of the largely note-perfect cast, and the film is all the more watchable for it (we can only wonder if the star's earnings from this gig came anywhere near to what he made on any of his many Hammer films).

Periodically, Flemyng descends to his dingy basement, where he keeps *SOMETHING* locked away behind a heavy door... gee, wonder *what* it could be? A giant, blood-slurping moth-monster, perchance? You see, the bug specialist's "daughter" Clare (played by highly prolific actress Wanda Ventham, who made her screen debut in the fish'n'chips JD ["juvenile delinquent"] drama **MY TEENAGE DAUGHTER** [a.k.a. **TEENAGE BAD GIRL**, 1956, UK, D: Herbert Wilcox]) can change at will into a mutated weremoth; a deceptively humanoid she-monster whose genes have been spliced with those of a death's-head hawkmoth (*Acherontia atropos*), a species identifiable by a skull-shaped marking on the back of the thorax. Having been created by her "father", if by no means via the natural procreative method, she periodically transforms into her insectoid alter-ego to put the fatal bite on local yokels, thus explaining the recent sharp increase in the death-rate locally, as well as all those shiny scales found scattered about (shed from the creature's wings). Director Sewell (he of last issue's **CURSE OF THE CRIMSON ALTAR** [1968, UK]) stages some effective set-pieces and sequences, such as when the alluring Ms. Ventham—who is unusually protective of her little winged insect friends, and has a pronounced aversion to fire—coquettishly plays a game of nocturnal "catch-me-if-you-can" with randy nature boy Wilde in the woods, strongly implying that her body will be his prize if he succeeds in catching her. After luring him off

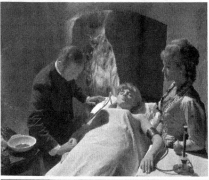

Mother Of All Moths: When galvanism fails to even get a twitch out of it, **THE BLOOD BEAST TERROR**'s obsessively dedicated mad entomologist Prof. Mallinger resorts to more desperate measures to bring his mutant mothster to life... or so he hopes! The girl on the operating table is Vanessa Howard

deeper into the trees with a series of cooily come-hither siren calls, she suddenly rushes at him from out of the underbrush, startling him with her now-monstrously-mothy mug (complete with antennae and big red faceted bug-eyes; the effective mask was the work of Brit SFX ace Roger Dicken, who also worked on such other variable Brit horror / monster / fantasy fare as **WITCHFINDER GENERAL** [1968, D: Michael Reeves], **SCARS OF DRACULA** [1970, D: Roy Ward Baker], **THE CREEPING FLESH** [1973, D: Freddie Francis] and **THE LAND THAT TIME FORGOT** [1975, D: Kevin Connor], latter of which has long been a not-so-guilty pleasure of mine ever since I first laid eyes on it as a schoolboy at the spacious Albert Hall cinema in Swansea, Wales upon its initial theatrical run, roughly a year prior to my family and myself lighting-out for greener pastures over in Canada).

The overall plot of **TBBT** was clearly derived from the previous year's Hammer horror **THE REPTILE**, with—by no means a bad thing, in this unrepentant monstrophile's personal opinion—a large dose of Rog Corman's **THE WASP WOMAN** (1959, USA) injected for good measure; amounting to a minor if serviceable enough effort from the lower echelons of British shock cinema. Up until its release by Redemption on digital disc in recent years (in a sumptuous widescreen transfer print at that), it had remained one of the lesser-known/seen entries in Cushing's expansive horror filmography and British horror cinema in general, so we can at least be thankful it has at long last become much easier to see, and in a near-as-dammit to optimum format to boot, which makes it that much easier on the eye.

Novelist-screenwriter Peter Bryan had formerly provided scripts for the likes of **THE BRIDES OF DRACULA** (1960, UK), **THE PROJECTED MAN** (1966, UK, Ds: Ian Curteis, John Croydon [see p.12]) and **THE PLAGUE OF THE ZOMBIES** (1966, UK, D: John Gilling [see *M!* #10, p.25]), and would go on to pen the original story for Freddie Francis' notorious **TROG** (1971, UK), as well as the novel on which "Anthony M. Dawson"/Antonio Margheriti's Italo *giallo* **SEVEN DEATHS IN THE CAT'S EYE** (1973) was based. He provides a literate enough scenario for the present title, which, while heavily derivative of other (sometimes arguably better) movies, holds its own quite adequately, all things considered, regardless of all its well-trod tropes. Composer Paul Ferris also scored such prime Brit horrors as **THE SHE BEAST** (1966), **THE SORCERERS** (1967) and **WITCHFINDER GENERAL** (1968, all D: Michael Reeves), as well as Freddie Francis' **THE CREEPING FLESH** (1973), lattermost three

of which all involved input at some level from the present film's producer Tony Tenser. While sometimes a tad on the weak side herein, Ferris' tuneage hereon is mostly more than adequate to the context.

Playing one "Smiler", comic actor Roy Hudd guest stars as a character that has since become a cliché in horror movies: that of a morgue attendant who thinks nothing of eating his supper in the presence of corpses. Indeed, he even goes so far as to wipe his fork on the sheet covering one of them before digging into his nosh no more than a foot from the corpse's greyish bare feet; as an amusing extra sight-gag, he makes a disgusted look when he spots a stray hair stuck to a chunk of his chicken pie. It's a cinch to picture Hammer character-acting stalwart Michael Ripper in Hudd's comic relief role here, although latter actor (born in Surrey in 1935 and still occasionally active today, mostly acting on the telly) does a perfectly fine job in his place, mugging it up animatedly while displaying flawless comedic timing.

In a nicely-done bit of period detail, we are treated to a lengthy, statically-framed sequence—which we view from the P.O.V. of other audience members in the second row—showing scenes from a stage play about an experimenter in galvanism who acquires a fresh corpse from a pair of Burke & Hare-inspired body snatchers and attempts to revive it via electricity, Frankenstein-style. Clearly, if the filmmakers went to the trouble of staging this extraneous theatrical sequence, some care and attention must have been expended on the production. None other than the film's heroine played by Ventham doubles as the heroine in the play, albeit as a brunette rather than as her blonde Clare Mallinger character (I personally thought she looked a lot sexier in her jet-black wig than with corn-colored ringlets, but she only appears that way for just one scene, more's the pity). The galvanist proceeds to revive her comely "corpse", only to have her momentarily come back to life in order to fatally throttle him, then return to death's domain once more herself. All-in-all, this whole sequence makes for a most welcome addition indeed. Having been left suitably inspired by this performance, which is staged right in his own home, Prof. Mallinger wonders whether a Wimshurst machine might aid him in his own research (said gizmo, a high-voltage electrostatic generator, was developed by a British inventor named James Wimshurst circa the early 1880s). The professor thereafter begins incorporating "galvanic stimulation" into his experiments, although to precisely what end we haven't been made privy to yet. After the galvanism angle proves to be a bust in seeing the final fruition of his pet project, Mallinger is forced to resort to other, far-less-legal means in order to realize his dream experiment.

Down in his cellar, (quote) "behind the green door", Flemyng stashes a suitably eerie-looking, six-foot-high moth cocoon (more Dicken work) that strongly resembles something out of an old *Dr. Who* episode, but which actually succeeds in being slightly ominous in appearance. This chrysalis, the doc's scientific pride and joy, needs intermittent injections of nubile girl-blood in order to flourish; for the purpose, Ventham preys on Insp. Quennell's virginal daughter Meg (wholesomely fresh-faced blonde Vanessa Howard, who subsequently appeared opposite Cushing in Robert Hartford-Davis' sadistic sci-fi shocker **CORRUPTION** [1968, UK], which has also recently received a stunning Blu-ray release). The cocoon contains Flemyng's brainchild: a supermoth hybrid that is the result of intricate cross-breeding / genetic tampering with other exotic moth species (including an evidently fictional XL species called *Lepidoptera Africana*). During the grand finale, Ms. Howard learns the hard way that one should never run pell-mell in panic around a darkened building with a lighted oil lamp in hand, coming *that* close to having her lovely golden curls set ablaze when she stumbles and falls in the process (she *is* a Victorian damsel-in-distress in a pre-PC era melodrama, after all!).

In my original *Killbaby* review, I rather cursorily dismissed the film, saying "this flick definitely lacks much in the line of real flair or personality". I also opined that "With the identities of the 'bad guys' obvious right from reel one, absolutely no suspense or tension are generated, so all we're left with is a by-the-numbers, vacuous time-killer. It's not bad enough to rate as prime 'camp' or 'trash,' but not *good* enough to really warrant a second viewing either; just another undemanding stroll in that no man's land of formulaic, mediocre second features. This is probably the cause of the film's remaining so seldom seen—I taped it off Canada's SuperChannel a couple of years back, where it played in a few 4 a.m. time-slots for a month or so, then fluttered off somewhere to hibernate for perhaps another twenty years... Events wind down

Right: 3 scenes from **THE BLOOD BEAST TERROR**. The mothster in action *[top & center]* and a nice close-up still of Roger Dicken's funky monster mask *[bottom]*, scanned directly from Denis Gifford's must-have tome *The Pictorial History of Horror Movies* (UK: Hamlyn, 1973)

to a predictably melodramatic finish, with the title monstrosity revealed in only titillatingly fleeting glimpses. All the 'build-up' and superficial character development culminate in the rather anticlimactic climax, ultimately having all the impact of a mildly annoying insect getting zapped by a backyard bug-light... **TBBT**, while it probably didn't ruin any careers, sure as hell didn't advance any, either. It must remain as another of those elusive films whose title lingers in your brain for years—promising lurid thrills—but, when you finally call its bluff, you realize it's largely all talk and precious little action." (Surprisingly enough, though, I didn't make an obvious "moth-eaten" joke!)

I'm only quoting all of the above to illustrate what I see as a valid point: how sometimes our opinions of something (be it a film or whatever [or even *somebody*, for that matter]) can change over time, at times even quite drastically by comparison to our initial impressions.

"Blood Monster": The deceptive Italian '70s reissue *locandina* for **THE BLOOD BEAST TERROR** (art by Renato Casaro). No, Chris Lee *isn't* in it!

Yes, I must say that viewing **TBBT** on Blu was like seeing it in a whole new light—almost as if for the very first time again, as a matter of fact—and this time around I was far better able to appreciate all the (mostly) careful attention to period detail (etc.) on view. Although, that said, in such a high-definition presentation, certain of the film's shortcomings also become more apparent (that aforementioned metal "log" canoe most immediately springs to mind). However, all nitpicking aside, I was more than happy to revisit this movie after so many years, especially in its revelatory new millennial reincarnation from Redemption, which, appropriately enough, really redeemed it in my eyes. Contrary to the old saying, first impressions aren't *always* last impressions.

CULT OF THE COBRA

Reviewed by Michael Hauss

USA, 1955. D: Francis D. Lyon

Onscreen introductory text: *"Slender hangs illusions. Fragile the thread to reality. Always the question: is it true? Truth is in the mind and the mind of man varies with time and place. The time is 1945. The place is Asia."*

Get Smart's future "Chief" Edward Platt, in an uncredited bit part as an irate Lamian cultist, to the intrusive protagonists: *"The Cobra Goddess will avenge herself! One by one, you will DIE!"*

Six U.S. Air Force buddies are on furlough for the last time in an unnamed Asian city, and while doing touristy things like taking pictures and buying trinkets, they stumble onto a talkative native snake charmer named Daru (played by Leonard Strong, an obvious Caucasian who speaks perfect English, without even a hint of any Asiatic accent or dialectic). One of the servicemen, Paul (Richard Long), reveals he's heard of a secret sect that worships snakes and how some of its members can actually physically change themselves into serpents; these shape-shifters are called "Lamians", he says.[5] After listening intently, Daru informs the Americans that he himself is a Lamian. To provide proof of his claims, he offers to sneak them into one of the cult's private religious rituals, where they will see a woman who—while yet still a woman— is also a snake. For $100 US dollars, Daru will

5   The word "Lamian" comes from ancient Greek mythology about a serpent with the head and breasts of a woman, who devoured children and—being also a vampire— sucked the blood of men.

STARRING
FAITH DOMERGUE
RICHARD LONG
MARSHALL THOMPSON
KATHLEEN HUGHES
with
WILLIAM REYNOLDS
JACK KELLY
MYRNA HANSEN
DAVID JANSSEN

US lobby card

smuggle them past the temple guards at great risk to both himself and the men, as no outsiders have ever witnessed this top-secret sacred ritual, where no non-members or cameras are allowed. The buddies consume much alcohol beforehand then, disguised in cultists' robes, follow Daru into the nocturnal gathering of Lamians at their temple, where all the attending worshippers are dressed in hooded white cloaks like themselves. During the ritual, one of the airmen, Nick (James Dobson), sneakily separates from the rest of the group of trespassers and, after observing what is obviously a human female dressed in a skintight snakeskin (i.e., spandex) outfit performing a sinuously slinky ritualistic dance, he recklessly snaps a picture of the show. No sooner has the flash-bulb gone off than the place goes crazy, and during the ensuing melee, before making a desperate dash for the exit, Nick grabs up the basket which the snake-suited woman had slithered out of then back into after her dance performance. During this scene is when the aforementioned Platt yells the above-quoted death threat at the intruders, thus establishing the main thrust of the story.

The five remaining comrades escape from the resultant free-for-all that had ensued following their discovery after jumping in their jeep and driving off, shortly spotting Nick lying unconscious on the side of the road, as well as noticing a woman's shadowy form slipping furtively into a dark passageway nearby. Having been bitten on his neck by a snake, Nick is saved (at least temporarily) when the venom is sucked out. He is seemingly on the road to a full recovery at the military hospital, but that same night *something* slithers in through the open window of his hospital room, whereupon he gets bitten once again and this time dies. Having been demobilized, his five surviving buds ship-out the next day, returning back home to their civilian lives in New York City. The two male leads, Paul and Tom (latter played by Marshall Thompson) are both in love with a girl named Julia (Kathleen Hughes), and when Julia finally chooses Paul over him, the heartbroken Tom—"on the rebound", so to speak—quickly becomes smitten with his new across-the-hall neighbor Lisa Moya (Faith Domergue). This mysterious, exotic and beautiful woman at first discourages Tom's amorous advances, although she eventually falls in love with him. Only problem is that (in a plot development that is made more than obvious right from the outset) Lisa is a Lamian—no less than the acting earthly vessel of the Cobra Goddess herself—and she is going around exacting revenge in the deity's name, killing-off the men responsible for violating the sanctity of her temple one by one...

COTC's cast is loaded with talented young actors and actresses, some of whom would go on to find

limited mainstream success in television and film. The six air force buddies were played by Richard Long (as Paul Able), Marshall Thompson (Tom Markel), Jack Kelly (Carl Turner), David Janssen (Rico Nardi), William Reynolds (Pete Norton) and James Dobson (Nick Hommel). Long is best-known for appearing in the western television series *Big Valley* (1965-69, USA), as well as opposite Vincent Price in **HOUSE ON HAUNTED HILL** (1959, USA, D: William Castle), plus he also appeared in **TOKYO AFTER DARK** (1959, USA, D: Norman T. Herman). Thompson is most famously known to many for his part as an animal doctor in the family-friendly, African-set TV series *Daktari* (1966-69, USA). The actor's credits total 115 film and television appearances, including the sci-fi classic **IT! THE TERROR FROM BEYOND SPACE** (1959, USA, D: Edward L. Cahn) and the geriatric aquatic monster movie **BOG** (1979, USA [see *Monster!* #18, p.19]). David Janssen, who amassed some 99 credits over the course of his career, was best-known for two television series in which he starred, *The Fugitive* (1963-67) and *Harry-O* (1973-76, both USA). Kelly became known as Bart Maverick, brother of James Garner's title character in the popular western series *Maverick* (1957-62, USA), and he also appeared in the sci-fi films **FORBIDDEN PLANET** (1956, USA, D: Fred McLeod Wilcox) and **SHE DEVIL** (1957, USA, D: Kurt Neumann [see *M!* #16, p.46]). Reynolds appeared regularly in the TV crime series *The F.B.I.* (1966-74, USA), and also has the notable "headless" horror movie **THE THING THAT COULDN'T DIE** (USA, 1958, D: Will Cowan) among his credits. Dobson has around 90 credits, mostly in television episodes, but he did appear in a few notable exploitation films, including the swashbuckling creature feature **CAPTAIN SINDBAD** (1963, USA/W. Germany, D: Byron Haskin) and the effective zombie film **DARK ECHO** (a.k.a. **DARK ECHOES**, 1977, USA/ Yugoslavia, D: George Robotham).

Female leads Faith Domergue (as Lisa Moya) and Kathleen Hughes (as Julia), while both beautiful, do come across as a bit vapid in their roles. Hughes, the more "traditional" beauty of the two, has a hard time conveying any emotion beyond stock naïve 1950s starlet reactions. The actress has 61 credits on her résumé, with the classic SF feature **IT CAME FROM OUTER SPACE** (1953, USA, D: Jack Arnold) being the most notable, on whose famous ads and posters she featured predominantly. Domergue was a drop-dead gorgeous woman whose acting style typically came across as disjointed and disengaged, as here (although in this case it rather fits her character). She plays the snake goddess in mortal bodily

Starlet-Into-Serpent: Faith Domergue as Lisa Moya undergoes her less-than-stunning metamorphosis in **CULT OF THE COBRA**

form, who can change into a King (make that *Queen!*) Cobra when needed to exact revenge. A onetime lover of the famous Howard Hughes, Domergue appeared in a number of fine 1950s sci-fi films—including **THIS ISLAND EARTH** and **IT CAME FROM BENEATH THE SEA** (both 1955, USA) and **THE ATOMIC MAN** (1955, UK)—before settling into a steady regimen of episodic television work. Francis D. Lyon, the present film's director, was formerly a film editor (who won an Academy Award for editing the film **BODY AND SOUL** [1947, USA, D: Robert Rossen]) before turning his attention to directing in 1952. Lyon directed 34 films, including the pulp SF exploitationers **CASTLE OF EVIL** (1966) and **THE DESTRUCTORS** (1968, both USA).

CULT OF THE COBRA was an independently-produced film which was initially released by Universal-International paired-up as the second feature to **REVENGE OF THE CREATURE** (1955, USA, D: John Sherwood), the first "gillman" sequel. The present film is decent enough in that 1950s-style "fake reality" way, which includes men and women who are always immaculately dressed and groomed who will have a drink and/or a cigarette at the drop of a hat. The film is definitely merely middle-tier quality-wise, but the premise of six buddies who stay true to one another and all look out for each other is a decent enough idea, as is the woman turning into a snake angle. However, the general shallowness and cheap execution of the film unfortunately weighs heavily on its overall outcome. Marshall's poor sap Tom Markel character gets jilted not just once but *twice* by his equal number of would-be lady loves; firstly by Julia, who chooses his best friend Paul over him, and then a second time when he also loses the Lisa character, because she must fulfill her preset destiny and kill. As their doomed relationship builds and develops, Lisa falls in love with Tom, a feeling she has never felt before, for which she comes off as a victim of her unfortunate destiny, prompting some audience sympathy with her plight. But ultimately she *is* a literally cold-blooded killer, who when in her (rubber) cobra form, murders four out of the six buddies and, as the film concludes, also has designs on killing Julia, too.

All the characters, while paper-thin, are enjoyable enough, if only at the surface level, but the actors had me buying into their portrayals, allowing me to overlook some obvious character flaws in the script. For its "action highlights", **COTC** boasts a couple of kill-shots that utilize the phony prop cobra from a "snake-eyed" POV perspective, which provides the film with an interesting "killer killing as seen through their own eyes" concept. I found this film

The sexy snake-girl's (Ruth Carlsson) dance routine amounts to about **COTC**'s liveliest sequence

35

ema.blogspot.ca/2015/02/cult-of-cobra.html*). And while you're at it, have a browse around at some of the other material there, too! – SF.*

IN THE MOUTH OF MADNESS

Reviewed by Brian Harris

USA, 1994. D: John Carpenter

Do you read Sutter Cane?

John Carpenter is a hard director to peg down; he goes effortlessly from horror, sci-fi, action and back. He doesn't seem interested in sticking to just one genre. Which is great for film lovers who crave variety, not so pleasing to those who want the man to continue doing sequels to his most popular films. The quality of his productions also varies from outlandishly entertaining (**BIG TROUBLE IN LITTLE CHINA**, 1986) to "Wait... *what?!*" (**GHOSTS OF MARS**, 2001, both USA). I think most would agree though that, while his work is hit-or-miss, the hits far outweigh the misses. So where in the hell does his homage to H.P. Lovecraft, **IN THE MOUTH OF MADNESS**, fall? Let's find out...

Snake-Eyed: Grant Williams *[top]*, as seen from the were-serpent's P.O.V. in **CULT OF THE COBRA** (note that serpentine shadow on his shirt!). A virtually identical "shimmering bubble" optical effect *[above]* had been used previously by Uni in 1953's **IT CAME FROM OUTER SPACE** (the actor is Russell *"Gilligan's Island"* Johnson)

to be a perfectly fine time-filler/killer and, while totally superficial and disposable, it does present an at times pleasantly sugar-coated alternate version of reality that's hard not to swallow.

*EDITOR'S NOTE: For a second opinion (I don't like it quite so much as Mike does!), check out my review of COTC at regular Monster! contributor Dennis Capicik's mighty fine and eclectic cult movie blog Unpopped Cinema (@ http://unpoppedcin-

As the film begins we're introduced to protagonist John Trent (Sam Neill), a relatively nice guy despite that crazy look in his eyes and the occasional outburst of violence, as he's being checked into a city mental health facility. After a few nasty flashbacks, Trent is introduced to Dr. Wrenn—presumably sent from the government—and asked to recount the events that landed him there.

We learn that John works as a fraud investigator, working for insurance companies to sniff-out crooks looking to bilk companies out of their money. One afternoon, his friend Robbie, an insurance man he does jobs for, assigns him to a case filed by a publishing company; seems their biggest author, Sutter Cane, has gone missing. Before they can get into any details, an ax-wielding psycho walks across the street and swings his weapon through the plate glass window they're eating next to, sending glass flying everywhere and people running for the exit. The question he poses to Trent is simple: "Do you read Sutter Cane?" Explosions of gunfire end the exchange.

Sam Neill enters into a strange new world during **IN THE MOUTH OF MADNESS**, one of John Carpenter's most fanciful concoctions

The next day, Trent is in the Arcane Publishing company's office for a sit-down with bigwig

Jackson Harglow (Charlton Heston) and head editor Linda Styles. It would seem that Cane went missing two months prior and, with the police making no headway, Arcane are interested in having Trent track him down and bring his newest book, *In the Mouth of Madness* to the publisher. Unfortunately, the only real lead he had to find him was Cane's editor, and he went mad and got gunned-down by the police... while swinging an ax at Trent. Skeptical that the entire situation may be nothing more than a publicity stunt, Linda suggests Trent check out Cane's work—which he does—in order to grasp just how important this job is to them.

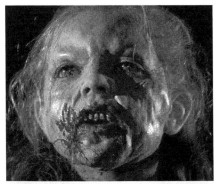

The next day while reading the books—and suffering through some intense nightmares—he discovers that, if assembled together, the different art on all the book covers form a map, leading to a town called, Hobb's End. Though it's not shown on any maps, Trent is convinced it's in New Hampshire and he's still just as skeptical, though he takes the job. Linda is assigned by her boss to accompany him on the trip.

When they finally reach Hobb's End—under rather *odd* circumstances—things really take a turn for the weird, as Linda takes notice of many details in the town that fit Cane's works, right up to paintings on walls and the names of townsfolk! Convinced something is definitely awry, she heads out to a mysterious cathedral where she believes Cane might be. Trent, on the other hand, begins to get what he thinks is a clear picture of what's really going on at "Sutter Cane Tourist Village." His attitude changes quickly when Linda returns barely coherent, ranting about having read the book and warning John not to read it himself. Rushing out to find help, he finds the innkeeper hideously transformed, tentacles and all. Intent on leaving, he heads back up to collect his things and get Linda; instead he's greeted with yet more tentacles and a brisk trip through a closed door.

With no hope of saving Linda, Trent jumps in his car and heads out of town, but no matter what he does, his car ends up careening right back into the Hobb's End town square: right in front of an angry mob of homicidal, monstery townsfolk! There's no hope for escape, as all roads lead back to him, Cane.

IN THE MOUTH OF MADNESS is one of those films you need to watch a few times in order to grasp all the cool little nuances that one might miss the first, second or even third time. For instance, up until my last viewing,

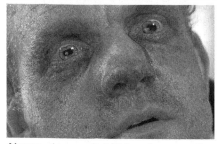

Above: As occult-dabbling horror author Sutter Cane in **ITMOM**, Jürgen Prochnow *[second from bottom]* is responsible for some pretty weird shit; just a fraction of which is depicted in these screen-grabs

I'd never noticed how Cane's agent had double pairs of irises and pupils in each eye, or that Lovecraftian painting on Harglow's wall, either. Cool. Anyhow, Carpenter has really scored with this film. I think it's definitely one of his hits. He created a convincing Stephen King-esque writer—played by the always-intense Jurgen Prochnow—on the verge of unlocking the doors to a new dimension, and I'll be damned if it didn't get my heart pumping! The town was creepy as hell, the denizens were gruesome looking and downright menacing, while the occasional oddball "**GROUNDHOG DAY** (1993, USA, D: Harold Ramis)"-style moments definitely ratcheted-up the tension for me.

I've read and heard many people complain about the musical score and how inappropriate the rock tracks were, and I'd normally agree with them, but the rock really only plays through the opening and closing credits. Otherwise, Carpenter, and co-composer Jim Lang, kills it with some great mood music. If you haven't seen this and you've come across mentions of the shit music, no worries.

For some not paying close attention, I can see you losing your way. The film occasionally eats its own tail, and sequences are looped. It doesn't happen often, but when it does, you'll need to give things your undivided attention. There are also some reality shifts, as the narrative jumps from the present-day to flashbacks and, towards the finale, back to the present-day... *sorta*. One particular sequence involving Trent watching **IN THE MOUTH OF MADNESS** may have some people scratching their heads, and all I can tell you is—that's what makes this film so damn cool. And you may want to give it another view.

Though **IN THE MOUTH OF MADNESS** only shares a few passing similarities and winks to Lovecraft's *At the Mountains of Madness*, there's more than enough Lovecraft—and even Stephen King—here to satisfy the literary nerds looking for cool references.

If you're one of those folks who hasn't seen this and you're on the fence, as Carpenter has disappointed you before (but all directors lay a few eggs). This one here is of the golden variety though: a really strange, exciting, mind-bending journey that's well worth owning. This is such a visual treat, as it's filled with beautiful buildings, angles, shadows, and original art. I think it's time for me to give up my DVD and upgrade this film to BD, as I can't wait to see what extra little details

Top to Bottom: Such things as a haunted painting and various monstrosities from a place other than reality—which is entirely subjective in the film—help make **IN THE MOUTH OF MADNESS** an unpredictable motion picture experience

are hiding in the high definition. I won't go so far as to say that I *love* this film, but it entertains to the fullest with a great cast of super-talented actors, an interesting story… and it's overflowing with monsters!

ÁREA MALDITA

Reviewed by Martín Núñez

Colombia, 1979. D: Jairo Pinilla

Thanks to the mass media worldwide, many people think of Colombia as a dangerous country ruled by drug lords and *guerrilleros*, but reality says otherwise. Colombia is one of the richest countries in Latin America when it comes to culture. Its influence can be seen in literature, their wonderful popular music (*cumbia* and *porro*, to name a few afro-influenced crazy beats), and also in cinema. And with any country's movie industry there's the official variety and an underground one, and Jairo Pinilla fits squarely into the latter. He is one of the weirdest filmmakers *ever* to have come out from Colombia… I daresay the *entire world*?!

Jairo Pinilla is a self-made filmmaker who abandoned his former profession as an electric engineer after living in México for a spell. While in that country, he fell in love with the movies after working for the once-famous Estudios Churubusco, a sort of Latin American Hollywood

where an entire star system was developed before the demise of popular Mexican Cinema in the early 'Eighties.

Once in México, Pinilla taught himself how a camera works, and what attracted his attention was the capability of translating his amateur comics to film along with his obsessions. However, there was one last hurdle to clear first, and that was funding his projects.

As you may guess, shooting a movie in Latin America is a huge enterprise, since there are no large studios unless you are involved in the Mexican, Brazilian, or Argentinian industry. Almost every film project made outside those countries turned into a battle against the odds, but Pinilla our hero was so determined to succeed that he spent his life savings in order to produce his first feature film. That film was **FUNERAL SINIESTRO** (1977, Colombia), a movie that tells the story of a young girl who must watch over a coffin (with a corpse inside, of course) during a lonely night after the other mourners leave. Based on an experience Pinilla had in his childhood, **FUNERAL SINIESTRO** remains his best work, mainly due to its atmosphere, which was filled with creepy things that scare the shit out of children. The movie has great sound design considering its nonexistent budget, and everything within it relates to the deepest human fears. Technique and narrative walk together down a frightfully good path to achieve the film's simple goal: to *scare* its audiences. However, be advised that if you're not into slow-paced, atmospheric movies, then said movie may not be for you.

Special thanks to Fernando Cháves for supplying this *über*-rare admat for **ÁREA MALDITA**

Well, as a third world production, extra cinematographic stuff must be considered to understand the whole thing. **FUNERAL SINIESTRO** was the first Colombian modern-day horror film and, as we may expect, the critics totally hated it. Pinilla was not to be dismissed however, because he is a mule-headed guy who spent the rest of his savings paying for a humble ad-mat that ran for but a single day in the most popular Colombian newspaper. Sadly, with this type of totally non-aggressive advertising campaign it was obvious people weren't going to pay any attention to the movie (how could they, if they didn't even know it existed?), and it turned out to be a total failure after a couple of weeks. However, as these things go, this then angered the critics even more, especially since they considered Pinilla a self-made, non-intellectual guy merely "playing" at being a filmmaker. But the returns on his first film ultimately proved to be decent enough that he was able to produce his second movie, **ÁREA MALDITA**, one of the *weirdest* Latin American movies ever made.

Simply put, **ÁREA MALDITA** is about a moralist snake killing as many potheads as it can!

The deadly snake can be seen before the second minute of footage, when we see a girl smoking weed before she drifts off to sleep. This sequence is a perfect example of Pinilla's naïve non-academic filmmaking in action: he mixes several unusual shots (which they would not have taught in film schools), but if you are into weird cinema, you will have an instant crush on this movie.

After this first sequence and the main credits unfold, Pinilla introduces the main characters: the sister of the first victim, who's trying to get some clues about the killing (and the marihuana found alongside the corpse), and a drug lord who's pushing *ganja* in town. The drug dealer is pretty much every cliché known when it comes to Latin American drug moguls: he lives surrounded by girls, luxury, and has armed-to-the-teeth bodyguards. It's difficult to describe the plot here, since there practically isn't any, and Pinilla fills the between-killing sequences with dull (and annoyingly overdubbed) dialogue which is utilized only to develop a plot that really needs none, because it actually works well in its own simplistic way.

Pinilla is a fan of detective movies, and one can spot this interest with the assorted of *noir*ish elements which he weaves into **ÁREA MALDITA**, such as the drug underworld and the investigation conducted by regular people as well as the police. A point worth mentioning is that in this film Pinilla developed a style which would become his "trademark", so to speak: namely, POV dialogues that result in endless minutes of people talking into the camera. Luckily for the viewer, though, in **ÁREA MALDITA** he rarely uses this uncomfortable narrative device.

Fortunately, the film has some interesting horror sequences that are filled with atmospherics that needs no plot to back them up. These unusual sequences show how Pinilla is a director who understands the "language" of horror cinema, but translates it to suit his own personal vision; which, of course, is a plus since we're dealing with "auteur cinema" here, no less.

Well, going back to the story: while the sister of the first victim is gradually uncovering the truth, she discovers that the monstrous snake was born and fed in a vast cannabis plantation out in the nearby jungle. She overhears the drug lord's intense debate with his people about whether they should plant coffee or weed! They even talk about producing cannabis-based food! And not only that, but there's even a sequence where the cops discover the pot smuggling, and one of them says: "Nice work! Marihuana and coffee, our two greatest exports" (!), then a well-shot gunfight follows.

ÁREA MALDITA is filled with out-of-context sequences, which is great. For example, there is a scene where Spanish singer Juan Erasmo Mochi, who was really popular in some Latin American countries in the late 'Seventies, performs an entire song. Obviously, his performance was intended to attract his fans into theaters, but the sequence itself is a pain in the ass if you're not into his music. As the mishmash continues, we get to see drug dealers' vendettas, girl gunfights, innocent people killed, dead animals (bitten by the snake), which all ends with the classic good guys vs. bad guys final battle.

After the final credits roll we notice how cheated we were, because the snake is nothing but a Mc-Guffin! But the journey was worth it, really, because the animal monster is the only thing that ties everything together, giving **ÁREA MALDITA** its horror edge. Which helps, as it moves back and forth between several genres, not belonging to any genre in particular. After all, Pinilla has his own distinctive artistic style—not unlike Jess Franco, to name only one other visionary filmmaker—although his is a naïve vision on how movies should be made. Pinilla's work borrowed a lot from old matinée serials, those wonderful short chapters in which anything can happen beyond the limits of logic; that is what makes his cinema so unique. It's obvious that Pinilla didn't give a shit about what others would say. After all, his films were minor successes until Colombian governmental policies regarding cinema changed in the early 2000s, after which independent filmmakers had an even tougher time producing their product. Pinilla himself was one of the victims, since he wasn't able to produce another movie following the change. This is sad, because he *deserves* more recognition.

He has been often compared with Edward D. Wood, Jr. Even local journalists have called him "The Colombian Ed Wood", but that comparison is pretty unfair, since Pinilla comes from the third world, where shooting a movie is way more difficult than it is in the States. This is especially true in the 1970s-2000s. It is true that both Wood and Pinilla had their own highly personalized approach to making movies, but they approached it in very different ways. If you want to check out more of his work, may I strongly recommend **27 HORAS CON LA MUERTE** (*"27 Hours with Death"*, 1982), a science fiction thriller about scientific experimentations dealing with life and death. It's curious how much **27 HORAS CON LA MUERTE** has in common with Joel Schumacher's **FLATLINERS** (1990, USA) except that the former was made eight years prior to the latter film!

Also, you could search for **TRIÁNGULO DE ORO** (*"Golden Triangle"*, 1984), a no-budget adventure "super-production" which remains to this day his only movie suitable for children… and that must be seen to be believed!

Please, give Pinilla's work a try, you won't regret it (*if* you're into weird cinema, that is).

Top: Director, crew, and snake-wrangler on the set. **Above:** Things get snaky in Jairo Pinilla's out-to-lunch Colombian horror flick **ÁREA MALDITA**

THE PROMISE KEEPER

Reviewed by Tim Paxton

USA, 2006. D: Martin Whitehead

Monster movies by African-American directors have always been a rarity, although they have been around since the early days of the industry. The most obvious example from way back when would be **SON OF INGAGI**, a film about a monstrous ape-man made in 1940 by director Richard C. Kahn (and covered by Mr. Steve F in *Monster!* #25 [p.48]). The two most obvious films that readily come to mind

Not the most imaginative DVD cover, nor
does it really represent the film within

Last issue I wrote extensively about the Indian witch/ghost film **CHUDAIL: THE WITCH** (1997/98, D: P. Chandrakumar), and in it I discussed the magical aspect of using iron nails in black magic. In **CHUDAIL** and other Asian horror films—most notably those from Hong Kong and Taiwanese directors—nails are used to "drive home" or tap magical energy when they are hammered into wooden fetishes, or even actual human (or zombie) skulls. This usage of iron in magic is an ancient one, which is even apparent in European witchery (of both the white and black kinds), and some of the remaining African traditional religions[7] include nails in various power rituals and incantations. Martin Whitehead's **THE PROMISE KEEPER** is a monster movie that took a commonly-used form of Congolese power magic and introduced it into American cinema.

The use—that is to say, their *proper* use—of magical rituals and items from such countries as Togo, the Republic of the Congo, Burundi, and Nigeria in films has been a rarity stateside and elsewhere. I first became aware of the horror aspects of their proper use in William Girdler's **ABBY** (1974). In that film, William Marshall (fresh off his *Blacula* two-pack) starred as Bishop Garnet Williams, an archaeologist who, while on a dig in Nigeria, unearths a magical box and unwittingly unleashes a West African *orisha*. This evil entity—a wild aspect of the Yoruba god *Olorun* (although this fact isn't readily made clear by the conclusion of the movie, maybe *Eshu/Èṣù/ Elegbara*, a trickster spirit, which is something common to many of the world's religions)— then possesses William's wife Abby (Carol Speed, who was subsequently seen opposite Rudy Ray Moore in **DISCO GODFATHER** [1979, USA, D: J. Robert Wagoner]. **ABBY** was also responsible for my formable interest in African religions, as its script was peppered with references to the Yoruba people's *Olódùmarè* beliefs, as well as those of Vodun (a.k.a. Vodon, Vodoun, Vodou, Voudou, Voodoo)

Over the past 70-odd years, other cinematic projects and TV shows have taken bits and pieces of *Olódùmarè* (and Vodun) beliefs and mixed them up for dramatic effect. Got a "spooky" *ori inu* mask made of wood or clay? Then you got

for viewers into movies of more recent vintage (as opposed to the aforementioned more obscurely ancient antique **SON OF INGAGI**) are the *Blacula* duo (which were covered in *M!* #14 [p.34] by Troy Howarth). The first of those, **BLACULA** (1972), was directed by the black filmmaker William Crain, who also helmed the seemingly supernatural film **BROTHER JOHN** (1971), as well as the more exploitive **DR. BLACK, MR. HYDE** (1976, both USA).[6] Rolling on into the '80s and '90s, fewer black-owned films were being made, though we did have **DEF BY TEMPTATION** (1990, USA, D: James Bond III), and even the shot-on-video and completely psychotic **BLACK DEVIL DOLL FROM HELL** (1984, USA, D: Chester Novell Turner). I'm sure many of these films will be discussed in *Weng's Chop* #9 and its Blaxploitation Roundtable (that particular issue should be out in June of this year).

There have been other "black" horror films, but this review is about one which I happened to discover serendipitously.

---

6   I would love to include coverage of some of my favorite "Blaxploitation" horror films in this review, but considering they were made by white directors, that wouldn't quite fit this review. For those interested, those titles include William A. Levey's 1974 **BLACKENSTEIN: THE BLACK FRANKENSTEIN** (a very entertaining although incredibly disjointed monster movie), William Girdler's Nigerian **EXORCIST** rip-off **ABBY** (1974), Paul Maslansky (of the *Police Academy* series fame)'s 1974 voodoo/zombie film **SUGAR HILL**, and Arther Marks' **J.D.'S REVENGE** (1976).

7   "Traditional" meaning *indigenous*, which are those religions still practiced today that existed *prior* to the intrusion of the Abrahamic religions of Christianity, Islam, and Bahá'í. Judaism, although far older than the other three, never really took hold in the continent. This may be due in part to its very exclusive nature, although the Beta Israelites from Ethiopia are black Africans and practice a very old form of Judaism (this was been a problem for the State of Israel, but I won't drag out my soapbox here!).

yourself some *voodoo* happening, man! **THE PROMISE KEEPER** introduces the viewer to one of the more violent or aggressive spiritual forms of the Kongo people's Bantu religion.

The film begins with a sexual tryst between two of a law firm's three partners, Bernard (Ric Walker) and Ranada (Terrina Reese). For Ranada, it's a booty-call and nothing more, and she wishes to remain friends with Bernard. It's rather obvious that he wants more, but she will have nothing of it. The firm is a young one, and all three of its partners are lean and hungry, and there is a constant sexual tension and conflict between Ranada and the two men. Bernard is conflicted about his ex-wife and teenage daughter (who has been skipping school), and hasn't been keeping his mind on the game. Ranada is the "modern woman", a go-getter who wants to be part of a successful law firm *and* get more out of life; she wants a man in her life worthy or her prowess. Miguel is worried about his status in the firm, as well as his insecurities as a heterosexual (he's short, and constantly tosses sexual innuendos towards Ranada, who constantly shoots him down). Yes, it's a simmering mess!

It's obvious that they were all once friends, and even lovers, but the strain of keeping the business going has begun to fry their nerves. In an effort for corporate togetherness, and to celebrate their recent landing of the Puerto Rican Trade Association on their roster of clients, Miguel buys a "Western African nail fetish" for the firm's lobby. As he describes it, "These were used in villages to seal bargains and deals".

(The staff looks more than a little uncomfortable at the unveiling.) "When a promise was made, a nail was driven in as a way of making an oath". Of course, this rather *Twilight Zone*-like introduction of the wooden figure already has us set up for the events to come.

The nail fetish is an actual religious and magical tool used by the West African Kongo people. It is known as a *nkondi*, and it is a male figure carved out of wood with iron nails sticking out if it. Like the wooden box that Dr. Williams unearthed in **ABBY**, this figure comes with a Bantu *nkisi/nkishi* spirit inside it. All of these types of fetishes do, and they are a type of magic that is not to be taken lightly. *Nkondi* are an aggressive subclass of *nkisi* that, once activated by hammering a nail into its body and an oath or name is spoken, they "hunt down and attack wrong-doers, witches, or enemies".[8]

Of course, Dan Curtis' 1975 made-for-TV horror movie **TRILOGY OF TERROR** inevitably popped into my head, and I imagined we were in store for something akin to that film's "Zuni fetish doll" which scared the crap out of TV viewers back in '75. However, that was *not* going to happen...

Early on in the film, Miguel's Auntie Ripol has a psychic bond with the *nkondi*, and she is able to disarm the spirit by removing its hex bag (sometimes called a *juju*) from a compartment carved into the back of the statue, then stores it in her purse. I imagine she has some sixth

8 *https://en.wikipedia.org/wiki/Nkondi*

Miguel introduces the staff to the office's new Nail Fetish statue...

sense about the forbidding nature of the *nkondi*, because she is part of the African diaspora and knows "the tradition of the Promise Keeper. They can be abominations, and that one is a *killer*". Bernard rolls his eyes and promises to take care of the matter by removing the statue from the lobby.

We are then introduced to Bernard's daughter Tina (Lakeisha Woodard), a bright high school student who is easily bored, so she tends to skip classes. After having a heart-to-heart with her father, she makes a promise to him that she will be good, hammering a nail into the top of the *nkondi*'s ugly head to make it official. She remarks to Miguel, who watches her nailing the statue, "It's like praying. It can't hurt".

Oh No!

Our three partners begin bickering and quarreling, and eventually grievances and gripes come to a boiling point, so something must be done to keep the firm from coming apart at the seams. Ranada suggests that all three of them should make promises to each other, so that cooler heads will prevail and work will resume as usual. "We all have flaws, that we created out of our strengths. The biggest challenge is making sure those flaws don't destroy us". Bernard gets an idea and leads his partners out into the lobby where the statue stands, a hammer and nails by its base. "Let's put our money where our mouth is, and make a bargain to change something about ourselves". One by one they approach, make a (secret) promise and hammer a nail into the wooden creature's roughly-carved frame:

Miguel in the statue's hand, Ranada into its neck, and lastly Bernard, who adds his promissory nail to the *nkondi*'s chest.

Later that night, Bernard recalls that Miguel's auntie had mentioned how the statue's spirit will only become activated if the owner adds a personal *juju* to the fetish. He decides to create his own by wrapping some Lemonhead candies and aspirin in a handkerchief then placing it inside the compartment. Once in place, he seals the statue then leaves the office to go home.

Dumb move, dude!

You *know* what's going to happen next. One by one the promisers break their vows, causing a monstrous giant to appear at their door. This creature, seen only as a silhouetted shape in rooms filled with a red haze, is that of a muscular African man with hundreds of iron nails protruding out of his skin. The action during these sequences is blurry, the editing quickly cut, and what effects there happen to be in creating the monster are very low-tech. As Kristoffer "Krist" Neumann, the film's makeup and effects man mentioned in a brief conversation, "...the fetish spirit was purposefully designed to be seen mostly in silhouette".

Of course, the monster does manage to kill one of the "promise-breakers", and although I won't reveal who it is, I wasn't all that surprised, since that character—like in many horror films—acted outside of the "social norm" and was too self-serving and mean-spirited to survive, given Whitehead's *Tales from the Darkside*-style approach to the tale. Nevertheless, the film does end on a lighter note as the surviving members of the legal firm manage to unload the fetish off on one of their competitors "as a gift".

THE PROMISE KEEPER was near-impossible to find once I read about it on Wikipedia. Googling didn't help matters, as I was typically guided towards a Christian YouTube documentary called **THE PROMISE KEEPERS**. (*Not* really what I was looking for!) A little more searching and I found that the present film was available from Amazon, although not as a streaming option as I hoped, so I bought the DVD. (Support the indie filmmaker and all!)

THE PROMISE KEEPER is definitely an independent production, and somewhat reminiscent of other low-budget monster movies, including **THE RUNESTONE** (1991, USA, D: Willard Carroll). It's obvious that the film was made on a meager budget, and was no doubt shot on location at various offices, restaurants, and apartments in and around Chicago, IL. Not that something like that should *ever* turn you off from renting, buying or streaming an unknown film (I mean, I'm a guy who has sat through *hundreds* of micro-budget Indian horror and action films over the past couple of years!). However, maybe something like the very odd **GANJA & HESS** (1973, USA, D: Bill Gunn) would be more in line as a comparison. In that African American-made indie, Dr. Green (played by Duane Jones of **NIGHT OF THE LIVING DEAD** fame) is a professor who becomes infected by an ancient vampirism bacterium when he is stabbed with an old African sacrificial blade. Gunn's gem is one of the genre's most fascinating entries, as we witness Green's transformation and thirst for blood—something he shares with a female companion (Marlene Clark)—and its associations with African vampirism (which is sketchy at best, though Gunn does manage to stay within plausible socio-anthropological logic). For those interested, **GANJA & HESS** has only recently been reissued in its full unedited format. The movie was previously recut and released theatrically as **BLOOD COUPLE** in an effort to make it more commercially viable. It was also out on domestic VHS as **BLACK VAMPIRE**, which is how I first saw it.

THE PROMISE KEEPER is Whitehead's sole feature outing, although some of the actors from it have been active in TV roles; most notable is Rick Vargas (a.k.a. Ric Arthur), who played the hothead Miguel. He has gotten rather steady, albeit minor, work in the Chicago indie scene, including Salvador Barcena's angel-

based horror/thriller **FALLEN SOULS** (2010), Junk Kajino's and Ed Koziarski's drama **THE FIRST BREATH OF TENGAN REI** (更多资料 / *Rei, saisho no kokyû*, 2009, USA/Japan), and Brian Caunter's crime actioner **CHICAGO OVERCOAT** (2009). Ric Walker's first role was in the "cult classic" gang flick **DEADBEAT AT DAWN** (1988, USA, D: Jim Van Bebber), which I must confess to having never seen. Lastly, Terrina Reese had a minor role in the Chicago indie **CUP OF MY BLOOD** (2005, D: Lance Catania), which sounds like a horror film about possession and exorcism, but I have yet to locate a copy of the film for review.

Monster! co-editor Tim has a collection of ritual masks, idols, statues, reliquaries and all sorts of "spooky" stuff in his house, including this Congolese nail fetish

Fernando Bilbao as "FM" in a Spanish lobby card for **DRACULA, PRISONER OF FRANKENSTEIN**

I wish to extend my special thanks to Alain Petit and Stephen Thrower, the leading voices in the small but fervent choir of pro-Franco enthusiasts, whose extraordinary books on Jess provided some essential information on the making of these films.
~ Troy Howarth

THREE MONSTER MASHES... FRANCO-STYLE!

by Troy Howarth

Lab assistant Uncle Jess cranks up the juice in **THE EROTIC RITES OF FRANKENSTEIN**

"I have a physical need for making movies. It's not just about directing but also the planning, the editing, everything. It's my whole life and I truly believe that I'm better off pursuing this career any way I can rather than just waiting around in a gilded cage for someone to come and get me. I don't like gilded cages and I don't like vacations. I like making movies and if I get the chance to make a big budget movie, that's great! But if I have to make do with low budget erotica, so be it, as long as I get to direct it myself. Any action is preferable to inaction." – Jess Franco (excerpt from an interview conducted by Philippe Rège)[1]

---

1   Petit, Alain, *Jess Franco: ou les prospéritiés du bis*, (Paris: Artus Films, 2015), p.20.

Another Spanish lobby card for **DRACULA, PRISONER OF FRANKENSTEIN**. Paca Gabaldón and Howard Vernon rise from their coffins for a late-night bite

The above quote from Jess Franco (birth name: Jesús Franco Manera [1930-2013]) is something of a mission statement. To understand it is to understand the impulse which guided the director through an unbelievably prolific career where the dizzying highs and stultifying lows blend into one big impressionist painting. For Jess Franco, making movies was not a job—it was an all-consuming *passion*. This passion resulted in a hectic workload, the likes of which we have seldom seem in other filmmakers. Directors like Stanley Kubrick (1928-1999) and Terence Mallick (1943-) are renowned for taking *years* to plan their films—and for taking

A candid behind-the-scenes shot from **DRACULA, PRISONER OF FRANKEN-STEIN** of Dennis Price and Howard Vernon

all the time in the world to make and then assemble them, sweating over every frame and obsessing over every edit in their quest for absolute perfection. For viewers who see this as the only admirable approach to making movies, a director like Franco is intolerable. Franco seldom devoted all of his energies to any one project. Even while he was in the throes of making one film, he had his mind on other projects, as-yet-unwritten. He would hastily jot down ideas, throw together sketchy screenplays and sell producers on backing these projects by the sheer force of his charismatic personality—as well as by the promise that the film wouldn't cost very much, thus minimizing the risk for all concerned. Franco had absolutely no interest in striving for perfectionism. It simply wasn't a part of his DNA. On those occasions when the films came together in a satisfactory manner, the end results demonstrated that Franco had the ability to make a conventionally well-crafted movie, with a clear and coherent narrative; but much of the time, what we were left with was something of a grab-bag of wild ideas done up in an air of impoverished desperation, but still pulsing with raw energy and conviction nonetheless. Not all Franco films were created equal and I, for one, do not hold with the idea that they are *all* worthy of being defended; for some of the more fervent fans, the bad films are an essential part of the puzzle and, as such, they demand our respect—but for me, to put the likes of **INCUBUS**

(2002, USA) on the same playing ground as **SUCCUBUS** (*Necronomicon—Geträumte Sünden*, 1967, West Germany) is to undermine the artistry and imagination evident in every frame of the latter. Let's be frank here: Franco *loved* to experiment, and he was also too hyperactive to focus on any given project for very long, and this could result in films which were only half-formed…to say nothing of half-baked. Franco was also prone to doing "survival projects," which is to say movies he had very little emotional interest invested in, which he undertook purely in the interest of paying-off his bills. The worst of Franco's films seem to be to be utterly indefensible: shoddy, lethargic and about as engaging as the worst home movies of anybody's childhood trips to Yellowstone Park. But it's the *best* of Franco—along with the wide array of films stuck in between the two extremes—which assures his reputation as one of European cinema's most interesting mavericks. Like him, love him or loathe him, there's only *one* Jess Franco!

In 1970, Franco endured a personal tragedy: his ideal "fetish actress" Soledad Miranda (1943-1970) died in a car crash. Franco had found an ideal artistic muse in the young actress, and was excited by the prospect of continuing to work with and build vehicles around her unique presence. Following her death, he threw himself into a string of mostly unremarkable movies, culminating in the truly remarkable **A VIRGIN AMONG THE LIVING DEAD** (*Une vierge chez les morts vivants*, 1971; see *Monster!* #23 [p.59]). **VIRGIN** found Franco working at the absolute top of his game, exploring the boundaries between life and death, and reality and fantasy, with a sure and steady hand. After completing the independently produced and financed VIRGIN, Jess signed on to work for the producer Robert De Nesle. De Nesle (1906-1978) set up the company Comptoir Français du Film Production in the 1950s and first entered Franco's universe when he contributed some money to the production of the tongue-in-cheek French/German/Israeli adventure romp **SEXY DARLINGS** (*Robinson und seine wilden sklavinnen*, 1971). De Nesle was impressed by Franco's ability to think on his feet and make films in a fast and efficient manner, so he persuaded the director to come and work with him. De Nesle would allow Franco the sort of creative freedom which had often been denied to him—on his Harry Alan Towers productions, for example—and the films he made during this period were emblematic of the explosion of unfettered creativity which typifies the director's "golden period" of the early-to-mid-1970s.

The first of Franco's De Nesle productions was **DRACULA, PRISONER OF FRANKENSTEIN** (*Drácula contra Frankenstein*, 1971, Spain/France).

Filmed in Portugal in November of '71[2], it opens with Count Dracula (Howard Vernon) putting the bite on his latest victim. Dr. Seward (Alberto Dalbés) decides that the time has come to put a stop to the killings, so he goes to Castle Dracula and stakes the vampire in his coffin. The peaceful respite is interrupted by the arrival of Dr. Frankenstein (Dennis Price), who revives the vampire and uses it and his man-made creature (Fernando Bilbao) to try and take control of the village.

DRACULA, PRISONER OF FRANKENSTEIN is absolutely indebted to the expressionist horror films of the 1920s, as well as to the Universal horror films of the 1930s and '40s. By his own admission, Franco was not a fan of the output of Hammer Films, so his movie inevitably looks quite different compared to the films they were producing around that same timeframe. Not surprisingly, given that the end result was so out-of-step with what was popular at the time, Franco's film encountered a great deal of hostility among fans and critics alike, many of whom failed to understand what he was striving for. The film is one part update of the "monster mash" approach of films like **HOUSE OF FRANKENSTEIN** (1944) and **HOUSE OF DRACULA** (1945, both USA, D: Erle C. Kenton) and one part homage to German

2 All shooting dates given herein are taken from Thrower, Stephen and Julian Grainger, *Murderous Passions: The Delirious Cinema of Jesús Franco, Volume One*, (London: Strange Attractor Press, 2015).

Belgian poster for **DRACULA, PRISONER OF FRANKENSTEIN** (art unsigned)

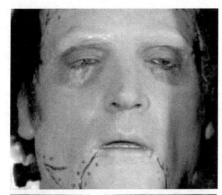

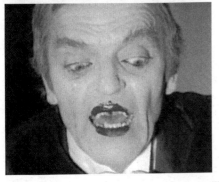

expressionism, all done up in Franco's usual off-the-cuff style. In a sense, it is basically his response to the disappointment of **COUNT DRACULA** (*El Conde Drácula*, 1970, Spain/West Germany/Italy/Liechtenstein), which Franco directed for Harry Alan Towers (1920-2009). That earlier film was a sincere but hopelessly compromised attempt at "faithfully" dramatizing Bram Stoker's novel, and it found the director trying his damnedest to stamp his personality on the material while being straitjacketed by a producer who had lost faith in his abilities; the end product was met with derision and disappointment and, despite being heavily promoted in fanzines of the period, it barely secured a theatrical release in the US or the UK. When the time came to make **DRACULA, PRISONER OF FRANKENSTEIN**, Franco was allowed creative freedom to do as he pleased, though inevitably he was still working within the restraints of very tight budgets and schedules.

The opening scenes play out in such a way that one would be forgiven for thinking the movie is a period piece—but when Frankenstein arrives in his limousine, it's clear that the action is actually set in the present-day. The contrast between the past and this sudden intrusion of the present is surreal, and sums up the movie's offbeat mentality. Frankenstein's motivations are sketchy at best, but hinge on the old supervillain motif of world domination; by enslaving the resurrected Dracula and using him and his brutish monster to terrorize the villagers, he hopes to put himself in a position of power which will allow him do as he pleases. As played by an ailing Dennis Price (1915-1973), Frankenstein is a sad shadow of his former glory; indeed, the use of a former star-on-the-skids like Price is essential in completing this image. It is well-known that Price's problems with alcohol were very much in evidence by this stage in his career, and indeed there are some moments when he appears to be weaving a bit. Even so, Price's inherent dignity helps to give the character a bit of gravitas. The film is not especially focused on character, however, being more of a mood piece at the end of the day. Franco has a lot of fun playing around with the classic monsters and mashing them up together for his own amusement. The director's long-time collaborator Howard Vernon (1908-1996) plays Dracula as a sort of grotesque pantomime figure. He never speaks a word and is often shown with his face frozen in a weird sort of grimace, with his

Left, Top to Bottom: "4 Faces of Death" – Fernando Bilbao, Britt Nichols, him known only as Brandy, and Howard Vernon as **DRACULA, PRISONER OF FRANKEN-STEIN**'s multiple monsters

fangs exposed; if anything, he looks more like Lon Chaney in **LONDON AFTER MIDNIGHT** (1927; see *Monster!* #25 [p.77]) than any of the other screen Draculas, from Béla Lugosi (1882-1956) to Christopher Lee (1922-2015). Stylization is the key here, rather than the sort of realism favored by the filmmakers at Hammer. Franco often spoke of his dislike of the films by Hammer's biggest hit-maker Terence Fisher (1904-1980), and this is a point worth considering. Fisher was a first-class storyteller, and his goal was always to root the supernatural in a sense of reality; the situations may be absurd, but the people and the way they interact with each other is as matter-of-fact as possible. In Franco's mind, this sort of approach robbed his films of the magic of fantasy, and spoke of a general dislike for the fantastic potential of genre cinema. As such, Franco's approach couldn't be any more different. He highlights the absurd, allows things to go off in completely unexpected directions, generally relegating the characters to the background while focusing on mood and atmosphere as much as possible.

DRACULA, PRISONER OF FRANKENSTEIN is not necessarily top-tier Franco, but it's one of those films that works exceedingly well in sections. Franco himself was very proud of the picture, and would defend it as one of the best he ever made. It's easy to see why he was so fond of it, though it's debatable whether it really deserves to be placed among his best works. In a sense, it is pure Franco in the best sense of the term: a succession of striking images set to a vaguely wonky sense of tempo

with an underlining sense of humor. That there are imperfections aplenty hardly seems important, especially since precious little effort is made to cover them up; instead, Franco hopes that we will simply go with the flow and appreciate it as a sort of comic book-style fever dream.

As a final, curious aside, it has to be noted that the film, as it commonly exists, is among the tamest in Franco's filmography. There is very little violence, and absolutely no sex; there aren't even any bare breasts on display, and that is very unusual indeed for Franco in the early '70s. Now, it can be argued that the film didn't call for eroticism. Fair enough. However, some stills exist which seem to confirm that an alternate "nude" version was prepared, though it was never released anywhere in the world, to the best of my knowledge. The English-language dub, prepared by Richard McNamara (1915-1998), adds on some voiceover narration by Drs. Frankenstein and Seward (though neither Dennis Price nor Alberto Dalbés [1922-1983] did their own dubbing) which disrupts the dreamy flow of the imagery. The Spanish version plays mostly like a silent movie, with lots of weird sound effects and music cues taken from Bruno Nicolai (1926-1991)'s scores for Franco's own **JUSTINE** (*Marquis de Sade: Justine*, 1968, Italy/USA/West Germany/Liechtenstein) and his aforementioned '70 effort **COUNT DRACULA**, with only a minimum of dialogue. Unless a more transgressive "nudie" version should ever surface, the Spanish edition will likely remain the gold standard by which all others must be judged.

Eye-Teeth:
One of **DRACULA, PRISONER OF FRANKENSTEIN**'s
numerous bizarre images

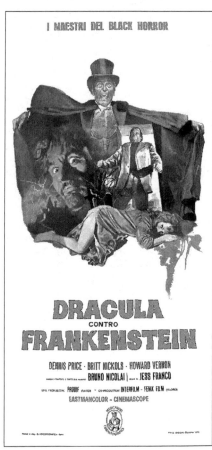

Inside poster:
I MAESTRI DEL BLACK HORROR

DRACULA
CONTRO
FRANKENSTEIN

DENNIS PRICE · BRITT NICKOLS · HOWARD VERNON
BRUNO NICOLAI | · · JESS FRANCO

PRODIF · INTERFILM - FENIX FILM
EASTMANCOLOR - CINEMASCOPE

Italian *locandina* for **DRACULA, PRISONER OF FRANKENSTEIN** (art by Rodolfo Gasparri)

Franco followed **DRACULA, PRISONER OF FRANKENSTEIN** with a second De Nesle production, the woman-in-prison opus **DEVIL'S ISLAND LOVERS** (*Los amantes de la isla del diablo*, 1972; see *Weng's Chop* #6 [p.42]), after which he continued to explore the classic movie monsters with the back-to-back productions of **DRACULA'S DAUGHTER** and **THE EROTIC RITES OF FRANKENSTEIN**, both produced in Portugal in '72. Together with **DRACULA, PRISONER OF FRANKENSTEIN**, the three films form a sort of unofficial trilogy—though any attempt at linking them together by strict chronology is doomed to failure.

DRACULA'S DAUGHTER (*La fille de Dracula*, 1972, France/Portugal) is generally regarded as the dud of the trilogy, and with good reason. It's not a *bad* film, and its best moments have the magic one associates with Franco when he is firing on all cylinders, but the pacing is lax, and it builds to a complete non-climax. The story deals with Luisa Karlstein (Britt Nichols), who is summoned to her family home to see her dying grandmother. The grandmother dies, but before expiring she tells Luisa of a family curse involving the former Count von Karlstein, also known as Dracula (Howard Vernon). Luisa thereafter falls under Count Dracula's dark spell, and helps to revive him. A series of murders follow, before the family retainer, Jefferson (Jess Franco), sets out to destroy the vampires and lift the curse.

Filmed around January to February of '72, on the same locations and with much the same cast and crew as **DRACULA, PRISONER OF FRANKENSTEIN**, **DRACULA'S DAUGHTER** suffers from an inability to sustain the same kind of dreamlike ambiance. Part of the problem is in the material, which plays out like a rather pale retread of the director's earlier Gothic film **THE SADISTIC BARON VON KLAUS** (*La mano de un hombre muerto*, 1962, Spain). The plotting is cumbersome and gets in the way of the sort of free-association of images found in the films which bracket it. By situating the action in a more "realistic" context, Franco introduces the need for more developed characterization—and on this front, in particular, the movie is definitely lacking. The actresses are attractive, but they don't have much to hang onto: Luisa is the usual wide-eyed horror film heroine, and she lacks the presence of mind typically found in Franco's most interesting female protagonists. Britt Nichols (born 1950) can hardly be blamed for this deficit: she does what she can with what she has to do, but ultimately she is little more than decorative window dressing. The film's best sequence is undoubtedly her seduction of her cousin Karine, played by the equally-fetching Anne Libert (1946-). In the rush to lionize the likes of Soledad Miranda and Lina Romay (1954-2012), Libert and Nichols have been somewhat overlooked in the canon of Franco's major "fetish actresses". They both figured prominently in some of the director's best films of the period, they both had no ambivalence about showing-off their bodies, and they both displayed a real flair for playing everything from heroines to villains. Neither of them get ideal showcases here, but Libert would be rewarded with a fantastic role in **THE EROTIC RITES OF FRANKENSTEIN**, while Nichols was given ample chance to shine not only in **A VIRGIN AMONG THE LIVING DEAD**, but also in another upcoming De Nesle/Franco gig, the nunsploitationer **THE DEMONS** (*Les Démons*, 1972, France/Portugal). The big seduction scene in **DRACULA'S DAUGHTER** is incredibly erotic, with the two actresses exploring each other's bodies in a way that feels both carnal and genuine. The action is intercut with Max Karlstein (played by Franco's favorite composer, Daniel J. White [1912-1997]) playing a beautiful piece of classical music on the piano. The intercutting adds immeasurably to this scene's tempo and the sequence is as breathlessly beautiful as it is erotic. Franco's fusion of sex and horror is at its peak here; unfortunately, nothing else in the rest of the film comes close to matching its impact, but it is still worth seeing for this scene alone.

DRACULA'S DAUGHTER is not one of Franco's more accomplished films, but that is not to say it's a total failure. Some of the photography is quite striking, the locations are as atmospheric as one could hope for, and Franco gives a good performance as the savant figure who understands all about vampires. Howard Vernon is completely wasted here, unfortunately, but he would soon get another stellar showcase in **THE EROTIC RITES OF FRANKENSTEIN**. The present film is a good deal sexier than **DRACULA, PRISONER OF FRANKENSTEIN**, but it never scales the heights of sublime absurdity achieved by its follow-up feature. Seen on its own terms, it is reasonably engaging and has enough going for it to warrant a viewing or two, but when put in the context of its companion features, **DRACULA'S DAUGHTER** simply feels too *ordinary* and run-of-the-mill.

The same cannot be said of **THE EROTIC RITES OF FRANKENSTEIN** (*La maldición de Franken-stein*, 1972, Spain/France). As Franco would later say, *"DRACULA, PRISONER OF FRANKEN-STEIN wasn't enough for me so I directed a second opus even crazier and more baroque than anything I'd done so far: LA MALDICIÓN DE FRANKEN-STEIN. That's why I love those two so much."*[3] The film is among the most "out-there" of Franco's ca-reer, and if you know anything about his movies, you will know: that is saying a *lot*. Dr. Frankenstein (Dennis Price again) and his assistant Morpho (Fran-co) succeed in giving life to a silver-skinned creature (Fernando Bilbao). The mad magician Cagliostro (Howard Vernon) sends his minion, the bird-wom-an Melissa (Anne Libert), to kill the doctor and his assistant and to kidnap the creature. Cagliostro plans to use the creature to abduct women on his behalf so that he can use their body parts to create his ide-al woman. Frankenstein's daughter, Vera (Beatriz Savón), resurrects her father using his methods, and he explains how Cagliostro had him murdered. She sets out to avenge him with the assistance of Dr. Seward (Alberto Dalbés), but Cagliostro does not prove to be an easy foe to defeat...

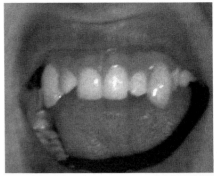

Britt-Bit! In the prologue to **DRACULA'S DAUGHTER**, lead actress Nichols bares her canines as she attacks a bathing starlet

DRACULA, PRISONER OF FRANKENSTEIN was strange, but it looks positively *staid* compared to **THE EROTIC RITES OF FRANKENSTEIN!** Latter film presents Franco at his most freewheeling, mixing-and-matching elements from his favorite pulp scenarios and serials to create a heady cocktail that is absolutely without comparison in the annals of European Cult Cinema. As is so often the case, the end product is rough around the edges and suffers from various technical imperfections which are sure to draw guffaws from less-sympathetic viewers. Those who are on the same wavelength as Franco, however, should find much to savor here. The atmosphere is every bit as intoxicating

Britt Bites Again! Belgian poster for **DRACULA'S DAUGHTER**

3   Petit, Alain, *Jess Franco: ou les prospéritiés du bis*, (Paris: Artus Films, 2015), p.545.

Spanish pressbook ad for **THE EROTIC RITES OF FRANKENSTEIN** (art by "Jano"/ Francisco Fernández Zarza)

as it had been in **DRACULA, PRISONER OF FRANKENSTEIN**, but the scenario is even wilder and the characterizations are gloriously over-the-top. The film is dominated by Howard Vernon, playing his third truly great role for Franco, following the original Dr. Orlof in **THE AWFUL DR. ORLOF** (*Gritos en la noche*, 1961, Spain/France) and the mysterious Uncle Howard in the above-cited **A VIRGIN AMONG THE LIVING DEAD**. Vernon truly gets into the spirit of the thing, playing the cackling, megalomaniacal Cagliostro with just the right touch of camp. He is not so far over-the-top as to be unbelievable, however. Cagliostro's attempts at creating a super race obviously align him to a real-life monster like Hitler, and Vernon's charismatic and super-intense presence coupled with his flair for delivering a good monologue helps to cement the comparison. Dr. Frankenstein is written-out of the action early on, though Dennis Price gets to come back for a few scenes of "reanimated" action.

Price has less screen-time overall compared to **DRACULA, PRISONER OF FRANKENSTEIN** and he really isn't at his best here, but his dignified presence still adds an extra something special to the proceedings; following the film's production *circa* March-April of '72, he would appear in a handful more films (including Douglas Hickox's superb **THEATRE OF BLOOD** [1972] and Antony Balch's **HORROR HOSPITAL** [1973, both UK]) before his premature death in October of '73. Best of all here is Anne Libert, who gets the role of her career as the cannibalistic bird-woman, Melissa. Melissa is blind and has a special psychic bond with Cagliostro, thus allowing her to communicate on his behalf as a sort of receiver. Libert looks fantastic: she is completely naked throughout, save for some plumage affixed to her skin. She is meek and subservient in her scenes with Cagliostro, but is capable of unleashing savage and frightening fury when she goes in for the kill, pecking her victims to death and tearing at their flesh like one of George Romero's zombies.

The timeframe is unclear once more, but it seems as if this time it really is intended to be the 19th Century. Franco makes exceptional use of the locations and cinematographer Raúl Artigot (1936-2014) captures some magnificent images, with heavy use of wide-angle lenses and colored gel lighting. The scenes of Cagliostro's sect gathering in the dungeons manage to rise above the tacky dime-store masks and makeup effects to achieve a real hallucinatory sort of delirium. The whole film plays out like a half-demented fantasy, with elements of the Italian *fumetti* (adult comic book) merging with the naïve dramatics of the 1940s Hollywood monster mashes to create something wholly different from any other film you are ever likely to see.

Frankenstein's monster and victim from **THE EROTIC RITES OF FRANKENSTEIN**

Owing to the film's increased erotic content, it was necessary to film alternative takes for the Spanish market. Spain was then still under the iron rule of Generalissimo Francisco Franco (1892-1975), so the kind of nudity and "perversion" depicted by Franco in this film would never have been permitted in that country. In addition to filming clothed takes, Franco was also forced to go back and add in a subplot to make up for some material that was sacrificed to appease the Spanish censors. The added scenes were filmed nearly a year after the original shoot and feature Lina Romay (birth name: Rosa María Almirall Martínez) in one of her earliest screen appearances. She plays a mute gypsy girl named Esmeralda who falls under Cagliostro's spell. The scenes with Romay are attractively filmed and have a poetry of their own, but on the whole they merely serve to slow the action down. The original French version ran a very lean 75 minutes, while the Spanish version with these added scenes clocks-in at 90 minutes. Franco and Romay completists will want to see this version for the sake of comparison, but the French version remains the ideal version of this most unorthodox gem.

THE EROTIC RITES OF FRANKENSTEIN does not represent Franco's final encounter with the classic horror film monsters, but it can be said to be his definitive statement on the genre. This is not a film that will win over ambivalent viewers to the Franco cult; on the contrary, it's probably assured to scare many people off from pursuing his movies any further. But for those who can appreciate its wild sense of imagination, humor and poetry, it offers proof positive of the director's unique personality as expressed in his work. And the trilogy of De Nesle/Franco retro-homages stands out as some of the most intoxicating and divisive work in the whole wide and wonderful world of European Cult Cinema. Whether you like them or not, chances are—you won't forget them!

French newspaper ad for **THE EROTIC RITES OF FRANKENSTEIN** (art unsigned)

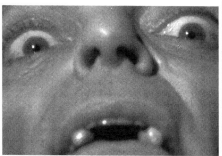

Howard Vernon as Drac rises from his coffin in **DRACULA'S DAUGHTER**, giving Britt Nichols quite the fright in the process

Uncle Jess as Jefferson the vampire-savvy savant in **DRACULA'S DAUGHTER**

DARK INTRUDER (1965):

A Synopsis *[Spoiler Alert]*

San Francisco, 1890: A series of Ripper-like murders by a taloned, monstrous stranger in a black cloak who leaves a bizarre miniature demonic carving with each body prompts Police Commissioner Misbach (Gilbert Green) to seek the help of wealthy bachelor occult investigator Brett Kingsford (Leslie Nielsen) and his manservant Nikola (Charles Bolender), who have assisted the police before. With each of the four killings to date, the carved idol's Janus-like head has subtly changed, as if a more human visage were emerging from the back of the reptilian skull. Eerily aligned with the murders has been the peculiar behavior of Kingford's friend, antique dealer Robert Vandenburg (Peter Mark Richman), whose socialite fiancé Evelyn Lang (Judi Meredith) visits Kingsford to request he check up on Vandenburg, whose mysterious 'blackouts' are beginning to alarm her. Vandenburg—born 30 years earlier under odd circumstances to his archeologist parents during an expedition near Baghdad, leaving him with a large inexplicable scar on his back—fears the murders may be related to his blackouts; furthermore, the victims were either acquaintances or persons connected to his birth.

Kingsford covertly consults elder Asian antiquities dealer and mystic Chi Zang (Peter Brocco), showing Zang one of the enigmatic carvings. Zang identifies the ivory likeness as that of *"a Sumerian god, ancient before Babylon, before Egypt... the essence of blind evil, with its demons and its acolytes, so cruel, so merciless. All were banished from the earth, and they are forever struggling to return."* Offering further explanation, Zang shows Kingsford a rare wrapped-and-preserved miniature, one which appears to be the sculpture of a bestial humanoid bound to a seven-spoked "demon's wheel." Though Zang cautions against it, Kingsford reaches out to hold the miniature; it is warm to the touch and scratches his palm, drawing blood. It is not a carving, it is a mummified creature with claws, craving blood and life. Zang explains that the demons who worship the ancient Sumerian god seek to possess a human or animal host, a ritual requiring seven sacrificial killings corresponding to the seven spokes of the "demon's wheel."

Meanwhile, Evelyn Lang convinces Vandenburg to consult a psychic known only as Professor Malaki (Werner Klemperer, voiced by Norman Lloyd) who sits in the shadows, his visage beneath a hooded robe. Vandenburg is shaken by the cryptic encounter and hastily departs; once alone, Malaki's clawed hands reach into the light: he is the killer, and Vandenburg is his intended "vessel." Kingsford and Nikola's investigations reveal that the odd circumstances of Vandenburg's birth and the scar on his back as evidence of a deformed twin sibling, surgically removed from the newborn Vandenburg. The nurse instructed to dispose of the body of Vandenburg's stillborn Siamese twin had instead rescued the deformed infant— not realizing the once-dead child's reawakening was due to possession by a Sumerian demon—and raised it as her own. The now-adult monster twin Professor Malaki has located Vandenburg and must complete the necessary ritual killings, the seventh allowing Malaki to finally exchange souls and bodies with his handsome biological brother. Orchestrating the possession and the immediate dispatch of his monstrous body—now host to the human Vandenburg's mind and soul—Malaki assumes Vanderburg's place in society and the wedding, but not before Kingsford rushes to expose the truth and rescue Evelyn, and restore the real Vandenburg to his rightful place in the family tomb.

BLACK-AND-WHITE INTRUDER

The Lurker at the Threshold of Made-for-TV Horror Movies
Part 2: The Hitchcock Connection

by Stephen R. Bissette

"Omnia Exeunt In Mysterium"
(Everything Ends in Mystery)

- Latin motto in Brett Kingsford's study in *Black Cloak* / **DARK INTRUDER** (1965)

The original subtitle for *Black Cloak*, the pilot, was on its shooting script: "Something With Claws," referring to the demonic murderous brother and to this pint-sized mummy of an actual Sumerian demon, which Chi Zang (Peter Brocco) has in his collection of the occult and arcane. The seven spokes of the "demon's wheel" it holds represent the seven ritualistic killings necessary if the monstrous brother Malaki (Werner Klemperer) is to transfer his spirit into a desirable host body—his more human sibling, Robert Vandenburg (Mark Richman)

We'll likely never know what the deciding factor was in Universal's decision to release **DARK INTRUDER**[1] (1965), to theaters; the decision had to have come from the top, MCA/Universal mogul Lew Wasserman. That's the *only* way any money would have been spent on the promotional materials and cost of prints essential to even the most meager theatrical run.

We can, however, explore the terrain surrounding **DARK INTRUDER**'s production and eventual release, excavating enough to possibly connect-the-dots.

First of all, despite the presumption that there were no made-for-TV horror or fantasy/science-fiction movies before **FEAR NO EVIL**'s telecast in 1969, nothing could be further from the truth. There were precursors and predecessors, and *Black Cloak /* **DARK INTRUDER** was among them.

Genre television's humble beginnings have been charted elsewhere,[2] but the origins of made-for-TV movies has been less thoroughly explored. In short, in the US, Arch Oboler's horror anthology radio series *Lights Out* made the leap to television in 1946 via producer Fred Coe as four live TV specials on NBC-TV; *Lights Out* became a weekly NBC series in 1949, still broadcast live until 1952. Likewise making the leap from radio to television, the thriller/horror series *Suspense* (CBS, 260 episodes, January 6, 1949-August 17, 1954), also broadcast live, followed. Note that *Black Cloak /* **DARK INTRUDER** star Leslie Nielsen appeared in both *Lights Out* (four episodes, 1950-1952) and *Suspense* (six episodes, 1950-53). *Captain Video* (June 27, 1949-April 1, 1955) launched science-fiction TV series the year before **DESTINATION MOON** (1950) kicked-off the American SF movie cycle of the 1950s; there was even an original **CAPTAIN VIDEO: MASTER OF THE STRATOSPHERE** theatrical serial from Columbia Pictures (1951). While pioneers like John Newland and Ivan Tors straddled theatrical motion picture production and producing original episodic television—but not yet telefeatures, per se—TV pilots were being polished, reedited, and/or repackaged to become theatrical releases like **TWO LOST WORLDS** (1950), **SUPERMAN AND THE MOLE-MEN** (1951), and **PROJECT MOON BASE** (1953). In the UK,

when BBC was the only television network, a writer named Nigel Kneale and producer/director Rudolph Cartier galvanized viewers with the serialized six-chapter *The Quatermass Experiment* (July 18, 1953-August 22, 1953), which Hammer Films adapted into their breakthrough theatrical hit **THE QUATERMASS XPERIMENT** (1955, US title: **THE CREEPING UNKNOWN**); Kneale, Cartier, and the BBC would produce and broadcast two more remarkable *Quatermass* serialized adventures before 1959, which yielded two more Hammer Films adaptations [See Louis Paul's "Professor Quatermass to the Rescue!" in *Monster!* #11, pp.51-61]. In France, the great Jean Renoir directed two intended-for-TV feature films, using techniques unique to TV production, to be simultaneously released theatrically even as they premiered on French networks; one of these innovative films was his adaptation of Robert Louis Stevenson's 1886 novella *Strange Case of Dr. Jekyll and Mr. Hyde*, entitled **LE TESTAMENT DU DOCTEUR CORDELIER** (a.k.a. **THE DOCTOR'S HORRIBLE EXPERIMENT** or **EXPERIMENT IN EVIL**, 1959). *[For more on the real history of pre-1969 genre telefeatures and variations on the format, see our accompanying "DARK INTRUDER Sidebar: A Made-For-TV Horror Pre-History" – ed.]*

In this, Renoir anticipated what Alfred Hitchcock himself was up to in 1959, spurning the conservative Hollywood studio *refusals* to produce his proposed adaptation of Robert Bloch's new novel *Psycho*. Hitchcock had his own weekly TV anthology series, and his own TV production company; why not make **PSYCHO** as he would a longer made-for-TV telefeature?

This brings us, at last, to Shamley Productions—the company that made both **PSYCHO** and *Black Cloak /* **DARK INTRUDER**—and the birth of made-for-TV horror movies.

The escalating conflict, conflation (via the licensing of old movies for TV syndication and broadcast), and collusion between cinema and television—as media and as industries—was made quite explicit in a 1957 issue of *Film Culture* that featured as its cover *"A reel of motion picture film on nitrate stock in one of the final stages of chemical deterioration, in the vaults of the Museum of Modern Art Film Library."*[3] A more tactile representation of the jeopardy cinema was in by 1957 could not be imagined—clearly, the point of the cover—and the jeopardy posed by television was explicitly addressed in the opening volley of essays and interviews in the same issue of *Film Culture*, in a

---

1 The title of this film when it was a TV pilot was *Black Cloak*; the title it was theatrically released as was **DARK IN-TRUDER**. When I am referring to its pre-release period—when it was a pilot—I will refer to it as *Black Cloak* / **DARK INTRUDER** (or *BC/DI*). Any reference to the feature after its July 1965 release, it will be **DARK INTRUDER** (or **DI**).

2 *Fantastic Television: A Pictorial History of Sci-Fi, The Unusual and the Fantastic* by Gary Gerani and Paul H. Schulman (Harmony Books, 1983; UK edition Titan Books Ltd., 1987).

3 "Our Cover," *Film Culture*, No. 2 (12), 1957.

HE KILLED with the POWER of DEMONS a million years old!

DARK INTRUDER

LESLIE NIELSEN · JUDI MEREDITH · MARK RICHMAN

Copyright © 1965 by Universal Pictures Co., Inc.   Country of Origin U.S.A.   Printed in U.S.A.

Occult detective Brett Kingsford (Leslie Nielsen) studies the carvings left by each murder victim, which Chi Zang tells him is that of "a Sumerian god, ancient before Babylon, before Egypt... the essence of blind evil, with its demons and its acolytes, so cruel, so merciless. All were banished from the earth, and they are forever struggling to return"

special section entitled "The Impact of Television on Motion Pictures." *Film Culture*'s Television Editor Gilbert Seldes edited and presented the special section with introductory comments, noting,

"Some fifteen years ago when I began asking studio executives what they planned to do when television arrived, the general reply was a laugh and ten years ago the prevalent attitude was 'television is pictures, so they'll have to come to us.'...At present, Hollywood has unloaded onto television hundreds of the very pictures which destroyed the box-office. But this will help Hollywood only if the new pictures it makes have some freshness in every department."[4]

Seldes followed up with interview excerpts by Gideon Bachmann (from a radio series of interviews

Bachmann conducted on WFUV-FM, New York) with movie directors Fred Zinnemann, Boris Kaufman, Stanley Kramer, Fritz Lang, John Houseman, and Otto Preminger. Missing from this celebrity lineup was one of *the* premiere veteran filmmakers of the decade (along with Walt Disney[5]) who had already busily invested himself—as an artist, a businessman,

---

4   Gilbert Seldes, "1. Introductory Notes," "The Impact of Television on Motion Pictures," *Film Culture*, No. 2 (12), 1957, p.3. *Film Culture* was paying rather close attention to television dramas in the late 1950s; also see "What's Wrong with Television Drama?," a transcript of David Susskind's November 11, 1958 forum on the talk show *Open End*, in *Film Culture* #19 (1959/1960), pp.18-37.

5   No history of telefeatures is complete without considering Walt Disney's innovative television series, which began as *Walt Disney's Disneyland* on ABC on October 27, 1954. For the purposes of this article, and its focus on Shamley Productions and **DARK INTRUDER**, I've excluded the vital role and chronology of Disney's programming, the conversion of serialized episodes of his ABC TV series to feature films—the *Davy Crockett* phenomenon primarily among them, launched with the three-installment *Davy Crockett* miniseries (December 15, 1954-February 23, 1955), edited together into the smash-hit feature **DAVY CROCKETT, KING OF THE WILD FRONTIER** (premiered May 25, 1955)—and vice versa, and the example he said for all who followed, including Alfred Hitchcock and Lew Wasserman. *Every* telefeature released after 1955 wished it would succeed like the Disney *Davy Crockett* films! In its first year alone, the *Davy Crockett* films had earned $2,150,000 in 1955 boxoffice dollars (*Variety Weekly*, January 25, 1956); only **PSYCHO**—not a telefeature or composite telefeature-to-theatrical release, but produced by Shamley as an expanded telefeature production-wise—topped it, with $12,000,000 earned on release (1960 boxoffice dollars).

and a celebrity—in the brave new competitive world of television: Alfred Hitchcock.

This was a major oversight, to say the least. Then again, Alfred Hitchcock was likely too busy talking about his television and film crossover career with *Cosmopolitan*, reaching a much wider readership. When asked by *Cosmopolitan* whether Hollywood's or TV's *"approach to the subject-matter"* was *"more mature,"* Hitchcock replied,

"Surprisingly enough, where I expected to find in TV a generalized simplicity because of the enormous range in the age of the audience, I discovered that I was able to use many more off-beat stories with unhappy endings than I had ever been able to use in movies. The children love them."

Addressing the *"challenges a director has to overcome in TV, as compared to the challenges in movie-making,"* Hitchcock said,

"Time is an important consideration. The approach to making a TV film involves a complete change of thinking. A half-hour TV film must be made in three days, because the nice mogul who gives us the money can't afford any more than a certain amount. He is a poor mogul. In motion pictures the final return is greater, so that much more money is spent; and in any case the small TV

Alfred Hitchcock himself hosted every episode of *Alfred Hitchcock Presents* and *The Alfred Hitchcock Hour*—ten years, from October 2, 1955 to June 26, 1965, over 250 episodes—until MCA's Lew Wasserman gave Hitch enough rope to hang himself, so to speak, with the exclusive contract of 1964

screen does not require anything like the amount of expensive production that the modern motion picture demands."[6]

In fact, at about the same time as that very issue of *Film Culture* was either published or about to be published, trade magazines were chronicling Hitchcock's ongoing television production efforts, which were extensive.

Hitchcock's entry into television was highly unusual for such a prominent filmmaker, as was that of Walt Disney at about the same time. As Hitchcock biographer Patrick McGilligan noted,

"The financial shortfalls and anxieties Alfred Hitchcock had experienced during the 1930s and 1940s were over and done by 1954. His salary was rising steadily, and had been augmented for the first time at Warner Bros. by profit-sharing arrangements... Yet it wasn't until he signed a contract with Paramount that he truly began to make dizzy money. ...The dizzy money began in 1954, courtesy of [his agent] Lew Wasserman, MCA, and Paramount... It was supposedly Wasserman who had the idea—and whoever had it, it was a hell of an idea—to put Hitchcock on television. Hitchcock always said it was Wasserman's idea... But it was also true that [Hitchcock] had spent years trying to launch a national radio series, and just as true that he was already choosing favorite suspense stories, writing introductions, and lending his name as editor to an anthology series of books.

"However it transpired, Hitchcock made a show of reluctance when Wasserman brought up the idea in the spring of 1955. He himself wasn't a big TV watcher (he liked quiz shows, he told one interviewer, and public affairs programs 'of an international nature'). He saw the epidemic popularity of television as a threat to the film industry, to which he was unreservedly loyal. And no other director of his caliber had dared defect to the small screen.

"Yet it hadn't escaped his notice that MCA was a growing power in television, packaging programs with talent and advertisers... When Wasserman suggested (or so Hitchcock always said) that another old friend, Joan Harrison, might help with a Hitchcock series, it sealed his interest. Although it was important that Hitchcock himself supervise the launch of the series, Harrison could shoulder much of the day-to-day work....

6 Both Hitchcock quotes are from "*Cosmopolitan* Exclusive Interview: 'Hitchcock Speaking'," *Cosmopolitan* (October 1956, Vol. 141, No. 4), pp.66-67. This rarely-mentioned interview perfectly encapsulates Hitchcock's public statements about his jump into television.

"With Wasserman oiling the gears, CBS offered Hitchcock a state-of-the-art contract. He would lend his name to the series, serving as host and producer and directing a set number of episodes. His salary would be higher than he received for many of the feature films he directed—reportedly $125,000 per episode. And in one of those clauses that were Wasserman's specialty, all rights to the series would revert to him after first broadcast."[7]

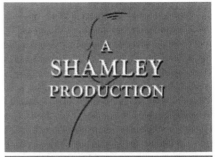

Alfred Hitchcock established his own firm explicitly designed to produce new dramatic programming for television, Shamley Productions. If any evidence were necessary how close these projects were to his heart, Shamley derived its name from the village in his native country of England where the Hitchcocks own a beloved country retreat (Shamley Green).

Shamley Productions remains a bit of an enigma to many, who often conflate Shamley (when it is acknowledged at all) with Revue Studios a.k.a. Revue Productions, a subsidiary of MCA that later became Universal Television, a subdivision of NBC Universal. Even the prestigious British Film Institute botches Shamley's legacy, listing **DARK INTRUDER** along with two single episodes of *Alfred Hitchcock Presents* and two of *The Alfred Hitchcock Hour* as being Shamley Productions— curious, that.

Make no mistake, Shamley was Hitchcock's own production outfit until 1964.

But by the time Shamley produced and filmed *Black Cloak* / **DARK INTRUDER** in November/ December 1964, it was independent no longer.

So, let's clear this up.[8]

Revue Studios was founded by the talent agency MCA (Music Corporation of America) in 1943 as Revue Productions, Inc., when MCA was producing live shows. By the fall of 1950, Revue was in partnership with the National Broadcasting Company aka NBC; Revue was overtly credited with the production of NBC's *Armour Theatre* TV series. As of 1952, Revue's Revue Productions subsidiary was cranking out TV series, leasing space at Republic Studios.

Alfred Hitchcock's Shamley Productions and its alliance with MCA (the talent agency) and Revue Studios (owned by MCA) made Hitch a millionaire many times over—and provided the autonomy in 1959-1960 for Hitchcock to make the film no studio wanted him to make: **PSYCHO**

---

7   Patrick McGilligan, *Alfred Hitchcock: A Life in Darkness and Light* (Regan Books, 2003), pp.475, 477, 514-515. Joan Harrison became the series' full producer as of the 1956-57 season (McGilligan, p.543).

8   And, yes, despite *Monster!* proudly trumpeting "No slashers!" since its first issue, we have to bring **PSYCHO** into the picture, along with a couple of Robert Altman serial killers, a killer who fixes weaponry fashioned for the stump of his severed hand, and a ghost. *Deal* with it; my editors have to! We'll still be discussing plenty of monsters.

Hitchcock's Shamley Productions was independent of Revue, active in and of itself by 1955, already a great success, without having slowed Hitchcock's output as a theatrical motion picture director and producer/director. Shamley *remained* independent of Revue, though Hitchcock/Shamley's partnership with Revue for television distribution invited some confusion. Furthermore, Hitchcock's and Shamley's relations with MCA were even more intertwined:

"MCA would help with the stories, the writers, and the casting. With Wasserman powering its growth, the firm was evolving into a superagency, an octopus with long tentacles. 'I am entering television,' Hitchcock joked to the Los Angeles Times, *'because I am the tip of a tendril. I am a slave to MCA.' But* Alfred Hitchcock Presents *would boost the director's fame and wealth in ways neither he nor Wasserman could have guessed."[9]*

As for Revue, MCA purchased the Universal International Studios 360-acre lot from Universal-International Pictures[10] for $11.25 million on December 18, 1958 and changed Revue's name to Revue Studios; thus, MCA entered the feature film production industry, which *"cemented Lew Wasserman as the most powerful man in Hollywood, at once the head of the biggest talent agency and the head of a major studio (albeit one fallen on hard times),"* which also *"intensified the Justice Department's ongoing investigation of the agency's strong-arm practices."[11]* once MCA merged with/acquired Decca Records (owner of Universal-International Pictures) in 1962, Universal-International became Universal Pictures, and Revue was renamed Universal Television.[12]

If anything, the Shamley diversions seemed to fuel the increasingly experimental nature of his feature film productions, while as contracted with CBS Hitchcock himself directed a number of episodes of *Alfred Hitchcock Presents*, including the premiere episode "Revenge" (which debuted on CBS on October 2, 1955), less than six months after the program had been brainstormed. The almost instantly-successful ongoing anthology series on CBS led to Hitchcock, Shamley, and Revue launching *another* anthology series—for NBC.

The same year that *Film Culture* was pondering the fate of cinema in the era of television, *Broadcasting* magazine blithely noted in its "Networks" section that Hitchcock was one of "Three Producers Set for '*Crisis*'":

"Three producers are set for Crisis. *NBC-TV series of mystery-suspense dramas to start Sept. 30 as a Monday. 10-11 p.m., program. Alfred Hitchcock will personally produce 10 filmed dramas through his Shamley Productions in Hollywood; Alan Miller, head of all production at Revue Productions, will produce another 10 on film, and S. Mark Smith, formerly producer of the* General Electric Theatre *live programs, will be executive producer of the 22* Crisis *shows to be produced live in New York."[13]*

That series was retitled *Suspicion* (September 30, 1957-July 21, 1958) before it debuted. The Shamley Productions episodes were executive produced by Hitchcock and produced by *Alfred Hitchcock Presents* producer Joan Harrison. Though he was never on-camera (the series was hosted by Dennis O'Keefe), Hitchcock directed *Suspicion*'s debut episode, "Four O'Clock," based on a Cornell Woolrich story (first published in *Detective Fiction Weekly* [October 1st, 1938]).

It's astonishing to consider just how much creative energy Hitchcock was personally marshaling

9   Ibid., pg. 515. For an in-depth analysis of the program itself, see McGilligan, pp.522-528, and especially *Alfred Hitchcock Presents: An Illustrated Guide to the Ten-Year Television Career of the Master of Suspense* by John McCarty and Bruce Kelleher (St. Martin's Press, 1985) and *The Alfred Hitchcock Presents Companion* by Martin Grams, Jr. and Patrik Wikstrom (OTR Publishing, 2001).

10 Universal-International was known as such from August 1948 until May, 1964; see *http://www.closinglogos.com/page/Universal+Studios*

Harry Townes sees his inner self in a mirror when he dared to wear "The Cheaters" in the still-stunning December 27, 1960 episode of *Thriller*, makeup by Jack Barron, who was part of the makeup team for **DARK INTRUDER**

11 McGilligan, *Ibid.*, p.578.

12 *See http://www.closinglogos.com/page/Revue+Studios*

13 "Three Producers Set for '*Crisis*,'" *Broadcasting*, June 17, 1957, p.84. This incarnation of *Crisis* never saw broadcast; NBC did broadcast a series entitled *Crisis* from October 5, 1949 to December 28, 1949, and a later MCA/Universal color series entitled *Kraft Suspense Theatre* (October 10, 1963-July 1, 1965) was syndicated under the title *Crisis*. More on that later in this article.

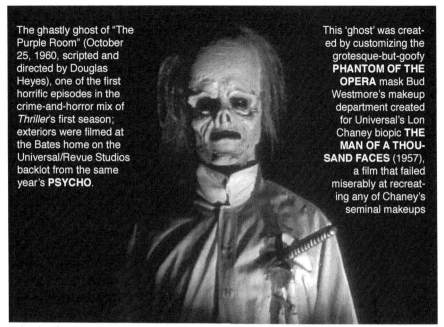

The ghastly ghost of "The Purple Room" (October 25, 1960, scripted and directed by Douglas Heyes), one of the first horrific episodes in the crime-and-horror mix of *Thriller*'s first season; exteriors were filmed at the Bates home on the Universal/Revue Studios backlot from the same year's **PSYCHO**.

This 'ghost' was created by customizing the grotesque-but-goofy **PHANTOM OF THE OPERA** mask Bud Westmore's makeup department created for Universal's Lon Chaney biopic **THE MAN OF A THOU-SAND FACES** (1957), a film that failed miserably at recreating any of Chaney's seminal makeups

and, via Shamley Productions, channeling and overseeing others in the decade between 1954 and 1964 (not counting the licensed subsidiary projects Hitchcock did *not* manage, like the ongoing print anthologies bearing his name and likeness and the newsstand digest magazine *Alfred Hitchcock Mystery Magazine*, which debuted in 1956). Shamley Productions handled the entire run of *Alfred Hitchcock Presents* (for CBS, October 2, 1955 to September 1960, and thereafter on NBC from September 13, 1960 to June 1962) and *The Alfred Hitchcock Hour* (NBC, September 20, 1962 to May 10, 1965)—*and* their respective contribution to *Suspicion*. According to Hitchcock biographer Patrick McGilligan regarding *Suspicion*, *"The financial incentives were attractive, but so was the hour-long format."* As for his own series, *"Hitchcock still approved the stories and writers, helped with script problems, discussed the major casting of all the television shows—even working Sundays when his weekdays were crowded. He regularly met with James Allardice to cook up his monologues, and watched all the finished episodes before they were aired, although his postproduction suggestions were usually diplomatic."*[14]

Most importantly, Hitchcock's boxoffice smash **PSYCHO** was famously produced via Shamley Productions using the autonomy and resources of Hitchcock's television outfit when Paramount Pictures balked at Hitchcock wanting to adapt

Robert Bloch's taboo-busting novel to the screen.

Paramount had, in fact, invested $200,000 already in the film they wanted Hitchcock to make, "NO BAIL FOR THE JUDGE", but Hitchcock wanted no part of it when his insistence upon a rape sequence led to prospective star Audrey Hepburn dropping out (she was also pregnant at the time, the reason publicly given for her departure from the production)—and he had decided on **PSYCHO** regardless, despite the misgivings of both Paramount and Hitchcock's agent Lew Wasserman: *"...at home on June 3, 1959, after talking it over with Lew Wasserman, Hitchcock convened the initial production conference for PSYCHO."*[15] Wasserman's aim to consolidate Hitchcock's creative product with MCA/Universal played into Hitchcock's own plan: *"The cancellation of 'NO BAIL FOR THE JUDGE' opened the door for Universal to recruit Hitchcock, which was Wasserman's goal. But Wasserman had to accept PSYCHO; that was Hitchcock's clever gamble."*[16]

Previously, *"Hitchcock tried to draw a line between his television and film companies. They were supposed to be distinct operations, even headquartered in separate locations—the film offices at Paramount, the television shows produced on Revue stages at Universal. But inevitably, the*

14 McGilligan, *Ibid.*, pp.551-552.

15 *Ibid.*, p.578.

16 *Ibid.*

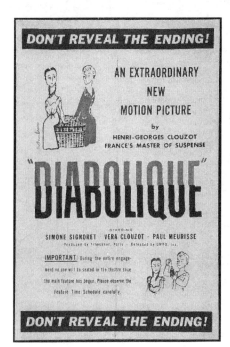

The 1955 American ad campaign for the stateside release of Henri-Georges Clouzot's **LES DIABOLIQUES** aka **DIABOLIQUE** made the French film a surprise hit; the gimmick was adapted (into insurance against "death-by-fright") by William Castle's **MACABRE** (1958) and adopted entirely by Hitchcock for **PSYCHO** (1960)

1955 and throughout 1956, as it was rolled out across the US, *and* the profits and lines-at-the-boxoffice William Castle had scored with the low-budget **MACABRE** (1958). Paramount wanted no part in such a film, so Hitchcock mobilized the autonomy and shelter Shamley Productions provided and proceeded regardless. *"Hitchcock first presented PSYCHO to his agents, his staff, and Paramount... as a simple, low-budget American shocker, in the style of his TV series... PSYCHO would be the ultimate Alfred Hitchcock Presents, the director told his staff: gruesome and scary and darkly humorous. He might even save a little money by shooting the film with his television crew. Shooting it in black and white would also keep costs down... All the filming could be done in the studio—on a quick, TV-style schedule."[19]* In the end, **PSYCHO** cost more than a typical episode, and took two months for principle photography to complete, but it was the success and existence of Shamley Productions that made it possible for **PSYCHO** to exist at all.

It was a gamble, for sure, and a history-making moment.

You all know the rest of the story; if you don't, there is a veritable library of books and countless online articles to enlighten you. Hitchcock made precisely the movie he wanted to make. With a full half-decade of sturdy Shamley Productions success to draw upon, Hitchcock rolled the dice and won the casino. With his own powerful TV-fueled celebrity to work with, Hitchcock cannily emulated, amplified, and made his own the promotional gimmick invented for the US release of **DIABOLIQUE**. That film's UMPO, Inc. American release ballyhoo—*"IMPORTANT: During the entire engagement no one will be seated in the theatre once the main feature has begun. Please observe the Feature Time Schedule carefully."[20]*—was revamped. Hitchcock also emulated the aggressive ad campaign for William Castle's shameless **MACABRE** hucksterism (with its Lloyds of London insurance policy *"for $1000 AGAINST DEATH BY FRIGHT!"*), taking it up a notch to make **PSYCHO** a major international hit which broke box office records across the globe, and became a phenomenon.

In writing about the history of made-for-TV horror, everyone seems to handily forget **PSYCHO**—the ultimate "made-for-TV" movie that was *not really* made for television, but only existed because

two spilled back and forth... "[17] Hitchcock played that spillover card, too, in his shrewd power-play to make the film he wanted to make, Paramount and Wasserman be damned.

Hitchcock had told *Cosmopolitan* magazine back in 1956, when asked if *"the growing trend toward independent productions"* made *"for better pictures,"* that *"The custom-made item, be it a dress or a sports-car is always better than the assembly-line job."[18]*Hitchcock cannily appropriated the readily-available aspects of Shamley's assembly line—those that suited his immediate needs—to produce his unique *"custom-made item."*

As has been repeatedly documented in a plethora of texts, Hitchcock eyed with envy the surprise success the French import Henri-Georges Clouzot's **LES DIABOLIQUES** (a.k.a. **DIABOLIQUE**) had enjoyed upon its stateside release in November

---

17 *Ibid.*, pp. 527.

18 *"Cosmopolitan* Exclusive Interview: 'Hitchcock Speaking'," *Cosmopolitan* (October 1956, Vol. 141, No. 4), p.66.

19 McGilligan, *Ibid.*, pg. 579.

20 See the original US release promotional campaign at *http://originalvintagemovieposters.com/wp-content/up-loads/2013/07/Diabolique.jpg*

Hitchcock independently funded and produced the feature under the same conditions a made-for-TV movie would have been filmed.

PSYCHO was the pseudo-made-for-TV-horror-movie that absolutely rocked the world—and yet, to the present day, no one includes even a mention of it in any made-for-TV genre movie overviews or discussions.

How is that even *remotely* possible?

As already noted, there is only *one* other Shamley Productions theatrical feature film:

DARK INTRUDER.

Somehow, in some way, Alfred Hitchcock was necessarily involved.

Many reviewers have noted the similarities between *Black Cloak* / **DARK INTRUDER** and the celebrated TV series *Thriller*; the same could be said for other Hitchcock teleplays in its final seasons. *Fantastic Television* co-author Gary Gerani once noted, *"That final NBC season of* Alfred Hitchcock Presents *played a lot like* Thriller, *which is why 'Something With Claws' would have been a decent fit. Most episodes were suspense mysteries rather than supernatural tales, of course, but there were notable exceptions... 'The Monkey's Paw* [A Retelling]' [April 19, 1965] *and 'Where the Woodbine Twineth'* [January 11, 1965], *for example."[21]*

The tangle of Universal, Revue Studios, and NBC resulted in an inevitable conflict of interest when Hubbell Robinson Productions collaborated with Revue and NBC on a new crime/horror anthology series in 1960, *Thriller* (September 13, 1960-April 30, 1962), hosted by the great Boris Karloff. After his departure from the competing network CBS, former CBS executive Hubbell Robinson created *Thriller* for MCA/Revue Studios, tapping much of the talent (behind the cameras and onscreen) that had already fueled *Alfred Hitchcock Presents, Suspicion*, and Rod Serling's hit CBS series *The Twilight Zone*. In fact, NBC positioned the one-hour *Thriller* to *precede* the half-hour *Alfred Hitchcock Presents* (by then in its sixth season) on Tuesday nights; for its second season, *Thriller* was moved to Monday nights, 10 to 11 p.m., after *Alfred Hitchcock Presents*. While the two anthology series seemed to NBC programming perfect companions conceptually, friction was inevitable.

---

21 Gary Gerani, personal email to the author, April 1, 2016; quoted with permission.

Conflict-of-interest #1 was the fact that back in 1962, Robinson *"collect*[ed] *$5,000 a week for having thought up and sold the idea of* Thriller... *Robinson, now back at CBS, is embarrassed by these riches, but only because they are on NBC."[22]*

This made *Thriller* more vulnerable to cancellation once the program became expendable to NBC.

Conflict-of-interest #2 was Alfred Hitchcock's

---

22 Eugene Paul, *The Hungry Eye* (Ballantine Books, 1962), p.133.

Boris Karloff was the host of *Thriller* (September 13, 1960–April 30, 1962), a Hubbell Robinson Productions/Revue Studios series for NBC that succumbed to conflict-of-interests with Hitchcock's alliance with MCA/Universal/Revue/NBC. Karloff also starred in five episodes, including the second season's "The Incredible Doktor Markesan" (February 26, 1962; directed by Robert Florey, makeup by Jack Barron)

Graphic designer Tony Palladino's cover art for the first edition of Robert Bloch's *Psycho* (1959) was licensed by Hitchcock to headline the 1960 film adaptation's titles and ad campaigns, establishing a relationship between innovative book graphic design and film adaptations that proved particularly effective and lucrative in the 1970s (i.e., **THE GODFATHER, JAWS**, etc.)

ongoing program, stature, and relationship with MCA/Universal/NBC. Hitchcock had in fact moved his offices from Paramount to Universal in 1962, in *"the biggest, best bungalow... on the Universal lot."[23]*

Thriller associate producer and story editor Doug Benton stated for the record:

"[Thriller] was never a top-ten show. In those days, a 30 rating was enough to keep you on the air, and we would do 28, 29, 30, 31—just around enough to be considered viable in terms of attracting advertising. But it wasn't a huge hit. (It's strange, there're a lot of other programs like that, Star Trek, for instance, or Rod Serling's Twilight Zone, that were never huge hits, either. All of these shows were kept on for 'prestige,' they were considered 'literary.') We were on the same network, and being made at the same studio, as Alfred Hitchcock Presents, and although I never heard this directly, I did hear it from people who worked on both shows: Hitchcock resented Thriller and he thought that Hubbell Robinson had infringed on his franchise. He thought that if he were doing this type of material for MCA and NBC, then we shouldn't be. Actually, we weren't doing the same thing he

was; he was doing some very sophisticated, 'twist' material. Hitchcock was doing the sort of thing that they started out to do on Thriller, but were not successful with. We... came along and improved the ratings considerably and got a tremendous amount of press, and Hitchcock didn't like the competition. I don't think he ever came out and said, 'Get rid of 'em!', but he did allows them to enlarge his show from a half-hour to an hour, and that made it more difficult for us to stay on. Also, Hubbell Robinson was a CBS executive operating on NBC, so there were network rivalries there, too; the NBC executives resented Hubbell showing up on their network with an hour franchise. And the fact that Thriller wasn't an out-and-out, blockbuster hit—all of these were factors in the fact that we all got nice letters saying, 'Good try, but...'...*"[24]*

Thriller scholar Alan Warren was less soft-spoken in his account, quoting *Thriller* producer William Frye:

"For some time Thriller *had been drawing consistently higher ratings than* Alfred Hitchcock Presents, *the show it had originally attempted to emulate, and this fact was not lost on the Master of Suspense. 'Don't think that Hitchcock and Joan Harrison [the producer of* Alfred Hitchcock Presents*] weren't watching* Thriller,' *says Bill Frye. Hitchcock, irked by* Thriller's *consistent high quality, issued an ultimatum: he wouldn't go on unless* Thriller *was withdrawn for one year. This was tantamount to cancellation: the network hesitated, but as Frye ruefully recalls, 'Hitchcock's clout at NBC was greater than Karloff's.' The decision was made to axe the series."[25]*

Though he'd only directed one episode for the season (his last for the half-hour format, the memorable boy-Billy-Mumy-with-a-loaded-gun "Bang! You're Dead," October 17, 1961—a shocker in '61 that would barely raise a goosebump in our current "toddler-shooting-news-story-per-week" present day 2016), Hitchcock still had a vested interest in his TV series in 1961-62, when the network verdict against *Thriller* was rendered.

Then, things changed.

While pouring his energies into his new feature film project **THE BIRDS** (1963)—in many ways, the most daring and experimental of all his studio films—Hitchcock had also considered helming

23 McGilligan, *Ibid.*, p.608.

24 Doug Benton interviewed by Tom Weaver, pp.98-99; quoted with permission.

25 Alan Warren, *This is a* Thriller*: An Episode Guide, History and Analysis of the Classic 1960s Television Series* (McFarland, 1996), p.23. This narrative of events was also covered by Martin Grams, Jr. and Patrik Wikstrom in *The Alfred Hitchcock Presents Companion*, pp.47-48.

a film version of *"the Robert Thomas play* Piège pour un homme seul... *Paul Stanton's novel* Village of Stars, *set aboard a plane carrying an atomic bomb liable to detonate below a certain altitude*[26] ... *as well as James Barrie's supernatural play* Mary Rose... *a project Hitchcock had long wanted to realize since seeing a stage version during his youth,"*[27] in 1920.[28]

Remember that title: "MARY ROSE".

As **THE BIRDS** postproduction got underway in July 1962, Hitchcock helmed his last-ever television production, "I Saw the Whole Thing," for *The Alfred Hitchcock Hour* (the debut episode of the new one-hour program, broadcast October 11, 1962). As for his next feature film, Hitchcock settled on an adaptation of Winston Graham's new novel *Marnie* as his followup to **THE BIRDS**, but *"Lew Wasserman and other Universal executives hoped that the director would return to the glossy thrillers of the 1950s that had become his trademark."*[29]

PSYCHO had been a Shamley Productions film; for **MARNIE**, Hitchcock created a new business entity, evidence of a shift already strong enough to require such a decision. After all, Hitchcock had the means to do anything after **PSYCHO**:

26 Hitchcock dodged a bullet. An apparently unrelated (or simply uncredited) early TV movie with a very similar plot—emerging from Wasserman/MCA/Universal/NBC's "Project 120" telefeature production line—was THE DOOMSDAY FLIGHT, scripted by Rod Serling, directed by William Graham, first broadcast on December 13, 1966. Alvin H. Marill wrote, *"Serling's screenplay was so detailed—creating a device that would explode below 5,000 feet—that a subsequent real-life incident using an almost identical premise caused this film to be withdrawn from distribution for a number of years..."* (Marill, *Movies made for Television*, p.13). That removal from broadcast was in the summer of 1971, upon "urging" from the US Federal Aviation Administration (Robert F. Buckhorn, "TV stations asked to ban 'Doomsday Flight'", *The Bryan Times* [Bryan, Ohio], August 11, 1971, p.5, archived online (@ https://news.google.com/newspapers?nid=799&dat=19710811&id=dJpPAAAAIBAJ&sjid=WFIDAAAAIBAJ&pg=873,2464342&hl=en).

27 Tony Lee Moral, *Hitchcock and the Making of Marnie* (Scarecrow Press Inc., 2002), p.4.

28 McGilligan, p.650.

29 Tony Lee Moral, *Ibid*. On a similar note, McGilligan writes, *"Wasserman felt that Hitchcock should return to the Paramount formula of beautiful people and beautiful scenery—that coincided with Wasserman's vision of the program Universal should be developing..."* (McGilligan, p.661). That glossy agenda spawned Hitchcock's lackluster **TORN CURTAIN** (1966) and **TOPAZ** (1969); only with the significant departure of **FRENZY** (1972)—a murderous gob of spit in the face of Wasserman's *"beautiful people and beautiful scenery,"* filmed far from Universal's Black Tower, in the seedier sections of Hitchcock's native country—did the Master of Suspense deliver the goods one last time. It was the culmination of a project Hitchcock had been gestating since the mid-1960s, and which Wasserman, MCA, and Universal *"had been opposed to... all along..."* (McGilligan, p.687). Of course.

"During its first year of release, **PSYCHO** *had earned $15 million in domestic sales, and Hitchcock himself earned well in excess of the same amount from the film...* **MARNIE** *was the first and only Hitchcock film to be produced under Geoffrey Stanley, Inc., which was incorporated on September 26, 1961. ...Geoffrey and Stanley were the names of Hitchcock's white Sealyham terriers that he cherished and featured in his cameo during the opening sequences of* **THE BIRDS.** *"*[30]

Hitchcock still drew from Shamley Productions and the TV series' cast and crew—Alfred Hitchcock Presents assistant director Hilton Green was unit manager on **MARNIE**—but something fundamental was changing. The control Wasserman held over Hitchcock, as his agent, prior to the 1960s was one thing. The power Wasserman and MCA/Universal wielded as the calendar moved toward 1964 was quite another:

"Wasserman personified the power of the front office, the business end of filmmaking, and brandished the authority Hitchcock both respected

30 Moral, *Ibid.*, pp.1, 55-56.

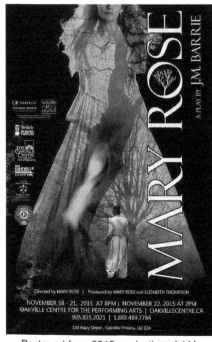

Poster art for a 2015 production of J.M. Barrie's still-popular 1920 romantic ghost play *Mary Rose*, which Alfred Hitchcock aimed to adapt to the screen—but Lew Wasserman deep-sixed at every opportunity

Right: Cover of the program booklet for the December 1920 New York City premiere stage production of J.M. Barrie's *Mary Rose* (SpiderBaby Archives). **Below Left:** a monstrous "twin"/brother unveiled in the climactic page from "The Ventriloquist's Dummy" in *Tales from the Crypt #28* (EC Comics, February-March 1952), script by Al Feldstein, art by Graham "Ghastly" Ingels, possibly inspired by Robert Bloch's "The Mannikin" (*Weird Tales*, April 1937). **Below Right, Top to Bottom:** Cine-siblings… of a sort! Peter Dyneley slowly undergoing "the split" in George Breakston's & Kenneth G. Crane's **THE MANSTER** (双頭 の殺人鬼 / *Sôtô no Satsujinki*, 1959/62, Japan/USA); Malaki from **DARK INTRUDER**; and Belial from Frank Henenlotter's **BASKET CASE** (1982)

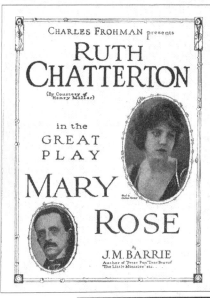

Hy Averback/Stephen Kandel/Ray Russell's **CHAMBER OF HORRORS** (1966) enjoyed international distribution and was a real moneymaker for Warner Bros.—though we've always wondered if (?) the foreign prints featured gorier footage unseen in the US. **Top Right:** While they were reedited and sold directly to television in the US, the Japanese *tokusatsu* **SUPER GIANT** (スーパージャイアンツ / *Sūpā Jaiantsu*) serialized telefilms were released theatrically through much of the world; this was the Italian condensation of the 2-parter スーパー・ジャイアンツ怪星人の魔城 / *Sūpā Jaiantsu – Kaiseijin no Majō* and スーパー・ジャイアンツ地球滅亡寸前 / *Sūpā Jaiantsu – Chikyū Metsubō Sunzen* (October 1 and 8, 1957), both directed by Teruo Ishii, syndicated to US TV as **INVADERS FROM SPACE** (1965)

and resented. The result was that both men endured a love-hate relationship, with Wasserman exercising a control over Hitchcock's career. The director often said when justifying his later projects, 'Oh, well, I'm doing it for Wasserman.' ...

"Universal Studios first began to play watchdog over Hitchcock during the production of **THE BIRDS**. Although, Hitchcock's agent and long-standing friend Lew Wasserman had been elevated to being the head of Universal, this didn't stop Hitchcock from making sarcastic comments about 'the front office,' even when that office was Wasserman's. As Jay Presson Allen surmises, 'Wasserman had been Hitchcock's agent; now he was his boss. That's a very big shift in authority, and I think Hitch resented it—I know he did. Nevertheless, it was a fact of life.' ... "[31]

Filmmaker and cinema scholar Joseph McBride wrote the definitive article on Hitchcock's planned production of "MARY ROSE", which I would steer curious *Monster!* readers who wish to know more to; McBride noted, *"This ghost story would have taken Hitchcock's characteristic mingling of eroticism and death into dimensions beyond which any he had explored on the screen."*[32] In many ways, "MARY ROSE" informed the ghost/love story Hitchcock's first American producer David O. Selznick had filmed as **PORTRAIT OF JENNIE** (1948), from the novella by Robert Nathan; though a beloved film today, **PORTRAIT OF JENNIE** had been a boxoffice disappointment, which may account in part for studio disdain for "MARY ROSE". In short, all evidence points to the development and abject studio rejection of "MARY ROSE" being the straw that broke Hitchcock's back, in many ways; ironically, it was central to his greatest business success as well, and Lew Wasserman was of course essential to both. McBride provided Hitchcock biographer Patrick McGilligan access to his research files (and his personal insights), and of this turning point McGilligan wrote,

"As late as March 1964, even as he was finishing **MARNIE**, *Hitchcock was still looking forward to making 'MARY ROSE'.... Hitchcock had tried over the years to interest various producers in a film of the play. He had pitched 'MARY ROSE' to Twentieth Century-Fox in the 1940s, and mentioned it to Paramount as a possibility for Grace Kelly in the 1950s. He and [his wife] Alma had discussed the adaptation and scouted the locations. He had invested his own money in*

31 *Ibid.*, p.1, 121-122.

32 See Joseph McBride, "Alfred Hitchcock's MARY ROSE: An Old Master's Unheard Cri de Coeur," *Cinéaste* Vol. 26, No. 2 (2001).

preproduction... Before Hitchcock could realize his dream project, however, 'MARY ROSE' was killed by Universal. 'I don't know whether it was because it was costume stuff, maybe marginally intellectual, I have no idea,' recalled Jay Presson Allen, 'but Lew Wasserman was on record as not being interested in it to begin with. Hitch never had a green light for the project, never. He just went ahead on his own.' ... "[33]

As he had with **PSYCHO**—but this time, Hitchcock didn't have the flexibility and speed of the production facilities of Shamley at his beck and call.

Despite the fortune which **PSYCHO** had reaped for Wasserman as well as Paramount and MCA/ Universal (who soon owned the property, as part of their renegotiated contract with Hitchcock), Wasserman had never approved of **PSYCHO**, and wasn't about to let Hitchcock get his way again. The supernatural romanticism and eroticism of "MARY ROSE" was completely out-of-line with Wasserman and MCA/Universal's plans for Hitchcock. The new contract was negotiated in August 1964—three months before filming commenced on *Black Cloak /* **DARK INTRUDER**.

Under the terms of the new contract, *"all future Hitchcock films would be produced and owned outright by Universal. The salary and benefits guaranteed by the new contract... reportedly made Hitchcock the highest-paid director in Hollywood history; but more important, the contract made him a part-owner of the studio. He and Alma became the third largest stockholders. In exchange for the stock transfer, Universal assumed all rights to* Alfred Hitchcock Presents, *the reverted Paramount films* [**ROPE, REAR WINDOW, THE TROUBLE WITH HARRY, THE MAN WHO KNEW TOO MUCH,** *and* **VERTIGO**], *and future marketing of the name 'Alfred Hitchcock.'*

"Although it was immensely satisfying to become a part-owner of the Hollywood studio that first showed interest in bringing him to America back in 1931... there were still tensions in Hitchcock's relationship with Universal. While Lew Wasserman was trying to transform the once lowly studio into a first-class operation, it would prove a long, slow process, and Universal would cling to television and television-style filmmaking far into the 1970s... And while his amended contract was generous, friends say that both Hitchcocks resented its strictures and, in sour moments, complained that he had been robbed of his golden opportunity to film 'MARY ROSE'...

33 McGilligan, *Ibid.*, p.652.

"... Hitchcock had done substantial preproduction work, along with his work with [**MARNIE** screenwriter Jay Presson] *Allen on the script, and* [matte painter/production designer] *Albert Whitlock, who drew 'a lot of sketches' for 'MARY ROSE' before it was canceled, asked the director why he had succumbed to front-office pressures and abandoned the project. 'They believe it isn't what audiences expect of me,' Hitchcock explained. 'Not the kind of picture they expect of me,' he repeated.*

"Later, Hitchcock would make a sad boast to interviewers: an actual clause had been inserted into his Universal contract, he said, stating he could make any film for the studio that he wanted, as long as it was budgeted under $3 million—and as long as it wasn't 'MARY ROSE'."[34]

One can only conjecture how *any* supernaturally-themed project in the pipeline—much less a pilot like *Black Cloak* / **DARK INTRUDER**—may have played for Hitchcock, given whatever resentments he quite naturally would harbor after having so dear a pet project crushed by Wasserman and MCA/Universal. Would the fact the *Black Cloak* pilot was written by a venerable British

fantasist like Alfred Edgar/Barré Lyndon—even his penname echoed that of *Mary Rose*'s celebrated playwright J.M. Barrie—added to the sting?

Still, Hitchcock *had* to have personally approved Edgar/Lyndon's participation in *The Alfred Hitchcock Hour*, scripting the second episode "Don't Look Behind You" (September 27, 1962) and the Robert Bloch adaptation "The Sign of Satan" (May 8, 1964), co-starring Christopher Lee; with its contemporary Hollywood studio exploiting involvement with a European devil worshipper, "The Sign of Satan" in particular was a clear precursor to Lyndon's deft handling of supernatural themes in *Black Cloak* / **DARK INTRUDER**.[35] Hitchcock biographer Patrick

---

34 *Ibid.*, pp.652-653.

35 Fandom, particularly Lovecraft fandom, has until recently underestimated Lyndon's importance to *Black Cloak* / **DARK INTRUDER**; with few exceptions, since all are only using hindsight in their assessments, the opinion stated by authors Andrew Migliore and John Strysik sums up the general consensus, noting *the "film's slender connection to Lovecraft, probably by way of* **DARK INTRUDER***'s producer Jack Laird who six years later would get serious about adapting HPL for* Rod Serling's Night Gallery....," Migliore and Strysik, *The Lurker in the Lobby: A Guide to the Cinema of H. P. Lovecraft* (Armitage House, 2000), p.10 (Night Shade Books, 2006), p.45. On the contrary, it may be that Lyndon was the one who turned Laird onto Lovecraft's body of work; see Rick Lai's exhaustive "The Sources of **DARK INTRUDER**," *Monster!* #27, and online

The demonic Professor Malaki (Werner Klemperer) prepares to exchange souls with his brother Robert Vandenburg (Peter Mark Richman), leaving his sibling trapped in the monstrous form of Malaki—just in time to die!

71

McGilligan specifically noted that in the summer of 1964 *"Hitchcock held meetings with Norman Lloyd and Joan Harrison about the final television season,"* but McGilligan also notes the health issues and deaths of loved ones that plagued Hitchcock that same year.[36]

Like most of the *Alfred Hitchcock Presents* and *Hitchcock Hour* writers, Lyndon was a prestigious creative feather-in-the-cap: Lyndon was the playwright whose debut play *The Amazing Dr. Clitterhouse* had been adapted into the successful Edward G. Robinson film (1938), and who subsequently scripted a procession of memorable and remarkably successful thrillers. These had included his scripting not one but *two* remakes of Hitchcock's first breakthrough success, the 1926 **THE LODGER** (both adapted from Marie Belloc Lowndes' 1913 Jack the Ripper novel)—Lyndon's were **THE LODGER** (1944) and **MAN IN THE ATTIC** (1953)—followed by Lyndon's bracing screenplays for **HANGOVER SQUARE** (1945), **THE MAN IN HALF MOON STREET** (1945, remade by Hammer Films as **THE MAN WHO COULD CHEAT DEATH**, 1959), **THE HOUSE ON 92ⁿᵈ STREET** (1945), **NIGHT HAS A THOUSAND EYES** (1948), brilliantly adapting and updating H.G. Wells' *The War of the Worlds* (1898) for producer George Pal (1953), and much more. Hitchcock may have even taken perverse pride in having "rescued" Lyndon from *Thriller*'s impressive writing collective immediately after the demise of that program: Lyndon had done three adaptations for *Thriller*, scripting one of the three tales in "Trio for Terror" (March 14, 1961), as well as "Yours Truly, Jack the Ripper" (April 11, 1961) and "Flowers of Evil" (March 5, 1962). *Black Cloak* / **DARK INTRUDER** was Lyndon's penultimate-screen credit; he scripted only on more episode for television ("The Plague Merchant" for *The F.B.I.*, October 30, 1966) before his own death in October 1972.

With MCA/Universal's acquisition of Shamley, Hitchcock gradually severed relations with the production studio he'd poured his energies into for a full decade—and the very operation that had provided the freedom of movement that had resulted in **PSYCHO**, another project that had not been "what audiences expected" of Hitchcock. By the time **DARK INTRUDER** opened wide theatrically in late fall of 1965, Shamley Productions was a shell of its former self, a mere subsidiary of Universal handling syndication of the still-popular-in-reruns *Alfred Hitchcock Presents*. In another context entirely—but most relevant here—21ˢᵗ Century actor/screenwriter/director/

novelist Mark Gatiss (*The League of Gentlemen, Doctor Who, Sherlock*, and the actor playing Tycho Nestoris in *Game of Thrones*) recently said, *"it's all about control, isn't it? I know from my own experiences, that's the most important thing if you have a vision. It's obviously great if you collaborate with people who share your vision and that you trust, but if you suddenly find yourself in a situation with people whose opinions you don't respect, it's deadly."* [37]

The extent of Hitchcock's divestment, and of MCA's complete ownership, was publicly revealed in 1966, when Hitchcock found his hands tied when CBS planned to censor **PSYCHO** for a forthcoming prime-time broadcast. Whereas Hitchcock was still able to contractually forbid NBC cutting **REAR WINDOW** and **VERTIGO**,

"... The fate of PSYCHO... as far as its upcoming CBS-TV showing is concerned, is up to the undetermined provisions of that web's deal with MCA... CBS-TV is understood contemplating some excisions. PSYCHO was made under Hitchcock's Shamley Prod. Banner, a company since sold outright to MCA. Hitchcock's vidseries plus the pic were included in the sale, so the director no longer has any rights in the product involved. He is still at MCA-Universal, but operating under a different corporate name there." [38]

That divestment was further evidenced in a letter signed by Hitchcock that has popped up for sale online. The letter was dated January 18, 1967, a reply to a Mrs. Cleta Pollock of Santa Monica, CA, who was evidently inquiring about film

37 "A Conversation with Mark Gatiss," interviewed by Neil Snowden, *We Are the Martians: The Legacy of Nigel Kneale* (Spectral "Horse Hospital Edition," December 2015), p.284.

38 "Hitch Restrains NBC From Cutting Up His Features" (Hollywood, July 26), *21ˢᵗ Annual Radio-TV Variety Review and Preview*, Wednesday, July 27, 1966, p.28. Special thanks to Tom Weaver for finding and sharing this article. I vividly recall the announced September 1966 broadcast, and my frustration with it being postponed—I'd never had the chance to see the film—and many family arguments about it not being suitable viewing followed (what? I was *eleven years old* now!). It was going to be on TV! I *had* to see it!). It never was broadcast on CBS in the 1960s, nor on any network we could get in northern VT; it premiered on late-night (11:30 p.m.) TV only in New York markets, edited, on WABC-TV on June 24ᵗʰ, 1967. I finally got to see it when Universal reissued PSYCHO theatrically in 1969-1970, with the previously-nonexistent "M" (for "Mature") rating ("See It the Way It Was Originally Made! Uncut! Every Scene Intact! The Version TV Didn't Dare Show!"). For the details, see "CBS and PSYCHO," *Television Obscurities*, archived at http://www.tvobscurities.com/articles/cbs_and_psycho/ ; for information on the MPAA more recently re-rating PSYCHO with an "R" rating, see "The Old PSYCHO Gets A New Rating," *Deseret News*, October 14, 1984, archived online at http://www.hicksflicks.com/-/the-old-psycho-gets-a-new-rating

at *http://lovecraftzine.com/2015/06/30/dark-intruder-a-little-known-lovecraftian-1965-movie/*

36 McGilligan, *Ibid.*, pp.655-656.

rights to the famous first-season *Alfred Hitchcock Presents* episode Hitchcock himself had directed, "Breakdown" (November 13, 1955):

"I am afraid I cannot be of much held in regard to the film rights of 'Breakdown' because I no longer control these. 'Breakdown' was made for the Alfred Hitchcock Presents *show which was controlled by Shamley Productions, Inc. This company has now been taken over by M.C.A. Inc., whose headquarters is here at Universal Studios. I would think the best thing to do is to write to a Mr. Elliott Witt, who is the head of the legal department of M.C.A."*[39]

Hitchcock's emotional detachment had to have been inevitable. It was reflected in the change in his relations with his long-time agent and professional confidant Lew Wasserman. Hitchcock biographer Patrick McGilligan noted how after the August 1964 contract revisions, *"the personal bond between Hitchcock and Wasserman was transformed and aggravated by their professional realignment. Once Hitchcock's agent, Wasserman was now his employer... Universal had been forced by the U.S. Justice Department to divest itself of MCA in 1964, and Arthur Park was Hitchcock's main contact at the agency now; still, despite Wasserman's efforts to put intermediaries between himself and Hitchcock in the decision-making process, either at MCA or Universal, there was no question who was the boss of bosses... His new contract made him a bird in a gilded cage. At Universal he would be worry-free from financially, but creatively he had sacrificed his power and freedom."*[40]

As already noted, there is evidence that Hitchcock still had *something* to do with the television productions—for Shamley, certainly, and possibly for MCA/Universal's "Project 120" in its formative stages—as Hitchcock biographer Patrick McGilligan noted the final straw in Hitchcock's waning relationship with Tippi Hedren, his star of **THE BIRDS** and **MARNIE**, came when *"the director asked her to appear in a Universal telefilm, and she refused."*[41] But I have fruitlessly scoured every single available book and article in the English language about Alfred Hitchcock over four decades; unless I have missed something—with the very notable exception of *The Alfred Hitchcock Presents Companion* by Martin Grams, Jr. and

Among the many Universal productions slated for made-for-TV status but rerouted to theatrical release instead was **MUNSTER, GO HOME** (1966), which rolled out in late spring of that year to mediocre boxoffice

Patrik Wikstrom (OTR Publishing, 2001), which dedicated three pages to **DARK INTRUDER**—I have never seen even a passing reference to either *Black Cloak* or **DARK INTRUDER** in any other Hitchcock biography or book.

And yet, while *Black Cloak* / **DARK INTRUDER** was being filmed, it was referred to as "Alfred Hitchcock's *Black Cloak* series" at least once in the

39 At the time of this writing, this letter's text was provided at its sale site with Houle Rare Books in Los Angeles, CA, linked at *http://www.abebooks.com/servlet/Book-DetailsPL?bi=7269194022&searchurl=kn%3DSham-ley%2520Productions%26sts%3Dt*

40 McGilligan, *Ibid.*, pp.653-654.

41 McGilligan, *Ibid.*, p.649.

trades—perhaps Universal was testing how easily they might be able to market the Hitchcock name on product lines he *didn't* personally supervise?—with evidence of considerable series ambitions on Universal's part:

"Universal is monster-happy. The success of The Munsters—*which has a new horror character skedded to join periodically—encouraged the studio's vidarm to launch Alfred Hitchcock's* Black Cloak *series, starring Leslie Nielsen—and a horror character in each seg; add to this gimmick fact that Nielsen plays a Frisco playboy which means there's also lotsa sex in the series... First to don horror makeup in the* Cloak *will be Mark Richman... "[42]*

The fact remains that *somewhere* amid all this activity—over two years after the final episode of *Thriller* had been broadcast (April 30, 1962), perhaps in a bid to resurrect the more overtly

supernatural flavor of that series as its own proposed new property, and only six months after the broadcast of the Barré Lyndon-scripted *Hitchcock Hour* Robert Bloch adaptation "The Sign of Satan"—Shamley Productions nurtured, developed, filmed, and quietly shelved the pilot episode of a proposed new series, *Black Cloak.* Per Hitchcock biographer Patrick McGilligan's most thorough account of almost every month of the director's life at this time, Hitchcock most like had approved the story, the writer, *"helped with script problems, discussed the major casting,"* and most likely previewed the pilot once it was completed, since it was Hitchcock's habit to screen *"all the finished episodes before they were aired."[43]* But what of the Shamley Productions that never were broadcast?

At some point, the pilot was entitled "Something With Claws." TV and genre scholar Martin Grams, Jr. turned up *"a 'revised pilot script' dated 11/17/64... in the script collection of the AFI's Louis B. Mayer Library; three titles appear on the cover, in this order:* The Alfred Hitchcock Hour, The Black Cloak, Something With Claws." [44]

42 Army Archerd, "Just for Variety," *Daily Variety,* Monday, December 14, 1964 (Vol. 126, No. 6), p.2; ellipses were in the original text. Major thanks to Tom Weaver for turning this up; this suggests Universal might have originally intended to imitate *The Outer Limits* first season's "monster of the week" format, which Irwin Allen's *Voyage to the Bottom of the Sea* and *Lost in Space* also emulated. Gary Gerani added, "TV Guide *listed "Something with Claws" as an upcoming episode of* The Alfred Hitchcock Hour." (Gerani, personal email to the author, April 1, 2016, quoted with permission).

43 McGilligan, *Ibid.,* p.552.

44 Personal email from Tom Weaver, March 7, 2016; quoted with permission of both Tom Weaver and Martin Grams, Jr. This script's existence, and the order of these titles on the script's title page, were documented in Martin's writeup of

Norman Lloyd hangs on for dear life from the torch-hand of the Statue of Liberty in the unforgettable climax of Alfred Hitchcock's **SABOTEUR** (1942); Lloyd survived to become a key player in Hitchcock's inner circle at Shamley Productions

By all available evidence, the pilot was filmed in December 1964. *Variety* announced on November 30th that *"Leslie Nielsen was cast over the weekend in 'Something With Claws' episode of* Hitchcock Hour, *a projected hourlong series to be called* The Black Cloak..."*[45] The cast and crew were comprised in part of veteran *Alfred Hitchcock Presents, Suspicion,* and *The Twilight Zone* talent. In his book on the *Alfred Hitchcock* television series, author Martin Grams specified the Hitchcock episodes each cast member had appeared in:

"Most of the cast... were veterans of other Shamley productions. Mark Richman ('Man with a Problem'), Leslie Nielsen ('The Magic Shop,' 'Ambition,' and 'The $2,000,000 Defense'), Werner Klemperer ('Safe Conduct' and 'The Crystal Trench'), Bill Quinn ('How to Get Rid of Your Wife'), and so on. Mike Ragan played numerous supporting roles in Alfred Hitchcock Presents episodes, including an escaped convict in the episode 'Breakdown' and a plumber in 'The Horseplayer.'..."[46]

Prior to 1964, Lew Wasserman's MCA handled a plethora of such seasoned players, many who were TV staples of the era, with Shamley and Revue providing constant gainful employment; as of 1964, despite the intervention of the U.S. Justice Department, MCA/Universal still effectively controlled talent *and* television and movie production, with a lock on major talents and employment. Just off the top, Leslie Nielsen had starred in the first episode of *Thriller,* "The Twisted Image" (September 13, 1960) as well as *Alfred Hitchcock Presents, The Alfred Hitchcock Hour,* and *Kraft Suspense Theatre.* Mark Richman (Peter Mark Richman) had already appeared in episodes of *Alfred Hitchcock Presents, The Twilight Zone,* and both Nielsen and Richman had appeared on *Ben Casey* (a series Jack Laird had a hand in), where Judi Meredith later had a supporting role (in the final season, 1966).

Black Cloak was a genuine Shamley Production, either the last of the Hitchcock Shamley era or the first of the post-Hitchcock era—though one might suspect it was the last of the Hitchcock Shamley productions, given the role played by

German-born stage, movie, TV actor Werner Klemperer (March 22, 1920–December 6, 2000) co-starred in **DARK INTRUDER** as Professor Malaki, but his face and hands were invisible under Bud Westmore's makeup and his voice was overdubbed by Norman Lloyd!

one of the most trusted players and producers of Alfred Hitchcock's inner circle. That key player was Norman Lloyd—the titular **SABOTEUR** of Hitchcock's classic 1942 feature, support player in Hitchcock's **SPELLBOUND** (1945), associate producer (and sometimes actor/narrator) for *Alfred Hitchcock Presents* since the summer of 1957, executive producer of *The Alfred Hitchcock Hour,* and occasional director of episodes for both series. It was Norman Lloyd who provided the voice of the demonic Professor Malaki in *Black Cloak /* **DARK INTRUDER,** *sans* credit.

Genre expert Tom Weaver had something to say about this:

"Werner Klemperer did the voice of the monster originally but [Mark] *Richman told me the decision makers didn't think a German-accented monster seemed to work, so Norman Lloyd was brought in to provide the new voice. Richman and Klemperer had already worked together in a stage production of* Detective Story *and I got the impression Richman liked W.K. because, when he told me about the voice substitution, he made it sound like Klemperer got a raw deal, that that wasn't very nice of Universal (pretty much eliminating Klemperer's performance).*

DARK INTRUDER in *The Alfred Hitchcock Companion* by Martin Grams, Jr. and Patrik Wikstrom (OTR Publishing, 2001), pp.76-78.

45 "Leslie Nielsen in Hitchcock Pilot," *Daily Variety,* Monday, November 30, 1964, pg. 10; special thanks to Tom Weaver for confirming the December 1964 filming of *Black Cloak /* **DARK INTRUDER** via the *Daily Variety* notices.

46 Martin Grams, Jr., *Ibid.,* p.76; quoted with permission.

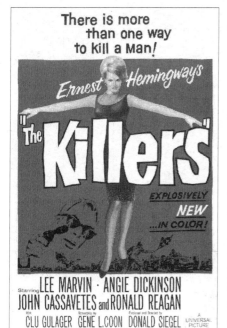

There is more than one way to kill a Man!

Ernest Hemingway's

"The Killers"

EXPLOSIVELY NEW ...IN COLOR!

Starring LEE MARVIN · ANGIE DICKINSON
JOHN CASSAVETES and RONALD REAGAN
With CLU GULAGER · GENE L. COON · DONALD SIEGEL
A UNIVERSAL PICTURE

The now-classic MCA/Universal made-for-TV "Project 120" feature that was bumped to a theatrical release due to concerns over its violence quotient: Don Siegel and Gene L. Coon's **THE KILLERS** (1964), co-starring Lew Wasserman's politician-in-the-pocket Ronald Reagan in his final screen role

---

"Norman Lloyd had no idea what I was talking about, when I asked about Black Cloak / **DARK INTRUDER**. *I sent him a VHS of the monster scene and he confirmed that it was his voice—but apparently he had nothing to do with it other than provide the voice."*[47]

Given Norman Lloyd's *lack* of recall on the production, it's increasingly unlikely Hitchcock had any direct involvement with any meaningful aspect of *Black Cloak* / **DARK INTRUDER**. By the end of 1964, and definitely by the pilot film's leap to theatrical release in 1965, there was simply nothing left to even vaguely interest Hitchcock in something like *BC*/**DI**, for a multitude of reasons he succinctly summarized at the time for anyone who was really listening:

"Among Hitchcock's future plans is R.R.R.R.R., about Mafia type gangsters whose activities center around a luxury hotel. Eventually, he plans to start work on Sir James 'Peter Pan'... Barrie's 'MARIE ROSE', but not as a ghost fantasy. Hitchcock feels that 'You can't sell customers on ghost stuff these days. To be effective, 'MARIE ROSE' will have to be adapted to science fiction.' He recently sold his TV interests to MCA and doesn't consider going into boob-tube work again. He feels that TV anthology dramatic shows aren't in demand by audiences anymore; rather, the TV public is primarily interested in a long-term continuing character each week, 'and to do that would be too much of a grind.'... "[48]

Hitchcock was also pragmatic when asked by the press about the cancellation of *The Alfred Hitchcock Hour*: *"We must be philosophical about this. As we all know, TV is a great juggernaut and we're all nuts and bolts attached to it. Sometimes the nuts and bolts fall off."* An NBC spokesman was less sage: *"We merely found Mr. Hitchcock a little too costly."*[49] NBC didn't even make note of the program's passing.[50] Given this attitude, perhaps it was projected per-episode costs that led to all three networks passing on the proposed *Black Cloak* TV series.

To the end, Hitchcock still picked his own pocket, appropriating key collaborators from Shamley: Hitchcock carried over *Alfred Hitchcock Presents* cameraman John F. Warren (who'd been with Hitchcock since **REBECCA**) and editor Bud Hoffman (landing his first feature film gig) to work on **TORN CURTAIN**. And yet—about his own continuing filmmaking, Hitchcock told a journalist in 1966, *"the industry's run by accountants and businessmen and agents. Agents are the worst, because they've no interest in the film, only in getting work for their artists."*[51]

We can be fairly certain Hitchcock saw *BC*/*DI*. As already noted, it was Hitchcock's habit to screen *"all the finished episodes before they were aired."*

---

47 Tom Weaver, personal email to the author, April 2, 2016; quoted with permission.

48 Calvin T. Beck aka "Cal Beck," "Movie Noose Reel," *Castle of Frankenstein* #9 (November, 1966), p.45. For a fuller account of the properties Hitchcock was weighing during this time period, see McGilligan, pp.656-662; for the fate of R.R.R.R.R., see pp.662, 668, and 676.

49 Both quotes are from John McCarty and Brian Kelleher's *Alfred Hitchcock Presents: An Illustrated Guide to the Ten-Year Television Career of the Master of Suspense* (St. Martin's Press, 1985), from pp.53-54.

50 Martin Grams, Jr. and Patrik Wikstrom quoted *TV Guide* as writing, *"As of May 10, Alfred Hitchcock presents no more. After ten year on CBS and NBC, the series leaves the air without fanfare—NBC did not even announced its departure, [they] simply failed to announce a renewal. The ratings of* The Alfred Hitchcock Hour *have gradually slipped, although not catastrophically, and, according to an NBC source, 'We merely found Mr. Hitchcock a little too costly.'"* (Grams, Jr. and Wikstrom, p.53).

51 McGilligan, pp. 666-667.

Furthermore, *"Hitchcock was a lifelong devotee of studio screenings,"* biographer Patrick McGilligan wrote, and after the August 1964 contract revisions, *"now he had his own private screening room... he kept up loyally with the output of anyone with whom he was acquainted.... and tried dutifully to sit through everything produced by Universal.* "[52]

We'll never know for certain what Hitchcock's role was in **DARK INTRUDER**'s eventual fate. Unless material evidence ever surfaces to prove Hitchcock asked a favor of Wasserman—would he have jeopardized the precarious balance of power with Wasserman over a trifle like **DI**?—we can't presume anything. One way or another—as a potential episode of the final season of the anthology program branded with his name, or as a Universal theatrical feature (he watched all Universal releases out of a sense of loyalty to the studio he owned a third of)— *BC*/**DI** was most likely privately screened by Hitchcock, once.

In hindsight, particularly given Lew Wasserman's aversion to allowing Hitchcock or Shamley (in what little time it had left) to involve themselves with supernatural narratives of any significance, it might seem a miracle **DI** was made it all, much less released theatrically to whatever acclaim and boxoffice it earned in 1965.

Anyone wishing to know more should read Dennis McDougal's essential *The Last Mogul: Lew Wasserman, MCA, and the Hidden History of Hollywood* (Crown, 1998/Da Capo, 2001) and/or screen the documentary **THE LAST MOGUL: THE LIFE AND TIMES OF LEW WASSERMAN** (2005) which Barry Avrich adapted from McDougal's book. Before his death in 2002 at age 89,[53] Wasserman had effectively altered the American commercial, corporate, and government (state and Federal) landscapes. We owe the relaxing of regulations controlling corporate media monopolies, and the 21ˢᵗ Century consolidation of concentrated corporate ownership of so much in our lives, to Wasserman.

But for the purposes of this article on this movie— **DARK INTRUDER**—all you must understand is that Lew Wasserman pulled all the strings; every

string, at every juncture—and that among those puppets-on-strings was Alfred Hitchcock at a critical and very vulnerable point in his life and career.

At the very peak of his career and powers, Wasserman had effectively neutered both Hitchcock and the soon-to-be-completely-absorbed Shamley Productions.

To cinéastes, the radical notion that Alfred Hitchcock was one of the great artists working in commercial cinema was spreading from the pages of *Cahiers du Cinéma* and *Film Culture* into wider acceptance: Peter Bogdanovich and Carl Belz praised **THE BIRDS** in their *Film Culture* reviews,[54] while in 1963 alone four revivals of Hitchcock's earlier works played in London's West End cinemas and the Museum of Modern Art hosted a near-complete retrospective of Hitchcock's films (May 5-November 19, with a published monograph by Bogdanovich, *The Cinema of Alfred Hitchcock*). French director Francois Truffaut presented Alfred Hitchcock to the world as an artist with the 1966 publication of their historic book-length interview *Hitchcock/Truffaut*.

This was all very gratifying, but to MCA/Universal and Lew Wasserman, Hitchcock wasn't an artist:

He was, like everything else they owned, a commodity.

―――――――

It is impossible to overemphasize Lew Wasserman's role in the nurturing, production, and eventual launch of made-for-TV features in the three-network American television marketplace. Within Universal Wasserman called this ambitious plan "Project 120," referring to telefeatures intended for two-hour (120 minute) timeslots, and the first of these MCA/Universal/NBC "Project 120" projects was to be **THE KILLERS**. Director Don Siegel himself noted,

"...in 1963, I was in Lew Wasserman's office at Universal. He was President of the company and wanted me to direct a new version of 'The Killers.' *It was going to be the first two-hour movie made for television... The only idea from the* [1946] *picture I wished to use was the catalyst of a man knowing he's going to be killed and making no attempt to escape sure death. Not one word of* [Ernest] *Hemingway's dialogue would be used, nor would there be any scenes similar to those in the* [1946] *movie. Wasserman and I enthusiastically*

52 *Ibid.*, pp.552, 656, 677, and 696; while working with novelist Leon Uris on adapting Uris' own *Topaz*, Uris noted that whenever Hitchcock was not privately screening for the writer *"a Hitchcock film, they watched... 'some other Universal junk,' in Uris's words..."* (McGilligan, p.685).

53 See Jonathan Kandell, "Lew Wasserman, 89, Is Dead; Last of Hollywood's Moguls," *The New York Times*, June 4, 2002, archived at *http://www.nytimes.com/2002/06/04/business/lew-wasserman-89-is-dead-last-of-hollywood-s-moguls.html?pagewanted=all*

54 Bogdanovich's appeared in *Film Culture* #28 (Spring 1963), pp.69-70; Belz's in *Film Culture* #31 (Winter 1963-64), pp.51-53.

agreed on telling the story from the killers' point of view...

"THE KILLERS was supposed to be the first two-hour TV movie. However, it was much too violent for the time. Wasserman liked it, particularly when it was shown on 16mm. It sold more than any other 16mm picture of its time, and when it was released as a feature it did very well critically and at the box office. The reaction to the violence in THE KILLERS was one of shock in 1964, although later the film was considered to be quite tame."[55]

Siegel's THE KILLERS became, in fact, iconic of its genre: the climactic image of the mortally wounded Lee Marvin with his pistol in both hands, about to cut down Angie Dickinson ("Lady, I just haven't got the time"), was the cover for the Museum of Modern Art's monograph *Violent America: The Movies, 1946-1964* by Lawrence Alloway (1971).

Violence on television had repeatedly flared into national controversies and even a procession of U.S. Senate Subcommittee hearings, with flash points like TV westerns, crime programs like *The Untouchables* (see Sidebar #1), and singular eruptions like Robert Altman and Ellis Kadison's *Bus Stop* episode "A Lion Walks Among Us" (December 3, 1961) occasionally fanning the flames. Starring teen idol Fabian Forte as a sadistic nomadic sociopath, "A Lion Walks Among Us" was a particularly volatile hour of television, broadcast once and only once[56]; its production team at 20th Century Fox and the network ABC-TV suffered in the wake of its broadcast, which 25 ABC affiliates refused to air after previewing the episode. Despite the immediate pre-emptive backlash among its own regional broadcasters, ABC President Oliver Treyz nevertheless chose to broadcast the episode. Treyz paid dearly: after weathering testimony and cross-examination before Senator Thomas Dodd's Congressional Committee investigation into TV violence, Treyz was fired from ABC, *Bus Stop* was

cancelled, and the show's executive producer Roy Huggins was a pariah at Fox.

And just when it appeared the early 1960s hubbub over violence on television might subside, President John F. Kennedy was assassinated in Dallas, Texas, on November 22, 1963. In the madness that followed, the controversies over violence on television spilled fresh blood, and the studios, networks, censors, critics, and the public were on high alert.

In the wake of the JFK assassination, the violence quotient of any proposed programming or made-for-TV feature became a sore spot for all future Universal/MCA/NBC coproductions. Don Siegel noted such in his account of Wasserman's ire concerning Siegel's proposed next project, "CRIME WITHOUT PASSION" (1964), from a screenplay by THE KILLERS co-star John Cassavetes, which Wasserman countered with *"How could you submit a script like this, knowing that NBC hates violence?... I don't want to go through another fiasco like THE KILLERS."* Siegel noted, *"THE KILLERS could never be made to pass the odious television censor code."*[57] Wasserman buried the Cassavetes script, didn't permit Siegel or anyone else to buy the property back for independent production. Siegel subsequently shot the Robert Culp suspenser THE HANGED MAN (November 18, 1964, considered the second made-for-TV movie to air in the US after producer Jack Laird's SEE HOW THEY RUN [Oct. 7, 1964, starring Leslie Nielsen], though it was made *after* THE KILLERS). After all, Siegel helmed his final NBC-TV movie, STRANGER ON THE RUN (October 31, 1967), starring Henry Fonda.

Siegel was then tapped to direct an episode of MCA/Universal/Revue Studios/NBC's prestige 90-minute police drama series *Arrest and Trial* (30 episodes, September 15, 1963-September 6, 1964). Siegel refused. It took Siegel going over the series' producer's head to the vice-president in charge of television for Universal to free himself to helm the theatrical feature MADIGAN (1968)—for the same producer, which kept Siegel on tenterhooks throughout the production. This culminated in yet another tangle with *"the censor board of NBC,"* initially cutting seven minutes—*"the entire beginning of MADIGAN"*—from the film; Siegel suggested a compromise to Wasserman, to *"save the opening sequence by taking out a few frames of film,"*[58] and Wasserman approved. MADIGAN

55 Don Siegel, *A Siegel Film: An Autobiography* (1993, Faber and Faber Limited), p.235, 259.

56 Ironically, given the plethora of TV series episodes retro-fitted into feature films, Fabian Forte claimed in interviews that Fox and the *Bus Stop* producers had intended to shoot additional footage to expand "A Lion Walks Among Us" into feature film length for oversea theatrical release, but Fabian himself declined to participate (see "'Bus Stop' Flop Flips Fabian Into High Gear" by Hal Humphrey, *Los Angeles Times*, Jun 17, 1962, p.N6). Had this come to ex-ist, it would have been Robert Altman's third feature film, an almost certain boon to Fabian's acting career, and a most significant entry in the post-PSYCHO sweepstakes. In later years, Fabian bemoaned his decision and the loss (see *Robert Altman: The Oral Biography* by Mitchell Zuckoff [Knopf, 2009], p.117). I will be writing a definitive overview of "A Lion Walks Among Us" at a future date.

57 Siegel, *Ibid.*, p.263.

58 *Ibid.*, pp.275-276, 293.

became a breakthrough success for Siegel, leading to his first hit collaboration with actor Clint Eastwood with his next theatrical feature project, **COOGAN'S BLUFF** (1969). The rest is history, but the grueling process demonstrated how the Universal/MCA/NBC combine could make or break careers.

Kraft Suspense Theatre (59 episodes, October 10, 1963-July 1, 1965) provides another sterling example of Universal's ongoing made-for-TV/TV-to-film production line. A select few of the *Kraft Suspense Theatre* episodes were released by Universal as theatrical films, overseas and domestically: the Season 1 debut two-parter "The Case Against Paul Ryker" (October 10 and 17, 1963) starring Lee Marvin was theatrically released as **SERGEANT RYKER** (1968) to cash in on the surprise box-office success of Robert Aldrich's Lee Marvin WW2 actioner **THE DIRTY DOZEN** (1967).[59] Robert Altman's extraordinary-for-its-time *Kraft Suspense Theatre* serial killer drama "Once Upon a Savage Night" (April 2, 1964, for a 60 minute time slot, based on William P. McGivern's titular

novella in *Killer on the Turnpike and Other Stories* [Pocket Books, 1961]) was expanded and repackaged as the 81-minute feature film **NIGHTMARE IN CHICAGO** for limited theatrical release in the Midwest, Canada, and overseas (which Universal subsequently folded into its TV movie syndication packages, which is how I originally saw it); thus, **NIGHTMARE IN CHICAGO** became Altman's third feature film, though it isn't included in many of the director's filmographies.[60]

Kraft Suspense Theatre's two-part "In Darkness, Waiting" (January 14 and 21, 1965), directed by Jack Smight, became **STRATEGY OF TERROR** (1969). Meanwhile, MCA/Universal/NBC's *Bob Hope Chrysler Theatre* aka *Bob Hope Presents The Chrysler Theatre* (107 episodes, October 4, 1963-May 17, 1967) was also spawning episodes-reedited-into-movies: the two-part "Memorandum for a Spy" (April 2-9, 1965) became the feature **ASYLUM FOR A SPY** (1966), the two-part "Code Name: Heraclitus" (January 4-11, 1967, co-starring Leslie Nielsen) became **CODE NAME: HERACLITUS** (1967), and so on.[61] If anything, this program only mutated and expanded in subsequent years under the helm of Lew Wasserman's long-time associate/toadie Harry Tatelman, whose hybrid MCA/Universal/NBC hybrid telefeatures-carved-from-TV-series were often incomprehensible, but always made money—and that was all that Wasserman and MCA/Universal cared about.[62]

---

59 This kind of opportunism in converting television series episodes into faux-feature-films for release overseas— and, occasionally, into Canada and into select domestic markets—reached lunatic extremes. MCA/Universal/Revue Studios concocted the loopy **THE MEANEST MEN IN THE WEST** (1978) from two completely unrelated episodes of *The Virginian*, "It Tolls For Thee" (November 21, 1962) guest starring Lee Marvin, and "The Reckoning" (September 13, 1967) guest starring Charles Bronson, just to fleece audiences hungry for an otherwise non-existent Lee Marvin/Charles Bronson vehicle (which could also boast partial-script-and-directing by Samuel Fuller!); having co-starred in **THE DIRTY DOZEN** (1967), the two stars wouldn't actually appear together in the same theatrical feature film again until **DEATH HUNT** (1981). The incoherent sow's ear **THE MEANEST MEN IN THE WEST** was released on DVD in the US by Goodtimes way back in July, 1998. TV historian/archivist Stephen Bowie noted, "*...'On its own it was a very good episode and I was horrified when I saw it,' said Joel Rogosin of* The Meanest Man in the West, *which combined one of Rogosin's episodes of* The Virginian *with one produced by another unit, in Paul Green's* A History of Television's The Virginian *(McFarland, 2010)*" (quoted from https://classictvhistory. wordpress.com/2012/02/25/procrustes-comes-to-syndication/). In the western genre, the most infamous example of such shameless hucksterism may be **MALEDETTO GRINGO / EL MAGNIFICO EXTRANJERO / THE MAGNIFICENT STRANGER** (1967), comprising two *Rawhide* episodes ("Incident of the Running Man," May 5, 1961, and "The Backshooter," November 27, 1964) that Jolly Films (coproducer of Sergio Leone's **A FISTFUL OF DOLLARS** (*Per un pugno di dollari*, 1964/1967) cobbled together and released in Europe with co-star Clint Eastwood headlined to cash in on the surprise success of the Sergio Leone 'Man With No Name' spaghetti westerns. According to "*After a legal action, the film was withdrawn. Soon after this, Lucas Film tried a similar trick, this time calling the result* EL GRINGHERO*... Again, Eastwood took the matter to court, and won his case. It was, he maintained, a question of protecting his image.*" (Christopher Frayling, *Spaghetti Westerns: Cowboys and Europeans from Karl May to Sergio Leone* [Palgrave MacMillan/I.B. Tauris & Co. Ltd., 1998/2006], p.169).

60 16mm color prints of **NIGHTMARE IN CHICAGO** still circulate and occasionally are screened on the college circuit; see the Harvard Film Archive's August 30th, 2015 showing at the Carpenter Center for the Visual Arts listing online, archived at http://hcl.harvard.edu/hfa/films/2015/junaug/altman.html#nightmare and http://www.thebostoncalendar.com/events/nightmare-in-chicago

61 And there are some of these transmutations that defy research. Rod Serling's Hollywood exposé "A Slow Fade to Black" starring Rod Steiger in an Emmy Award-winning role as a fading Hollywood mogul became **THE MOVIE MAKER**—which TV movie expert Alvin H. Marill cites as a two-parter from *Bob Hope Chrysler Theatre*, but is listed online (including IMDb) as two separate movies, one from 1964 and another from 1967, with two different directors! However, I cannot find any Bob Hope TV anthology series of the 1960s with an episode entitled "A Slow Fade to Black" or "Fade Out to Black." Gary Gerani wrote to me about this, saying, "'*Fade Out to Black*' *was originally an hour presentation on NBC's* Bob Hope *anthology; it was expanded to feature-length for 16mm syndication as* THE MOVIE MAKER, *with a new cast playing the main characters in their youth via flashbacks, for padding.*" Gerani, personal email to the author, April 1, 2016, quoted with permission.

62 See Stephen Bowie, "Procrustes Comes to Syndication," *The Classic TV History Blog*, February 25, 2012 (@ https://classictvhistory.wordpress.com/2012/02/25/procrustes-comes-to-syndication/). Also note that Four Star Productions (the studio behind TV series like *The Dick Powell Theatre*, *The Big Valley*, *Burke's Law*, *Honey West*, etc.) plot for a proposed prime-time soap opera entitled *Royal Bay* starring Joan Crawford failed to find a network, so the 68-minute pilot was theatrically released in some markets (domestic and overseas) as **DELLA** (US pre-

AN ENTERTAINMENT FIRST THAT MAY WELL SET A NEW PATTERN FOR ALL FUTURE SHOCKERS!

A motion picture with an audio-visual warning system to protect the timid and the fearful...

Here's how it works: At the start of certain scenes that many may consider too shocking, a red **FEAR FLASHER** will begin its signal on the screen to alert you to the terror ahead. When you hear the **HORROR HORN**, shut your eyes and hold your ears!

CHAMBER OF HORRORS

The unspeakable vengeance of the crazed "Baltimore Strangler."

STARRING
CESARE DANOVA · WILFRID HYDE-WHITE · LAURA DEVON · PATRICE WYMORE · SUZY PARKER ALSO STARRING TUN TUN PHILIP BOURNEUF
and PATRICK O'NEAL as "JASON" · Story by Ray Russell and Stephen Kandel · Produced and Directed by Hy Averback · Screenplay by Stephen Kandel · TECHNICOLOR® FROM WARNER BROS.

Recognizing there was gold in the new 1960s graphic gore films like **BLOOD FEAST** (1963), but unwilling to revel in Herschell Gordon Lewis-style mayhem, Hy Averback and Stephen Kandel's unsold pilot *House of Wax* was revamped by Warner Bros. into the theatrical release **CHAMBER OF HORRORS** (1966) with a bold ad campaign that promised and sold "the sizzle"—though there sure wasn't much "steak" to be seen onscreen!

This was the production line environment out of which **DARK INTRUDER** was conceived, produced, shopped around to all three networks, shelved, and eventually released theatrically. As *Thriller* associate producer/story editor Doug Benton told interviewer Tom Weaver, *"They were the packing house of television. Do you remember the Armour* [Bacon] *slogan, 'We use every part of the pig but the squeal'? Well, that's the way MCA was with television—the sets would be repainted and turned upside-down and shot sideways. Believe me, that Indian was squealin' on every nickel [laughs]!"[63]*

The fact is, after the unexpected success of **THE KILLERS** and **DARK INTRUDER**, Wasserman/MCA/Universal was hustling *a lot* of "Project 120" telefeatures into theaters instead. Gone was the moniker "Project 120" Don Siegel referred to; as *Fantastic Television* author and TV movie expert Gary Gerani explains,

"To the world at large, there was no 'Project 120.' The brand name was World Premiere, *used with great fanfare in 1966 to promote* **FAME IS THE NAME OF THE GAME** [November 26, 1966] *which ran on NBC's* Saturday Night at the Movies *and did extremely well in the ratings.[64] More two-hour World Premiere offerings followed, run on the network's Saturday and Tuesday prime-time movie slots, including feature length pilots for* Dragnet [January 27, 1969] *and* Ironside [March 28, 1967] *(and* Columbo *in its earliest form,* **PRESCRIPTION: MURDER** [February 20, 1968]). *ABC approached Universal to develop a series of 90-minute telefeatures, but the studio balked at producing TV movies with the reduced budgets ABC had in mind. So ABC went to Aaron Spelling, Fox, etc., for their 90 minute* Movie of the Weeks, *which wound up doing better in the ratings than many WPs, even though most were of inferior quality... almost like B-movie second features to the* WPs. *But the funky format and subject matter caught on. Universal would eventually throw in the towel and make cheapie 90-minute MOTWs*

---

miere: August 1964), a.k.a. **FATAL CONFINEMENT**, and syndicated to television as a feature.

63 Doug Benton interviewed by Tom Weaver, *Ibid.*, pp. 92-93; quoted with permission.

64 The weekly TV series *The Name of the Game* followed (76 episodes, September 20, 1968-March 19, 1971).

for ABC a year or so later as Movie of the Weekend (Saturdays), most but not all inferior to their NBC telefeatures. Most famous of these was Steven Spielberg's DUEL [November 13, 1971]."[65]

Unlike **DARK INTRUDER**, all the other MCA/ Universal telefeatures rerouted into theatrical runs were in color. According to telefeature expert Alvin H. Marill—who wrote the definitive, first-ever book on made-for-TV movies—Wasserman's "Project 120" yielded a string of Universal theatrical releases, some of which proved quite lucrative. Of these, *"diverted into theatrical release instead of having intended television premieres—although they all subsequently took their natural route to TV,"* Marill headlined Don Siegel's **THE KILLERS**, along with **HOT RODS TO HELL** (1967), *"Rod Serling's adaptation of Irving Wallace's* **THE MAN**" (1972), **WARNING SHOT** (1967), Lamont Johnson's atmospheric thriller **YOU'LL LIKE MY MOTHER** (1972), **SCOTT JOPLIN** (1977), and **BUCK ROGERS IN THE 25th CENTURY** (1979).

"Among others which Universal diverted to theatrical release first were remakes in the 1960s of **THE PLAINSMAN** [1966], **BEAU GESTE** [1966], **THE PALEFACE** *(newly titled* **THE SHAKIEST GUN IN THE WEST** [1968]*),* **AGAINST ALL FLAGS** *(retitled* **THE KING'S PIRATE** [1967]*), and* **MAN WITHOUT A STAR** *(as* **A MAN CALLED GANNON** [1968]*); assorted hoss-operas* **RIDE TO HANGMAN'S TREE** [1967], **JOURNEY TO SHILOH** [1968] *and* **GUNFIGHT IN ABILENE** [1967]; *action dramas* **JIGSAW** [1968], **COMPANY OF KILLERS** [1977], **THE YOUNG WARRIORS** [1967], **LOST FLIGHT** [1970] *and* **VALLEY OF MYSTERY** [1967]; *and comedies* **NOBODY'S PERFECT** [1968], **ROSIE** [1967], **MUNSTER GO HOME** [1966] *and* **THE RELUCTANT ASTRONAUT** [1967]."*[66]

Across town from Lew Wasserman's vast, ever-prolific MCA/Universal/Revue/Shamley arena, other studios were energetically leaping into the fray with similar productions. The one that was thematically and narratively closest to **DARK INTRUDER** was the Technicolor period shocker with the Fear Flasher and the Horror Horn, **CHAMBER OF HORRORS**.

Warner Bros. bankrolled producer/director Hy Averback and writer Stephen Kandel's pilot for a

HOUSE OF WAX-based series entitled—ahem— *House of Wax* (1966); as Kandel can best recall, it was produced as a 90-minute pilot for ABC on the still-standing Warner **HOUSE OF WAX** sets.

As I stated earlier, I believe *this* is the programming whose actual history is erroneously conflated with that of **DI**; in fact, the promise of violence was central to its entire conception and presentation. *This* was the TV pilot that actually was *"deemed too strong for TV,"* in the words of Tom Weaver:

"The setting is Baltimore, circa 1880, and a killer prowls the foggy night streets: Jason Cravette, a mad blue-blood who once strangled his bride-to-be with her own hair and then forced a clergyman to perform the wedding ceremony anyway. With the help of Anthony Draco and Harold Blount, criminologists and operators of a local wax museum Chamber of Horrors, Cravette had been apprehended, tried for her murder and condemned—but en route to prison, he escaped. Now he stalks the city again, deadlier than before: During his getaway, Cravette had to hack off his own shackled right hand, which he now replaces with a series of grisly instruments of murder.

"This was the bizarre plot of the TV pilot for House of Wax, *a proposed 1966 Warner Bros. series starring Cesare Danova and Wilfrid Hyde-White as the sleuthing showmen and guest star Patrick O'Neal as the homicidal (but otherwise impeccably mannered) 'Baltimore Strangler.' Gruesome, sometimes verging-on-kinky, the Hy Averback-directed shocker was deemed too strong for TV, and the idea of a series was scrapped..."*[67]

According to screenwriter Stephen Kandel, had the *House of Wax* series pilot sold, each episode would have been one hour, and *"every episode would have involved a horrible crime. Dismemberment, rape, Jack the Ripper, impalements, horrors... that was the idea! Think of Hannibal the Cannibal as a regular! I would have been a regular writer on the series—I would have been the* head *writer,"* Kandel penned to interviewer Tom Weaver. Kandel very specifically recalled the sequence that dealt the pilot the death-blow:

"I watched the movie again just the other night, and I noticed that a shot was missing—a shot which sent the network over the edge. It was a cut from Patrick O'Neal's cleaver hand descending at the judge [Vinton Hayworth a.k.a. Haworth], to a piece of rare roast beef being sliced in an upscale restaurant. It was very *effective—at the screening*

65 Gary Gerani, personal email to the author, April 1, 2016, quoted with permission.

66 Alvin H. Marill, *Movies made for Television: The Telefeature and the Mini-Series 1964-1979* (Arlington House, 1980), p.10.

67 Tom Weaver, *Earth vs. the Sci-Fi Filmmakers: Twenty Interviews* (McFarland, 2005), p.212; Kandel noted the ABC-TV connection on pg. 216 of the same interview. Quoted with permission.

What Do *You* Think? The Martians in **THE THREE STOOGES IN ORBIT** (1962, makeup by Frank McCoy) sure look to us like blood-brothers to Professor Malaki in **DARK INTRUDER** (1965, makeup by Bud Westmore)!

house where we tested the pilot, with an audience of civilians enticed in off the street to watch and rate the show, there were screams. Which was the idea, I thought! But the network said, 'That's it! No chance!' Jack Warner, because of this flap, saw it, and he said, 'Hell, [we'll make it] a feature.' And he said, 'Let's put some more money in it.' Eleven cents [laughs]! I wrote more and Hy Averback shot

more. I wrote, for instance, the wedding scene at the beginning, to help pad it out.''[68]

Warner bankrolled the necessary additional material—including onscreen cameos by contracted Warners stars Tony Curtis, Patrice Wymore, Suzy Parker, and Marie Windsor, and narration by William Conrad—yielding the September 1966 wide theatrical release of **CHAMBER OF HORRORS.**[69]

Despite fan presumptions over the years, the film's gimmick of "The Fear Flasher and the Horror Horn" wasn't added to the revised feature; it was, Kandel remembers, part of the TV pilot, and would have been part of the TV series:

British fantasist Alfred Edgar wrote for the screen under the penname Barré Lyndon, including the first adaptation of his own play **THE MAN IN HALF MOON STREET** (filmed 1944, released 1945); Eve Brandon (Helen Walker) falls for 120-year-old Dr. Julian Karell (Nils Asther), who reverts to his true age without the human gland transplants that keep him looking young

68 Kandel interviewed by Weaver, *Earth vs. the Sci-Fi Filmmakers*, pp.216-207; quoted with permission. The re-edit is apparent on the uncut Warner DVD of **CHAMBER OF HORRORS**: the film was softened prior to theatrical release so that O'Neal's cleaver hand descending to attack the victim judge fades instead to the marquee of the House of Wax (timecode: 45:39). The closeup of the bloody roast beef being cut was moved to 1:00:25, to meaninglessly conclude a fade from the trio of detectives in their coach (1:00:20) to close-ups of hands playing the strings of a harp, which quickly fades to the close-up of the roast beef being sliced. Silly, really—they should have left it as Kandel remembers it!

69 I've researched numerous American newspaper archives to verify this; see, for instance, *The Cincinnati Enquirer* online archives, evidencing a mid-September opening in Ohio for **CHAMBER OF HORRORS**, a full month before its New York City premiere: https://www.newspapers.com/search/#lnd=1&dr_year=1966-1966&query=chamber+of+horrors&offset=10&t=844&oquery=1966+chamber+of+horrors

"Oh, it would have been the show's trademark [every week]... I really resisted that, and I got absolutely nowhere. Finally I said, 'Look, let's use it only in the moment when something horrible is gonna happen, so the audience is cheated of its vision of the exploding viscera? They see the Fear Flasher instead and it enables them to visualize what's hiding behind that red glowing splash on the screen.' They sort of went for that. So, yes, the Fear Flasher and the Horror Horn would have been seen and heard every week."[70]

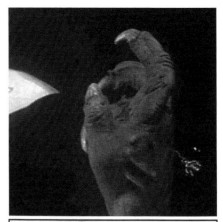

Thus, despite the aggressive promotion for the theatrical release and promise of gore (the ad art prominently featured a severed hand, with veins jutting from the severed stump like a Pre-Code horror comic image), there is *no* real onscreen gore—in fact, the gimmick is perversely *not* blared or flashed from the screen before the only splash of real onscreen bloodshed, during the climax. The pilot screened for the network was, according to Kandel, more grisly than the film Warner Bros. released to theaters:

MONSTER HAND
These colorful rubber claws fit right over your hand like a glove. Enough to scare the wits out of your victims. (The werewolf on the cover of #3 issue is wearing them.) Full price only $1.50 each hand, or $3.00 for a complete pair. Circle No. 4 in coupon.

"There was originally a much better underwater sequence, and I don't know what happened to it. You see the Strangler [at the bottom of the river] wrap that chain around a rock, forcing his hand on top of the rock and chopping it off. Just then, a cloud of little fish comes by, attracted by the blood. And that's it. The last thing you see is the anchored hand on the rock, bleeding, and the fish swimming around this cloud of blood. Which I thought was a great shot.... I shot it! Hy didn't care, he said, 'All right, look, we're out here [in the studio tank] anyway. If you want to try and sneak a second unit shot...' I said, 'Yeah, let me take a whack at it.'... So, yes, there were things that were shot that [weren't used], like the roast beef slice and a better amputation scene."[71]

CHAMBER OF HORRORS was a seasonal hit for Warners, and an early entry in the 'body count' horror subgenre popularized in subsequent years. Along with Columbia's release of William Castle and Robert Bloch's **STRAIT-JACKET** (1964), it was also arguably the first Hollywood studio response to Herschell Gordon Lewis and David Friedman's **BLOOD FEAST** (1963); both films were timid by comparison, but both shamelessly played up the promise of bloodshed in their advertising. Returning to one of our barometers for how mainstream critics responded to these made-for-TV horrors making the leap to the big

When filmed as a pilot episode for the proposed series *Black Cloak*, **DARK INTRUDER** was subtitled "Something With Claws"—and it sure looks to us like Bud Westmore's makeup department used the same "Monster Hand" you could mail-order from monster magazines in 1964!

screen, note that the week of its Manhattan area debut (double-billed with the western **THE MAGNIFICENT SEVEN** sequel **RETURN OF THE SEVEN**), *The New York Times'* Vincent Canby wrote:

"For all its sickening, chop-chop text, "Chamber of Horrors" does have some neat professionalism about it. The color is excellent (red included) and beguilingly enhances the ripe settings and costumes that simulate turn-of-the-century Baltimore. Add to the atmosphere, the director Hy Averback's easy clipped pacing. Mr. O'Neal hams it up like Vincent Price, but people like Cesare Danova, Philip Bourneuf and Marie Windsor perform sensibly and well. But that cleaver—yipe!"[72]

70 Kandel interviewed by Weaver, *Ibid.*, p.221; quoted with permission.

71 Kandel interviewed by Weaver, *Ibid.*, pp.217-219; quoted with permission.

72 Vincent Canby, "Screen: 'The Fortune Cookie,' Funny Fantasy of Chiselers, Begins Its Run:3 Manhattan Theaters Have Wilder's Film Walter Matthau Stars As Farcical Villain A Western and a Horror Film Also Open Here," *The New York Times*, October 20, 1966, archived online at *http://www.nytimes.com/movie/review?res=990DE5D-D1530E43BBC4851DFB667838D679EDE*

As for the TV movie guides, the first to include **CHAMBER OF HORRORS** in its capsule reviews was the 1969 edition of Leonard Maltin's *TV Movies*:

"**CHAMBER OF HORRORS** *(1966) C-99m. * ½ ... Wax museum provides setting for uneven mystery about mad killer on the loose. Intended for TV, it has mark of low-budget film. Uses gimmick of horn sounding before each murder.*"[73]

It's easy to see how **DARK INTRUDER** and **CHAMBER OF HORRORS**, and their production and distribution histories, were conflated: released only one year apart, both share similar 19th Century urban settings (San Francisco, Baltimore), both feature private criminologists (both aided by a dwarf assistant) specializing in the bizarre covertly aiding the police, both involve a series of mysterious murders executed by cloaked killers.

House of Wax / **CHAMBER OF HORRORS** writer Kandel stated for the record, *"As far as I know, nobody involved in* Black Cloak *had a hand in* House of Wax.*"*[74]

As for the monster in *Black Cloak* / **DARK INTRUDER**, screenwriter Barré Lyndon and director Harvey Hart tease out his origin with skill. We are told at one point of the birth of Kingsford's friend Robert Vandenburg (Mark Richman) in 1860; that a "fleshy mass" was removed from his side a week after birth, which we come to understand has grown up to be Professor Malaki, Vandenburg's brother. This gruesome concept was still quite novel in any movie at the time, as much an echo of H. P. Lovecraft's "The Dunwich Horror" as it recalled the more immediate contemporary **THE MANSTER** (双頭の殺人鬼 / *Sôtô no Satsujinki*, a.k.a. **THE SPLIT**, 1959/1962). It was also as a precursor to Frank Henonlotter's **BASKET CASE** (1982). The enigmatic Janus-faced demon carvings left by each body, and the gradual progressive *separation* of the bestial and human visages in the carvings noted by Kingsford, is the strongest visual cue we're given as to the methodology and goal of Malaki's murderous sacrifices. Malaki's quest for immortality also draws from Lovecraft's *The Case of Charles Dexter Ward* and Lyndon's own **THE MAN IN HALF MOON STREET** (1945), among other precursors.

Director Harvey Hart uses brief point-of-view handheld shots during the murders, lending immediacy to the attacks while keeping Malaki's features invisible; this became a hoary cliché of future slasher films. This opener still seemed comparatively fresh in 1965, though it employed a visual and narrative device Barré Lyndon and director John Brahm had utilized twenty years earlier *[see Sidebar #3: "The* Monster*! POV – ed]*. Gaslights and lanterns dim in Malaki's presence, accompanied by an odor, "musty like a graveyard" (echoing and echoed in references to the unpleasant smell of Kingsford's potted Mandrake plant in his study), and a guttural gurgling and growling; his power and malignance are strongly conveyed via this effective shorthand. Persistently hiding himself beneath a dark pull-down brimmed hat and the titular black cloak, Malaki initially comes across like another variation on a parade of cinematic cowled and caped killers, particularly Ivan Igor (Lionel Atwill) in **MYSTERY OF THE WAX MUSEUM** (1933) and especially the 3D color remake's Professor Henry Jarrod (Vincent Price) in **HOUSE OF WAX**. The latter film had reinvigorated the archetype and was much-imitated around the world, particularly in the early horror films coming out of Mexico in the 1950s; Mario Bava would overtly imitate Price's Jarrod for **BARON BLOOD** (*Gli orrori del castello di Norimberga*, 1972), and Joe Dante, Jr. would in turn gleefully cop Bava's appropriation for a sequence in Dante and Allan Arkush's **HOLLYWOOD BOULEVARD** (1976).

DARK INTRUDER gave this venerable Gothic icon its own twist, as implied by the unused subtitle of the shooting script. There are two beings that fit the description of "Something with Claws": the miniature, mummified creature lashed to a seven-spoked wheel that the Chinese antiquities dealer Chi Zang (Peter Brocco) shows to Kingsford to explain Malaki's existence, curse, and need for seven sacrificial victims. Casually picking up the mummy despite Chi Zang's warning, Kingsford is startled to find it searing to the touch, and drops the damned thing when it scratches his hand. The other "Something with Claws" is Malaki himself, whose clawed talons are the most visible onscreen manifestation of his true monstrous nature; we first glimpse them in the film's opening minutes as Malaki claims another victim in a darkened alley.

Bud Westmore was credited with the makeup, which was for the most part quite startling and effective—a snaggle-toothed creature with angry, deep-set eyes and a monstrous forehead, echoing the look of the Martians in **THE THREE STOOGES IN ORBIT** (1962, makeup by Frank McCoy)

73 *TV Movies*, edited by Leonard Maltin (Signet, September 1969), pg.83. Those of us who saw it in the theater *knew* there was almost no onscreen gore, but those who first saw it on TV presumed they were seeing a censored version. The original uncut theatrical version was released on DVD by Warner Home Video in September, 2008, co-featured with **THE BRIDES OF FU MANCHU** (1966).

74 Kandel interview by Weaver, p.215; quoted with permission.

and a clear forerunner to the Gene Roddenberry "gnarly forehead" school of *Star Trek* alien beings.[75] Unfortunately, the emphasis throughout the film on Malaki's taloned hands showcase the makeup's greatest weakness: the latex mold seams have always been all-too-visible on the demon's claws and wrists, which look almost identical to the rubber "monster claws" sold via mail order in many 1960s newsstand magazines.

The finale's transformation effects were filmed in the penultimate week of December 1964:

"Six Universal makeup-men, including Bud, Perc and Mike Westmore,[76] worked on Mark Richman from 7:15 ayem until 10 p.m. Tuesday [December 29, 1964] *for his horror transformation in the Hitchcock pilot,* 'The Black Cloak,' *more horrible than* 'Dr. Jekyll and Mr. Hyde.' *Richman admits he came close to passing out...* "[77]

---

75 Later TV horror films, particularly Dan Curtis/William F. Nolan's **THE NORLISS TAPES** (February 21, 1973) and Gene Roddenberry/Clive Donner's **SPECTRE** (May 21, 1977), also echoed **DI**'s Malaki makeup design. Gary Gerani notes, *"I always though John Chambers created the demonoid make-up, as he did the 'Pickman's Model' creature for Night Gallery a few years later. As a kid when I saw DARK INTRUDER theatrically (at the Marboro theater in Bensonhurst Brooklyn, doubling with I SAW WHAT YOU DID), I thought the monster looked like something out of The Outer Limits more than anything else (forehead and cheekbones)."* (Gerani, personal email to the author, April 1, 2016, quoted with permission).

76 Tom Weaver confirms Michael Westmore's involvement, saying, *"I have a one-page interview I did with Mike Westmore (never published) where he talked about being part of the team for the transformation scene."* Weaver, personal email to the author, April 2, 2016, quoted with permission.

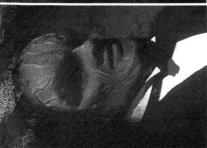

77 Army Archerd, "Just For Variety," *Daily Variety*, Thursday, December 31, 1964, p.2; special thanks to Tom Weaver for this information. Tom Weaver added via email on March 8, 2016, writing, *"I found a… trade paper gossip column item that said it was a big multi-makeup man job accomplished two days before, and that Mark Richman 'nearly passed out' (or something like that). (He didn't mention 'almost passing out' to me so probably that part was just to make the story better.)"* Richman *did* tell Weaver during their interview about how terrible the experience was of having his face cast for the makeup appliances: *"You sit in a makeup chair and they pour over your face plaster of Paris, or some other material that hardens quickly, in order to make a life mask. Your only source of life are your two nostrils—there's a straw sticking out of each nostril, and that's your source of air. When they were doing this, one of the straws got plugged, and I only had one nostril to breathe from. And I was in a panic, and absolute panic. It's a horrifying experience, because you can't move for about*

According to the actor under this transformation makeup, Mark Peter Richman, **DARK INTRUDER**'s climactic transformation was executed by the makeup effects team of Bud, Mike, Perc and Wally Westmore, working with Hank Eads and *Thriller*'s Jack Barron

Mark Richman later recalled that effects shoot in an interview:

"At the end, I was in the graveyard [about to transform into a demon]. I turned toward the approaching police, and I did a physical transformation I was so proud of. I did physical movements, from a normal person into a monster—I contorted my shoulders and my hips and my arms and my neck, and the facial thing. And they pretty much cut *the damn thing. I was so pissed when they put the picture together—they cut right to the point where they shoot me, they didn't give me the time to develop this whole thing, which was horrific because it happened* on the film. *And I was* so-o-o *angry!*

"I had five or six men working on me at one time when I 'transformed.' Bud, Mike, and Wally Westmore; Perc Westmore who was a hair specialist, Hank Eads and Jack Barron. They had to work fast because there was a lot to do, and they had all these prosthetic pieces to gradually add on. They'd put some devices on me and we would go on the stage and shoot about 15 or 30 seconds, and then I'd go back to the makeup room. Each thing took an hour, two hours to do; They'd take off these pieces and then put on the new stuff, and then I'd go back to the stage and get set exactly where I needed to be. They'd shoot that, and then back to the makeup...! It took a lot of time, we did it all day long—it took about 15 hours. And I always questioned the way Harvey Hart shot that scene. It was a very effective transition, but it would have been so much better if he had a better angle on it, maybe if he had had the camera directly above. He had it sideways, *and you had to turn your head to see it happen!"* [78]

The makeup effect appliances Richman and Klemperer wore had an unusual afterlife, too, eventually being publicly displayed by Universal in the very city that had been so receptive to the film, critically and at the box-office, back in July, 1965. According to Gary Gerani, co-author of the seminal *Fantastic Television* (Harmony Books, 1983), the original transformation masks were displayed in a New York City department store sometime after the film's release.

"Funny thing about the distinctive monster make-up created for Black Cloak / ***DARK INTRUDER.*** *Sometime in the late '60s, Universal and one of the top department stores in Manhattan (Macy's?) got together to put on a limited-engagement display of studio movie costumes and such. Among the artifacts were all the appliances for the transformation stages from* ***DARK INTRUDER****, with showcased heads evolving from sinister-looking human into the full-fledged demon that adorns the poster. But instead of labeling this display Mark Richman as the* ***DARK INTRUDER****, a sign identified it as 'Rock Hudson as* ***DR. JEKYLL AND MR. HYDE.****' Tells you a lot about how relatively unimportant authenticity was back in the day; the studio obviously figured that a famous actor and a famous title would play better for mainstream visitors. Have to admit, it was fun studying those transformation sculpts up front, whatever this show chose to call them."* [79]

Some fans have argued over the years about that final transformation: as Malaki successfully completed the ritual and swapped bodies with Vandenburg—meaning it was Vandenburg's spirit in the demonic Malaki body that plunges from the tower to his death—how is it that once the possessed Vandenburg is shot in the true finale, Vandenburg's body is shown to transform at the moment of death into the hideous Malaki? This cue recalls the final moments of the many film and TV adaptations of *Dr. Jekyll and Mr. Hyde* and Universal's own **THE WOLF MAN** (1941); it is an inversion of the classic "monster changes to man at the point of death" iconography, closer to *The Portrait of Dorian Gray*'s revelation of Gray's corrupt inner self manifest in the flesh when Gray succumbs. The metamorphosis makes dramatic *visual* sense, and is satisfying as such; the internal logic would seem to be that even though the second body was once that of Vandenburg the man, once possessed it became a mere vessel, and once the possessed brother was shot and killed, the demonic being possessing the vessel revealed its true nature, revealing the irrevocable nature of its dominion over mere flesh; all supernatural illusions evaporate in death. Thus, an early device of later demonic possession movies (which proliferated in the 1970s, in theatrical films and telefeatures) was codified.

In the coda, Kingsford and his manservant Nikola plot the necessary "correction" of burial sites, since his late friend Vandenburg's true self was

---

45 minutes—it's the closest thing to being buried alive." (Richman interviewed by Tom Weaver, *Monsters, Mutants and Heavenly Creatures: Confessions of 14 Classic Sci-Fi Horrormeisters!* [Midnight Marquee Press, Inc., 1996], p.176; quoted with permission.

78 Mark Richman interviewed by Tom Weaver, *Monsters, Mutants and Heavenly Creatures: Confessions of 14 Classic Sci-Fi Horrormeisters!* (Midnight Marquee Press, Inc., 1996), pp.175-177; quoted with permission.

79 Gary Gerani/Gerani53, November 15, 2015, comment #57 (archived @ *http://monsterkidclassichorrorforum. yuku.com/topic/60953/The-Night-Walker-and-Dark-Intrud-er-Are-Coming-on-DVD?page=3#.VtRszRzDZlY*); quoted with permission.

relegated to a pauper's grave in Potter's Field while the demonic brother that claimed Vandenburg's human body will wrongfully be laid to rest in the family tomb. They will, of course, have to rectify this situation—at which point the Mandrake plant begins to quiver anew, suggesting the next adventure to come, if there were another episode of *Black Cloak* to accommodate one.

The wild card in the production of *Black Cloak* / **DARK INTRUDER**—the man who was *never* a part of the Shamley Productions inner circle—was its credited producer, Jack Laird. Perhaps there were greater stakes in a pilot like *BC*/**DI** for Lew Wasserman than meets the eye—stakes that had nothing to do with Alfred Hitchcock.

Wasserman always played the long odds in Hollywood—and by the end of 1964, when the final transformation special effects shots for *BC*/**DI** were being lensed, Hitchcock was already in Wasserman's pocket, as was Shamley Productions, which was no longer a going concern for either Hitchcock or Wasserman, accept as the definable, finite asset Hitchcock had sold off to MCA/Universal.

Perhaps *BC*/**DI** director Harvey Hart (August 30, 1928-November 21, 1989) was the apple in MCA/Universal's eye? Hart had been a creative powerhouse at the CBC (Canadian Broadcasting Company) in the 1950s, directing episodes of series like *Scope* (1955), *Folio* (1955-59), *Encounter* (1959), and *First Person* (1960), TV movies like **THE DOUBLE CURE** (1958) and **A VERY CLOSE FAMILY** (1964), and producing the CBC *Festival* one-shot *The Luck of Ginger Coffey* (June 19, 1961, adapted into a Montréal-shot feature film by Irvin Kershner in 1964). As Canadian genre and cinema scholar Caelum Vatnsdal wrote,

"...the Canadian Broadcasting Corporation was teaching itself the television ropes... providing experience and instruction the technicians and creative personnel alike. Young directors such as Sidney Furie and Harvey Hart were working for the CBC, while Don Haldane was cutting his teeth at the [National Film Board a.k.a. NFB]. All of these men were more than a little interested in creating a self-supporting industry in Canada, but for the moment it simply didn't happen... Harvey Hart and Don Haldane (later to direct, respectively, the Canadian horror features **THE PYX** and **THE REINCARNATE**) continued slogging it out in Canada, though Hart would soon head to the States, and in the meantime independent production companies were springing*

Lewis Robert "Lew" Wasserman (March 22, 1913–June 3, 2002), the power behind MCA and the eventual MCA/Universal/Revue Studios dynasty; the man who made Hitchcock his fortune, but after 1964 kept Hitchcock's creative fortunes in golden handcuffs

up to provide product for the hungry medium of television."[80]

Hart moved to Hollywood in 1963 to sign on with a new filmmakers program MCA/Universal announced. This was publicly announced as a talent-development program at Revue, primarily seeking actors and actresses but also filmmakers, as described by Vice President in Charge of Production Alan J. Miller, and note the key role Jack Laird played in Hart's arrival:

"We inaugurated a plan nearly five years ago... Revue felt that new talent was one of the primary ingredients of success for studio operation.... Our development of young talent hasn't stopped with actors. Writers and directors are also being given opportunities at Revue. For instance, a recent Channing *episode*[81] *was directed by Harvey Hart,*

80 Caelum Vatnsdal, *They Came From Within: A History of Canadian Horror Cinema* (Arbeiter Ring Publishing, 2004), pp.30-31; quoted with permission. Due to his Hollywood career arc, even Harvey Hart's Canadian TV and feature film work has been essentially ignored in almost all Canadian film histories; Caelum Vatnsdal provides one of the precious view reference points in past or current texts. For the best analysis of Hart's **THE PYX** in any English language text, see Caelum's overview in *They Came From Within*, pp.67-70.

81 *Channing* a.k.a. *The Young and the Bold* (26 episodes, September 18, 1963-April 8, 1964), produced by Jack Laird for Revue Studios, starring Jason Evers (**THE BRAIN THAT WOULDN'T DIE**, etc.) and Henry Jones (**THE BAD SEED**, etc.), for ABC-TV. Hart directed four episodes of the program in all: the premiere episode "Message from the Tin Room" (September 18, 1963,

Barré Lyndon collaborated with director John Brahm on his first Jack the Ripper outing (an adaptation of Marie Belloc Lowndes' 1913 novel), **THE LODGER** (1944); Lyndon adapted the play again as **MAN IN THE ATTIC** (1953), and returned to the Ripper theme once more for *Thriller*'s adaptation of Robert Bloch's "Yours Truly, Jack the Ripper" and for *Black Cloak* / **DARK INTRUDER**

brought here from Canada by producer Jack Laird, who had admired his work on taped shows for the Canadian Broadcasting Company. He never before had directed a filmed program. He'll be doing more... We have great faith in our industry. We intend to develop talent to the best of our ability."[82]

Along with directing a quartet of *Channing* episodes for Jack Laird, Hart directed five episodes of *Alfred Hitchcock Presents* and *The Alfred Hitchcock Hour* before his theatrical feature debut helming William Inge's script **BUS RILEY'S BACK IN TOWN** (1965) for producer Elliott Kastner. Despite positive reviews, **BUS RILEY**

failed to find an audience, and the new directors' program Harvey Hart had signed on for failed to materialize the hoped-for boxoffice hits.[83] Despite his excellent work on **BUS RILEY'S BACK IN TOWN** and the surprisingly positive reviews for **DARK INTRUDER** later that same year, MCA/Universal relegated Hart to television, including *Laredo* (1965), *Ben Casey* (1965-66), *Court Martial* (1965-66), *Peyton Place* (1966-67), and others—including an episode of *The Wild Wild West* guest-starring Mark Richman ("The Night of the Dancing Death," November 5, 1965). Producer Jack Laird's satisfaction with Hart's work on *Channing*, and Shamley's with Hart's quintet of *Alfred Hitchcock* episodes, no doubt initiating his involvement with *BC*/**DI**; there also may have been some comfort in a Canadian director working with a fellow expatriate Canadian talent, Leslie Nielsen. Hart was, for numerous reasons, an ideal choice for both production camps.

Despite the quality of his 1960s TV and film efforts, it must be said that Hart did his best work *after* completing his contract with MCA/Universal—*he* wasn't their long-term investment associated with **DARK INTRUDER**. After helming **THE SWEET RIDE** (1968) for 20th Century Fox, Hart made the move back to Canada in 1970 to direct features as he'd originally intended, making his mark anew with playwright John Herbert's controversial prison drama **FORTUNE IN MEN'S EYES** (1971), co-directing (with Alexis Kanner) the back-to-the-country **MAHONEY'S LAST STAND** (US title: **MAHONEY'S ESTATE**, 1972), the Montréal-set occult thriller **THE PYX** (1973, scripted by Robert Schlitt from John Buell's 1959 novel), and the sleeper **SHOOT** (1976), among others. Hart settled into a comfortable groove directing television, features, and made-for-TV movies and mini-series for Canadian and American producers and studios, scoring especially with the Golden Globe-winning three-part mini-series adaptation

---

guest starring John Cassavetes), followed by "Exercise in a Shark Tank" (September 25, 1963), "Collision Course" (November 6, 1963), and "The Face in the Sun" (February 19, 1964).

82 Alan J. Miller, "Does TV Nurture New Talent?", *Daily Variety*, October 29, 1963, p.160; special thanks to Tom Weaver for turning this up in time. I know I have another industry trade reference to the same Revue/MCA/Universal program for young filmmakers malingering in my own library/files, but couldn't lay my hands on it in time for this publication. Thanks, Tom!

83 MCA/Universal/Revue's young talent program had also pegged high hopes on **BUS RILEY** star Michael Parks, who Revue Vice President in Charge of Production Alan J. Miller had touted in 1963 as one of Revue's *"exciting new talents... on the verge of national acclaim... a dynamic actor who has done exceedingly well in character juvenile roles and now is being groomed for more diversified opportunities to show his skill. Revue believes he will become an important name in entertainment..."* (Miller, "Does TV Nurture New Talent?", *Ibid.*). After a burst of mid-1960s theatrical features—**BUS RILEY'S BACK IN TOWN**, **WILD SEED** (1965, for Marlon Brando's Pennebaker Productions), John Huston's **THE BIBLE: IN THE BEGINNING...** (1966), **THE IDOL** (1966), and **THE HAPPENING** (1967)—MCA cast Parks in Don Siegel's final TV movie **STRANGER ON THE RUN** (October 31, 1967) and then it was back to TV series work until the 1970s. As with Hart, disappointing boxoffice results from the 1960s young talent program as a whole led to MCA/Universal letting their contracts run their course via television work, without further significant investment.

of John Steinbeck's **EAST OF EDEN** (February 1981) and the Gemini Award-winning **PASSION AND PARADISE** (February 1989).

But Jack Laird—ah, back in 1964, in the eyes of Wasserman, Jack Laird still had promise, with prospects for a rich future ahead for and with MCA/Universal.

Curiously enough, in describing the production history of **DI**, *Castle of Frankenstein* published a version of events that was ever so slightly different than *Variety*'s account:

*"Here's the inside info on Universal's **DARK INTRUDER**, which was probably the outstanding horror pic of 1965: It was originally planned as the pilot film for a prospective tv series. Under the title of* 'BLACK CLOAK', *the idea was rejected by all three major networks. Universal then planned to make it for screening on the Alfred Hitchcock show. When NBC vetoed this also, the studio finally decided to film it anyway. Finally, unable to find any video outlet, they showed it in theaters... "*[84]

Note the slightly different sequence of events when compared to the July 23rd 1965 *Variety* report: planned as a pilot, rejected by the networks, planned for production for *The Alfred Hitchcock Hour*, rejected *again* by NBC—*then* filmed "anyway." Did the three networks reject a script, or a filmed pilot? Was *Black Cloak* the pilot in the can *before* the three networks rejected it, or *after* the second rejection by NBC? Was *Black Cloak* shot as a pilot to be presented to the networks for consideration—or did Shamley Productions film it for MCA/Universal/Wasserman *after* the title and script suffered its rounds of rejections, intent on *either* finding a broadcast venue or release it theatrically if it was up to snuff? After all, the summer dumping ground of *Cloak of Mystery* (where **THE 13th GATE** was disposed of) was available, if nothing else. Gambling on a theatrical release for **DI**, however tentative, would mean Wasserman had done a favor for his new producer Jack Laird—it was a reward for work well done, and a *favor*, a promise for future work—*and* a generous grace note with which to wrap up operations at Shamley Productions. Laird would owe Wasserman and MCA/Universal. Besides, what did Wasserman/MCA/Universal have to lose? *BC*/**DI** had *already* profited MCA/Universal in any case, just by being put into production.

There's a reason a property like *BC*/**DI** was slotted into the production line of a program like *The Alfred Hitchcock Hour* (at *whatever* point in its gestation-to-completion it entered that production line). Consider not so much the cost of producing an hour of television in the early-to-mid 1960s, but rather what MCA earned off that hour. Author and industry analyst Eugene Paul broke it all down back in 1962, in the context of producing a single episode of *Thriller* in the MCA/Revue Studios production line:

"What does it all cost? Standard estimate for an hour filmed show on television [in 1961-62, filmed within one week] is $92,000. Costs run something like this: ...[there is] a maximum budget for supporting cast of $1,800 for the week. [The guest star] may have cost as much as $3,500, probably was contracted for half that. Cast costs were less than $5,000 for the week. The crew, which is on yearly contract, and the assistant directors, also on yearly contract, cost the production about $7,800 for the week. The sets were repainted and rebuilt, if necessary, at what may have been $1,500 but was probably billed to the production at $6,000. The producer gets around $1,000, the executive producer gets $5,000 each week. The director is probably around $750. Script cost in toto, about $3,500. Studio rental $1,000 a day, lighting and equipment rental another $500 per day. The art director, $600, the set decorator $300, the production manager, $350, the script girl, the same. The whole thing roughs out to less than $40,000 for an hour show. Add fifteen percent advertising agency commission, plus 10 per cent to the packager, and the total goes up to around $63,000.

"When one considers that MCA, the company owning Revue Studios, was also the agent for most of the actors, the writers, the directors, and producers, and collected agents' fees from all of them for rendering services to them, in securing employment for them, in making employment for them, the earnings were quite sizeable. MCA thus garnered around $30,000 from this one show each week. Compound this several times, and you will see why MCA has often been called 'The Octopus.' ... "[85]

Remember, in this context, the July 23 1965 *Variety* article citing *Black Cloak* / **DARK INTRUDER** having been completed at a *"cost of about $250,000"*—four times the cost of the 1962 *Thriller* episode Eugene Paul itemized—and do the

---

84 Ken Beale, "Movie Noose Reel," *Castle of Frankenstein* #8 (January 1966), p.48.

85 Eugene Paul, *The Hungry Eye* (Ballantine Books, 1962), pp.142-143. For more on the hard economics of American television production, broadcast, and business in this period, including the 'payola' and quiz show scandals of the 1950s, also see *TV in America: The Morality of Hard Cash* by Meyer Weinberg (Ballantine Books, 1962).

Professor Peabody (Carl Reiner) paid a price for ridiculing the *Necronomicon* and student Mr. Lovecraft (Johnnie Collins III) when he delivered "Professor Peabody's Last Lecture" (November 10, 1971) in one of the comedic short episodes producer Jack Laird also scripted for *Night Gallery*; Jerrold Freedman directed.

math. Even before its theatrical release, MCA had earned about $120,000 from the pilot; a successful theatrical run (even given the cost of mounting that release) was a sure bet. And when actor Mark Richman told interviewer Tom Weaver that the decision to open **DI** in theaters garnered him an additional "*100% of my salary for the theatrical*

Kingsford (Leslie Nielsen) consults one of his occult library's essential texts—authored by a demonology expert whose name reads suspiciously like that of **DARK INTRUDER** producer Jack Laird, who went on to produce *Rod Serling's Night Gallery* in the 1970s!

release," don't forget that MCA would earn *its* percentage off that additional 100% due every other cast, tech or crew member contracted for such a windfall.

It was a win/win, all around.

If Wasserman sanctioned the decision to release *BC/* **DI** to theaters in part to reward, or as an incentive, for producer Jack Laird, that paid off, too.

———

Jack Laird entered Hollywood as an aspiring actor, and indeed continued teaching acting into the 1960s, after he shifted his career arc into writing for television and becoming a story editor and associate producer for *Ben Casey* (153 episodes, October 2, 1961-March 21, 1966). MCA/Universal lured Laird away from the series, which had been produced by Bing Crosby Productions at Desilu Studios for ABC. Scott Skelton and Jim Benson's *Rod Serling's* invaluable tome *Night Gallery: An After-Hours Tour* offers the most succinct published account of **DARK INTRUDER**'s production, and indicates that the production of *Black Cloak* the pilot was perhaps independent of Shamley's usual production line for Hitchcock:

"In 1963, Laird was offered a full producer's post on Ben Casey *but declined when he was given a chance to write and produce independent projects for Universal Studios. One of them was his introduction to dark fantasy—a stylish plot, written by Barré Lydon (*THE LODGER, HANGOVER SQUARE*) and directed by Harvey Hart, at first titled '*BLACK CLOAK*'. A precursor in spirit to* The Wild, Wild West*, its main character (played by Leslie Nielsen) is a wealthy playboy living in nineteenth-century San Francisco who investigates*

a series of weird murders scientifically, a la Sherlock Holmes. 'It did not get bought as a series,' recalls Nielsen, 'but it turned out to be such a well written and directed piece that the studio saved all the material that had been shot, recut it to about seventy minutes—enough to sneak it into motion picture category—and released it as a feature." Retitled *DARK INTRUDER*, the feature ran on a double bill with William Castle's *I SAW WHAT YOU DID* and garnered impressive reviews. The making of *DARK INTRUDER* escalated Laird's interest in the science fiction and fantasy genre, and led the way to his helming of Night Gallery five years later."[86]

How "independent" was the project? Independent of—*what?* A regular TV series—and if so, did that indicate a flirtation on the part of Shamley to produce something separate from Hitchcock's series for Universal and NBC? How was it that Shamley and Laird came together, other than through MCA and Universal?

The particulars of how Jack Laird did or didn't mesh with the veteran *Alfred Hitchcock Presents/ The Alfred Hitchcock Hour* creative team have never been discussed, to my knowledge. Judging by the superior results, and MCA/Universal's subsequent relations in following decade with Laird, it must have gone well indeed. Laird cast as the pilot's hero Kingsford one of his favorite performers, Leslie Nielsen. Nielsen told interviewer Scott Skelton,

"I looked upon Jack as my patron. I did a tremendous variety of work for Jack Laird. He cast me in different roles, sometimes as a sort of last resort... he knew I could do it, he took a risk [on my talent]. That's why I look upon him as my patron." [87]

They'd already worked together on the first-ever MCA/Universal/NBC telefeature to actually debut on television, **SEE HOW THEY RUN** (premiering on October 7, 1964, only a few weeks before *BC/DI* was filmed). They went on to work together on the *Bob Hope Presents the Chrysler Theatre* two-parter "Code Name: Heraclitus" (1967) mentioned earlier, Laird's series *The Bold Ones: The Protectors* (February 22, 1969-March 8, 1970), in which Nielsen starred as California Deputy Chief Sam Danforth, and **THE RETURN**

OF CHARLIE CHAN (1973), which Laird co-produced with John J. Cole. *[Also see Sidebar #2: **THE RESURRECTION OF ZACHARY WHEELER** – ed.]*

Jack Laird's affinity for *BC/DI* was playfully manifest in the film itself: note the book Kingsford takes from shelf in his occult library: *The Cabala of Demonic Possession* by J. Drail—get it? Laird/ Drail? If one needs confirmation of how much Laird himself valued **DARK INTRUDER**, consider the fact that Laird later incorporated a nod to it in *Night Gallery*:

*"... 'The Dear Departed' offers clues that others, most probably Jack Laird, had tampered with Serling's script. In one scene, the dialogue reveals a subtle bit of self-referentiality: Joe tries to persuade Mark and Angela to go with him to the movies, a double bill. The two films? **DARK INTRUDER** and **DESTINY OF A SPY**, a pair of telefeatures that Jack Laird had produced in the 1960s, a prideful aside for two of his better efforts. Although Serling is listed as sole author of the teleplay, it is doubtful he would have made this reference. A review of Serling's original draft proves it."* [88]

DARK INTRUDER's surprise theatrical run could have only increased MCA/Universal's interest and faith in Jack Laird. As one of the four producers of *Bob Hope Chrysler Theatre*, Laird was already

88 Ibid., pg. 212; quoted with permission.

Jack Laird directed the *Night Gallery* adaptation of H.P. Lovecraft's "Pickman's Model" (December 1, 1971, teleplay by Alvin Sapinsley); John Chambers scored an Emmy Award nomination for his design of the titular "model" (shown here), played by Robert Prohaska

86 Scott Skelton and Jim Benson, *Night Gallery: An After-Hours Tour* (Syracuse University Press, 1999), p.31; quoted with permission.

87 *Ibid.*, p.30; Skelton's footnote in the book indicates this was from a phone interview he conducted with Neilsen in 1995. Quoted with permission.

spinning-off reedited telefeatures for MCA/Universal/NBC. No surprise, then, that Laird was a key player in Wasserman/MCA/Universal's "Project 120" (pre-1966) and World Premiere (1966 onward) telefeatures. A quick scan of the credits of the first three years of Project 120/World Premiere features broadcast on NBC proves Laird was crucial to Wasserman's plans, yielding a procession of completed features from Laird's department: Laird produced the very first MCA/Universal/NBC TV feature broadcast as such, **SEE HOW THEY RUN** (October 7, 1964). Laird followed this with **HOW I SPENT MY SUMMER VACATION** (January 7, 1967, released theatrically in the UK and Europe to solid boxoffice earnings as **DEADLY ROULETTE**), **SHADOW OVER ELVERON** (March 5, 1968), **TRIAL RUN** (January 18, 1969), **DESTINY OF A SPY** (October 27, 1969, filmed in London), **THE MOVIE MURDERER** (February 2, 1970), and **HAUSER'S MEMORY** (November 24, 1970, adapted from Curt Siodmak's nominal 1970 sequel to his novel *Donovan's Brain* [1942]).

By 1970, a multitude of other MCA/Universal producers—including former Hitchcock associate and the voice of Malaki, Norman Lloyd—were cranking out made-for-TV features to fill multiple weekly time slots on all three networks. World Premiere had worked, in spades, rapidly breeding formidable competitors like Thomas/Spelling Productions (TV star Danny Thomas and producer/mini-mogul Aaron Spelling) and others.

By then, MCA/Universal had also responded to the ratings success of one of its more unusual genre TV features Laird hadn't had a hand in—the three-story portmanteau **NIGHT GALLERY** (November 8, 1969), from writer Rod Serling, producer William Sackheim, and directors Boris Sagal, Barry Shear, and a young Universal upstart named Steven Spielberg—by developing it into a weekly series, Rod Serling's *Night Gallery*.

Jack Laird was assigned the series, and the rest, as they say, is history.

Laird and Serling clashed over the direction of *Night Gallery*; it was not a happy collaboration. Under contract to MCA/Universal, Laird produced and/or wrote for *Kojak* (Laird was supervising producer for the series), *Switch* (1977), *What Really Happened to the Class of '65?* (1978), and more TV movies and mini-series-format made-for-TV features like **PERILOUS VOYAGE** (1976), **TESTIMONY**

"...aid your servant in the name of Shaitan and Opun, Father and Mother of Mindless Chaos...": Professor Malaki begins the climactic possession ritual to claim the handsome body of his brother Robert as his own in **DARK INTRUDER**

OF TWO MEN (1977), **THE DARK SECRET OF HARVEST HOME** (1978), **BEGGARMAN, THIEF** (1979), and **HELLINGER'S LAW** (1981, which Laird executive produced and co-wrote). Laird reportedly suffered emotionally under the corporate yolk, though he remained in television into the 1980s; he succumbed to cancer at age 68 in December 1991, still hoping to launch a series based on work by best-selling novelist Robert Ludlum. Struggling with Universal studio edicts, aesthetic and budgetary constraints, timidity and adherence to the formulaic in the face of any true innovations, Laird nevertheless produced a lot of solid work for MCA/Universal but reportedly became disenchanted with the industry and his own part in it. According to Scott Skelton and Jim Benson in the only substantial biographical information on Laird to see print:

"Although Laird was happy in his marriage and well compensated at Universal, the passage of time and opportunity effected an abrupt change in his outlook. 'All of a sudden, after he got a contract at Universal, Jack got bogged down,' Johnson recalls. 'To tell you the truth, I think he gave up his dream... Jack felt he'd sold out—hacking it out at Universal every day. That's when he started withdrawing... ' "[89]

Thriller's Doug Benton didn't care to discuss Jack Laird's legacy with interviewer Tom Weaver, save to say, "De mortuis nihil nisi bonum—*I was a loyal member of WGAW. He wasn't. Although some of my best friends were scabs, I couldn't forgive Laird. He was a very good writer and a good producer, however."*[90] It could be argued that, just as they had done with and to Alfred Hitchcock after 1964, Lew Wasserman and MCA/Universal/NBC drained any love for the industry, and perhaps the creative juices, out of Laird.

In the end, Jack Laird's main claim to genre history, *Rod Serling's Night Gallery*, was subjected to the worst abuses of Wasserman's MCA/Universal/NBC profit schemes. It suffered quite the opposite fate of those 1950s and 1960s TV pilots and two-part episodes that were padded and re-edited into telefeatures and theatrical films: *Night Gallery* suffered the afterlife of a thousand cuts. It's no wonder Lovecraft fans and scholars so despise the *Night Gallery* adaptations: most of them never had a chance to see those adaptations (for good or ill) in their original form.

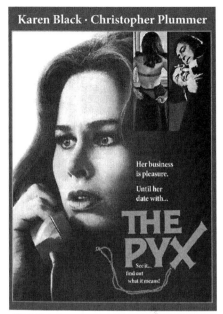

Karen Black · Christopher Plummer

Her business is pleasure.

Until her date with...

THE PYX

See it... find out what it means!

DARK INTRUDER director Harvey Hart went on to helm the sleeper **THE PYX** (1973); interviewed for *Cinema Canada*, Hart claimed **THE PYX** was more about "the horror of our everyday lives... To try and outdo that would have been an attempt to top myself with horror"

Film and television historian/archivist Stephen Bowie summarized the fate of *Night Gallery*, which further compromised the posthumous reputations of not just the program but also of both Rod Serling and Jack Laird:

"The most invasive of these reworkings remains infamous among TV fans: Universal turned Night Gallery, *the hour-long horror anthology, into a half-hour syndication package, slicing out large sections of the longer segments and adding stock footage to others to achieve a uniform length. Then the studio took* The Sixth Sense, *a one-season occult drama,*[91] *edited its hour-long episodes down*

89 Skelton and Benson, *Ibid.*, pp.31-32; quoted with permission.

90 "*De mortuis nihil nisi bonum*": it is socially inappropriate to speak ill of the dead. Doug Benton to Tom Weaver, related to me in a personal email from Tom Weaver, April 2, 2016, quoted with permission.

91 Concerning the TV series *The Sixth Sense*—not to be confused with the 1999 M. Night Shyamalan theatrical feature—*Night Gallery*, and the proposed series *Bedeviled* (for which the TV movies **FEAR NO EVIL** and **RITUAL OF EVIL** were pilots), genre TV expert Gary Gerani notes, "Although The Sixth Sense *was technically piloted by the independently-produced* **SWEET, SWEET RACHEL** [see sidebar], *it became more like a variation of* Bedeviled *(the two 'Evil' pilots) once Universal helmed the series, with psychic phenomena replacing demonology as the supernatural subject matter. The formula and structure created for* Bedeviled *was retained (handsome, understated investigator of paranormal events helping cosmically besieged guest stars every week), along with* Billy Goldenburg's 'Evil' *themes and background music;* Lalo Schifrin *stock music from* **EYE OF THE CAT** [1969] *was also used in* SS's Season One, *although none of his*

HORROR DOUBLE FEATURE

Finally on DVD after decades of home video bootlegs, **DARK INTRUDER** is as part of the TCM Selects DVD-R series, using Universal's PAL transfer from 16mm, not a proper 35mm restoration; excellent sound, OK image

Harry Tatelman, a Universal vice president whose department oversaw, among other things, the recutting of feature films to meet television censors' requirements. Tatelman was a kind of self-hating corporate yes-man, an old-time Lew Wasserman lackey who had started with MCA as a literary agent in the forties. Tatelman left to produce feature films and some of the Warner Bros. westerns and detective shows in the fifties, returning to the bustling Universal shortly after MCA purchased the studio in 1959. 'Lew made me crawl when I came back,' Tatelman said in Dennis McDougal's The Last Mogul: Lew Wasserman, MCA, and the Hidden History of Hollywood *(Da Capo, 2001), but his fealty to the company was such that he had no compunction about hacking up other filmmakers' work behind their backs. 'The resulting pictures were not good, but Harry was widely praised by the financial people for his ability to turn otherwise useless film into money,' said producer and television executive Frank Price in* A History of Television's The Virginian. *'By the time anyone had learned what had happened with the old episodes, it was pretty much too late to change anything.'*

"Although it likely turned a modest profit in the short term, Universal's thinking seems totally backward in the current vintage television market. Short-lived television series have become marketable again on niche cable networks like TVLand, Trio, Encore, ALN, RTN, and MeTV; to some extent, they have even displaced played-out behemoths like Wagon Train *or* The Adventures of Ozzie & Harriet, *which had so many episodes that some were omitted from syndication just to make the packages manageable. And while many remarkably obscure television series have enjoyed successful DVD releases, the made-for-television film has remained an almost wholly uncommercial prospect. (Only the Warner and Sony manufacture-on-demand DVD-R initiatives have, in the last three years, attempted to release vintage TV movies in any number.) Any number of the series that Universal once chopped up for TV-movie scrap have a hook that a licensor like Shout! Factory or Timeless could use for a DVD release:* Get Christie Love! *(blaxploitation);* Mister Terrific *(superheroes);* The Outsider *(Roy Huggins' first draft for* The Rockford Files*);* The Psychiatrist *(early work by Steven Spielberg); and so on."[93]*

to a half-hour form, and married them to the recut Night Gallery *in order to hit the magic number (100 episodes) that syndicators supposedly desired.* Night Gallery *was restored to its original form for a home video release back in 1991, but the uncut* Sixth Sense *episodes emerged (on the Chiller Channel and then Hulu) only a couple of years ago.*

All this effort on Universal's part ran counter to the creators' intentions for these shows. 'All the rhythms are off, and it doesn't play so well any more,' said Night Gallery *director John Badham in Scott Skelton and Jim Benson's* Rod Serling's Night Gallery: An After-Hours Tour *(Syracuse University Press, 1999)."[92]*

These half-hour syndication hack-jobs were carved from *Night Gallery* and *The Sixth Sense* under the couldn't-give-a-shit hand of Wasserman toadie Harry Tatelman. I do not use that term unadvisedly:

"The man responsible for this butchery was

After decades of syndication in grossly mutilated form, it reportedly took the intervention of Guillermo del Toro to ensure *Rod Serling's Night Gallery* finally see light of day on DVD in as close as reconstituted form as possible; the first

---

DARK INTRUDER *score was tapped (Laird was too busy recycling it for* Night Gallery *at the same time)."* Gerani, personal email to the author, April 1, 2016, quoted with permission.

92 Bowie, "Procrustes Comes to Syndication" (@ *https://classictvhistory.wordpress.com/2012/02/25/procrustes-comes-to-syndication/*).

93 *Ibid.*

season boxed set hit the market in August 2004, the second in November 2008, and the last in April 2012. That process proved daunting, due to the manner in which the Tatelman regime had treated the original episodes and elements, but Jack Laird's legacy—however compromised the series remains in the eyes of all but devoted fans—was partially restored.[94]

If anything, the fate accorded **DARK INTRUDER** was far kinder.

As with every production in the MCA/Universal assembly line, elements of **DI** were inevitably recycled. Lalo Schifrin's music score certainly was used elsewhere; Gary Gerani notes,

*"The **DARK INTRUDER** score is most famously repeated in various* Night Gallery *episodes, which were produced by Jack Laird. But this same music can be heard in 1965 episodes of* The Alfred Hitchcock Hour, *most notably "The Monkey's Paw"* ["The Monkey's Paw: A Retelling," April 19, 1965]. *That's because "Something with Claws" was considered a* Hitchcock *episode, and it was standard practice at the time to use music composed for one of the show's episodes in other episodes, as stock. That practiced stopped around 1978."*[95]

In every other significant way, however, MCA/Universal more or less forgot about the movie. That benign corporate neglect inadvertently preserved the film from alteration, colorization, or destruction.

DARK INTRUDER was folded into a limbo of another sort after the completion of its first, second, third theatrical runs, quietly slipping into odd timeslots on morning, afternoon, and late night regional broadcasts of Universal's various 1960s syndication movie packages. It was the kind of limbo that seemed to evaporate completely at the end of the 1970s.

During its time in limbo, however, **DI**'s stature began to rise. Mainstream critical reassessment of the film (by those who bothered to note its existence at all) can be summarized by the revised capsule

review offered for the film in the 1975 edition of Leonard Maltin's *TV Movies*. This was the first revision of the 1969 capsule review (the Scheuer movie guides never revised their curt dismissal); the film gained a star (moving from "fair" to "good" in the star ratings system standardized by the Steven H. Scheuer movie guides), a retrial, and a bold new verdict:

*"DARK INTRUDER (1965) *** ...Uneven performances major liability in near-flawless supernatural thriller. Occult expert called in by San Francisco police in connection with series of weird murders. Lavish production, intricate plot, exceptional use of time period blending with suspense. One-of-a-kind movie."*[96]

This reflected horror fandom's growing affection for the film, as more and more folks lucked into rare TV broadcasts of **DI**. One of the first genre capsule review books on the market, *John Stanley's Creature Features Movie Guide* (1981), was the first to make the H. P. Lovecraft connection outside of zine circles: *"Above average for the supernatural genre, reminiscent of the themes of H. P. Lovecraft and atmospherically photographed... "*[97] The Saturday night *Creature Features* KTVU-TV (Channel 2 out of Oakland, CA) horror host knew his stuff.

There was no official home video release of **DI** on either Beta, VHS, or laserdisc; there were plenty of bootlegs and gray market releases (taped from regional television broadcasts) on the convention and mail order circuits. The best of these I ever purchased was from Sinister Cinema (transferred from a worn 16mm TV print). It only occasionally played on cable movie TV channels; that 58-minute running time was still problematic.

This changed late last year. For years, I know that Tom Weaver had been suggesting to the Universal Pictures Home Entertainment division (in association with his writing liner notes, credited and uncredited, for Universal's laserdisc and DVD releases) a home release of **DI** was long overdue, perhaps as a double-bill with an appropriate genre studio co-feature like **THE THING THAT COULDN'T DIE** (1958) or **THE NIGHT WALKER**. At last his wish was granted: the Turner Classic Movies/Universal Studios DVD-R

---

94 For more on the restoration of *Night Gallery* for the DVD sets, see: *http://nightgallery.net/night-gallery-on-dvd/* , *http://www.tvshowsondvd.com/news/Night-Gallery-Season-3/16412* , and *http://www.sandiegoreader.com/weblogs/big-screen/2012/jan/22/rod-serlings-night-gallery-local-wrote-the-book-up/#* . The series has finally been released on UK DVD this year; see *http://www.ukhorrorscene.com/rod-serlings-complete-night-gallery-released-on-uk-dvd-from-fabulous-films-jan-11th-2016/*

95 Gary Gerani, personal email to the author, April 1, 2016; quoted with permission.

96 *TV Movies: 1975 Edition*, edited by Leonard Maltin, associate editors Mike Clark, Dennis Fine, Drew Simels (Signet, November 1974), p.125. The review was excised from the later editions of the book, since the film essentially dropped out of public view; the review was *not* included in the final edition of Maltin's text, *circa* 2015.

97 John Stanley, *John Stanley's Creature Features Movie Guide* (Creatures at Large, 1981), p.48.

Day George and her demon-possessed mirror in the "first" made-for-TV horror feature, **FEAR NO EVIL** (March 3, 1969). There's now an entire book on this movie, *Fear No Evil* (Bear-Manor Media, 2012) by Richard A. Ekstedt and Gary Gerani, highly recommended!

release of **DI** arrived in late 2015 (paired with **THE NIGHT WALKER**, as Weaver suggested), further preserving and showcasing Jack Laird's legacy as a genre producer and creator of merit. Here's how they dressed it up:

*"Turner Classic Movies and Universal are proud to present **THE NIGHT WALKER** AND **DARK INTRUDER**: HORROR DOUBLE FEATURE. The name Universal has long been synonymous with the horror genre, starting with famous monster movies of the 1930s and continuing through to contemporary films. While many of these movies feature supernatural elements, they also share a penchant for moody atmosphere and suspense that slowly draw viewers into the mystery until the final terrifying reveal. Included in this collection are two films that showcase not only these horrific thrills, but also such stars as Barbara Stanwyck, Robert Taylor and Leslie Nielsen.*

*"**THE NIGHT WALKER**: Dreams have been a recurring theme in film from its earliest years, but in director William Castles hands the question of what dreams mean becomes a terrifying story of the line between fantasy and reality in **THE NIGHT WALKER** (1964). Barbara Stanwyck, in her final feature film, stars as a woman haunted by dreams of an imaginary lover dreams that increase in intensity after her husband dies. Robert Taylor*

co-stars as the attorney determined to help her solve the mystery.

*"**DARK INTRUDER**: While most famous for his later work in comedy, Leslie Nielsen had a long career as a leading man in a variety of genres, including horror. **DARK INTRUDER** (1965) stars Nielsen as an Occult expert who is brought in by police to help solve a series of murders in which a mystical statue is left at each crime scene. Nielsen is on the case, until he discovers the mysterious connection between the victims in this gothic horror tale."*

Sans extras of any kind, the 2015 TCM/Universal Studios MOD DVD release of **DI** is the first opportunity audiences have had since 1965 to see this feature anywhere except on television, or on bootleg videocassettes or DVDs. While the 1:33 image is unremarkable—sourced from 16mm, not 35mm, elements and some argue online the transfer is slightly sped-up, possibly working from a PAL studio transfer—the soundtrack is the best I've ever heard for **DI**, highlighting Lalo Schifrin's excellent score and the effective sound effects throughout.

Speaking of the soundtrack, Gary Gerani sums up the circumstances concerning the DVD transfer and access to the original elements thusly:

*"I've been doing a documentary about composer Billy Goldenberg, who scored the first TV horror film, Universal's 1969 **FEAR NO EVIL**. That film has not been available in 35mm since 1970; Universal provided me with a 16mm-derived PAL DVD for reference. **DARK INTRUDER** was in many ways the forerunner of **FEAR NO EVIL**, and they offered me exactly the same thing: a PAL version of a 16mm transfer, probably identical to the TCM release. As I understand it, the 35mm film elements for both films do indeed exist in the Uni-vaults, so they aren't actually 'lost' in their original format. It just may not be cost-effective to resurrect them when handy 16mm transfers are readily available. That adds up to the same thing, sadly... we don't get to see these films as they were meant to be seen."* [98]

Gary adds, *"In some 16mm prints of **DARK INTRUDER**, the font used for Harvey Hart's director credits dissolves into a less stylized font, which I believe was* The Alfred Hitchcock Hour

98 Gary Gerani aka "Gerani53" posting on the Monster Kid Classic Horror Forum on November 8, 2015, comment #71, archived at *http://monsterkidclassichorrorforum. yuku.com/topic/60953/The-Night-Walker-and-Dark-Intruder-Are-Coming-on-DVD?page=4#.VtRuLRzDZIY* (quoted with permission). Gerani's documentary in production is entitled **ROMANTIC MYSTICISM: THE MUSIC OF BILLY GOLDENBERG**; best of luck, Gary, we're looking forward to seeing it!

type face... as if new credits had been layered over old ones. You won't find this anomaly in the TCM and Sinister Cinema editions, although they are also 16mm transfers. For the record, **DARK INTRUDER** has not been seen in 35mm since its 1965 theatrical presentation."[99]

At last, the **DARK INTRUDER** is resurrected, lurker at the threshold no more. We can still hope for a proper restoration from the original 35mm elements, someday, but for now—in whatever rough form, however shabby its guise—let it be reborn!

"O Utuq, God of the Night... Broosha, Ruler of the East... Demons Asmodeus, Azazel, Maskim, and the banished gods Nyoghta and Garoth, aid your servant in the name of Shaitan and Opun, Father and Mother of Mindless Chaos..."

---

99 Gary Gerani, personal email to the author, April 1, 2016, quoted with permission.

©2016 Stephen R. Bissette, with extra special thanks to Tom Weaver, Gary Gerani, Martin Grams, Jr., Scott Skelton, David J. Schow, Mike Davis, Rick Lai, and Joseph A. Citro, and eleventh-hour monster magazine research assistance by Mike Howlett, David Horne, and Daniel Best. This article incorporates material originally researched and written for my *GoreZone* column "With My Eyes Peeled" two-parter "TV Terror: An Introduction," way back in 1992; *GoreZone* editor Tony Timpone rejected my proposed series on made-for-TV horror movies, prompting my decision to end the column with an abbreviated two-part overview of my personal favorites (*GoreZone* #21-22, 1992), concluding forever my association with the magazine and publisher. Consider this a taste of what might-have-been—and a reason why I love writing for *Monster!* and *Weng's Chop*!

The murders in **DARK INTRUDER** committed by "Something With Claws"—the demonic Malaki—were hardly the first of their kind in movie history; see the following Sidebar #3, "The *Monster!* P.O.V.", on page 115

THE TV TERROR CONTINUES WITH THREE ADDITIONAL EXCLUSIVE SINISTER SIDEBARS!!

A MADE-FOR-TV HORROR PREHiSTORY:

Key Genre TV Movies
(or TV Pilots Released as Movies)
Predating **FEAR NO EVIL** (1969)

Most texts (books and articles) on made-for-TV movies cite Paul Wendkos/Guy Endore/Richard Alan Simmons' Universal/NBC-TV prime-time feature **FEAR NO EVIL** (March 3, 1969) as the first horror telefeature, which is correct as far as that goes.[100] But there was and remains a relatively unexplored prehistory that is long overdue attention. Calling your attention anew to the notable early TV movies and planned-and-produced-as-TV-movies titles already cited in my article, here is a partial listing of additional key predecessors and precursors to **FEAR NO EVIL** and the 1970s made-for-TV horror boom. There are notable *exclusions* (for reasons of space) of Walt Disney's key position and product in this history (Disney's *Davy Crockett* episodic-installments-to-theatrical-feature-films-and-merchandizing-empire was *the* primary example of what

was possible), of British TV serials and telefeatures (which are adequately covered in other books and articles) and of numerous French, Belgian, Spanish, Italian, and Canadian telefeatures (a subject requiring much more research; did you know the Canadian Broadcasting Network [CBC] produced telefeatures like **THE OTHERS** [1965] that eventually appeared on American television?[101]). I'd also include the original *Star Trek* pilot, **THE CAGE** (February, 1965), in my personal list of best 1960s made-for-TV genre features pre-dating **FEAR NO EVIL**; however, **THE CAGE** remained unavailable to the public until 1988, having been extensively re-edited and reworked for the two-part *Star Trek* season one episode "The Menagerie" (November 17-24, 1966) and never otherwise released in its original form overseas or domestically, hence its exclusion from this list.

A subject for further research…

---

00 For more on **FEAR NO EVIL**, see *The Rakashi File: 'Fear No Evil'* by Richard A. Ekstedt and Gary Gerani (Bear-Manor Media, 2012). Interested *Monster!* readers seeking a starting point for reading about made-for-TV genre films might begin with *Fantastic Television: A Pictorial History of Sci-Fi, The Unusual and the Fantastic* by Gary Gerani and Paul H. Schulman (Harmony Books, 1983; UK edition Titan Books Ltd., 1987), *Cyborgs, Santa Claus and Satan: Science Fiction, Fantasy and Horror Films Made for Television* by Fraser A. Sherman (McFarland, 2000), *Television Fright Films of the 1970s* by David Deal (McFarland, 2007), and *The ABC Movie of the Week Companion* by Michael Karol (iUniverse, Inc., 2005).

101 Bob Allen cited this in "A Critical Reference Guide to Television II" in the fanzine *Spectre* #12 (September-October 1966): *"THE OTHERS—This was a telefilm produced by the CBC in '65 and again shown on* The Chrysler Theater, *hosted by Bob Hope. This was one of the classic ghost stories presented in an excellent, semi-Gothic atmosphere, brilliantly acted and directed, and perfectly presented…"* (p.13). Oh, so much unexplored terror-terrain!

Let me establish a handy marker, using adaptations of Robert Louis Stevenson's *Strange Case of Dr. Jekyll and Mr. Hyde* (1886) as a reference point to begin and end with:

The first known US TV adaptation was broadcast on NBC on June 4, 1940. The script adaptation was by Warren Wade; starred Winfeld Hoeny as Dr. Jekyll/Mr. Hyde, Paula Stone as Alice, Judson Laire as Utterson, Anne Crosby as Prima Dona. It is a lost slice of television and made-for-TV horror history; though it likely doesn't count as an actual "made-for-TV movie" in the traditional sense, it was likely the first American genre telefeature.

TWO LOST WORLDS (1950)

61-minute compilation of a two-part pilot by Sterling Productions, Inc., produced by Boris Petroff, filmed in part in Red Rock Canyon State Park in Cantil, CA. Petroff collaborated with (Argentina-born) Australian film pioneer/director Norman Dawn on **TWO LOST WORLDS**, *"a slightly crazy adventure that begins with pirate ships, continues with the hero stranded in Australia, and wraps up with dinosaurs"* integrating stock footage *"from two swashbuckling Hal Roach productions,* **CAPTAIN FURY** (1939) *and* **CAPTAIN CAUTION** (1940)" and *"another Roach source,* **ONE MILLION B.C.** (1940)" with some of Dawn's Australian-filmed material.[102] For more on **TWO LOST WORLDS**, see my article "Carnosaur Cinéastes: Quit Your Bitching!" in *Monster!* #19 (pp.57-59).

This kind of pilot-compilation, or padded pilot, was common in the 1950s: for related genre-specific 1950s pilot-compilation features that were released theatrically, also see James Wong Howe/Ben Parker/John Sledge's **INVISIBLE AVENGER** (1958, a compilation of two episodes of a 1957 licensed *The Shadow* TV pilot from Republic Pictures, re-issued in 1962 as **BOURBON STREET SHADOWS**) and Charles Haas/Sandy Howard/H. Bruce Humberstone's **TARZAN AND THE TRAPPERS** (1958/1960, a b&w compilation feature cobbled together from a trio of color TV pilot episodes produced by Sol Lesser; this was shown theatrically overseas starting in 1960, unseen in the US until it was sold as part of a TV package of Tarzan titles in 1966), among others.

SUPERMAN AND THE MOLE-MEN (1951)

The first feature film based on Jerry Siegel, Joe Shuster, and National Periodicals/DC Comics' best-selling superhero comic book series was also the pilot for the proposed *Adventures of Superman* TV series.

102 Anders Runestad, *I Cannot, Yet I Must: The True Story of the Best Bad Monster Movie of All Time 'Robot Monster'* (self-published via Radiosonde Books, 2016), pp.280-281; for more on Petroff, also see Runestad, pp.52-53.

Clocking in at a brisk 58 minutes, the feature was produced independently by Barney A. Sarecky, shot in 12 days by director Lee "Roll 'Em" Sholem from a script by *The Adventures of Superman* radio show (2088 episodes, February 12, 1940-March 1, 1951) producer/writer/director Robert Maxwell and National Periodicals/DC Comics editor and movie/TV studio point man Whitney Ellsworth (credited to the singular pen-name "Richard Fielding"). This came on the heels of Ellsworth representing DC's interests for producer Sam Katzman's Columbia Pictures *Superman* serials, **SUPERMAN** (1948) and **ATOM MAN VS. SUPERMAN** (1950), both starring Kirk Alyn. Having earlier worked with Columbia as DC's representative and consultant on the serials **BATMAN** (1943), **BATMAN AND ROBIN** (1949) and **CONGO BILL** (1949)—the latter two produced by Sam Katzman—Ellsworth had higher ambitions than continuing to work with infamous cheapskate Katzman, setting himself up instead as the producer, writer, and script editor for a proposed live-action

The first *Superman* feature film was first experienced by the first TV generation in slightly reedited form as the only two-part episode of *The Adventures of Superman,* "The Unknown People" (August 10-17, 1953)

TV series. **SUPERMAN AND THE MOLE-MEN** was the pilot for the series starring George Reeves as Clark Kent/Superman. **SATMM** was a boxoffice success, released by Lippert Pictures, Inc. Ellsworth wasn't going to wait and see how the film would do, however; the Lippert Pictures theatrical release had been arranged to ensure recovery of production costs, if nothing else.

By the time **SATMM** opened in late November 1951, filming of the TV series had already begun in the RKO-Pathé studios and on the RKO Forty Acres lot under the sponsorship of Kellogg's; *Adventures of Superman* was an instant hit, running 104 episodes (September 19, 1952-April 28, 1958) and in almost perpetual rerun syndication for over two decades thereafter. Two of those 104 episodes were the adapted-for-the-series reedit of **SATMM**, broadcast as the series' only two-part episode, "The Unknown People" (August 10-17, 1953). It was released on VHS and laserdisc in 1988 and later included as a bonus feature on Warner's *Adventures of Superman: The Complete First Season* DVD set, the *Christopher Reeve Superman Collection*, and *The Complete Superman Collection*. This was also character actor Jeff Corey's final screen role before the House Committee on Un-American Activities blacklisted him, derailing his career for almost a full decade.

PROJECT MOON BASE (1953)

Variety's review opened *"This science-fiction entry originally was planned as a TV series, but following producer's look at the pilot it was decided to expand it into a feature. Result is a ridiculous offering, which even juve audiences won't accept... Jack Seaman, who co-authored with Robert Heinlein, must the rap for this one, as the producer."*[103] The pilot was for the proposed TV series *Ring Around the Moon*, scripted by the great science-fiction author Robert A. Heinlein, who had recently co-scripted and acted as technical advisor for the smash-hit **DESTINATION MOON** (1950); reportedly proceeding without Heinlein's knowledge or permission, producer Jack Seaman scripted and shot additional footage to pad it out to feature length (63 minutes). A Galaxy Pictures Inc. production, shot at Hal Roach Studios (Culver City, CA), released by Lippert Pictures, directed by Richard Talmadge. Bill Warren wrote, *"According to some sources, the pilot films turned out well enough that the producers decided to release them as a theatrical feature, but it's much more likely that the series simply didn't sell.... Reviews at the time were uniformly negative, however, and the picture isn't any good. I just don't like the thought that the film should not have been released,*

if only as a historical record of the last time to date that Robert A. Heinlein was personally involved in a motion picture."[104]

TALES OF FRANKENSTEIN, "The Face in the Tombstone Mirror" (1958)

This must be included for obvious reasons, though it never saw release in its day: this was the Hammer Films/Columbia Pictures pilot for proposed 26-episode US TV series, each studio to produce 13 episodes; only this never-broadcast, never-released theatrically pilot resulted. Columbia (who was handling the US release of **THE REVENGE OF FRANKENSTEIN** that year) had licensed the Universal *Frankenstein* movies as part of their Screen Gems "Shock!" TV syndication feature film package, wanted to use Universal's version of **FRANKENSTEIN**; Hammer's Michael Carreras wanted to use Hammer's version. According to various Hammer Films experts, Columbia rejected all half-dozen of Hammer's script proposals, prompting Carreras to abandon the project, leaving Anthony Hinds in charge of Hammer's interests, but soon Hinds, too, left. Columbia went with Henry Kuttner/C.L. Moore/Curt Siodmak's "Face in the Tombstone Mirror"—the pilot, the only episode filmed—with Hammer's choice of Anton Diffring as Dr. Frankenstein, Columbia's choice of Don Megowan (fresh from **THE CREATURE WALKS AMONG US**, 1956) as the Monster. Hammer later used elements of the scripts Columbia had rejected as the basis for **THE EVIL OF FRANKENSTEIN** (1964) and **FRANKENSTEIN CREATED WOMAN** (1967). Waste not, want not!

VARAN THE UNBELIEVABLE (大怪獣バラン / *Daikaijū Baran*, 1958/1962)

Back in 1994, pioneer Toho and *daikaijū-eiga* scholar Stuart Galbraith IV revealed that Toho's final black-and-white genre film was originally a coproduction with an unknown American TV interest: *"Shortly before his death, director Ishiro Honda told David Milner that VARAN was initiated by an American firm wanting to release the picture directly to U.S. television. This was very surprising for several reasons: While telefeatures date back to 1950, they were extremely rare until the mid-to-late sixties. Was a theatrical run considered? How was the project financed?"*[105] Galbraith's subsequent

---

103 Variety, September 2, 1953, reprinted in *Variety's Complete Science Fiction Reviews* edited by Donald Willis (Garland Publishing, Inc., 1985), p.101.

104 Bill Warren, *Keep Watching the Skies! American Science Fiction Movies of the Fifties, Volume 1: 1950-1957* (McFarland, 1982), p.143.

105 Stuart Galbraith IV, *Japanese Science Fiction, Fantasy and Horror Films: A Critical Analysis of 103 Features Released in the United States, 1950-1992* (McFarland, 1994), p.41. At the time, Galbraith concluded the opening paragraph of his **VARAN THE UNBELIEVABLE** review with the statement, *"To this day, VARAN's American origins remain a mystery."*

research and that of other *daikaijū-eiga* scholars revealed the active role of American TV producers ABC-TV[106] (as part of their subdivision AB-PT; read on) and their initial participation with Toho Studios. The AB-PT Pictures Corp.[107]—American Broadcasting-Paramount Theaters—emerged from Paramount's internal upheavals after the Supreme Court ruling forcing the separation of production and distribution. In its first five years of operation, AB-PT also produced Bert I. Gordon's **BEGINNING OF THE END** and Boris Petroff (as "Brooke L. Peters")'s **THE UNEARTHLY** (both 1957) before hitting real paydirt with their mid-1950s arrangements with Walt Disney for television and a share of the proposed new theme park, Disneyland. *"With the separation of production and exhibition forced by the U.S. Supreme Court, Paramount Pictures Inc. was split in two. Paramount Pictures Corporation was formed to be the production distribution company, with the 1,500-screen theater chain handed to the new United Paramount Theaters on December 31, 1949. Leonard Goldenson, who had headed the chain since 1938, remained as the new company's president. The Balaban and Katz theatre division was spun off with UPT; its trademark eventually became the property of the Balaban and Katz Historical Foundation. The Foundation has recently acquired ownership of the Famous Players Trademark. Cash-rich and controlling prime downtown real estate, Goldenson began looking for investments. Barred from film-making by prior anti-trust rulings, he acquired the struggling ABC television network in February 1953, leading it first to financial health, and eventually, in the mid-1970s, to first place in the national Nielsen ratings... ".*[108] It was the radical success and rapid growth of AB-PT that most likely derailed their interest in **VARAN**: production started as US/Japan co-production for planned ABC-TV broadcast, but for unknown reasons the American producers abandoned the project despite the film being almost completed. Toho shot additional scenes, and retroformatted the completed footage, in anamorphic widescreen TohoPanScope.

"...For the movie, Toho reunited most of the key players who worked on RODAN (1956), including director Ishirō Honda, producer Tomoyuki Tanaka, writer Shinichi Sekizawa, special effects director Eiji Tsuburaya, and composer Akira Ifukube. The film was intended to be shown through ABC for

106 Stuart Galbraith IV, *Monsters Are Attacking Tokyo: The Incredible World of Japanese Fantasy Films* (Feral House, 1998), p.179.

107 The AB-PT Pictures Corporation connection was clarified by August Ragone in his research and fanzine writings, and most widely disseminated in Ragone's excellent book *Eiji Tsuburaya: Master of Monsters* (Chronicle Books, 2007), p.55.

108 *https://en.wikipedia.org/wiki/Paramount_Pictures* ; for a candid assessment of AB-PT's origins and fortunes closer to the timeframe of their pulling out of the production of VARAN, see *The Hungry Eye* by Eugene Paul (Ballantine Books, 1962), Chapter 6, pp.91-101.

American audiences, and Toho constructed the picture accordingly: filming in black and white and on a full screen, 1.33:1, aspect ratio.

"However...the US backing for the project fell through. When this occurred, though, Toho had already finished most of the film. Ifukube's score was ready to go and most of the principal shooting was already completed. Consequently, Toho then prepared to adapt VARAN for a theatrical release in Japan, instead of throwing away the work and money that had already been spent on the project. To do this, Toho had the writers draft another screenplay, adding many new segments to the film. These segments included the early side plot with the butterflies and the struggle with the Iwaya villagers, while rewriting most of the scenes involving dialogue. More special effect shots were commissioned as well, including the lengthy water battles seen in the final product. Ifukube was also hired to re-score the film, allowing the composer to reconstruct the score utilizing a bigger orchestra, while also composing music for the added scenes.... The newly completed film was released in Japanese theaters on October 14th, 1958..."[109]

For the US theatrical version released by Crown International Pictures in 1962, much of Toho's 87-minute original was hacked down to make way for considerable new footage starring Myron Healey, directed by Jerry A. Baerwitz (shot by Jacques R. Marquette, edited by Rudolphe Cusumano and Jack Ruggiero) and released in a 70-minute version preserving little more than the monster highlights of the Toho original. Both Japanese and US (Tokyo Shock/Media Blasters) DVD editions offer a two-part (26 minutes per installment) Japanese TV version of BARAN/VARAN that Toho had prepared at some point in the film's bizarre post-production period.[110]

09 http://www.tohokingdom.com/cutting_room/varan_tv.htm, which also notes: *"...In 1996, Ifukube's score for the televised version of the film was released by Futureland as additional tracks on their Varan CD. In 2005, Toho released VARAN on DVD, including the televised version as an extra. As expected, the feature was incomplete, with some footage missing, although most of the audio had been recovered. The feature also revealed that the film was intended to be a mere 54 minutes in length, while also being broken down into two smaller episodes, each 26 minutes in length. Sadly, the footage was cropped for a 2.35:1 aspect ratio, instead of the TV version's original full screen dimensions. This feature was also reprinted on Tokyo Shock's 2005 release of the movie under VARAN THE UNBELIEVABLE."* Also see Glenn Erickson's review of the US VARAN DVD release at http://www.dvdtalk.com/dvdsavant/s1621vara.html and Keith Aiken's 5/09/05 Online DVD review archived at http://www.henshinonline.com/archive.html

10 Keith Aiken notes, *"Details about this cut are sketchy, but the commentary track reveals that this was the unfinished international export version that was recently remastered for Toho's R2 DVD of GIANT MONSTER*

Two decades later, Rankin/Bass Productions, Inc. had more successful collaborations with ABC-TV and Japan's Tsuburaya Productions on a number of made-for-TV features for US television that were released theatrically elsewhere in the world (i.e., THE LAST DINOSAUR, February 11, 1977; THE BERMUDA DEPTHS, January 27, 1978; and THE IVORY APE, April 18, 1980). Also see AGON THE ATOMIC DRAGON (幻の大怪獣アゴン / Maboroshi no daikaijū Agon / "Giant Phantom Monster Agon") below.

SUPER GIANT / STARMAN, MOONLIGHT MASK / PRINCE OF SPACE

American packager Walter Manley fabricated a unique variation on the made-for-TV genre telefeature, by purchasing US rights to original Japanese superhero films and TV series from 1957-1959 to create crazyquilt telefeatures he sold to US TV syndication markets in the early 1960s. These involved both theatrical features being dubbed and re-edited into telefeatures, and TV series being consolidated and dubbed to become telefeatures. The same year VARAN was completed, the 特撮 / tokusatsu movie super-hero genre was launched with the short theatrical feature film SUPER GIANT (スーパージャイアンツ, July 30, 1957), the first of nine tokusatsu features (running 39-57 minutes each) purchased by Walter Manley Enterprises and Medallion Films for sale to the US TV syndication market, dubbed and re-edited into four 74-87 minute telefeatures (ATOMIC RULERS OF THE WORLD, INVADERS FROM SPACE, ATTACK FROM SPACE, and EVIL BRAIN FROM OUTER SPACE, all 1964), changing its costumed hero Super Giant into the anglicized Starman.

Moonlight Mask (月光仮面 / Gekkō Kamen [130 episodes, February 24, 1958-July 5, 1959]) was the first original-to-TV tokusatsu (特撮) superhero; while the TV series was produced by the ad agency Senkosha, Toei produced six theatrical feature film adaptations of the TV series' story arcs, beginning with MOONLIGHT MASK (光仮面 / Gekko Kamen [July 30, 1958]). The second tokusatsu series produced in 1958 was Planet Prince (遊星王子 / Yūsei Ōji [49 episodes, November 4, 1958-October 6, 1959]), from which Toei produced two feature film adaptations, PLANET PRINCE (遊星王子 / Yūsei Ōji [May 19, 1959]) and PLANET PRINCE – THE TERRIFYING SPACESHIP (遊星王子

VARAN. The film has been edited down to two 27-minute "episodes"; each with complete opening credits. The first part condenses the first half-hour of the feature—including Varan's rampage in the village—down to barely three minutes of highlights and narration." Quoted from Aiken's 5/09/05 Henshin! Online "DVD Review: VARAN THE UNBELIEVABLE," archived at http://www.henshinonline.com/archive.html

– 恐怖の宇宙船 / *Yūsei Ōji – Kyofu no uchusen* [May 25, 1959]), which were sold to the US for TV syndication via Walter Manley Enterprise/Medallion Films, reedited into the single feature film **PRINCE OF SPACE** (1962).

THE SCARFACE MOB (1959/1962)

The Desilu pilot—originally broadcast as a two-part episode of *Westinghouse Desilu Playhouse* "The Untouchables" (CBS, April 20 and 27, 1959)—for *The Untouchables* was released theatrically (1962, via the Desilu Film Distributing Co.) internationally and domestically. CBS declined to broadcast the proposed series (on advice of CBS Vice President Hubbell Robinson, who later created *Thriller* for NBC), so *The Untouchables* premiered on ABC October 15, 1959. The series was a huge success, despite multiple controversies (including for violence) and ran four seasons (1959-1963); two other episode-compilation features were released overseas (**THE ALCATRAZ EXPRESS**, from 2-part "The Big Train," January 5-12, 1961, and **THE GUN OF ZANGARA**, from "Unhired Assassin," February 25-March 3, 1960). **THE SCARFACE MOB** is available on DVD as a bonus feature on Paramount's *The Untouchables Season 1, Volume 1* DVD.

LE TESTAMENT DU DOCTEUR CORDELIER / THE DOCTOR'S HORRIBLE EXPERIMENT / EXPERIMENT IN EVIL (1959/1961)

Written and directed by Jean Renoir, adapted from Stevenson's *Strange Case of Dr. Jekyll and Mr. Hyde*; cinematography by Georges Leclerc, music by Joseph Kosma; starred Jean-Louis Barrault as Dr. Cordelier/Opale, Teddy Bilis, Michel Vitold, Jean Topart, and Micheline Gary. The great Jean Renoir worked off and on throughout 1958 to prepare for the filming of **LE TESTAMENT DU DOCTEUR CORDELIER**, from a screenplay that went through "many transformations" (according to Renoir biographer Célia Bertin), and a second feature, **LE DEJEUNER SUR L'HERBE** ("Picnic on the Grass"), using state-of-the-art television techniques. Its Venice premiere was on September 8, 1959; the Paris premiere on November 16, 1961 (produced by Radio-Télévision Francaise (RTF)/ Société Financiére de Radiodiffusion-Sofirad/Compagnie Jean Renior; released by Consortium Pathé, 95 minutes).

This film has been unfairly ignored by almost all genre texts, including those specifically on made-for-TV features, though it is essential viewing. Renoir biographer Bertin explained,

"He had been thinking about them for a long time.... France had gone from 60,000 [TV] sets in 1954 to 680,000 in 1958. It was time to use them. Inspired by his theatrical experience, Jean want-

Our hero "Starman" a.k.a. *Super Giant* (スーパ ージャイアンツ) tangles with the alien creature from the series' seventh original telefeature, スーパー・ジャイアンツ 宇宙怪人出現 / *Sūpā Jaiantsu – Uchū Kaijin Shutsugen* / "The Space Mutant Appears" (April 29, 1958), which was dubbed and reedited for American TV as **EVIL BRAIN FROM OUTER SPACE** (1964)

ed to use four or five cameras (he even went up to eight!), not for shots, but for whole scenes acted from beginning to end without interruptions, as in the theater, with microphones scattered all over the set. This meant working methods that were completely different from those he had used before. Even more than in a regular movie, this kind of filming requires teamwork and professional technicians who have master their art.

"No television/movie coproduction had ever before been attempted in France. Jean Renior's idea was to release the film simultaneously on television and in movie theaters. But he had a struggle on his hands. The National Federation of French Cinemas was against it... Fortunately, Jean Renoir did not allow himself to get discouraged... With his usual powers of persuasion, he succeeded in convincing the director of French TV that he should undertake this unprecedented experiment. Pathé, which was supposed to distribute the film, advanced the necessary funds."[111]

Never having had a legal home video Beta or VHS release, it finally was made available on DVD in

111 Célia Bertin, *Jean Renoir: A Life in Pictures*, translated by Mireille Muellner and Leonard Muellner (1986/1991, The John Hopkins University Press), pp.303-304.

France in February 2003 from StudioCanal, and in the US by Criterion's Eclipse imprint as part of their April 2007 *Jean Renoir Collector's Edition* boxed set.

—

Two unique TV specials produced by David Susskind also fit the bill. Though these were among the many one-shot productions to air on anthology TV series of the day, these were impressive predecessors to the now-classic made-for-TV horror telefeatures of the 1970s, and both prominently featured unforgettable makeup effects by the late, great Dick Smith:

THE DEVIL AND DANIEL WEBSTER (NBC, *Sunday Showcase*, February 14, 1960)

Philip Reisman, Jr. script from the 1939 Broadway play by Stephen Vincent Benet and Douglas Moore, directed by Tom Donovan, makeup by Dick Smith; starred Edward G. Robinson as Daniel Webster, Da-

vid Wayne as Scratch, Tim O'Connor at Jabez Stone, Royal Beal as Justice Hawthorne.

PICTURE OF DORIAN GRAY (CBS, *Golden Showcase*, December 6, 1961)

Script by Audrey Gellen and co-producer Jacqueline Babbin, directed by Paul Bogart, makeup by Dick Smith; starred John Fraser as Dorian Gray, Louis Hayward as Basil Hallward, George C. Scott as Lord Henry Wotton, Susan Oliver as Susan Vane, Robert Walker Jr. as James Vane.

The Haunted / THE GHOST OF SIERRA DE CO-BRE (1964/1967)

This Daystar Productions/Villa Di Stefano pilot/TV-movie-released-theatrically-overseas was related in part to the convoluted *The Outer Limits* history behind the unsold pilot Joseph Stefano-scripted, Gerd Oswald-directed *The Unknown*. After ABC-TV rejected the pilot's proposed series, that uncanny slice of Gothic SF was reedited to become the

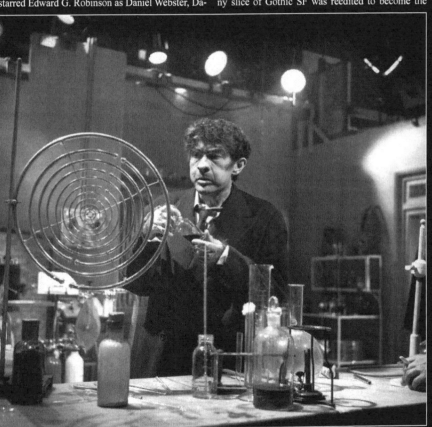

The great French actor/mime Jean-Louis Barrault starred as both Dr. Cordelier and his sadistic alter-ego Opale (shown here) in Jean Renoir's pioneer telefeature **THE DOCTOR'S HORRIBLE EXPERIMENT** (*Le testament du Docteur Cordelier*, a.k.a. **EXPERIMENT IN EVIL**, 1959/61, France) *[Note top of set and lighting visible in this photo]*

final first season *The Outer Limits* episode "The Form of Things Unknown" (May 4, 1964). But CBS was interested in Joseph Stefano cooking up a pilot for them, and the result was *The Haunted* (1964), revolving around a psychic investigator played by Martin Landau; according to *OL* expert David J. Schow, *"Stefano wrote the script after wrapping production on the first season of* The Outer Limits, *and unexpectedly found himself in the unintended position of... writer-producer-director, when his original choice for director* [Robert Stevens] *bowed out."* This was Stefano's only directorial effort; cut down in a marathon editing session from approximately 100-120 minutes to approximately 60 minutes, the initial reaction from CBS was positive, but a major management change at CBS killed the series. David J. Schow explains:

"The Haunted was actually scheduled to premiere in a Tuesday night, 10:00 PM slot on the CBS fall schedule for 1965-66, but when Jim Aubrey was fired as the head of that network, his replacement flushed all the shows originated during Aubrey's tenure except one—The Wild Wild West. ... *A feature-length recut of* The Haunted *was proposed for European release, to be titled* THE GHOST OF SIERRA DE COBRE. *Twenty minutes longer, it contained added shots, extended versions of some scenes,"* etc.

"Like Daystar's last feature film, INCUBUS [1966], The Haunted *was doomed to become 'lost' by history... Similarly to the fate that befell [Leslie Stevens' theatrical feature]* PRIVATE PROPERTY [1960], *there were precious few prints of* The Haunted *to begin with. Joe Stefano's own print was never returned to him. The show never aired, but apparently* THE GHOST OF SIERRA DE COBRE *version was televised in Japan as early as 1967. Viewers in Great Britain claim to have seen it on TV during the 1970s, and viewers in Canada, Australia, and as far away as Thailand reported seeing it on local television affiliates throughout the 1980s—under* THE GHOST OF SIERRA DE COBRE *title. It remained elusive and intractable."*[112]

The US premiere of *The Haunted* and *"very probably a world premiere for* The Unknown*"* [a rare complete 35mm print] was presented on Friday, February 26, 2011 by the UCLA Film & TV Archives at the Hammer Museum's Billy Wilder Theater in Westwood, CA.[113]

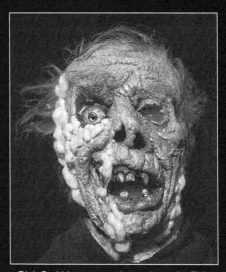

Dick Smith's eye-popping makeup for TV's Golden Showcase adaptation of Oscar Wilde's **PICTURE OF DORIAN GRAY** (CBS, December 6, 1961). This was about as gruesome as 1960s mainstream television could get!

AGON THE ATOMIC DRAGON (幻の大怪獣ア ゴン / *Maboroshi no daikaijū Agon* / "Giant Phantom Monster Agon") (produced 1964, broadcast January 1968)

This sepia-tinted black-and-white obscurity was made in 1964, and eventually broadcast in January 1968 as a four-episode (20 minutes per episode) miniseries; it was produced by Nippon Denpa Eiga (Japanese Radio Pictures). I first read about it in Greg Shoemaker's pioneer fanzine *Japanese Fantasy Film Journal* #9. Toho, parent studio of **GOJIRA**, had legally squashed this pre-*Ultraman* TV monster series because they considered the titular monster design too close to **GOJIRA**; rumor was that Toho relented after a few years because it turned out **AGON**'s creator—series co-director and special effects supervisor Fuminori Ohashi—had been among special effects maestro Eiji Tsuburaya's seminal effects crew who constructed the first Gojira/Godzilla monster suit back in 1954. **AGON** remains interesting as an artifact; Ohashi's monster and effects transcended anything in earlier Japanese sf television, but it's also worth noting that Eiji Tsuburaya had flirted earlier with the made-for-TV monster movie, **VARAN THE UNBELIEVABLE** (大怪獣バラン / *Daikaijū Baran*, 1958/1962 [see above]). Tsuburaya's **BARAN/VARAN** was superior in design and execution to **AGON**. **AGON** wasn't the first of his kind on Japanese television, as far as *daikaijū* go. The first ever TV *daikaijū* was probably "Mammoth

112 David J. Schow, "THE HAUNTED (1964)" draft chapter for a planned third edition of Schow's *The Outer Limits Companion* (previous editions 1986, 1999), as yet unpublished; quoted with permission. Also see *http://www.imdb.com/title/tt0312723/*

113 David J. Schow, "Inside the Dark & Stormy Nights of Joe Stefano," We Are Controlling Transmission, Sunday, February 27, 2011, *http://wearecontrollingtransmission.blogspot.com/2011/02/inside-dark-stormy-nights-of-joe.html*

Here comes romping-stomping **AGON THE ATOMIC DRAGON** (幻の大怪 獣アゴン /
Maboroshi no daikaijū Agon, 1964/68)—the first *daikaijū* to feed on radioactive fuel—which
was finally broadcast as a four-episode miniseries, but produced as a telefeature

Kong" (マンモスコング / *Manmosu Kongu*, October 19, 1958-December 26, 1958), from the first Japanese TV superhero series, 月光仮面 / *Gekko Kamen* (1958-59, see above). Nisan Productions' マリン コング / "Marine Kong" (1960) was the first TV *kaijū* with its own series; then again, Marine Kong *was* actually a robot. **AGON** pioneered a couple of concepts that only later became staples of the genre. This was the first *daikaijū-eiga* in which radioactive material was the food source for the monster. We also see, during an imagined "flashback" in Episode 2, Agon stirring from the ocean floor due to radioactive waste dumped in the ocean, the same year Del Tenney first depicted similar imagery in **THE HORROR OF PARTY BEACH**. Alas, **AGON** must have looked positively archaic when it was finally telecast in 1968 in the wake of Tsuburaya's colorful *Ultraman* and that show's weekly procession of imaginative monsters. Thus, Fuminori Ohashi's status as the first to imitate Toho's monsters has been derailed by the four-year delay between production and eventual broadcast. Ohashi also directed the final two episodes of **AGON**; Norio Mine directed the first two, though I assume Ohashi also directed the effects sequences in those. **AGON** was officially released on DVD in Japan in 2004.

THE MAN FROM U.N.C.L.E. feature films (1964-1968)

A number of feature films were prepared by MGM[114] from episodes of the popular MGM Television series *The Man from U.N.C.L.E.*, including the color pilot "The Vulcan Affair" (broadcast in

black-and-white on September 22, 1964; filmed November-December 1963, with additional color sequences filmed April 1964) which became **TO TRAP A SPY** (1964); "The Double Affair" (November 17, 1964) was expanded to the feature **THE SPY WITH MY FACE** (1965); the two-part "Alexander the Greater Affair" (September 17-24, 1965) became **ONE SPY TOO MANY** (1966); the two-part "The Bridge of Lions Affair" (February 4-11, 1966) became **ONE OF OUR SPIES IS MISSING** (1966); the two-part "The Concrete Overcoat Affair" (November 25-December 2, 1966) was edited into **THE SPY IN THE GREEN HAT** (1966); the two-part "The Five Daughters Affair" (March 31-April 7, 1967) became **THE KARATE KILLERS** (1967); the two-part "The Prince of Darkness Affair" (October 2-9, 1967) was compiled into **THE HELICOPTOR SPIES** (1968); and the two-part "The Seven Wonders of the World Affair" (January 8-15, 1968) became **HOW TO STEAL THE WORLD** (1968), guest-starring **DARK INTRUDER**'s Mark Richman. Though originally prepared for release overseas, these were almost all also released domestically, often as U.N.C.L.E. double-bills. There was also one MGM non-*Man from U.N.C.L.E.* feature film produced to capitalize on the series by casting series lead Robert Vaughn as the former CIA agent hero of **THE VENETIAN AFFAIR** (1967), co-starring Boris Karloff—fresh from his cross-dress guest-starring role in the spinoff TV series *The Girl from U.N.C.L.E.*, "The Mother Muffin Affair" (September 27, 1966)!

SPACE MONSTER (1965)

Some sources list this film as **SPACE PROBE TAURUS**, but the only title I ever saw it broadcast under (in both the US and Canada) was **SPACE**

114 Note that MGM was well-versed in this practice; for instance, MGM prepared three feature films for theatrical release from their TV series *Northwest Passage* (September 14, 1958-March 13, 1959), **FRONTIER RANGERS** (1959), **MISSION OF DANGER** (1959), and **FURY RIVER** (1961), with each feature comprised of elements from three TV episodes.

MONSTER. Tom Weaver wrote (in *A Sci-Fi Swarm and Horror Horde: Interviews with 62 Filmmakers;* see footnote attribution), *"In the mid-1960s, years before the concept of made-for-TV movies became a small-screen institution, American International Pictures [AIP] ventured down that unexplored avenue, commissioning a number of low-cost flicks that could be used to 'sweeten' the packages of older AIP titles they were preparing to offer to local TV stations... with his partner Leonard Katzman, [Burt Topper] signed on to produce for AIP-TV the science fiction adventure 'THE FIRST WOMAN IN SPACE' (ultimately released as* **SPACE MONSTER**). *Shot in March 1965 and set in the year 2000, the film featured Francine York, Jim Brown, Baynes Barron and Russ Bender as Earth astronauts streaking through space aboard the rocketship Hope 1 seeking a planet suitable for colonization—and instead encountering monsters and more monsters."*[115]

In an interview conducted just days before Topper's death, the producer told Tom Weaver *"After making two pictures for Allied Artists [***WAR IS HELL***, 1963, and ***THE STRANGLER***, 1964], I came back to AIP and made a deal with Sam to make some pictures, because AIP needed some product for televi-*

115 Weaver, *A Sci-Fi Swarm and Horror Horde: Interviews with 62 Filmmakers* (McFarland, 2010), p.318; quoted with permission.

sion. Leonard Katzman and I became partners and we made **SPACE MONSTER** *for AIP. I think it was Leonard who came up with the idea [to do an outer space picture]. His uncle was Sam Katzman, and for years Leonard had worked for his uncle as an assistant director and so on. Leonard and I were friends from the time we were in Fairfax High School. I produced* **SPACE MONSTER**, *and Leonard directed and wrote it."*

SPACE MONSTER's rocketship interiors were constructed by Topper and shot at Producers Studio, and the monsters included a 'gill man' (footage lifted from AIP's **WAR-GODS OF THE DEEP**, 1965), an actor (Al Kanter) wearing an alien suit and mask recycled from David Hewitt's **THE WIZARD OF MARS** (1964), which Topper and his team *"got... from AIP,"* and a few "giant" crabs. Producer (and uncredited co-director) Burt Topper noted, *"On a big tabletop there at my folks' place, we set up a fish tank, full of water, and we put in it the miniature Earth rocketship and some little Japanese crabs.... The rest of the underwater stuff was shot at Catalina off my boat... If you look at the monsters in* **SPACE MONSTER** *now, they look corny as hell. I can't believe some of the pictures we actually put out... But the kids were crazy about 'em.... We did* **SPACE MONSTER** *in 35mm, with a $50,000 budget, in five days. And it*

James Brown—not *the* James Brown, but low-rent **SPACE MONSTER** star James R. Brown!—steadies an alien (played by Al Kanter) in Leonard Katzman's and Burt Topper's madefor-AIP-TV space opera. (See page 90 for the truth about this alien!)

The alien and its creator. The big-eared, barebrained **SPACE MONSTER** extraterrestrial was actually created by Don Post *[right]* Studios for David H. Hewitt's **THE WIZARD OF MARS** (1964); note the glass bubble-dome is intact here; it was lost by the time AIP loaned the getup to Leonard Katzman and Burt Topper

was made all IA; if you notice, it has the seal on it. We made that IA in five days, except for the stuff I shot at Catalina and the miniatures, and we didn't have crews for that."

When asked "What did Nicholson and Arkoff think of **SPACE MONSTER**?" Topper replied,

"Well, hell, for that *price...I mean, what the hell [laughs]? It was for a television package. AIP made a lot of money on those TV packages. What AIP did was, they had a lot of good pictures...well, not good, but good for 'our market'...and a couple years after they played theatrically, AIP would put them in packages for television, and in the packages they would mix in a few of these little [made-for-TV] cheapos and get money for the whole package. That's the way they got away with these pictures that were very cheaply made."* [116]

HERCULES AND THE PRINCESS OF TROY
(September 12, 1965)

This was an ABC-TV and Joseph E. Levine/Embassy Television coproduction, filmed with Italian involvement (co-scripted by Ugo Liberatore, cine-

matography by Enzo Barboni, production managed by Giorgio Baldi), directed by Albert Band. It was filmed as a pilot for an intended series entitled *Hercules* (47 minutes), and eventually broadcast as a one-shot special on ABC-TV on September 12, 1965. This was apparently its only showing anywhere in the world; it was also historic for being star Gordon Scott's final peplum. The highlight of the film remains an uncredited Carlo Rambaldi constructed and operated state-of-the-art, full-sized animatronic monster—a caterpillar-like crustacean with crab-like pincers that emerges from the sea— that outdid any and all made-for-TV monsters, outside of *The Outer Limits*. It remains one of Rambaldi's finest 1960s monster creations.

THE EYE CREATURES (a.k.a. ATTACK OF THE EYE CREATURES, 1965), CURSE OF THE SWAMP CREATURE (1966), ZONTAR THE THING FROM VENUS (1966), CREATURE OF DESTRUCTION (1967), IN THE YEAR 2889 (1967), MARS NEEDS WOMEN (1967), HELL RAIDERS (1968), 'IT'S ALIVE!' (1969)

Dallas, Texas-based filmmaker and educator Larry Buchanan also cranked out a batch of super-low-budget color made-for-TV AIP-TV features in 1965-66, under Buchanan's Azalea Pictures masthead. Some of the films were remakes of 1950s AIP feature films (noted below), adapted from scripts AIP provided, revamped (stripped down) by Buchanan and his partners. According to Buchanan, AIP instructed him *"We want cheap color pictures, we want half-assed names in them, we want them eighty minutes long and we want them now."* [117] AIP production associate Burt Topper described AIP-TV's contract with Buchanan:

"There was a man named Larry Buchanan in Texas who did a lot of pictures for AIP to put into these TV packages. We paid him like $35,000 for each movie, and he made 'em in 16mm in Texas. I was head of production there at AIP when he made those things. Larry made these pictures with locals, non-union, and we'd send the star down. Francine did a picture down there [CURSE OF THE SWAMP CREATURE, 1966], *and John Ashley* [THE EYE CREATURES, 1965], *and John Agar* [CURSE OF THE SWAMP CREATURE, ZONTAR THE THING FROM VENUS, 1966, HELL RAIDERS, 1968]. *When Larry made a war story, HELL RAIDERS, I had a lot of equipment and uniforms and other stuff of my own, and I sent my whole 'armory' down to him to make that war story with John Agar. When you're makin' pictures for that money, you call in all your*

116 Topper interviewed by Weaver, *Ibid.*, pp.319-324, also archived online in part at *http://monsterkidclassichorrorforum.yuku.com/topic/11481/Burt-Topper-SPACE-MONSTER-THE-STRANGLER#.Vv_XAxzDZIY* (quoted with permission).

117 Buchanan, interviewed by Douglass St. Clair Smith, "How Bad Were They?," *Texas Monthly*, May 1986, p.211.

friends, all the people you know! You did whatever you had to do."[118]

ATTACK OF THE THE EYE CREATURES (yes, "THE" was actually printed *twice* on the title cards to some prints!) was a remake of **INVASION OF THE SAUCER MEN** (1957); **ZONTAR, THE THING FROM VENUS** was revamped by Buchanan and Hillman Taylor from Lou Rusoff and Charles B. Griffith's screenplay for **IT CONQUERED THE WORLD** (1956); Enrique Touceda rewrote **THE SHE-CREATURE** (1956) for **CREATURE OF DESTRUCTION; IN THE YEAR 2889** was a remake of AIP's first boxoffice hit, **DAY THE WORLD ENDED** (1955) with Harold Hoffman reworking Lou Rusoff's original screenplay and AIP finally using a Jules Verne-derived title they've

118 Topper interviewed by Weaver, *Ibid.*, p.324, also archived online in part at *http://monsterkidclassichorrorforum.yuku. com/topic/11481/Burt-Topper-SPACE-MONSTER-THE-STRANGLER#.Vv_XAxzDZIY* (quoted with permission).

registered in the early 1960s. Buchanan claimed the filmed-in-Uncertain, Texas **CURSE OF THE SWAMP CREATURE** to be original, but Tony Huston's screenplay owes an obvious debt to the Russ Bender and V. I. Voss script for Alex Gordon/Edward L. Cahn's AIP feature **VOODOO WOMAN** (1957), and recycles Ronald Stein's scores from **IT CONQUERED THE WORLD** and **INVASION OF THE SAUCER MEN**, and **MARS NEEDS WOMEN** surely was drawn in part from AIP's Tommy Kirk's Martian character in **PAJAMA PARTY** (1964). Dallas ad executive Jack Bennett constructed the monster suit for **CREATURE OF DESTRUCTION**, which Buchanan reused for the filmed-in-the-Ozarks cheapie 'IT'S ALIVE!' (1969), from an unproduced AIP script based on Richard Matheson's short story "Being."[119] **ZONTAR** holds

119 *http://www.imdb.com/title/tt0063145/trivia?ref_=tt_trv_ trv* (and note the first TV showing of **IT'S ALIVE!** was reportedly March 1970).

Carlo Rambaldi's marvelous full-sized animatronic crustacean constructed for **HERCULES AND THE PRINCESS OF TROY** (ABC-TV, September 12, 1965), the pilot for a never-realized Hercules TV series

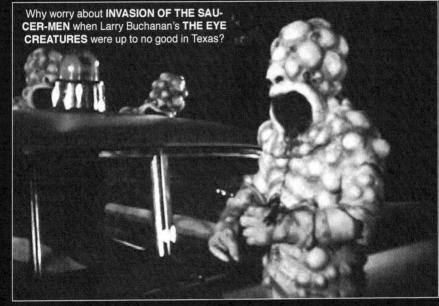

a position of honor as the only known made-for-TV movie to spawn a fanzine title, the Boston-based *Zontar the Magazine from Venus* (1981-1992). For more information, see Buchanan's autobiography *It Came From Hunger: Tales of a Cinema Schlockmeister* (McFarland, 1996) and *The Films of Larry Buchanan: A Critical Examination* by Rob Craig (McFarland, 2007).

There were other films made for AIP-TV by other filmmakers at this time (i.e., **VOYAGE TO THE PREHISTORIC PLANET**, etc.), but we'll note **SPACE MONSTER** and the Buchanan films as sufficient evidence of the AIP-TV program.

AGENT FOR H.A.R.M. (1966)

Shot by producer Joseph F. Robertson and director Gerd Oswald (*The Outer Limits*, etc.) as a pilot for a proposed sf-spy television series created and scripted by Blair Robertson (wife of the producer, screenwriter of **THE SLIME PEOPLE**, 1963), this was released by Universal as a theatrical feature film. *Variety* reported the production as launching in early 1965, under the title *"... the 'Harm Machine' pilot 90 mins. color, has Richman playing a James Bond-ish character for a projected hour-long series..."*[120] **DARK INTRUDER** co-star Mark Richman played secret agent Adam Chance, battling Russian agents wielding *"a sporegun blob that crawls... and creeps... and turns human flesh into fearsome fungus!"* (to quote the one-sheet poster, lobby card, and ad mat ballyhoo). Richman recalled that Gerd Oswald *"liked me a lot, and he came to my home and gave me the script. So that's how I got involved with it, when it was an idea for a series. It didn't turn out to be very good, I didn't think—the whole concept was kind of cheesy."*[121] The flesh-eating fungus component resonates with the appearance of co-star Martin Kosleck, fresh from the gorefest **THE FLESH EATERS** (1964); H.A.R.M. stood for "Human Aetiological Relations Machine", one of the most unwieldy acronyms in the 1960s 007-*Man from U.N.C.L.E.* pop landscape.

There were a multitude of spy/espionage pilots, many with sf elements, produced during the mid-1960s that did not sell to networks, but were eventually broadcast on TV anthology series, sold as telefeatures folded into syndicated packages of theatrical films, and/or released overseas theatrically. Others include Leslie Stevens/Marion Hargrove/Walter Grauman's **FANFARE FOR A DEATH SCENE** (1964, a pilot film originally titled *Stryker* from Stevens' Daystar Productions—of *The Outer Limits* fame—starring Richard Egan, Telly Savalas, and Tina Louise), MCA/Universal's **THE FACELESS MAN** (unsold pilot broadcast on *Bob Hope Presents The Chrysler Theatre*, May 4, 1966, script by Harry Kleiner, directed by Stuart Rosenberg, starring Jack Lord, L.Q. Jones, Shirley Knight, and Jack Weston), etc.

---

120 Army·Archerd, "Just For Variety," *Daily Variety*, Thursday, December 31, 1964, p.2; special thanks to Tom Weaver.

121 Mark Richman interviewed by Tom Weaver, *Ibid.*, p.177 quoted with permission.

ISLAND OF THE LOST
(November 10 and 17, 1967)

John Florea/Ricou Browning/Richard Carlson/Ivan Tors' ISLAND OF THE LOST (a.k.a. **IVAN TORS' ISLAND OF THE LOST**) did play some parts of the world as **DANGEROUS ISLAND, LOST ISLAND, LA ISLA DE LOS DESAPARECIDOS** (Spain, Universal Films Esp. S.A. distributed it there), and **AZ ELVESZETTEK SZIGETE** (Hungary). Producer Ivan Tors either produced this for television or *dumped* it there, after it was deemed unsuitable for theatrical US playdates by MGM. It was, ultimately, split into two parts and broadcast as part of the family ABC-TV series produced by MGM and Chuck Jones (executive producer), *Off to See the Wizard*. ISLAND OF THE LOST was also the first Bermuda Triangle a.k.a. Devil's Triangle movie, launching what became a made-for-TV and exploitation film staple in the 1970s. The convoluted history behind this dumped-to-US-television but released-theatrically-overseas oddity was detailed in my article in *Monster!* #19 (pp.59-66).

THE STRANGE CASE OF DR JEKYLL AND MR. HYDE (1968)

An US/Canadian coproduction shot on videotape by CBC/Canadian Broadcast Corporation and Dan Curtis Productions. It debuted on CBC on January 3, 1968, via an afternoon broadcast; two weeks later, it premiered for American audiences on ABC, January 17, 1968 (120 minutes). Because we got CBC via TV antennae on our home television set in northern VT at the time, I was able to see this twice—first on CBC, then on ABC—an *incredibly* rare opportunity for *any* movie on television at the time, which may be among the reasons this remains my favorite adaptation of *Jekyll and Hyde*. It began filming with Jason Robards as Jekyll/Hyde, but production was halted by a strike; production resumed with Jack Palance in the lead role; photos exist of Robards in Dick Smith's makeup, which Smith radically redesigned for Palance, giving him a strikingly original Satyr-like visage. Palance was magnificent in this production, and it was for its time surprisingly adult, including one moment of visceral horror (*"I don't think you'll want to show your face in public again—not with your nose a slit!"*) that was a shocker in 1968. This still packs a punch, and deserves to be seen. Adaptation by Ian McLellan Hunter, directed by Charles Jarrott, produced by Dan Curtis, makeup by Dick Smith, music by Robert Cobert (incorporating *Dark Shadows* music); starred Jack Palance as Dr Henry Jekyll/Mr. Edward Hyde, Denholm Elliott as George Devlin, Leo Genn as Dr. Lanyon, Torin Thatcher as Sir John Turnbull, Billie Whitelaw as Gwyn Thomas, and Oskar Homolka as Stryker.

There are more examples of this genre telefeature and made-for-TV-but-released-theatrically movie prehistory, but I trust this makes a convincing enough case that much came before FEAR NO EVIL.

~SRB

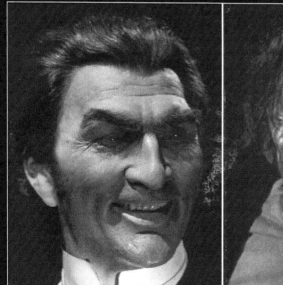 

Jack Palance in the satyr-like Mr. Hyde makeup by Dick Smith for **THE STRANGE CASE OF DR JEKYLL AND MR. HYDE** (1968); the production was originally slated to star Jason Robards (right, shown in a test photo of Dick Smith's makeup as Mr. Hyde) and to be filmed in England

THE RESURRECTION OF ZACHARY WHEELER

About six years after the release of **DARK INTRUDER**, Leslie Nielsen starred as a Carl Kolchak-like TV journalist investigating the mysterious disappearance of a mortally-injured US Senator in a most unusual mutation of this late 1960s/early 1970s wave of pioneer video-to-film productions. Nielsen co-starred in **THE RESURRECTION OF ZACHARY WHEELER** (1971), the first SF "clone" movie[122] spearheading what became a sporadic fad in the 1970s, predating **THE CLONES** (1973, the most widely-distributed of the initial clone SF exploitation features) and **PARTS: THE CLONUS HORROR** (1979). The clone beings were called 'soma' here; the term 'clone' dates back to 19th Century horticulture, but was first used in this context in 1963 by J. B. S. Haldane at the Ciba Foundation Symposium on "Man and His Future."

Though the film looked and was cast like a telefeature, it was prepared for theatrical distribution in 1971, which was modest at best; its videocassette release in the 1987 (Showcase Productions, Inc. and Fusion Video) and 1988 (Neon Video) was its first wide release (it became a PD staple thereafter, though still rarely come by). Leslie Nielsen, Bradford Dillman and Angie Dickinson starred; familiar 1960s character actor Robert J. Wilke played the Frankensteinian scientist operating a remote New Mexico medical complex, supervising covert operations growing generic human bodies sans fertilization as living organ donors. These 'soma' bodies mature but their brains do not, providing the film's most chilling imagery: with their blank eyes, bald heads, and baby-like features, the 'blank' soma are the soulless nominal zombie-like "monsters" of this SF sleeper. Nielsen's reporter risks his life to get to the bottom of the story, discovering that the soma are organically 'farmed' and mass-produced to supply organs and body tissues to those rich and/or powerful enough to be approached for rescue surgery, including the titular Senator (Bradford Dillman). The goal: by saving the lives of powerful politicians and world leaders, the scientists acquire affluence and power, the new coin of the realm. As Fielding (Wilke) says at one point, "As I said, it's a new kind of money."

---

122   Some might argue that Gordon Hessler and Christopher Wicking's **SCREAM AND SCREAM AGAIN** (1969), from the novel *The Disoriented Man* by Peter Saxon, is the first, but that gem involved removing limbs and organs from living humans to synthetically create a new "Master Race"—not the cloning of human organisms for organs and body parts.

THE RESURRECTION OF ZACHARY WHEELER was co-scripted by Tom Rolf and Jay Simms; the screenplay is a really solid piece of work, worthy at times of Larry Cohen's best from this period, and it culminates in a potent third. Rolf recalls:

"It all started with my reading an article in Esquire *magazine.[123] At that time I was working as a Production Coordinator on the TV series* Big Valley *and I mentioned it to Jay who was one of the writers and before we knew it we came up with the idea for a screenplay. It took about 3 weeks and when we finished it we gave it to Jays' agent who said 'It's too far out.' That turned out to be the general consensus and both Jay and I went on to different things. Eventually it was bought and produced with a very small budget, very evident in the final version but it did have a 'far out' premise. I never wrote another screenplay but went on to a career as a film editor but deep down there lurks a frustrated writer." [124]*

Variety touted the feature as the "first U.S. tape-to-film presentation," which isn't true—though it's likely the first tape-to-film theatrical genre narrative feature. Breakthroughs in video-to-film technologies were reaching critical mass by 1970-72, and *American Cinematographer* dedicated itself to coverage of this revolution in their October 1972 "Videotape & Film" special issue:

"The use of a videotape recorder to preserve the image of a scene which the cinematographer and director have created isn't new in theatrical motion pictures. In 1963, Richard Burton played HAMLET *before the vidicon cameras.* HARLOW *was produced in 1965. Both of these productions were made in a 'sound stage' environment and, when they were screened, had the look of a television kinescope.*

"THE T.A.M.I. SHOW (1965) and THE BIG T.N.T. SHOW (1965) were musicals staged before the vidicon cameras and later transferred to film for theatrical release. Evolutionary to these features were THE COMMITTEE (1969) and Frank Zappa's 200 MOTELS (1971). But in the traditional sense of the theatrical feature, these productions were mere exploitations in the music world.

"With the development of systems for transforming the image from a videotape recording to film, the technical feasibility of using vidicon cameras for an electronic motion picture became a reality. The picture quality is equal to conventional photography... In essence, this system has the efficiency and cost-reducing techniques of television and the 'wide-vista' photography and 'free-wheeling' portability of film... "[125]

Variety's reviewer "Tegs." had issues with the transfer, cited in his November 11, 1971 review:

"It is the first U.S.-made example of the video-tape-to-film process, developed by Vidtronics Technicolor and looks like a solid b.o. [boxoffice] *entry. A previous film, 200 MOTELS, now in release, was produced in the same process by Vidtronics' British subsid for U.A. Release. A note of reservation seems in order, however. Although the film looked as sharp and clear as that done by any process, with colors especially vivid, fine horizontal lines were occasionally visible on the screen, somewhat distracting from the film itself. Picture was previewed in the Technicolor screening room which does not simulate big theatre projection. The evidence of lines may be due to the fact that scansion with American video equipment employs fewer lines than the British system."[126]*

THE RESURRECTION OF ZACHARY WHEELER was shot in videotape, then transferred to 35mm for release (a Madison Productions, Inc. production, a Gold Key Enterprises release); I've yet to find any article on the making of this film, but the "Videotape & Film" special issue of *American Cinematographer* covered the making of a companion feature from the same production team, WHY? (1972), *"the New Hollywood's first feature film to be released at colleges across the U.S. before going into general theater bookings."* Co-producer John Bluth was President of the Vidtronics Division of Technicolor—which provided the shooting facilities and tape-to-film transfer technology for both THE RESURRECTION OF ZACHARY WHEELER and WHY?—and he noted that WHEELER involved the first use of a professional 35mm feature film cinematographer, Bob Boatman, for *"a tape-to-film feature... but there was a differentiation, to a degree. In* [WHEELER], *the cinematographer that we used had come out of broadcasting where he had been a lighting director. But he had also been a cinematographer for a period of time before we used*

123   For a chilling sequel to that 1960s *Esquire* article, see this June 2001 *Esquire* article: you've already been *sold*, baby! Wil S. Hylton, "Who Owns This Body?", archived at *http://www.esquire.com/news-politics/a1063/ esq0601-june-genes-rev/*

124   Tom Rolf, "A film way ahead of its time!," "Reviews & Ratings for **THE RESURRECTION OF ZACHARY WHEELER**," November 25, 2007, *http://www.imdb.com/ title/tt0067669/reviews?ref_=tt_urv*

125   James Willcockson, "Shooting Theatrical Features with Electronic Equipment," *American Cinematographer*, October 1972 (Vol. 53, No. 10), p.1140.

126   Tegs., *Variety*, November 17, 1971, quoted from *Variety's Complete Science Fiction Reviews*, edited by Don Willis (Garland, 1985), pg. 274. Also see the same volume's November 14, 1979 **PARTS THE CLONUS HORROR** review for some closure on the 1970s clone SF movie flap.

There is evidence (including promotional stills) of a truncated or very limited theatrical release for **THE RESURRECTION OF ZACH-ARY WHEELER** (1971), but most of us first discovered the film via its early 1980s VHS and Beta release to the home video market, including this 1987 Fusion Video edition

---

him... "¹²⁷ In fact, Boatman's only previous theatrical film credit was the video-to-film concert documentary **THE BIG T.N.T. SHOW**; he'd also been lighting director for American-International Pictures' TV special *The Wild Weird World of Dr. Goldfoot* (1965) and the TV specials *33⅓ Revolutions Per Monkee* (1969) and the super-patriot extravaganza *Swing Out, Sweet Land* (1970), and directed over 40 episodes of *Hee Haw* (1973-79). Director Bob Wynn was cut from the same cloth, having produced over a dozen TV variety specials from 1965-1979 and directed a dozen more from 1971-1994. Given his career, it's unfortunate Wynn didn't helm more narrative features; his only other genre feature credits were as producer on the dreadful TV special *Alice Through the Looking Glass* (November 6, 1966) and two Empire productions, John Carl Buechler's

CELLAR DWELLER (1988) and Jay Kamen's **TRANSFORMATIONS** (1988).

For the record, *Variety* praised the film when it was fresh out of the can:

"A solid sci-fi thriller about medical science. Outlook good. ...an above-average suspense melodrama of a secret medical team hidden in the desert of New Mexico which couples as intriguing plot line with expert pictorial pacing... It is a feasible story, similar in tone to **THE ANDROMEDA STRAIN***, and director Bob Wynn has unfolded the tight screenplay of Jay Simms and Tom Rolf in a manner that heightens anticipation of the final discovery of the center's secrets. With a thriller of this type, the screenplay is all important.* **ZACHARY WHEELER** *is so structured that each of the double plots, centering on the newsman and the senator respectively, works its way slowly and inevitably to the climax, leading the audience around blind corners, into dead ends, back-tracking and inching forward to the ultimate revelation at the end.... as a whole is a fine achievement, due in no small part to Bob Wynn's crisp direction. He had versatile actors to work with and all performed smoothly... All credits are very good, with Bob Boatman's camera work capturing the feel of the New Mexico countryside, adding to the excitement... "¹²⁸*

The efficient but programmatic direction by Bob Wynn gives **THE RESURRECTION OF ZACH-ARY WHEELER** its made-for-TV vibe; in many ways, it remains the best of the 1970s clone films. For me, this deceptively lackluster made-for-TV surface always enhanced to the subversive charge of the movie's final 15 minutes, lending surprising gravitas to the sequence in which Wheeler is "introduced" to his soma, a gray-skinned, dead-eyed, sugar-craving clone of the Senator (12 hours after the introduction of a patient's cellular sample into a "blank" soma, they begin to manifest the physical characteristics of their donor, much like the pod-people of Jack Finney's *The Body Snatchers* and its film version **INVASION OF THE BODY SNATCHERS**). The abrupt finale hinges on a line of dialogue that neatly turns the tables, though it may not play well for 21ˢᵗ Century viewers sans the context of post-Korean War/then-current Vietnam War tropes.

Why so much attention in *Monster!* to this clone curate's egg? **THE RESURRECTION OF ZACH-ARY WHEELER** was among the first SF narrative video-to-film feature films produced in the manner almost all SyFy Channel and direct-to-video genre films are made today—and that seemed worth a little *Monster!* love, don't you think? ~SRB

---

127 "**WHY?** and How This New Tape-to-Film Feature Motion Picture Was Produced," *American Cinematographer*, October 1972, p.1135.

128 Tegs., *Variety, Ibid.*

Point-of-view (POV) camera shots were inventively deployed in John Parker's experimental feature **DEMENTIA** (1953), which Jack Harris recut and added Ed McMahon narration to for theatrical release as **DAUGHTER OF HORROR** (1953/1955)—which Harris subsequently used as the movie shown in the theater attacked by **THE BLOB** (1958)!

DARK INTRUDER (1965) starts with a point-of-view (POV) Jack-the-Ripper-like attack in its opening minutes. In conversation with Tom Weaver, Tom and I wondered: was that camera direction in Barré Lyndon's script,[129] or was it entirely director Harvey Hart's decision? Until we know, I thought it worth looking at the precursors to **DARK INTRUDER** in his regard. Given the Lovecraftian context of these two issues of *Monster!*, please note the almost immediate successor **THE SHUTTERED ROOM** (1967, based on the story by August Derleth and H.P. Lovecraft), which exclusively showed attacks from the "monster" POV for almost all of its running time; director David Greene used the technique to keep his film's "monster" hidden until the (disappointing) finale's reveal. Despite this magazine's "no slashers!" policy, I can't help but wonder: prior to 1965, what movies featured, even fleetingly, a POV-of-the-killer shot in the movie (usually to hide the identity

129 The original script resides at the University of Southern California's Special Collections.

of said killer)? Here's a short off-the-top-of-our-head *Monster!* list, with a debt to Tom Weaver, and to Peter Marra's essay "'Strange Pleasure': 1940s Proto-Slasher Cinema" in *Recovering 1940s Horror Cinema: Traces of a Lost Decade*, which I will quote extensively to sort this through; Marra's article is, to date, the most thorough in print to discuss the pre-**JAWS** (1975)/pre-**HALLOWEEN** (1978) use of the device in the 1940s, with a focus on Barré Lyndon and John Brahm's films, making it particularly useful in the context of Lyndon's and Harvey's **DARK INTRUDER**. As with our other sidebars this time around, this is a subject for further research. We welcome updates, corrections, revisions—and note, *SPOILER ALERT!* Many of the following descriptions include plot spoilers.

———

* THE LODGER: A STORY OF THE LONDON FOG (1927) was the first film adaptation of Marie Adelaide Belloc Lowndes's 1913 novel, which Barré Lyndon later adapted (see below) and

P.O.V. In '42: The first onscreen werewolf victim *[top]* in **THE UNDYING MONSTER** (D: John Brahm), and another guest *[above]* succumbs to the surprise bedroom visit of the off-screen **NIGHT MONSTER** (D: Ford Beebe)

which informs **DARK INTRUDER** in a number of critical ways. Some cinema scholars note the opening scene in which the first onscreen murder victim faces the camera and screams, but Peter Marra argues this isn't actually use of a killer's POV—though director Alfred Hitchcock *did* use POV for one crucial shot in the film:

"Hitchcock's adaptation of the novel in 1927 introduced first-person from the perspective of the 'possible' killer... as he first approaches the [family renting rooms] Buntings' door. Murders often become visualized in this version only with close-ups of the screaming female victims, thereby preserving the anonymity of the killer without using POV."[130]

Note there were many silent-era uses of POV camera techniques—the most internationally renowned of the era being F. W. Murnau/Carl Mayer's *Kammerspielfilm* **THE LAST LAUGH** (*Der letzte Mann*, 1924), with Karl Freund's camera

130 Peter Marra, "'Strange Pleasure': 1940s Proto-Slasher Cinema" in *Recovering 1940s Horror Cinema: Traces of a Lost Decade*, edited by Mario DeGiglio-Bellemare, Charlie Ellbe, Kristopher Woofter (Lexington Books, 2015), p.43; the complete chapter runs from pp.27-45, and is most highly recommended.

even simulating the POV of its drunken protagonist (Emil Jannings).

* Rouben Mamoulian's **DR. JEKYLL AND MR. HYDE** (1932) dramatically opened with an extended introductory sequence from the POV of Dr. Jekyll (Fredric March), setting up the POV transformation sequence.

* The British sound remake of **THE LODGER** (1932, US title: **THE PHANTOM FIEND**) featured what Peter Marra notes as the *"final approach by the killer (Ivor Novello) toward the heroine, Daisy (Elizabeth Allan)... filmed as a POV push-in on the victim. The attack, however, does not end in murder."*[131]

* There are many crime and film noir examples—too many to cite—but we have to acknowledge the POV opening sequence—the shooting of Miles Archer—in John Huston's adaptation of Dashiell Hammett's **THE MALTESE FALCON** (1941)

* **NIGHT MONSTER** (October 1942) features three quasi-POV attacks on the targeted doctors in their guest rooms. These are not filmed with the you-are-there/you-are-the-killer immediacy of the same year's **THE UNDYING MONSTER**.

* **THE UNDYING MONSTER** (November 1942): the first werewolf attack (6 ½ minutes into the film) concludes with a brief but effective POV shot, which director John Brahm carries over in a way to the subsequent camerawork as the heroine (Heather Angel) commandeers a coach and insists on rushing out to the source of the screams; Brahm and cinematographer Lucien Ballard film the post-POV sequence with a subtly frenetic, almost staccato rhythm that stands apart from the stately imagery of the rest of the film. Until and unless someone can steer me to a previous example, I'll presently posit *this* as the first POV monster attack shot in American films.

* Jacques Tourneur's **THE LEOPARD MAN** (1943)—the Val Lewton production that evoked **CAT PEOPLE** (1942) with its title, but eschewed a supernatural 'monster' for a serial killer disguising his murders as the butchery of a renegade jungle cat—does not use POV per se, but Peter Marra points out that Tourneur and cinematographer Robert De Gresse "repeatedly photographs [the] young women walking down dark alleys and cemeteries, nervously reacting to sounds, and ultimately screaming at the sight of a thing which the audience is unable to see..."[132] (Ibid, pp.36-37)

131 *Ibid.*

132 *Ibid.*, pp.36-37.

* **THE LODGER** (1944) has one POV shot, from the killer's perspective, courtesy of the breakthrough collaboration of screenwriter Barré Lyndon and director John Brahm, adapting the venerable Lowndes novel. 46 minutes into the film, the hapless Jennie (Doris Lloyd) is attacked in her own room, seconds after she realizes she is not alone. It is a fleeting but potent moment, preserving audience doubts about the identity of the unseen Jack the Ripper (doubts Lyndon and Brahm retain to the end).

* Edgar Ulmer's **BLUEBEARD** (1944) *doesn't* use POV for its killings, but it does follow the cinematic adaptations of George du Maurier's 1894 bestseller *Trilby*—particularly **SVENGALI** (1931)—in its use of what Peter Marra's accurately refers to as *"First-person camera... throughout the film to accentuate the connection between the audience and Gaston's* [John Carradine] *dangerous gaze... a POV shot provides his perspective* [through a peephole] *as it finds and then locks upon Lucille in the audience... "*[133] Ulmer does not extend the use of POV to the murder sequences: Gaston's strangulations occur offscreen, with the camera fixed on Gaston's eyes. The killer's use of a secret peephole, and Ulmer's use of POV to directly involve the viewer in his lethal voyeurism, directly anticipates Norman Bates' peephole gaze in Alfred Hitchcock/Joseph Stefano's adaptation of Robert Bloch's **PSYCHO** (1960).

* Screenwriter Barré Lyndon and director John Brahm refined their use of POV for the harrowing opening two minutes of **HANGOVER SQUARE** (1945). The first murder is initially shown from the killer's POV—then Lyndon and Brahm whip the camera around to immediately reveal who the killer is. That's all three 20th Century Fox films directed by John Brahm utilizing killer POV shots, regardless of the writer or source material. Peter Marra parsed out the nuances of Lyndon and Brahm's refinement of the POV device in this film:

"Pre-figuring the famous opening sequence of **HALLOWEEN**, **HANGOVER SQUARE** *begins with an unidentified first-person murder which puts the audience in the position of the killer before we know his identity. Unlike* **THE LODGER**, *which simply recreates the gait and movement of an approaching male,* **HANGOVER SQUARE** *creates a full visualization of the act of murder from the killer's POV complete with a knife-bearing arm swinging down in front of the camera... "*[134]

* The finale of Alfred Hitchcock/Angus MacPhail/Ben Hecht's **SPELLBOUND** (1945) involves a still novel use of a killer's POV, intercutting a more straightforward filming of the confrontation between psychoanalyst Dr. Constance Peterson (Ingrid Bergman) and hospital director Dr. Murchison (Leo G. Carroll) with unusual POV shots of Murchison's (giant) hand, holding a (giant) gun, and a single red frame of film...

133 *Ibid.*, pg. 35.

134 *Ibid.*, pp. 35-36.

Top Right: 33 years before **HALLOWEEN**, Barré Lyndon and John Brahm concocted the POV opening murder for **HANGOVER SQUARE** (1945). **Above:** That same year, Alfred Hitchcock cooked up an inventive POV shot involving a giant prop hand-holding-a-handgun for the finale of **SPELLBOUND**

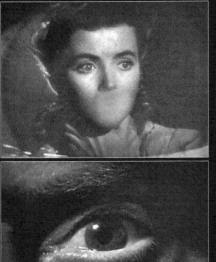

Imaginative use of the killer's POV showed what the killer imagined his victims looked like (top: mute Dorothy McGuire) superimposed within a closeup of his eye, in director Robert Siodmak's **THE SPIRAL STAIRCASE** (1945); Barbara Rush was the focal point when the POV monster-shot went space-age for the first time in Jack Arnold/Ray Bradbury/Harry Essex's **IT CAME FROM OUTER SPACE** (1953)

* Robert Siodmak/Mel Dinelli's **THE SPIRAL STAIRCASE** (1945) uses a POV shot to reveal the derangement of the killer: he sees the vulnerabilities of his victims as deformations (i.e., a mute victim is seen as having no mouth), but *not* for the murders. Also note that the POV shot is presented as a superimposition over a closeup of the killer's eye, revealing to the audience not what he sees, actually, but rather *what he imagines.*

* Robert Montgomery/Steve Fisher's adaptation of Raymond Chandler's **LADY IN THE LAKE** (January 1947) was presented entirely from its protagonist's POV—another novel 1940s variation on use of POV camera, though not of POV the killer(s).

* **DICK TRACY'S DILEMMA** (1947) showcased a POV murder-by-prosthetic-hook about three minutes into the feature, by which time the killer's face ("The Claw," Jack Lambert) has been shown. The device was used here to indelibly associate the killer with his weapon, his artifical 'hand.'

* Curtis Bernhardt/Sydney Boehm/Lester Cole's **HIGH WALL** (December 1947) presented a POV strangulation; an unstable WWII vet (Robert Taylor) strangles his wife (Dorothy Patrick) when he discovers she had an affair while he was at war, but he blacks out before the act is complete, awakening not knowing whether he actually killed her or not. The POV strangulation-to-blackout was used here to leave the audience wondering, like the hero, if a murder was completed/committed.

* Jack Arnold/Ray Bradbury/Harry Essex used extensive special-effects-enhanced POV shots for **IT CAME FROM OUTER SPACE** (1953), both revealing and hiding the extraterrestrials by only showing the audience what the aliens 'see.' This device implies the aliens are 'killing' the humans they cross paths with—thus adding to the suspense—but it turns out the aliens are not killing anyone, merely 'detaining' them and using their likenesses/bodies to move about as necessary and complete repairs to their damaged, downed ship. As Tom Weaver notes, "Universal loved POV in the 1950s, starting with **IT CAME [FROM OUTER SPACE]**."[135] Subsequent Universal POV 'monster attack' shots were included in Jack Arnold's **CREATURE FROM THE BLACK LAGOON** (1953) and **TARANTULA** (1955), Francis D. Lyon's **CULT OF THE COBRA** (1955), etc. *[See p.36 for POV images from both IT and CULT – ed.]*

---

135 Tom Weaver, personal email to the author, March 31, 2016, quoted with permission.

* **MAN IN THE ATTIC** (1953) was another adaptation of the Lowndes Jack the Ripper novel *The Lodger*, and this version preserves the POV technique John Brahm introduced and codified. Suffice to note that almost *every* Jack the Ripper-inspired film and TV show to follow—including *Black Cloak* / **DARK INTRUDER**, and the Barré Lyndon-scripted *Thriller* episode of "Yours Truly, Jack the Ripper" (April 11, 1961), adapted from Robert Bloch's 1943 short story and directed by Ray Milland—also used the killer's POV technique, primarily to hide the killer's identity and the horrific specifics of the actual murders.

* A most novel use of POV camera informed much of John Parker's experimental feature **DEMENTIA** (1953), which was re-edited and had a narrative track overdubbed for theatrical release by Jack Harris under the title **DAUGHTER OF HORROR**, 1953/1955).

* Gene Fowler, Jr./Herman Cohen/Aben Kandel's **I WAS A TEENAGE WEREWOLF** (1957) used POV for its initial werewolf attacks, building on **THE UNDYING MONSTER**'s use of the effect.

* **THE DEAD TALK BACK** (made in 1957, but unreleased until nearly 40 years later) featured an opening shot from the killer's POV.

* **THE BLOB** (1958) presented a few shots staged as sort-of from the titular (eyeless) monster's POV, though they cheated a bit by making sure the titular bright-red blob's form was partially-visible in the lower part of the frame. By 1958, fleeting actual or suggested (i.e., camera placement at the attacker's shoulder or above their head) POV monster attacks were almost *de rigueur* in the genre, if only to keep hidden or further delay the reveal of the monster (while keeping the budgets low and cameras grinding without special effects necessary for every 'shock' sequence).

I was another screaming POV victim of **I WAS A TEENAGE WEREWOLF** (1957, D: Gene Fowler, Jr.)!

* The once-reviled, now-celebrated opening sequence (presented as seen through a camera lens/viewfinder) of Michael Powell/Leo Marks's **PEEPING TOM** (1960) fused the voyeuristic nature of **SVENGALI/BLUEBEARD**'s POV shots to fixate upon their victims and the use of POV for attack/kills by an offscreen killer/monster. There was no going back after **PEEPING TOM**!

* Aside from the already-cited peephole POV shots of Norman Bates (Anthony Perkins), the shower scene in **PSYCHO** (1960) shifted rapidly between two (the killer, and victim Marion Crane) or maybe three (the omniscient camera eye) POVs in mere seconds of the entire three-minute sequence. Recent revelations about different edits of the film may reveal more; nevertheless, as with PEEPING TOM, there was no turning back after **PSYCHO**!

~**SRB** (with special thanks to Tom Weaver and Peter Marra; to John Scoleri and Ian Richardson for frame grab images; and for a Facebook "brainstorming" by Graham Gareld Barnard, Damin Toell, Craig Rogers, Matt Bradshaw, Tim McLoughlin, Craig Fischer, Jolyon Yates, and Jonathan Stover)

Lee Payton (as Kate, the nurse) sees and flings acid at **THE BLOB** (1958), which used this sort of *faux*-POV monster shot, keeping the titular red menace at the bottom of the frame whenever the eyeless amoebic mass was "seeing" a potential victim

DARK INTRUDER:
DARK ADDENDUM & ERRATA

Chicago's WNBQ late-night *Faces in the Window* host Ken Nordine read at least one Lovecraft story on Saturday nights back in 1952. (Backdrop: Michael Whelan's memorable "Lovecraft's Nightmare A" and "B" imagery, for Del Rey books, 1982-85)

* One big error in Part 1: Veteran composer and pop song writer Vic Mizzy did the music for **THE 13th GATE**, but *not* for *The Munsters!* I don't know how that brainfart cleared all our proofreaders; Mizzy, of course, composed the finger-snapping immortal *The Addams Family* TV theme, along with a plethora of other 1950s and 1960s TV themes (*Green Acres, Captain Nice*, etc.), the musical scores for all five of Universal's Don Knotts movies starting with **THE GHOST AND MR. CHICKEN** (1966), three of William Castle's mid-1960s theatrical features (**THE NIGHT WALKER** [1964], **THE BUSY BODY** [1967], and **THE SPIRIT IS WILLING** [1967]), and a whole lot more!

After the publication of Part 1 of this article, Tom Weaver shared research findings that require an extensive addendum to that text:

* It turns out there actually *was* a flurry of TV interest in H.P. Lovecraft before the 1970s! My apology for this oversight in Part 1.

There had been some television interest in Lovecraft as a wellspring for programming early in the 1950s, and briefly in the early 1960s. Chicago's WNBQ broadcast at least one reading of Lovecraft's fiction in 1952, as part of their then-innovative *Faces in the Window* late night (11:30 p.m.) show:

"WNBQ has come up with another conversation piece. One that may well stir up something like the attention gained by the recently launched 'Ding Dong School,' *morning half-hour aimed at the nursery set which has broken through as a solid local hit. However, this possibility and the fact that*

'Faces in the Window' *and* 'School' *are both single-personality, one-camera offerings are the only similarities.*

"'Faces,' slotted as the Saturday night finale, is designed to titillate the horror fans with Ken Nordine reading famous chiller yarns adapted by Marv David. The combination of Nardine's superb reading on the frame watched (13): some remarkable eerie effects by the solo camera, and he truly horrendous tale, 'The Rats in the Walls,' penned by H.P. Lovecraft, must have produced a bumper crop of goose pimples. The camera never left the reader's face and he remained sitting during the 40-minute unfolding of the tale, yet this very concentration increased the almost hypnotic fascination to really spine tingling proportions. Like the best of the old radio curdlers, the most potent quivers came from the viewers' imaginations.

"Specific details of the gruesome Lovecraft yarn were lost in the pervading mood…. Midnight snack, anyone?"[136]

Spoken-word presentations of Lovecraft's short fiction were back in the trade newspapers almost a decade later, with reports of *"Prestige Records* [adding] *an eighth label to its string called Prestige/Lively Arts… The label has been devised to showcase various talents in the arts, covering the fields of literature, poetry, humor, philosophy, legit and storytelling, among others…* [including] *Roddy McDowell… a legit and pix performer, reading classic horror stories by H.P. Lovecraft."*[137] [Note: We covered this Lovecraft LP (and others) in *Monster!* #6, pp.49-50].

In 1961-62, *Variety* reported at least twice about a potential series involving Lovecraft's fiction providing source material:

"Max Fortie, producer-director of the local TMF Productions, is prepping a tv series of H. P. Lovecraft horror stories in which Screen Gems and CBS have shown interest…"[138]

"Television is breaking with its past and falling into the habit of picture studios in buying pub-

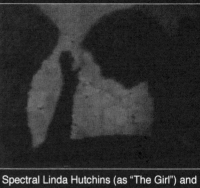

Spectral Linda Hutchins (as "The Girl") and unkissed shadows in John Newland's and Barry Trivers' adaptation of Robert Bloch's story "I Kiss Your Shadow", broadcast once and only once on *Bus Stop* (March 25, 1962); Stephen King called this "the single most frightening story ever done on TV"

---

lished material as basic concept for its teleplays. Growing trend away from originals has caught the eye of Robert Goldfarb, veepee of Frank Cooper Associates, who cites a block of recent sales on behalf of its literary clients. Tack is taken by most tv buyers that material in published form has the advantage of a built-in audience, according to Goldfarb, who has negotiated subsidiary rights of more than a half dozen properties in the past few weeks. Among them are… Series of fantastic and macabre stories by August Derleth and H. P. Lovecraft, sold to Merwin Gerard and John Newland and marked as a pilot spinoff on 'Bus Stop.'…"[139]

The *Bus Stop* TV series episode this proposal was probably spun from was the one-and-only season's finale, "I Kiss Your Shadow" (March 25, 1962), directed by TV genre veteran John Newland (*One*

136 'Dave.,' "Faces in the Window," Television Reviews section, *Variety*, Wednesday, December 17, 1952, p.27; special thanks to eagle-eyed Tom Weaver for turning this up. The credits noted the program was produced by George Heinemann and Marv David, and Bill Goodrich directed.

137 "8th Prestige Label to Showcase Arts," *Variety*, Wednesday, November 29, 1961, p.51; special thanks to Tom Weaver.

138 Forrest Duke, "The Las Vegas Strip," *Daily Variety*, Monday, June 26, 1961, p.5; special thanks to Tom Weaver.

139 "Note Vidpix Trend Toward Established Literary Material," *Daily Variety*, Wednesday, February 7, 1962, pg. 12 and "TV Seen Taking Cue From Pix in Buying Published Material: Hollywood, Feb. 27," *Weekly Variety*, Wednesday, February 28, 1962, p.39; special thanks to Tom Weaver.

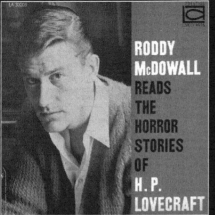

RODDY McDOWALL READS THE HORROR STORIES OF H. P. LOVECRAFT

Prestige Lively Arts and Roddy McDowall first brought H.P. Lovecraft to LP records in 1962 (LA 30003); give it a listen at *http://www.arkhamdrive-in.com/Blogarchive/sept-11.html* and see our coverage of the Lovecraft LPs in *Monster!* #6, pp.49-50

Step Beyond, *Thriller*) working from a script by Barry Trivers adapting the short story by Robert Bloch. Stephen King himself tagged "I Kiss Your Shadow" as *"...the single most frightening story ever done on TV... [Bus Stop* was] *a straight drama show... The final episode, however, deviated wildly into the supernatural, and for me, Robert Bloch's adaptation* [sic] *of his own short story 'I Kiss Your Shadow' has never been beaten on TV—and rarely anywhere else—for eerie, mounting horror."*[140] Was this the pilot for the proposed series? Perhaps; nothing else came of the reported Max Fortie/John Newland pilot or series.

This news was reported at the same time *Thriller* had effectively adapted stories by a few of Lovecraft's closest peers.

* I must revise one paragraph in Part 1 of this article in *Monster!* #27, and add new information relevant to that revision:

At the time **DARK INTRUDER** was produced, the three networks were still resistant to any primetime supernatural narrative programming other than anthologies—and they weren't too damned interested in those, either, by 1964-1965, given the flagging ratings and eventual cancellations of *One Step Beyond*, *The Twilight Zone*, *Thriller*, *The Outer Limits*, and even *Alfred Hitchcock Presents/ The Alfred Hitchcock Hour*. Comedic "monster" series—*The Munsters* (another MCA/Univer-

sal concoction), *The Addams Family*—were hot properties, however. Filmway, Inc. and ABC-TV's *The Addams Family* (64 episodes, September 18, 1964-September 2, 1966) was popular, but Universal and CBS scored consistently higher ratings with *The Munsters* (70 episodes, September 24, 1964-May 12, 1966). CBS *almost* launched *The Haunted*, an original psychic investigator series from PSYCHO screenwriter and *The Outer Limits* co-creator Joseph Stefano, for the upcoming 1965-66 season[141]; that was deep-sixed when new network management took over [see Sidebar #1: "A Made-For-TV Horror Pre-History" entry on *The Haunted* / **THE GHOST OF SIERRA DE COBRE**]. Whereas one *Variety* columnist linked the December 1964 production of *Black Cloak* with Universal's eagerness to build on the success of *The Munsters* (we'll get to that claim before we're done, I promise; if you're impatient, see footnote 86), the quiet implosion of more adult "monster," horror, and genre programming must have played a crucial role in convincing network executives that audiences were losing interest in *serious* ghosts, ghouls, monsters, demons, or anything bumping in the night, much less paranormal detectives.

Only *after* **DARK INTRUDER's** theatrical release was there a brief spark, but that spark never flared into a flame—or, more to the point, a brief point of light at the center of the picture tube (the TV screen) that never opened up into programming. *Variety* reported in February 1966:

"THE DARK INTRUDER [sic], *originally slated as an hour spin-off and later released as a theatrical feature, may yet make it as a tv series on ABC. Universal release, toplining Leslie Nielsen, had been made as a pilot and intended to be shown on the* 'Alfred Hitchcock Presents' [sic] *teleseries. Studio instead released it theatrically. Now ABC-TV is dickering for story as hour-long series."*[142]

Nothing further came of it.

* **FEAR NO EVIL** likewise had some initial interest reported as a pilot that might spawn a series, *Bedeviled*. *Variety's* reviewer 'Daku' wasn't enthusiastic about the pilot-broadcast-as-a-feature (which *Variety* referred to as a "longie"):

---

140 Stephen King, *Danse Macabre* (Berkley Books, 1981), p.219 (footnote).

141 CBS-TV's initial acceptance and 1965-66 seasonal plan for Stefano's *The Haunted* may be a previously unreported/ignored reason for CBS passing on *Black Cloak* for the same season; this is pure conjecture, but given the new information David J. Schow has shared with me on April 2, 2016 via personal email, that seems entirely possible. As noted, see Sidebar #1, and a special thanks goes to David J. Schow, who is a gentleman and a scholar.

142 "'Dark Intruder' May Retrace Steps From Theatres to TV," *Daily Variety*, Tuesday, February 1, 1966, p.6; special thanks to Tom Weaver.

"FEAR NO EVIL, filmed as a pilot for a potential series, deals with the supernatural, the occult, black magic, but despite the inbred fascination of this area of entertainment, is a disappointing longie. Suffering from obvious script padding, it's a loquacious film which plods along, relying on camera trickery, shadows and such, to seek suspense which simply isn't there. Consequently, although there must be a vast audience waiting for a series on the supernatural, producer-writer Richard Alan Simmons' exercise in exorcise fails dismally in its efforts to reach this audience... This might have been good as an hour show, but for two hours it was just too much conversation, too little dramatics... Producer Simmons doesn't have much to work with in writer Simmons' script. Tv's trek to the supernatural will have to wait for another time, another pilot. "[143]

However, a news item blocked amid Daku's review text noted:

"FEAR NO EVIL topped the N.Y. City overnight Neilsen, averaging a 27 rating and 41 share. CBS was next with a 19 rating and 29.5 share, ABC last with 9.2 and 14.2 share. "[144]

This prompted Universal to bankroll a sequel, announced in August 1969:

"Untitled sequel to last season's FEAR NO EVIL, being written by Robert Bloch, produced by William Frye. A potential series, it will star Louis Jordan, as did EVIL. "[145]

As noted in Part 1, what was eventually broadcast by NBC was the Emmy-Award winning **RITUAL OF EVIL** (February 23, 1970), from a script by Robert Presnell, Jr., directed by Robert Day, produced by **FEAR NO EVIL**'s associate producer David Levinson. Neither *Thriller* alumni William Frye nor Robert Bloch were credited.[146]

Bradford Dillman ponders his reflection in the possessed mirror of **FEAR NO EVIL** (March 3, 1969), pilot for the proposed series Bedeviled; the MCA/Universal/NBC World Premiere ad art for **FEAR NO EVIL**'s sequel (and the second *Bedeviled* pilot), **RITUAL OF EVIL** (February 23, 1970)

Neither **FEAR NO EVIL** nor **RITUAL OF EVIL** have ever enjoyed legal home video or DVD releases of any kind—sadly typical of made-for-TV genre telefeatures, though that has begun to change in the era of studio DVD-R releases. For more on **FEAR NO EVIL, RITUAL OF EVIL**, and *Bedeviled*, see *The Rakashi File: 'Fear No Evil'* by Richard A. Ekstadt and Gary Gerani (BearManor, 2012). ~**SRB**

143 'Daku', "Telepic Review: 'Fear No Evil'", *Daily Variety*, Wednesday, March 5, 1969, p.14; special thanks to Tom Weaver.

144 "Highly Rated in N.Y.," *Daily Variety*, Wednesday, March 5, 1969, p.14; special thanks to Tom Weaver.

145 "NBC Greenlights Into 1971-72 U's 'World Premiere' Series (Continued from Page 1)," *Daily Variety*, Monday, August 18, 1969, p.12. This was reported again by Dave Kaufman, "On All Channels: 'Chance' Heavy Is A Cop; Sequel To 'Fear No Evil'," *Daily Variety*, Tuesday, September 16, 1969, p.10: *"Producer Bill Frye working on a 'World Premiere,' the sequel to last year's FEAR NO EVIL pilot, at U [Universal], with Robert Bloch scripting the longie, starring Louis Jordan."* Special thanks to Tom Weaver.

146 Gary Gerani adds, *"One should also mention that FEAR NO EVIL received strong reviews elsewhere, including Steven Scheuer's Movies on TV book (three stars out of four). RITUAL OF EVIL fared less well with critics,* although it did win an Emmy for Best Cinematography (one of the few horror films to do so, on the small or large screen)."* Duly noted, Gary; Gerani, personal email to the author, April 1, 2016; quoted with permission.

For one of the earliest made-for-TV productions on the theme, see *Tales of Frankenstein*, see page 100

A TALE OF THREE MONSTERS: THE '70s TRINITY OF FRANKENSTEINS

by Seb Godin

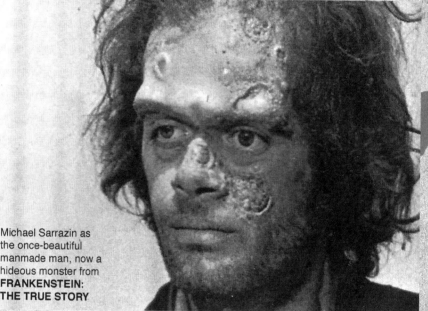

Michael Sarrazin as the once-beautiful manmade man, now a hideous monster from **FRANKENSTEIN: THE TRUE STORY**

The 1970s were a fascinating, exciting time for the horror genre. It was the dawn of a new wave of cinematic boogeymen. Slashers, zombies, possessive demons and spirits were exploding everywhere, imprinting themselves permanently in the psyches of both average moviegoers and hardened genre fanatics. But at the same time, the traditional monsters were showing no signs of disappearing. Hammer was still churning out their films to admittedly lukewarm reception, while Dan Curtis was presenting gothic horror to television with greater success, thanks to his immensely popular monster soap opera Dark Shadows *and his made-for-TV adaptations of Stevenson's* Strange Case of Dr. Jekyll and Mr. Hyde *(with Jack Palance), Wilde's* The Picture of Dorian Gray *(with Shane Briant) and Stoker's* Dracula *(again with Palance). With the success of these adaptations of classic horror stories, it only seemed natural for Mary Shelley's mad medical student and his patchwork creation to get some TV airtime.*

And so, in 1973, we got two televised Frankenstein *adaptations, and, in 1977, a Swedish theatrical feature that would get some real TV airtime under a different title. This will be a breakdown and assessment of each of these three notable adaptations, beginning with Dan Curtis' 1973 miniseries...*

This version was part of ABC's *Wide World of Mystery* program, an anthology series that was meant to fill in the late-night time slot. Shown as a two-parter with an absurd amount of commercial breaks to fill up the "extra" time, this adapts Shelley's novel with reasonable fidelity, only ever really breaking away from the source material on account of either budgetary constraints, or to add a slight flair of originality. Among these deviations is the exclusion of the Arctic segments (and therefore the character of Robert Walton is absent, too), the blind man is now a young blind girl (possibly to add a "Beauty and the Beast" angle?), and the inclusion of not one but *two* lab assistants for Victor Frankenstein (one of them played by *Dark Shadows*' very own John Karlen!).

Robert Foxworth is an intense (albeit, slightly miscast) Victor Frankenstein, while Bo Svenson is a gentler Monster than most people may be accustomed to seeing. Susan Strasberg does the best she can with the frankly do-nothing role as Elizabeth. The supporting cast is a bit on the dull side, with only Karlen bringing any sense of life to his (albeit short-lived) character.

It's worth noting that Dan Curtis himself did not direct this adaptation, taking on the role of solely

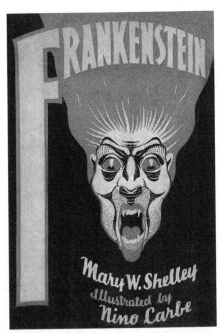

Slipcover for the Illustrated Editions Company's 1932 *Frankenstein*, with artwork by Nino Carbé. This was the edition that Tim P grew up on, and that he still owns

producing it instead. The direction was handled by Glenn Jordan, but it's noted in the audio commentary on the excellent Dark Sky DVD release that Curtis was still very involved through the entire production, though.

It's not a terrible adaptation and, despite the budgetary limitations from which it suffered, I'd argue that it's still one of the few adaptations that perfectly captured the heart, soul and essence of Shelley's original novel. It's certainly much more faithful in that sense than the next adaptation we'll be covering here...

The same year that Curtis' adaptation hit the airwaves, Universal unleashed one of the most (if not *the* most) lavish, big-budgeted TV miniseries of that time: *Frankenstein: The True Story* (1973, USA, D: Jack Smight). I'll get that little complaint out of the way right from the start... This *isn't* an accurate adaptation of the novel. Not at *all*. In fact, it might actually be one of the adaptations that deviates the most from the original plot.

Victor Frankenstein (sympathetically played by Leonard Whiting) meets the embittered Dr. Henry Clerval (played with scenery-chewing brilliance by David McCallum), who has mastered a way of reanimating the dead using the power of the sun! Clerval dies of a heart attack, leaving Victor to continue the experiment on his own. The result is a shockingly handsome Creature (gently portrayed by Michael Sarrazin), whom Victor immediately unconditionally accepts as a sort of surrogate brother. But not all is well, as the process that gave the Creature his beauty begins reversing itself, slowly turning him into a more recognizable (to Franken-fans) misshapen monster...

Right off the bat, this version deviates greatly from the novel. True, key points from the book are left intact (e.g., the old blind man, the intelligent creature, the ending in the Arctic, etc.) but beyond that, this film chooses to go down its own separate path. The greatest deviations (beyond the gradually degenerating nature of the Creature) would be the inclusion of two antagonists: John Polidori (James Mason, hamming it up), a former associate of Clerval's who uses the Creature to further his own megalomaniacal goals, and Prima (Jane Seymour at her catty best), a female creature who was designed to be a mate for the Creature but is ultimately used by Polidori to further his plans. The concept of a "Bride" for the Creature does originate from the novel, but she is never actually animated therein. I do appreciate that they put the character to good use here and mostly take full advantage of her as an antagonist, even if her subplot is resolved somewhat anticlimactically.

Bo Svenson as you-know-who in
Dan Curtis' TV adaptation

Despite the deviations made from the original story, some of you may be surprised to know that this is probably my personal favorite Frankenstein film. It's masterfully acted, brilliantly directed and written, and only suffers from a few faulty editing decisions (most notably in the film's opening, which almost feels like a recap from a television series). For years, the only way to see the film was in a condensed format that was sold to European distributors for theatrical screenings, but Universal has graciously released it on DVD in its uncut format, including an intro by James Mason (which boldly shows the film's finale!). It may not be anything close to what Mary Shelley had in mind when she wrote her novel, but it's well worth watching nevertheless, and is a genuinely great film in its own right, especially for a television miniseries from the '70s.

The final film in the Franken-trifecta that we will be looking at is a low budget Irish/Swedish co-production which was shot under the title **VICTOR FRANKENSTEIN** (1977, Sweden/Ireland, D: Calvin Floyd), but is probably better-known under the more exploitative title that Independent-International (I-I) Pictures gave it for its US television release, as **TERROR OF FRANKENSTEIN**.

Despite the more sensational title, **TERROR** is actually one of the most faithful adaptations of the book ever made. Some character omissions aside

The late Swedish actor Per Oscarsson as The Creature from **TERROR OF FRANKENSTEIN**

and certain events being condensed, it presents elements of Shelley's novel that are often left by the wayside. The appearance of the Creature (played with terrifyingly restrained anger by Per Oscarsson) is pale, black-lipped and longer-haired, which is pretty identical to what the novel described and which the vast majority of adaptations tend to ignore in favor of something more recognizable to those who may only know the character from the pop culture interpretations from over the years (typically the "Karloffian" concept, by Jack P. Pierce).

The film has an excellently dreary, dread-filled tone that perfectly matches that of the book. The performances vary between excellent (Leon Vitali as Victor and Oscarsson as the Creature) and dull (Stacy Dorning as Elizabeth). The slow pace may turn away some monster movie fans, but anyone who is a fan of the book or any other gothic horror aficionados will find plenty to appreciate here.

It would remain the most faithful adaptation of the book until 2004 when Hallmark would painstakingly produce a slavishly faithful mini-series *Frankenstein* starring Luke Goss, Alec Newman and Donald Sutherland directed by Kevin Conner.

And so ends our trinity of 70's Frankenstein movies. This isn't to say other movies featuring our favorite mad med student/scientist weren't released during this decade. Some other titles include **FRANKENSTEIN AND THE MONSTER FROM HELL** (1974, UK, D: Terence Fisher [see *Monster!* #13, p.22]), **THE EROTIC RITES OF FRANKENSTEIN** (*La maldición de Frankenstein*, 1973, France/Spain, D: Jess Franco [see p.53]), **FRANKENSTEIN'S CASTLE OF FREAKS** (*Terror! Il castello delle donne maledette*, 1973, Italy, D: "Robert H. Oliver"/Dick Randall [see *M!* #3, p.59]), and many, many more.

However, these above three are definitely the most noteworthy adaptations made during this time period, and the only ones that actually set out to properly represent the novel (to my knowledge). Each one has its strengths and each one has its flaws. But each one offers a different, unique take on the material. I'd say that alone is what helps keep each of these versions *ALIVE*!!

SUPER VIDEO

Horror's Classic Tale becomes a Strange and Shocking Nightmare!

TERROR OF FRANKENSTEIN

Starring LEON VITALI   PER OSCARSSON   NICHOLAS CLAY   STACEY DORNING
Produced and Directed by CALVIN FLOYD   in EASTMAN COLOR

US Video cover (art unsigned)

Leonard Whiting as Doc Vic goes out on a limb in **FRANKENSTEIN: THE TRUE STORY**.
(This image was scanned directly from Steve F's copy of Alan Frank's *The Movie Treasury: Horror Movies* [UK: Octopus Books, 1974])

A Late-Night Filipino Fright Flick Double-Bill:
BLOOD OF THE VAMPIRES
& THE TWILIGHT PEOPLE

by John Harrison

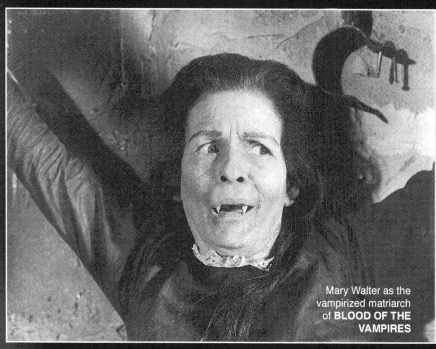

Mary Walter as the vampirized matriarch of **BLOOD OF THE VAMPIRES**

One of the things I miss most about growing-up in the pre-home video era of the late 'Seventies is having to actually stay the distance if you wanted to catch the screening of some fright flick on the late, late show. Sure, you had to fight the sandman a lot of the times, but that strange twilight world where you watched movies through bleary, half-closed eyes made the experience just that little bit more surreal and effective, and somehow more rewarding.

So, 2 a.m. on a recent Sunday morning seemed like the perfect time for me to indulge in a Filipino horror double-bill. With the darkness and late-night stillness outside, interrupted only by the odd screech of a catfight and the occasional rustle of wind through the surrounding trees—not to mention a strong cup of coffee in hand!—I decided to kick-off my double-bill with Gerardo de Leon's **BLOOD OF THE VAMPIRES** (1966), certainly one of the classier productions to come from the

Filipino horror factory, and somewhat different in tone and theme than the other low-budget genre films which the country was turning out at the time, such as **THE MAD DOCTOR OF BLOOD ISLAND** (1968) and **BEAST OF BLOOD** (1968), both of which were also directed by de Leon.

In **BLOOD OF THE VAMPIRES**, Eduardo (Filipino horror/exploitation veteran Eddie Garcia) and his sister Leonore (Amalia Fuentes) arrive at the musty old family castle after their father suffers a debilitating heart attack. When Pops announces that he is changing his will to ensure that the entire estate will be burned down to the ground immediately upon his passing, Eduardo—next in line to inherit the creaky old estate—is outraged and begins to explore the hidden passageways of the castle in order to discover the real reason for Dad's sudden change of mind. What he stumbles upon is the fact that his mother (Mary Walter), whom he had believed to be dead and at peace in

Alternate US ad for **BLOOD OF THE VAMPIRES**

the ground, is actually a vampire who is being kept chained-up in the castle's mausoleum. Eduardo stupidly takes pity on his undead mom, thinking he can save her soul, and soon pays for it by being bitten and turned into a vampire himself. This sets him off on a vampiric rampage throughout the castle and the surrounding area, killing his father (from fright rather than bite!) and sinking his teeth into his girlfriend Christine, before turning his unhealthy attentions towards his own sister, Leonore.

Filipino newspaper ad for **BLOOD OF THE VAMPIRES** (image courtesy of Video 48 [*video48.blogspot.ca*])

Often filmed with beautiful, bold color gels, **BLOOD OF THE VAMPIRES** possesses a lot of the same atmosphere and feel as a 1960s Italian gothic horror. Director de Leon brings a real sense of claustrophobia and tension to the film, with many of the actors' faces dripping with sweat (probably the result of hot studio lights combined with the tropical climate rather than any creative decision, but one which does help bring an extra degree of grimy *frisson* to the film). There are also some rather overt incestuous overtones throughout the movie, such as when Mother bites her son Eduardo on the neck then hungrily drinks and drains the blood from him; as well as Eduardo's obvious lascivious lust for his sister. The religious symbolism on display in **BLOOD OF THE VAMPIRES** is also rather potent at times, particularly during the film's climax, as villagers gather outside the castle and chant prayers while the place burns to the ground with Eduardo, Christine, Leonore and the vampiric female servants still inside (Leonore at this point has been bitten by Eduardo and is in the process of her own transformation). The sequence where Eduardo's father burns his wife on a funeral pyre is also effectively poignan,t and helps bring a real emotional core to the film. You actually *feel* for this cursed family. There are certainly some very hokey elements to it (such as the "African" servants at the castle clearly being Filipino extras in blackface!), but overall this is a genuinely interesting vampire film which deserves to be held in much higher regard than it currently seems to be by fans and students of the genre.

BLOOD OF THE VAMPIRES (a.k.a. **CURSE OF THE VAMPIRES** or **CREATURES OF EVIL**) was originally released in its home country as **IBULONG MO SA HANGIN** (*"Whisper to the Wind"*) before Hemisphere Pictures, a distribution company set up by Kane W. Lynn which specialized in importing product from the Philippines, picked up the movie for international release in 1970, sending it out to grindhouses and drive-ins under its more lurid and exploitable Anglo titles (tacking-on a great psychedelic-tinged opening credit sequence). At the time of its initial release, the film was well-regarded in its home country, garnering nominations for Best Picture and Best Director at the FAMAS (the Filipino equivalent of the Oscars) and a win for Amalia Fuentes as Best Actress.

With 4 a.m. now approaching and dawn slowly starting to loom, another jolt of joe was required before I could face the second part of my self-programmed Filipino double-feature: Eddie Romero's **THE TWILIGHT PEOPLE** (1972), which contains a lot more of that patented freakiness that we have come to associate from Filipino genre fare, and is essentially a lurid combination of H.G. Wells' 1896 novel *The Island of Dr. Moreau* and Richard Connell's 1924 short story of man as hunter's prey, "The Most Dangerous Game". Former teen idol John Ashley racks-up another Filipino exploitation credit, both as a producer and actor, playing Matt Farrell, a young man who is out for a brisk dive in the ocean when he is scooped up in a fishing net by a trawler and taken to a mysterious island run by the brilliant-but-deranged Dr. Gordon (Charles "**BLACULA**" Macaulay), who is consumed with the idea of creating a super race by combining human and animal biology. Gordon's experiments have already wielded such bizarre cross-pollinations as a panther woman, an antelope man, a wolf woman and a bat man (latter *not* the type that wears a cape, cowl and tights!).

Farrell demands to know of his captors, "Come on, goddammit, what *is* this circus?!" before realizing that his healthy physique has made him the perfect specimen for another of Dr. Gordon's experiments. As luck would have it, the doctor has collated extensive scrapbooks for Farrell to conveniently discover, which contain newspaper clippings detailing the controversial direction of Gordon's work and his discharge from the American Medical Association. Fortunately for our hero, the doctor's beautiful young daughter Neva (Pat Woodell) is starting to doubt her father's sanity and his

Fanged, Winged & Pissed-Off! Darmo the Bat Man (Tony Gosalvez) *[above & inset, below]* in **THE TWILIGHT PEOPLE** has much in common with the *Berbalang* (a bat-like humanoid vampire) of Philippine folkloric beliefs; similar creatures appear in a number of Filipino fright flicks

unhealthy obsession with his work after he botches another experiment, so she decides to help Farrell and the animal people escape their cages and flee the island. Most of these poor experimental subjects are killed in the ensuing chaos, though Darmo the Bat Man (Tony Gosalvez) is able to take care of the island guards, while Dr. Gordon himself is confronted and killed by the "tree woman" who used to be his wife before she agreed to volunteer herself as a subject for her husband's experiments.

Mexican lobbycard for **THE TWILIGHT PEOPLE** (art unsigned)

Farrell and Neva survive the carnage, of course, and watch on as Darmo spreads his wings and flies off into the distance (thanks to some primitive animation techniques).

Originally produced for Roger Corman's New World Pictures on a budget of $150,000, **THE TWILIGHT PEOPLE** was ultimately distributed by Lawrence Woolner and his Dimension Pictures

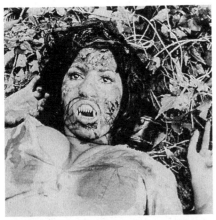

GRRRRRRRRIER!!! Before she hit the big time with action flicks like **COFFY** and other Blaxploitation classics, Pam Grier was "The Panther Girl" *[top and above]* in **THE TWILIGHT PEOPLE**

company, which Woolner founded after dissolving his partnership with Corman. The film is oft-ridiculed, but I have always found it to be a wildly entertaining hoot, with plenty of primitive but cool makeup designs, plus enough action and offbeat craziness to hold the interest throughout and keep things moving at a decent pace (something that cannot be said for a lot of other Filipino horror fare). Ashley, Woodell and Macaulay are all fun to watch, as is the supporting cast, which includes Eddie Garcia and Pam Grier (in an early role as Ayesa the Panther Woman), but it's Gosalvez as Darmo the Bat Man who steals the movie for me, looking quite impressive as he glides between the trees on large leather wings with the aid of wires that are sometimes visible but don't detract from the low-rent magic of the spectacle.

By now the morning sun was beginning to make its appearance over the horizon, casting a red glow through the slats of the venetian blinds behind the television set. I took it as a sign that it was finally time to retreat beneath the covers for some much-needed shuteye, and I drifted off into a restless sleep that was interrupted by dreams of vengeful man-beasts and sexy female vampires with strangely-dubbed voices who kept trying to entice me into some bizarre underground lair where I would be promised a new beginning and a life without end. I kept struggling to resist, though I'm not sure why. It seemed like the perfect world for someone like me to be at peace in!

GERBIL WITH A JETPACK

LOVECRAFT HOVERCRAFT.

© 2016 Matt Bradshaw

gerbilwithajetp..ck.com

HATYARIN (India, 1991, D: Vinod Talwar) lobby card—Well, what's *Monster!* without at least *one* reference to an Indian creature feature?!

BATHED IN BLOOD

A Cinematic History of Countess Elizabeth Báthory

by Andy Ross

Very much a product of turbulent times, the girl who would become one of history's most prolific serial killers emerged not from a deprived background, but from a wealthy and altogether noble heritage. Born (sources differ) in either 1560 or 1561, Erzsebet (Elizabeth) Báthory de Ecsed was one of four children born to George and Anna Báthory. In 1570, at the age of just 10, Elizabeth became engaged to the Hungarian noble Ferenc Nadasdy, and from the age of 11 (up until her marriage to him some three years later) the girl was schooled under the tutelage of Ferenc's mother, Orsloya. A devout Catholic, who instructed the girl in religious scripture, whilst Elizabeth was both intelligent and studious, she found Orsloya's presence to be painfully overbearing. It was during this engagement that Elizabeth, at the age of 13, became pregnant to a servant by the name of Laszlo Bende. For his part in the affair, Bende was castrated and fed (still very much alive) to a pack of hungry dogs. As for his illegitimate offspring, whilst some mystery surrounds the eventual fate of the child, it is widely accepted that cuckolded husband Ferenc (in his rage) would have had it rather conveniently "disposed of". Whilst she was initially opposed to the idea of marriage (and equally ill-at-ease with the idea of bearing more children), if nothing else, the wedding that took place at Varanno palace in May 1575 at least served to free Elizabeth from Orsloya's grip. Shortly after completing his education, the young Ferenc joined the ongoing campaign against the Ottoman Turks, thus leaving Elizabeth to rule in his absence. It has been suggested that throughout her formative years Elizabeth would have been no stranger to acts of human cruelty. Frequently flying into violent rages and physically abusive towards her household staff, in the years following Ferenc's death in 1608, the legacy of Elizabeth Báthory—infamously known to history as "The Bloody Countess"—would quite readily come to fruition.

Born of a lineage genetically prone to psychosis, by the time Elizabeth had entered her 40s (now a widow and with no one to rein-in her behavior), the Countess' curious relationship with her servant Darvulia was to fuel a morbid fascination with the occult. According to contemporary accounts, Elizabeth's sadistically sanguineous tendencies became manifest when one of her attendants, a young girl, accidentally tugged her hair whilst combing it. Although the Countess did not react immediately, the servant's transgression was thereafter never far from Elizabeth's mind. After interrupting the girl whilst she and a friend were pretending to sting each other with a needle, when Elizabeth joined in on the game, the frolics were to end on a far more serious note. Drawing blood from the girl (who assumed the act to be a punishment), the Countess was to experience her first taste of the salty, life-giving fluid. Becoming less involved in her estate and the management of its accounts, Elizabeth began to develop a dangerous interest in magic and the practice of witchcraft. Encouraged and tutored by her devoted Croatian servant Darvulia, the Countess was to increasingly glean sexual gratification from the torture and murder of young women. With the bloodbath representing a celebration of the accomplishment itself, as Elizabeth began to suffer from

Truthier Than Fiction? A romanticized portrait of the historical Countess Erzsebet (Elizabeth) Báthory de Ecsed *[left]*, and the cinematic variation in the guise of Paloma Picasso *[right]* wallowing in gore in the third segment of Walerian Borowczyk's **IMMORAL TALES**

crippling migraines, epileptic seizures, and bouts of severe depression, Darvulia was again on hand to add drugs to her list of addictions. Habitually choosing peasant girls as her primary targets, (as it was believed their poor parents could be more readily appeased via financial means), as accounts of missing teenagers increased so too did suspicion among the local populace. When these suspicions fell on the ears of Istvan Magyari, this Lutheran Pastor was swift to air his concerns with the aristocracy in Vienna. Whilst the powers-that-be were sluggish in addressing Magyari's complaints (Elizabeth was after all, of noble lineage), in 1610, King Matthias Corvinus II duly assigned Hungarian Palatine Gyorgy Thurzo to carry out investigations on his behalf. As the year drew to a close, Thurzo had successfully compiled over 300 signed testimonies from a variety of "reliable" sources and, on December 30th, the Countess, Darvulia, and a handful of household servants compliant to the crimes were duly arrested. As the sensational trial of Elizabeth's accomplices drew to a close, no less than 80 people had been found guilty either of direct involvement or of willful participation and, of this number, three of the closest aides (including the ever-loyal Darvulia) were summarily executed. Physical torture followed by hanging was to be the eventual fate of those involved, and it was not without some sense of irony that Elizabeth's accomplices were tortured by the same ruthless means as she herself had once championed. The fact that Elizabeth belonged to the ranks of the

nobility was the sole grace that saved her from the hangman's noose. Having been spared the indignity (let alone the political embarrassment) of being brought to trial herself, the Countess was to suffer a far more prolonged and insufferable sentence. Imprisoned in a windowless chamber in Cachtice Castle—an arrowslit in one wall now her only contact with the outside world—it was here that Elizabeth was to remain until her death in August, 1614.

How based in actual fact the murderous proclivities of Elizabeth Báthory sincerely were remains a matter of conjecture. Whilst history continues to be a casualty of bias on behalf of those who record it, in the 17th Century (where scribes were driven almost entirely by their own political agendas) this propensity was perhaps even more prevalent. If Elizabeth had direct involvement in the death of but one young woman, (let alone the calculated 300 she's been credited for) there remains the possibility that accounts of her cruelty were embellished in order to expedite her removal from power. Regardless, what filtered down throughout the centuries, whether wholly accurate or shamelessly doctored in an effort to denigrate her, was to make for a uniquely fascinating narrative.

Sexual depravity, systematic torture, vampirism, and cold-blooded murder. As elements that belonged in the darkest realms of horror fiction, that Elizabeth Báthory was a real person—who had (purportedly) voluntarily indulged in such vile and sadistic behavior—was to witness her story become the true stuff of horror legend. A fact-based yarn on par with that of her infamous ancestor through marriage, Vlad Ţepeş, or Vlad the Impaler, of the House of Drăculeşti (the inspiration behind Bram Stoker's *Dracula* [1897]), when Elizabeth's life story eventually crossed into cinematic territory, it did so with an almost complete disregard for historical accuracy.

Proffering a lightweight but typically gore-laden translation of the Countess' story, it was Britain's Hammer Films that were the first to venture into Báthory territory and, fresh from her horror début as the title character of J. Sheridan Le Fanu's 1872 novella *Carmilla* in **THE VAMPIRE LOVERS** (1970, UK, D: Roy Ward Baker), it was Polish-born actress Ingrid Pitt (**WHERE EAGLES DARE** [1968, UK, D: Brian G. Hutton]) who was to rise to the auspicious occasion. Arriving at a time when the studio was endeavoring to inject new life into their by-now-tried-and-tested archetypes, **COUNTESS DRACULA** (1971, UK, D: Peter Sasdy) was a deceptively-titled, non-canonical Hammer offering. Based *very* loosely on historical accounts, whilst **COUNTESS DRACULA** appeared determined to gloss-over the most insidious aspects of events, the end result was to deliver a rather well-rounded and enjoyable Hammer horror.

Arriving at the Báthory residence to witness the reading of the late Count's will, dashing hero Imrie Toth (Sandor Eles of **AND SOON THE DARKNESS** [1970, UK, D: Robert Fuest]) becomes the proud owner of the deceased man's well-stocked stables. Embittered that she has to share the remainder of her husband's estate with her daughter Ilona (Lesley Anne-Down of **THE FIRST GREAT TRAIN ROBBERY** [1979, UK, D: Michael Crichton]) when Elizabeth physically assaults a maid—and discovers that the girl's blood rejuvenates her long-faded youth—the Countess sets about orchestrating a devious and diabolical plot. Exploiting Captain Dobi's (Nigel Green of **ZULU** [1964, UK/USA, D: Cy Endfield]) unquestionable devotion to her, Elizabeth arranges for the abduction of Ilona, and (in her "refreshed" form) promptly assumes the girl's identity. Captivated by the charms of the young Imrie Toth and increasingly in need of blood to maintain the charade, the Countess commands the compliance of her daughter's one-time nanny Julie, (Patience

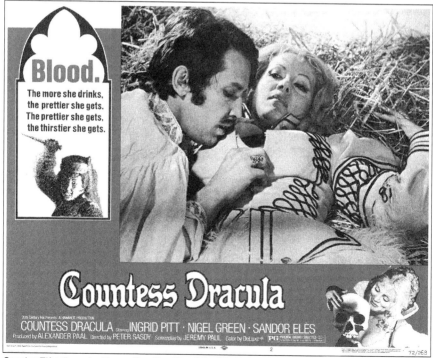

Sandor Elès (here looking rather like Ron "The Hedgehog" Jeremy!) and Ingrid Pitt get cozy in a US lobby card for Hammer's '70s vampire classic

As **COUNTESS DRACULA**, Ingrid Pitt is starting to look a tad rough-around-the-edges, and is in need of some new blood

Collier [**BABY LOVE** [1968, UK, D: Alastair Reid]). When the newly-arrived Ilona's uncanny resemblance to that of a young Countess ignites the curiosity of librarian Master Fabio (Maurice Denham of **SINK THE BISMARK** [1960, UK, D: Lewis Gilbert]), loyalties within the household are swiftly divided. With the kindly old man disposed of by Captain Dobi, when Imrie confronts the jealous former soldier, he deems to reveal the truth behind the Countess' continuous absence. Upon removing the screen that protects the bathing Countess from prying eyes, the truth as to why Elizabeth and Ilona are never seen in public together becomes readily apparent. Disgusted—however, trapped by the threat of being held accountable for a series of murders—Imrie has no choice but to comply with Elizabeth's wishes. Arriving at the castle to investigate the apparent suicide of Master Fabio, local constable Captain Ballough (Peter Jeffrey of **THE ABOMINABLE DR PHIBES** [1971, UK, D: Robert Fuest]) finds his work further complicated when the drained corpses of the Countess' victims are discovered in a wine cellar. Having arrested the shadiest-looking of Elizabeth's staff and ordered the women—both young and old—to leave the premises, the Countess' lack of fresh blood once again calls for the services of Captain Dobi. Growing weary of Elizabeth's constant abuse, and unbeknown to the

Countess, the virginal blood which Dobi acquires is none other than that of her own imprisoned daughter.

With an effectively shocking denouement, striking visuals and an evocative Harry Robertson score, **COUNTESS DRACULA** is by no means, a quintessential Hammer horror. With supernatural elements if devoid of a monster in the accepted sense of the word—rather, a mortal woman driven to commit atrocities out of vanity—whilst Sasdy's film might have lacked the physical presence of a "big bad", it was to prove no-less-effective. With her vocal performance curiously overdubbed (given that her Eastern European tones would have been far more authentic), Ingrid Pitt (in the dual role of older/younger Elizabeth) delivers a mesmerizing central performance. Particularly memorable for the scene in which Pitt is revealed in all her blood-drenched (read: naked) glory, as part of Hammer's '70s renaissance, **COUNTESS DRACULA** was a worthy (albeit, wholly historically inaccurate) addition to the studio's extensive horror pantheon.

Appearing the same year but somewhat overshadowed by Hammer's more mainstream offering, **DAUGHTERS OF DARKNESS** (*Les lèvres rouges*, 1971, Belgium/France/West Germany, D: Harry Kümel) was to volunteer a sublime and profoundly atmospheric take on the Báthory legend. With Lebanese-born actress Delphine Seyrig portraying an Elizabeth/Carmilla amalgam, Kümel's film rather artistically explored the sexual significance of the vampire myth. Set against the tranquil backdrop of an out-of-season hotel in Ostend, Belgium, **DAUGHTERS OF DARKNESS** relates an ill-fated encounter between a newlywed couple, a mysterious Countess, and her eerily-attentive secretary-*cum*-chauffeur. Presented in the *avant-garde* style synonymous with the continental horrors of Jess Franco (**VAMPYROS LESBOS** [1971, West Germany/Spain]) and Jean Rollin (**THE SHIVER OF THE VAMPIRES** [*Le frisson des vampires*, France, 1971]) Kümel's film is jointly provocative and overwhelmingly sinister. A film that writer/presenter Mark Gatiss (rightly) enthused about in his BBC documentary series *History of Horror* (2010, UK), Kümel's work was to take the stereotypical *femme fatale* and transform her into something cold, determined, and seductively evil.

Having missed their boat to England due to a train derailment *en route* from Switzerland, newlyweds Stefan (John Karlen) and Valerie (Danielle Ouimet) book themselves into a grand, albeit deserted, hotel along the Belgian seafront.

French poster for **COUNTESS DRACULA** (artist's name illegible)

As the couple enjoy their evening meal, the arrival of a black sedan portends the appearance of the Countess Elizabeth Báthory (Seyrig) and her beautiful assistant Ilona (Andrea Rau). Recognized by the hotel's concierge—who notes how her features always remain unchanged (i.e., ageless), despite the passage of time—Elizabeth's attempts to convince him otherwise fall on deafly suspicious ears. Reluctant to phone ahead and inform his wealthy mother of his recent marriage, Stefan seems determined to delay their return to England. Having enjoyed a trip on the canal in Bruges, the siren of an ambulance alerts the couple to a crowd gathering by the roadside. Not for the first time in recent days, the corpse of a young girl has been discovered with its throat slit and its body drained of blood. Seemingly mesmerized when the cadaver is loaded into the back of the ambulance, when Valerie attempts to pull her husband from the curious throng, she is rewarded

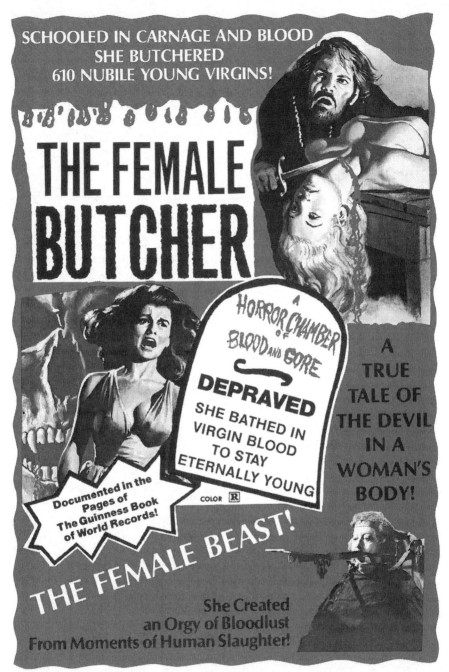

SCHOOLED IN CARNAGE AND BLOOD
SHE BUTCHERED
610 NUBILE YOUNG VIRGINS!

THE FEMALE BUTCHER

A HORROR CHAMBER of BLOOD and GORE

DEPRAVED

SHE BATHED IN VIRGIN BLOOD TO STAY ETERNALLY YOUNG

COLOR R

Documented in the Pages of The Guinness Book of World Records!

A TRUE TALE OF THE DEVIL IN A WOMAN'S BODY!

THE FEMALE BEAST!

She Created an Orgy of Bloodlust From Moments of Human Slaughter!

Alternately-titled US one-sheet poster for **THE LEGEND OF BLOOD CASTLE** (art unsigned)

for her troubles with a slap to the face. Something about the murder has struck a raw nerve in Stefan; as if once-repressed emotions are beginning to bubble up to the surface within him. Returning rain-sodden from their outing, the couple are met by the Countess, who insists they meet her for drinks in the lounge. Joined by the sullen Ilona (who is jealous of Elizabeth's increasing attraction to Valerie), as the conversation turns to the Countess' family history, so too does the dialogue take on a sick and sadistic turn. Having finally persuaded her husband to pass on the news of their union to his "mother" (bizarrely, a middle-aged man with a curious fondness for flora) that he's had to revisit his (rather peculiar) past leads Stefan—in a scene dramatically offset against a raging coastal storm—to horsewhip his terrified spouse. Determined to separate the couple, whilst Elizabeth uses Stefan's domestic violence as a wedge, Ilona sets out to seduce him by far more conventional means. When a post-coital shower turns into an accidental bloodbath (a scene so intense it serves to leave the viewer breathless!) the Countess' influence over Valerie grows stronger still. Having revealed Stefan in his most primal state (and to all intents, as a murderer, too) Elizabeth's plans to secure Valerie's affections have finally come to fruition. Or *have* they…?

Article author Andy Ross' stark impression of Danielle Ouimet and Delphine Seyrig in **DAUGHTERS OF DARKNESS**

Focusing on the Countess' fancy for blood and as such placing this particular portrayal firmly within vampire territory, that **DAUGHTERS OF DARKNESS** only fleetingly refers to the historical crimes of Elizabeth Báthory does not make it any less relevant. In the central role, Seyrig delivers a polished and truly spellbinding performance. Notable too, as her saturnine lady-in-waiting, is the Louise Brooks-inspired character of Ilona, a faithful companion who has been relegated to the role of a mere tertiary player in Elizabeth's ongoing intrigues. Whilst the majority of mainland European-produced horrors were to prove something of an acquired taste (and again, I feel compelled to refer to the works of Jess Franco), **DAUGHTERS OF DARKNESS**, despite its occasionally intrusive soundtrack, was to lose nothing in its overseas translation. An absorbing tale of lust, murder and seduction shot exquisitely against a stark, sparsely-populated backdrop, Kümel's film remains a true classic of contemporary vampire cinema.

A rather obscure entry that is no-less-loved by fans of the genre, **THE LEGEND OF BLOOD CASTLE** (*Ceremonia sangrienta*, a.k.a. **THE FEMALE BUTCHER** or **THE BLOODY COUNTESS**, 1973 Spain/Italy, D: Jorge "Jordi" Grau) was to astutely combine the legend of Elizabeth Báthory with the very real beliefs of Eastern European folklore. With its milieu borrowing heavily from Hammer but its style very much more in keeping with that of Continental cinema, **THE LEGEND OF BLOOD CASTLE** remains a rather noteworthy addition to Báthory's onscreen chronicle. In an age where recently-buried bodies are exhumed amid fears of vampirism

and where said corpses are then put on trial for their perceived posthumous misdemeanors, the Countess Erzsebet Báthory (Lucia Bosé of **THE STORY OF A LOVE AFFAIR** (*Cronaca di un amore*, 1950, Italy, D: Michelangelo Antonioni]) grows increasingly frustrated by her husband's lack of under-the-sheets attention. Preferring to spend time with his beloved hunting falcons rather than in the boudoir with her, that Karl (Espartaco Santoni of **THE HOUSE OF EXORCISM** [*La casa dell'esorcismo*, 1975, Italy/West Germany/Spain, Ds: Mario Bava, Alberto Citini]) has likewise developed a wandering eye leads Ezrebeth to lament the passing of her once-youthfully desirable appearance. Noticing that the blood of a clumsy maid gives her skin a seemingly

Censored German poster for **DAUGHTERS OF DARKNESS** (art unsigned)

la L. M. presenta

LE VERGINI
CAVALCANO LA MORTE

LUCIA BOSE' • EWA AULIN
SILVANO TRANQUILLI • SPARTACO SANTONI
Regie di JORGE GRAU
EASTMANCOLOR

Italian *locandina* for **THE LEGEND OF BLOOD CASTLE** (art by Morini)

Canada), for enthusiasts of good old-fashioned horror fare, the film is well worth tracking down. Less so however, is **THE DEVIL'S WEDDING NIGHT** (*Il plenilunio delle vergini*, a.k.a. **FULL MOON OF THE VIRGINS**, 1973, Italy, D: "Paolo Solvay"/Luigi Batzella), a decidedly lame affair wherein two brothers, Franz and Karl Schiller (both played by Mark Damon of **HOUSE OF USHER** [1960, USA, D: Roger Corman]) stumble blindly into satanic goings-on amidst the Carpathian Mountains. As part of his ongoing quest to locate the mystical ring of the Nibelungen, academic Karl finds himself at the gates of the infamous Castle Dracula. Seduced by the lady of the house, the darkly mysterious La Contessa Delingen de Vries (Rosalba Neri of **LADY FRANKENSTEIN** [*La figlia di Frankenstein*, 1971, Italy, D: Mel Welles]), Karl's arrival coincides with a half-centennial local event called "The Night of the Virgin Moon"; a satanic ritual in which five virgins are lured to the castle, thus allowing the Contessa to bathe in their blood. A film that is every bit as silly as it sounds, besides the obvious reference to Elizabeth Báthory, the rather messy presentation (co-directed by an uncredited Joe D'Amato) haphazardly throws a zombie maid, a hunchbacked vampire and even a resurrected Count Dracula into the mix. Visually, the film does have its artistic moments, however, with clever use of shadows and fantastic lighting effects adding a fleeting sense of menace to the proceedings. Taken at face value, the most aesthetically stunning facet of the film is Rosalba Neri's unnatural bathing habits. No doubt as charming as the actress is, a prolonged scene of Neri rubbing blood over her naked breasts is not something you want to hang an entire production on. (Who am I kidding? Of *course* it is!)

As a director who began his film career in the field of animation, Walerian Borowczyk has been widely-acclaimed as "a genius, who also happened to be a pornographer". Hailing from Kwilcz in Poland, after completing his degree in Fine Arts studies at Krakow, Borowczyk emigrated to France in 1959 and settled in the vibrant city of Paris. Best-known for his short films, whilst his catalogue of live-action features were often erotically-charged, Borowczyk's artistic background was to endow his polished productions with a rather unique aesthetic flair. Following his breakthrough presentation **GOTO, ISLAND OF LOVE** (*Goto, l'île d'amour*, 1968, France), Borowczyk was to take his fascination with the weird and the wonderful one step further in his first portmanteau offering, **IMMORAL TALES** (*Contes immoraux*, 1974, France). The third of four short stories— and, in this instance, based on the works of the

rejuvenated quality, Erzsebet (aided and abetted by her maid Nodriza) sets about procuring innocents to satisfy her mounting bloodlust. Duty-bound to support his (clearly insane) wife and exploiting the superstitions of the unkempt local yokels, Karl fakes his own death and, returning as a "vampire", seeks to seduce young virgins in the dead of night. Boasting similar production values to **COUNTESS DRACULA** but lacking the presence of an Ingrid Pitt, Grau's take on The Bloody Countess legend possesses a near fairy-tale quality about it. Wonderfully framed but rather plodding in the plot department, whilst **THE LEGEND OF BLOOD CASTLE** is by no means an ineffectual movie, it is a little rough around the edges. That said, the familiar trappings of the vampire film are very much on display here. From shadowy graveyards to imposing castles and from cozy little taverns to dark, dank crypts, the film boasts it all. Incredibly difficult to get a hold of in the UK (perhaps less so in the US and

surrealist poet Valentine Penrose—the segment entitled "Erzsebet Báthory" focused on two very distinct predilections of the infamous Bloody Countess. Opening with a long-distance shot of the Countess and her page riding across a green— albeit bleak—landscape, a lingering close-up of Paloma Picasso's hypnotic gaze is rapidly intercut with a scene of a young couple frolicking naked in a hayloft. Describing the day-to-day life of a 15th Century Hungarian village via fleeting scenes of unkempt individuals, a woman treading on grapes barefoot, and a semi-clothed toddler clambering over a mound of freshly-picked apples, the sudden peal of church bells prompts a mixed response of fear and excitement in the locals. Bringing with her the promise of a far better life in servitude, the Countess Erzsebet Báthory has descended upon the village to enlist the prettiest and most flourishing of its maidens. Circling those chosen before dismounting her horse to inspect them on a far less impersonal level, the Countess appears pleased with what the village has to offer. Leaving behind the preteens and infants (perhaps for another day?), upon arrival at the castle, the peasant girls duly strip down and indulge in a particularly drawn-out (and shamefully voyeuristic) bathing session. Amidst scenes of bared breasts, pubic mounds, in-fighting, and the wanton defacing of shower walls, the Countess

has been busily preparing a potent libation for her guests to partake of. Resplendent in luxurious silks and jewels, and with the gathering now drugged and in a state of lustful frenzy, Erzsebet makes her flamboyant entrance. Entering the fray and gleaning a great deal of pleasure from the girls' brutal probing, the Countess is soon stripped of her finery, and the next time we see her is when she is bathing languorously in their frothy, still-warm life's-blood. With the girls having all been systematically put to the sword by her (soon to be, for obvious reasons) fresh-faced page, Erzsebet has satisfied her wanton bloodlust, and clearly not for the first time, either. Showering herself down, she is joined in her bed-chamber by the young "male" servant who—rather abruptly—is shortly revealed to be a boyish-looking girl instead. Besides having betrayed the Countess to her lover (a Captain of the King's Guard), the page rather curiously complies to a *faux* marriage and same-sex union with the rejuvenated Erzsebet. As the sun duly rises and the King's Guard gatecrash the party, so too does the blood-soaked reign of the Countess come to an end.

An exercise in vanity, lust, and—ultimately— betrayal, Borowczyk's take on the Báthory legend was to breathe fresh life into the renaissance paintings of Titian, Caravaggio, and Michelangelo.

"Sara Bay" a.k.a. Rosalba Neri [inset, upper right] and her entourage in an Italian fotobusta for **THE DEVIL'S WEDDING NIGHT** (note hand-drawn "bikini" at left!). The actress with her hands up is Esmeralda Barros

A whole cornucopia of naked feminine pulchritude with absolutely nothing left to the imagination, whilst the shower and bed-chamber scenes belong entirely in sexploitation territory, it has to be said that they are rather attractively filmed. Focusing jointly on the Countess' abnormal fascination with blood and her reputed lesbian tendencies, given that a further episode of **IMMORAL TALES** was to feature the incestuous shenanigans of the Borgia family, it's hardly surprising that Borowczyk would opt for a no-holds-barred approach to the narrative. Whilst the movie itself might not appeal to the masses (there is after all a *lot* of female nudity on show), in true Borowczyk fashion, this particular episode surely smacks of the director's artistic brilliance. Despite its rather flat and uninspired storyline and a puzzling denouement—i.e., the cross-dressing page-"boy" is shown wiping blood from her sword and, as such, proves equally culpable in the Countess' crimes—as the Countess Erzsebet herself, Paloma Picasso (a fashion designer and daughter of acclaimed Spanish artist, Pablo, here in her sole dramatic acting role) delivers a regally sinister (and incredibly sexy!) central performance. As a director whose films were to divide both audiences and critics alike, Borowczyk's body of work adroitly reflected his understanding of dramatic detail. Originally intended as a five-part anthology, the proposed fifth segment—an erotic dream sequence detailing the violation of a young woman by a freakishly-endowed bestial monstrosity—eventually saw light at full feature-length as the controversial **LA BÊTE** (a.k.a. **THE BEAST**, 1975, France).

A direct sequel to **HOSTEL** (2005, USA, D: Eli Roth), the same director's **HOSTEL PART II** (2007, USA) was to focus almost entirely on the female of the species. Treading much the same path as its predecessor (i.e., American tourists fall foul of an agency in Eastern Europe which procures victims to satisfy the bloodlust of a wealthy elite clientele), for one of its most graphic sequences, this visceral body-shocker (I do so *abhor* the term "torture porn"!) was to glean direct inspiration from the historical murders purportedly perpetrated by Elisabeth Báthory. When three art students holidaying in Italy are persuaded by their life model to join her on a luxurious spa vacation in Slovakia, the attraction of a prolonged pampering session seems too good of a one to miss. After checking into a local hostel, the three friends, Beth (Lauren German), Whitney (Bijou Phillips), and Lorna (Heather Matarazzo) have little reason to suspect their lives might be in danger. With their passport details uploaded onto the auction site of the so-called "Elite Hunting" group, it is the socially-awkward Lorna who first succumbs to its vile agenda. Worse for wear after partying hearty

Article author Andy Ross' drawing of Paloma Picasso bathing in blood in the third segment of Walerian Borowczyk's **IMMORAL TALES**

Seyrig and Ouimet get better acquainted in a US lobby still for Harry Kumel's elegantly erotic '70s Belgian vampire classic

with the villagers at their harvest festival, Lorna dismisses the concerns of her colleagues to join the suave Roman on an impromptu midnight boat-trip. Having been whisked away to a clandestine location, when we next encounter Lorna, she is seen bound, gagged, and suspended upside-down like an animal carcass over a deep (and oddly, empty) sunken bath. Struggling vainly to free herself, Lorna looks on with increasing fear as two brutish men light a series of candles around the ornately-tiled bathing vessel. With the overhead lights now distinguished, the sound of stiletto heels can be heard reverberating through the cold and altogether practical chamber. Slipping off her shoes and discarding her robe, a genteel-looking woman eagerly lowers herself into the sunken receptacle. Naked, her chest rising and falling rapidly, the woman rather casually raises a scythe above her head. Scratching at the girl's exposed flesh, clearly oblivious to her muted pleas for mercy, as the woman's excitement grows, so too does the severity of her attack. Culminating with a scene worthy of a myriad "slasher" movies, whilst the final, throat-slitting act is undeniably shocking, there remains a dark and savage poetry to it. This is gruesome stuff, it has to be said, made even more disturbing by the murderess' near orgasmic

response to being spattered by her victim's showering blood.

Cherry-picking the more exploitative aspects of the Countess' backstory (and concentrating far more on its themes of bloodlust and lesbianism), what had remained elusive was a relatively faithful interpretation of Elizabeth Báthory herself. Given the Countess' familial history of mental illness, her early traumatic experiences, and her later downward spiral towards sadism, a more accurate account of her horrific reign had yet to come to fruition. With the mass appeal of the historical costume epic rejuvenated by the likes of **BRAVEHEART** (1995, USA, D: Mel Gibson) and **GLADIATOR** (D: Ridley Scott, 2000, UK/USA), that was an oversight that was soon to be addressed and, in part two of this article, we'll not only be looking at two international co-productions on the theme—namely Juraj Jakubisku's Slovakian-Czech-Hungarian-British **BÁTHORY: COUNTESS OF BLOOD** (*Báthory*, 2007) and Julie Delpy's French-German-American **THE COUNTESS** (*La comtesse*, 2009)—but also how the grotesque appeal of the Bloody Countess' character was to witness her media transition from feature film to documentary, through to comic-books and even musical opera.

PUBLISHING INFORMATION

MONSTER! is published typically monthly, but this here "Spring Special" is different, okay? Subscriptions are NOT available. © 2016 Wildside Publishing / Kronos Productions, unless otherwise noted. All rights reserved. No part of this publication may be reproduced, distributed, or transmitted in any form or by any means, including photocopying, recording, or other electronic or mechanical methods, without the prior written permission of the publisher, except in the case of brief quotations embodied in critical reviews and certain other noncommercial uses permitted by copyright law.

For permission requests, write to the publisher:
"Attention: Permissions Coordinator," at:
Tim Paxton, Saucerman Site Studios, 26 W. Vine St., Oberlin, OH 44074 •
kronoscope@oberlin.net.

MONSTER! contains photos, drawings, and illustrations included for the purpose of criticism and documentation. All pictures copyrighted by respective authors, production companies, and/or copyright holders.

GERBIL WITH A JETPACK presents

The Lost Children's Stories of H.P. Lovecraft

AUSTRALIAN GOTHIC

The Story of the 1929 *Dracula* Stage Tour
(Part 2)

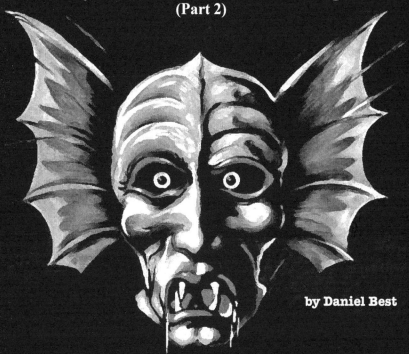

by Daniel Best

Theatre Royal: Melbourne,
20th July to 8th August
King's Theatre: Melbourne,
9th August to 16th August

"World's Greatest Dramatic Sensation."

Cast of characters in order of their appearance

Helga Rolunde	Maid
Ellis Irving	John Harker
Arthur Cornell	Dr. Seward
Ashton Jarry	Dracula
Andrew Money	Prof Van Helsing
Nat Madison	Renfield
Leonard Stephens	The Warden
Bertha Riccardo	Mina

Although being advertised for the Melbourne season, Bert Barton was engaged for the Sydney run only, and would be replaced with Leonard Stephens for the remainder of the tour. But before the Melbourne season could kick off, the cast and producers had to deal with a domestic scandal that saw Nat Madison being named in the media in regards to a divorce case. Norma Drayton, understudy to both Bertha Riccardo and Helga Rolunde, was being hounded by her estranged husband, John Gilfoy.

In what now reads like a classic case of domestic violence, Drayton had filed for divorce on the grounds of apprehended violence, claiming Gilfoy had threatened to shoot her, smacked her face, scarred her foot with a lighted cigar and threatened to throw acid in her face. Things had come to a head when Gilfoy drove up to where Drayton was staying, with the cast, in a hotel in Springfield. Accosting her, in front of witnesses, Gilfoy screamed, "I will go mad and shoot you dead!" Naturally, Gilfoy denied the claims, stating that he had merely

asked her where she went in a motor car after each performance.

The Judge looking over the case ordered Gilfoy to keep the peace for six months and fined him £20, but not before Gilfoy had written to Madison demanding that his wife be sacked from the cast for the Melbourne run. Madison duly ignored the request, Norma Drayton wasn't fired and remained with the cast as the female understudy.

A more pressing problem was being faced at the time. The train carrying vital parts of the scenery had failed to arrive, meaning the crew were working overtime trying to adapt what they could find for scenery, props and costumes. The props quickly became an issue as the bat failed on stage. The bat, a rubber bat on wires *[What else?! – ed.]*, snapped its strings and flopped to the floor during the first Melbourne performance, resulting in Madison apologizing to the audience at the show's end. Although the situation was handled with good grace, the embarrassment that was felt amongst the cast was acute.

The Melbourne run began at 8:10 p.m. at the Theatre Royal, with advertisements promising, *"A night of awe and mystery, fun and fantasy with thrills in plenty."* Reviews later claimed that the first-night audience didn't exactly get what was promised. The missing scenery was highlighted, as were bats dangling from strings. Despite praising Madison, Jarry and Riccardo, The Argus decried the play as, "...just another of the large family of rather crude 'mystery' pieces which are not taken seriously even by those who like to become exclamatory at the performances. If any theatre-goers arrived with hopes of being horrified, it seemed fairly evident that their hopes were not realised at the Royal." The Australasian panned the play as being "Unimpressive", and even went so far as to state that, as a drama, Dracula was a comedy. Other critics went on to attack the play as failing to live up to their expectations, while praising the cast members for doing the best they could with the material at hand.

With only six days remaining on the run, The Firm decided to move the play to the King's Theatre to accommodate the Melbourne premiere of *Journey's End*. *Journey's End* had originally been booked for the nearby Comedy Theatre, but advance ticket sales and interest, combined with falling sales for *Dracula*, necessitated the move. The matinees already booked for *Dracula* were duly cancelled, and tickets already sold were moved to the night performance or merely refunded.

GRUESOME PLAY

"Dracula" in Melbourne

"Dracula" will displace Harry Lauder at the Theatre Royal, Melbourne, tomorrow night. "Dracula" is the story of a vampire lady, who, under the evil influence of Count Dracula, apparently develops a thirst for the blood of her victims. This fateful role is to be undertaken by Bertha Riccardo, the pretty young South African, who, after making an engaging first appearance in "Tip Toes," went into comedy and drama, in which her gifts had a larger scope.

She will be recalled as one of "The Silent House" in which Maurice Moscovitch turned on a bland Oriental manner and a sinister smile, and she was also with Alan Bunce in "Pigs."

Alan Bunce and the ingratiating Ruth Nugent, by the by, have now turned their minds to sterner things in Sydney. They figure in the detective play, "The Perfect Alibi," at the Criterion.

Cover Art by Basil Gogos

Top: Bernard Jukes, who played "Renfield" in the 1924-27 British stage productions of *Dracula*. **Left:** Fans of *Famous Monsters* mag will recognize his visage on the cover of issue #18. **Above:** Australian news item (from Perth's *The Daily News* for July 26, 1929)

Melbourne was to see the introduction of a second play, Nat Madison's pet project, *No. 17*. Madison had been presenting *No. 17* for the past eighteen months, and the bulk of the *Dracula* cast, who had worked on the play previously in both Australia and New Zealand, reprised their earlier roles. *No. 17* had never been staged outside of Sydney, and the run attracted more interest than was previously expected. Despite the interest and strong ticket sales, the run had to end on the 24th of August, affording the casts of both shows a short break before they were due in Adelaide on the 30th.

Melbourne proved to be a happy city for the touring troupe—lost scenery, changing theatres and tepid reviews aside. Overall publicity was positive, resulting in good houses, the atmosphere was excellent and the troupe were starting to become very comfortable with their roles, and each other.

Theatre Royal: Adelaide, 4th September to 9th September

*"The amazing vampire play...
the world's biggest thrill."*

Cast of characters in order of their appearance

Helga Rolunde	Maid
Ellis Irving	John Harker
Guy Hastings	Dr Seward
Ashton Jarry	Dracula
Frank Royde	Prof Van Helsing
Nat Madison	Renfield
Leonard Stephens	The Warden
Bertha Riccardo	Mina

Advance advertising for the Adelaide run began in mid-August. Immediately after the culmination of the Melbourne run, the cast and crew made their way to Adelaide by train. As *No. 17* was to have a very limited run before *Dracula* began, the cast of both plays toured, with most acting as understudies for each other in their respective plays.

The negative reviews in both Sydney and especially Melbourne saw changes made to the cast and to the play. Guy Hastings (who appeared in *No. 17*, and had previously worked with Moscovitch) and Frank Royde were brought in to replace Andrew Money and Arthur Cornell. Cornell and Money were both moved to understudy status, and were now to focus on their familiar roles in *No. 17*. Also

Australian press item about the play's star Ashton Jarry (from Adelaide's *The Advertiser* for September 5, 1929)

BERTHA RICCARDO plays the role of the bloodless heroine in "Dracula," a weird play of vampires and reincarnated spirits, at the Theatre Royal.

BLOODLESS "DRACULA"

Weird Drama at Royal

One of the best jobs in Adelaide is that of the trained nurse who is present at every performance of "Dracula" at the Theatre Royal. In the advertisements she is one of the greatest attractions of the show; in the theatre she is not much in evidence. Although the company headed by Nat Madison does this weird play full justice, it is not the terrible affair that one expects. Interesting and exhilarating, yes; hysterical, overpowering, no.

In the book written by Bram Stoker the opportunities that the superstition of Southern Europe afford a writer of thrillers are fully used, but obviously these can not be repeated with such effect on the stage.

It is still believed in certain parts of Europe that some spirits leave their grave each night to suck blood from a loved one, and that the only cure is to impale the vampire on a stake. This is the plot behind "Dracula."

When a girl is stricken with a queer malady a vampire is suspected, and it is not long before they find that there is a man in the neighborhood who at night changes his form to that of a were-wolf, and enters houses as a bat.

A professor of the occult accuses him of vamparism, and declares that to prevent the dying girl developing into a vampire also, the bat man will have to be killed with a stake and a hammer. That is done, much to the distaste of the audience.

Nat Madison as a lunatic does much to add an eerie atmosphere to the play, and his characterisation is an outstanding one. Ashton Jarry has the unsympathetic role of Dracula, but it is to him and Frank Royde, as the professor, that the chief honors of the play go. The bloodless heroine is played by Bertha Riccardo.

touring as a featured player for *No. 17* and an understudy for *Dracula* was Campbell Copelin.

Bradford, England-born Frank Howroyd had an impeccable heritage, first appearing onstage with Herbert Beerbohm Tree. From there he featured in the play, *A Stranger in the House* alongside Sybil Thorndyke, then regarded as the best stage actress in the world. After changing his last name to Royde, he performed at the famous Garrick Theatre, and had been busily producing and performing in plays in South Africa, American and India since 1908. According to contemporary accounts, Royde's stage specialty was playing Oriental men, apparently aided by the fact that he had prominent front (buck) teeth. Royde was also serving as the stage manager and producer for both plays for Adelaide and Brisbane.

Irish-born Guy Hastings also came from England, where he began his stage life. He had extensive experience in live theatre and was originally employed by J.C. Willamson to star alongside Bert Bailey in the Steele Rudd play, *On Our Selection*. Hastings liked Australia enough to want to stay. He had worked with both Madison and Moscovitch and was a valued, and highly reliable, member of the Nat Madison company.

The cast of both plays arrived in Adelaide on the 30th of August. The change in climate, from the damp cold of Melbourne to the dry warmth of Adelaide, was appreciated by all. "We have been crouching over roasting fires in Melbourne," Riccardo was quoted as saying. But the warmth didn't come without cost, as South Australia was experiencing its worst drought in recorded history. The drought had caused much hardship in the state, as no serious rainfall had been recorded in that time, only light showers. This was acknowledged by Riccardo. "I suppose for the sake of the country I must be unselfish and hope for rain before we leave for Brisbane." The rain didn't come until December, and when it did it arrived in the shape of a monsoon that caused floods and created more hardship…but that was in the future.

No. 17 opened at the Theatre Royal on the 31st of August and closed on the 2nd of September, allowing the cast a break between the two plays. Riccardo was asked for her thoughts on the production of *Dracula* so far. "If the effect on the audience makes it necessary for a trained nurse to be in attendance each night you can imagine that some members of the company become rather jumpy," she said, before repeating her earlier line about having issues with sleeping in the dark. "At times, when playing in *Dracula*, I cannot go to sleep in the dark. I must have the light on."

Australian press item (from Adelaide's *The Mail* for September 7, 1929)

Imagination More Than Actors, Says Dracula Star

In the following article, specially written for "The Mail," Mr. Nat Madison discusses the psychological effect of mystery thrillers on the audience. The "Dracula" star declares that the success of the mystery melodrama depends as much upon the imagination of the audience as the acting of the players. He says that the actors merely suggest a situation and the audience does the rest.

"NONE OF YER SOBS, GUV'NOR," says Nat Madison in his role of Ben, of the Merchant Service, in an amusing moment of the thriller "No. 17."

"I have been asked to write on the melodramatic thriller and the psychological reasons for its great popularity. In view of the fact that my company's play 'Dracula' is sending cold shivers down Adelaide's spine, it is interesting to look into this matter and see just why these plays pack houses, while Shakespearean drama is given little support.

"Since 'Dracula' is regarded by dramatic critics to be the last word in thrillers, we have in this play a good chance to analyse the fascination that draws audiences night after night.

"Perhaps, in this case, it is the strangeness of the story. The plot is built around the ancient superstition of the human vampire. The chief character in the story is Count Dracula, a Polish nobleman who has the form of a human being by day and the shape of a vampire bat by night. He sows terror in every heart, until finally he is killed, and the evil spirit within him exorcised.

"Three things are responsible for the success of 'Dracula'—or for any mystery play that deals with the unknown. First, there is the deep-seated awe of the supernatural that lies at the bottom of every person's heart. Most of us retain the childish antipathy to being left alone in the dark.

"To sit in the ease and security of a comfortable theatre and watch a group of persons struggling with unknown horrors is, for many people, a most satisfying way of spending an evening. Although they know that it is all make-believe, there is always the feeling that it might be real. These are the people who are carried away by our play, and faint or become hysterical.

"The second reason lies in the fact that we are all born with a certain amount of curiosity in our mental make-up. That urge to see other men and women in dangerous situations and to wonder how they are going to extricate themselves from their plight, is a potent force which lies behind the popularity of the thriller.

"Then last, but by no means least, there is the escape from the grey monotony of everyday life that is offered by the thriller. In these mechanical times keen competition has made the fight for existence a thing of routine that leaves

little time for strange happenings. The world is a sadly overcrowded, familiar place, and romance and adventure are being crowded out.

"Yet mankind has not altered. Men still want romance and adventure, and being unable to get them in real life they seek them in the theatre.

"Members of the audience do almost as much work as the actors in a play of the type of 'Dracula.' They are led up to a certain point, and their imaginations do the rest. If you analyse any mystery play that has been a proven success you will find that it contains not so much action as suggestion. The actors work hard to suggest the required situation, and imagination supplies the action. Because every person's imagination supplies it in his own way, with himself in the limelight, the play has a personal appeal for everybody. Of course, we stimulate the imagination with trick effects, with wailing cries and dimmed lights, and our conversation puts members of the audience in a receptive state of mind; but, after all, they imagine much more than they really see or hear.

"Actors benefit by this knowledge. After a while you get a kind of sixth sense that enables you to gauge your audience and sway it as you will. Every actor knows how different it is when rehearsing before an empty theatre, with only the sheeted chairs and the vacant boxes in front. It is not a question of seeing his audience—the stage lights are so blinding that the darkness of the auditorium hangs like a black curtain in front

BEHIND THE MASK OF GREASE-PAINT—The smiling face of the man himself.

of the stage—but by that intimate sixth sense he can tell whether or not he is getting over with the people in front.

"Does the acting in such gruesome plays affect the nerves, is one of the questions I am often asked.

"Well, I believe that it would if one brooded on the part. For instance, in

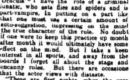

"'OO'S BIN FOOLIN' ABART WITH ME DRINK?" scowls, Ben, the cockney seaman of the play "No. 17." With a minimum of greasepaint and a few old clothes, Mr. Madison makes Ben an unforgettable study.

'Dracula'—I have the role of a criminal lunatic, who eats flies and spiders and is part-vampire. In putting on a part like that one must use a certain amount of auto-suggestion, impressing on the mind the true character of the role. No doubt if one were to keep this practice up month after month it would ultimately have some effect on the mind. But I take a keen interest in all sports, and away from the boards I forget all about the stage and uncanny roles. But there are occasions that the actor views with distaste.

"These are first nights, when the cues and lines are new to the actor, and the final nights of a long run. On the latter occasions the dialogue has become so mechanical that it is liable to go right out of the actor's mind and leave him standing speechless in the centre of the stage. This unfortunate experience happened to me when playing in 'The Great Lover' in London. I was forced to walk off the stage and get my lines from the prompter.

"Many persons have asked me how it was that I did not take my father's name when following a profession in which he was so well known. There is an interesting reason behind my action.

"My father, who was born in Russia, was a Moscovitch, but later in life he travelled to New York, where he entered into business with one of his brothers. While in New York my father changed his name to Masskoff, and it was while he was bearing this name that he married. I was born at Madison avenue, New York, and of course took my father's changed name, Masskoff.

"Some time later, when my father took up the acting profession he reverted to his true name, Moscovitch, the name by which he is known to the profession all over the world. When I decided to follow in his footsteps I determined to pick out a new name for myself so that I would not be accused of trading on my father's reputation I chose 'Madison' from the avenue in which I was born, and retained my Christian name."

Nat Madison

Australian press item about *Dracula* co-star Nat "Renfield" Madison (from Adelaide's *The Mail* for September 7, 1929)

Like Melbourne, reviews of the Adelaide run were mixed. The cast were beginning to hit their stride, and the relaxed atmosphere that provided allowed them to ease back into their roles. Jarry was again singled-out for his star turn as Dracula, as was Madison who was described as being, "...really powerful as a lunatic". Hastings had an immediate impact as he, and Ellis, too, drew kind reviews. The only exception was Riccardo, who was described as being, "...drawn on to do little except look pale and sick." Interestingly, a review in The Advertiser compared portions of the play with the earlier, 1908 play The Power of the Cross; the same publication, in 1908, had compared The Power of the Cross to Dracula.

However, there was a problem with the play here, too. Duke wasn't present, resulting in a crew member having to pretend that he was a werewolf. Sadly, the effect was muted, as the glowing lights, which were used to illuminate Duke's eyes, merely blinded the crew member and didn't have the same reflective effect. Luckily, Horace, the white mouse that Madison, as Renfield, eventually "ate", was present and accounted for.

The play wrapped on the 9th of September, an all-too-short run of just six nights, plus matinées. The last night saw Riccardo winning the rave reviews, along with Madison ("horribly convincing") and Jarry ("sinister").

From here the play moved to Brisbane...

His Majesty's Theatre: Brisbane, 21st September to 28th September

"Thrills beyond precedent and without parallel"

Cast of characters in order of their appearance

Helga Rolunde	Maid
Ellis Irving	John Harker
Guy Hastings*	Dr Seward
Ashton Jarry	Dracula
Frank Royde	Prof Van Helsing
Nat Madison	Renfield
Leonard Stephens	The Warden
Bertha Riccardo	Mina

*Andrew Money replaced Hastings for the last four performances.

A short break, this time of three days, was afforded to the cast and crew of Dracula before they were called upon to appear in Brisbane. As with Adelaide, Dracula was to be preceded by a run of No. 17. Unlike Adelaide, No. 17 was given a full week to run at His Majesty's, the same amount of time as Dracula ran. The play was now being advertised in New Zealand, with a run to begin in mid-October. It was in Brisbane that Madison was given word that he was to be given a screen-test in Hollywood, immediately after the Australian Dracula run was completed.

No. 17 opened on the 14th of September and ran until the 20th. The same cast that appeared in Adelaide appeared in Brisbane, in both plays. Reviews for No. 17 were good, with critics noting that the cast were very comfortable with each other and very settled in their roles. As they'd been with the play since it's conception at the beginning of the year, they knew that play far better than they did Dracula.

The latter opened on the 21st, with a matinée performance, and, as with the other states, the reviews were largely positive. By now it was clear that, no matter the interest in the Dracula play in America and England, the same couldn't be said for Australia. Although performances were packed, houses were not fully selling-out and mid-run shows were not selling as rapidly, or as well, as expected. This was noticed as far back as Melbourne, hence the shorter Adelaide and Brisbane runs. People were turning up, but the general masses, who would be expected to make an extended run, just weren't attending.

Despite all of the ticketing issues, the Brisbane premiere was sold out (ads promised such surefire ticket-sellers as *"Gleaming Eyes, Clammy Bats, The Were-Wolf, Mystic Women in White "*). The then-State Premier, A.E. Moore, was in attendance, along with several other notable people. The main review of the play concentrated on Riccardo and her wardrobe—or rather, her *lack* of wardrobe. During the performance there was excitement in the theatre as a woman duly fainted after a loud, piercing scream came from the stage. For the only time in the entire Australian run, the trained nurse in attendance had to do something more than just sitting at the front of the audience!

The more cynical of the audience cried *"Publicity stunt!"* only to be faced with the sight of the young woman laid out on a chair in the lobby at the intermission, white as a sheet with the nurse attending to her along with her escort for the evening. The resulting publicity produced a spike in ticket sales, and matinees were added for the following Wednesday and Saturday. J.C. Williamson's immediately pounced on the fact that a woman had (finally!) fainted during a performance, releasing an ad for the last four nights with a disclaimer stating that patrons attended the show at their own risk and that no responsibility would be accepted by the producers.

Adding to the woes of the play, there were yet more cast changes, causing disruptions. Guy Hastings made it known that his time with the play had to cease early, as he was already booked for rehearsals with the Nellie Bramley company, which was about to undertake a major tour of Australia. Arthur Cornell, the original Dr. Seward, had also left the company once the run of *No. 17* had concluded. As there were only four performances left, the original Van Helsing, Andrew Money, who was understudying, quickly stepped in as Dr. Seward.

The addition of the extra shows was in vain. Tickets sales were so poor that the Saturday matinee was cancelled. Tickets sold for the matinee were transferred to the evening show, ensuring that the last performance of *Dracula* in Australia was to a packed, albeit not sold-out, house. The reviews of the last show were very positive, but not as glowing as those in other cities.

So it came to be that, on the 28th of September, 1929, the first run of *Dracula* in Australia came to an end. Nat Madison gave his last performance on an Australian stage, although only he knew that at the time. The cast and crew dispersed, most believing that they would be gathering again in just over one week's time in New Zealand.

The (Cancelled) New Zealand Tour

A tour of New Zealand had been booked and promoted by J.C. Williamson to begin immediately following the Australian run. At the time it was common for an Australian stage production to tour New Zealand as The Firm had interests in that country, both in real estate (theatres) and also in promotion.

The idea was that the main cast of Jarry, Madison and Riccardo would make the trip, and the practice of performing *No. 17* and *Dracula* on alternate nights would continue. Theatres were booked and the season was to begin in Auckland on Tuesday, the 8th of October, 1929. It wasn't to be, however. After a flying visit to New Zealand, Madison left for America due to family reasons.

At the last minute the tour was postponed until the 21st of October, leaving The Firm's Auckland theatre, His Majesty's, "dark" until another play, *Journey's End*, began its run there on the 23rd. A further postponement pushed *Dracula* back until mid-November, then January, 1930, after which the play was then quietly cancelled. The reason for this postponement was a simple one: Nat Madison had "gone Hollywood".

Australian newspaper ad (from *The Brisbane Courier* for September 20, 1929)

Once he had received the news of an impending screen test and auditions in America, Madison began to wind-up his affairs both in Australia and New Zealand. If he had failed his screen-test he had intended to fulfill his New Zealand obligations, but the test proved positive, and a contract to appear in films was offered him, which h promptly accepted. This meant severing all ties with The Firm and its productions.

Top: US newspaper ad (March 1929) for a Pittsburgh performance of the Raymond Huntley-starring version of *Dracula*. **Above:** Billing for Lugosi's performance at England's Dudley Hippodrome (from May 28 to June 2, 1951)

Madison was the main draw-card in the play, both in Australia and New Zealand, despite others' involvement (notably Jarry and Riccardo, who enjoyed long careers there), and his absence left a hole that couldn't be immediately filled. The rest of the cast found other work. By the time The Firm was ready for another run at *Dracula*, everyone involved in the original production was engaged with other plays. The Firm then counted their losses from the production and shelved the play, deciding that it would be cheaper to send Mrs. Stoker the obligatorily contracted £100 per year for the next four years instead.

After Dracula

Once Universal's **DRACULA** feature, starring Bela Lugosi in the role that would forever define him, was released to cinemas in 1931, the idea of doing a fullscale stage revival of the play in Australia evaporated. Lugosi's performance in the movie was hypnotic and captivating, and no stage show could ever hope to compete with him—he *became* Dracula, as far as anyone was concerned. Decades would pass before anyone would attempt to mount a full-blown production of *Dracula* on the Australian theatre circuit again. The people directly, and indirectly, involved with the original *Dracula* had mixed fortunes after the play ceased.

Helga Rolunde, the Maid, who managed to give Bertha Riccardo a run for her money in the beauty stakes, left the stage in 1930 to become a theatre critic for the *Sunday Sun* in Sydney. She passed away, far too young, in 1935. She was the first of the *Dracula* principals to die.

Guy Hastings, Dr. Seward, remained in Australia and continued to act on the stage. He made the move over to radio and, eventually, film, where he flourished. He was a favorite amongst theatregoers and performers alike due to his range and reliability as a performer. In December 1940, while appearing onstage in *The Streets of London*, Hastings was struck down by a series of heart attacks. In hospital he was informed that his acting days were officially over. Such was his popularity that, once the news became public, benefits was quickly organized and staged in both South Australia and Victoria in order to assist him with his ongoing care while hospitalized.

The benefits took place over February, 1941, and were well-attended. In Victoria, a performance of *Streets of London* was staged and the proceeds handed to his fund. In South Australia, a cabaret was held at the end of February, with professionals turning out, performing and recounting stories of

Hastings. He passed away from a heart attack just over a fortnight after the testimonials, at his home in Olinda, outside of Melbourne, Victoria in March of 1941. He was 63 years old. His official obituary listed a number of plays and name-checked Moscovich, but there was no mention made of his turn in *Dracula*.

Also passing away in 1941 was the show's producer, Gregan McMahon. McMahon had broken away from The Firm after *Dracula* and formed the Gregan McMahon Players, a casual group that featured amateur and professionals who came together (or not) to stage plays as the mood took them. Unfortunately, the Players went bust and McMahon was forced to return to work for The Firm again in 1935, where he continued to produce shows. Tired of doing the same work for very little money, McMahon became bitter and disillusioned; he too died of a heart attack at the end of August, 1941.

Andrew Money, who did a double turn as both Van Helsing and Dr. Seward, remained as enigmatic after the play as he had been before. He had another featured role in *The Prince and the Pauper* in 1930 and then left the stage. He passed away in 1947. His death notice tellingly gave his occupation as "engineer".

"I did not leave the stage, the stage left me."
– Ashton Jarry, 1932

Ashton Jarry, Australia's first stage Dracula, continued to perform in Australia. He went from play to play and became one of the first ever radio presenters, performing on 3LO in Melbourne as far back as 1928. Ever the nomad, he settled in Adelaide for a few years, taking up residence at the Black Bull Hotel in 1931 and appearing at every opening night, where he cut an impressive sight in his dress suit accessorized with a six-inch cigarette holder. By 1932 he was giving indications that he was done with stage work. "I did not leave the stage," he told a reporter, "the stage left me. Suitable plays are not being produced."

Jarry continued his radio work in Adelaide. Radio, then still in its relative infancy in Australia, was popular amongst actors, as it provided a means to be heard by many with little physical effort, and the rewards could be great. Jarry also gave speeches at various functions, one of which saw him land in court as he, along with three others, were charged with having unlawfully obtained liquor during prohibited hours: they were caught, drunk and merry, on the premises of the Amateur Sports Club of South Australia. Jarry was ordered to pay £2 in total for his indiscretion.

Jarry had no reason to return to England after the death of his mother, Lucie, in 1931. By this time he had two brothers, and the late Albert had a family

Raymond Huntley as the Count in Hamilton Deane's mid-1920s pommy stage production

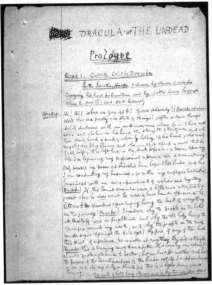

Written in Stoker's own hand, this is the first page of his manuscript for an onstage reading of *Dracula* performed on May 18th, 1897 at the Lyceum Theatre in London. It represents the first ever stage dramatization of the work, for which the author and others read aloud different characters' lines from the book

in Western Australia. It's not known if Jarry had any contact with his nephews and nieces.

After intermittent appearances in stage productions, Jarry made the move into film. He had resisted it for as long as he could, primarily because he simply wasn't fond of the medium. His film

Ex-Drac Ashton Jarry as an "ethnic" undercover G-man in the Oz outback melodrama **UNCIVILISED** (1936), seemingly channeling Leslie Banks as Count Zaroff from **THE MOST DANGEROUS GAME** (1932, USA) in the way he delivers his lines

career was short, he appeared in two movies, gaining rave reviews for his turn as an Afghan named Akbar Jhan in the 1936 Charles Chauvel film **UN-CIVILISED** (a.k.a. **UNCIVILIZED** or **PITURI** stateside). In a role that must have reminded him of his *Dracula* days, he endured two hours a day being made-up for his role. It was enough for him to call it quits, and he quietly retired from both the stage and screen, at the age of 60. He was financially secure, and no longer needed to work anymore, so he could play golf or build shelves all day if he wanted to.

Jarry settled into a flat at Rose Bay, Sydney, and lived out the remainder of his life the same way as he'd always done: alone and quietly. He took on the role of caretaker for the units, and his neighbors knew him as Leon Jarry; he had reverted back to his proper name once he retired from the stage. He was befriended by another tenant of the block of units, Reginald Eagar, and the two men would meet every day to talk, with Jarry regaling Eagar with stories of his time on the world stage.

Leon Henry Jarry passed away in his sleep on the 20th of September, 1949, at the reported age of 71, in Sydney; he had actually shaved three years off his official age, and was in fact 74 when he passed. As he passed away intestate, his estate was disposed of by the Public Trustee. He left £150 in the bank and his effects, photos, jewelry and other worldly possessions were sold for a total of £29 at a public auction. There was no public announcement of his death, although a notice did appear in the American *Billboard* magazine. His final resting place is currently unknown.

Leonard Stephens, the Warden, continued to work, appearing on stage and then radio, until he was struck down by a combination of old age and heart disease. A testimonial was staged for him, attracting the likes of Gregan McMahon, the producer of the 1929 *Dracula* tour, future country music legend Smokey Dawson, a host of actors and a professional wrestler who showed the audience how to grapple. Stephens died in 1953.

Only a year before he passed away, Ashton Jarry had nearly crossed paths with Bela Lugosi, *the* legendary Dracula himself. In mid-1948, Lugosi was asked to travel to Australia by Universal Studios to promote his latest film, **ABBOTT AND COSTELLO MEET FRANKENSTEIN** or, as it was titled in Australia, **MEET THE GHOSTS**. The movie, a comedy, saw Lugosi finally reprise his famous role on film—although he had appeared as other vampires in movies, he had not played the actual Dracula character since the original Universal film in '31. The plan was for Lugosi to fly to Sydney, promote the movie and appear onstage. The thought of the Australian Dracula meeting the most famous Dracula in the world is just too good to be true!

It *was* too good to be true, as it happens. Despite having changed into a flapping rubber bat onscreen a number of times during his career, Lugosi had a lifelong fear of flying, and flatly refused to come, no matter how much money was put before him. "I have never flown in my life," he told reporters, "and I don't intend to start now". The alternative was a boat trip, which would take up to three months. Lugosi couldn't afford to be at sea—both literally and figuratively—for six months, not when he had built up some momentum back in his adopted country. However, there was a darker reason as to why Lugosi couldn't spend that much time away on the ocean.

By this point in Lugosi's life, he was hopelessly addicted to morphine and methadone. A boat trip for that length of time would have required a lot of drugs to be smuggled onboard; if not, then the trip might very possibly have killed him. Lugosi couldn't, and *wouldn't*, take the risk.

This was not to be the only time that Lugosi would have to field an offer from Australia. In 1951, while he was undertaking a successful revival of *Dracula* on the English stage, Lugosi was offered the opportunity to revive the play in Australia. The initial offer would see Lugosi spend all of 1952 Down Under, staging the play across the country, beginning in Sydney in late January. Again, citing his fear of flying, Lugosi declined. The offer was then reduced to a two-week run, in Sydney alone, for the same guarantee. As tempting as it was, it was conditional on Lugosi flying to Australia, as he would not have had time to sail there. Faced with this dilemma, Lugosi again passed on the offer. He would never again be offered the chance to travel to Australia. He passed away in 1956.

Bertha Riccardo: I cannot find my Jimmy. You don't know where he is, do you?
Alfred Frith: I don't know where your Jimmy is. I hope you never find him.
-- from the stage play Sons o' Guns, *1ˢᵗ April, 1931*

Bertha Riccardo, the delightfully vivacious Mina, suffered the most as her personal life hit highs and crushing lows, but her career remained constant at a steady level. Once Madison left the country, his company was dissolved, so Riccardo found herself looking for work, not that she had to look far. She found herself employed in both light musical

US pressbook for the Australian wilderness adventure **UNCIVILISED** (1936), which costarred Oz Drac star Ashton Jarry *[far left, bottom]*. It was his sole film appearance

comedy and dramatic roles, her looks and sheer talent driving her forward. All the way through, her breezy outlook served her well, as did the many advertisements for beauty products she was commissioned to endorse. In the back of her mind was a desire to return to the London stages that she missed, and she cheerfully told anyone who asked that she wanted to go back and conquer the performing world there.

In 1931, Riccardo dropped a bombshell: she got engaged and married in just over a month. She had met Clyde Hood[1], a stage producer with Union Theatres, and they began a clandestine affair. This resulted in her announcing to her friends and cast-mates, at a party, their engagement. In a brilliant move for the pair, they tied the knot at midnight on New Year's Eve, 1931. Her plans now were to finish her current engagements and then move to break into Hollywood using Hood's connections. It truly appeared that Bertha Riccardo was blessed: with not only looks and talent, but now a well-connected handsome young husband who loved her dearly, too.

---

1 Hood was referred to, in contemporary accounts, as being called Colin, Clive and Clyde. The official name on the *Southern Cloud* memorial is Clyde Hood.

The fall was sudden, unexpected and utterly brutal. Riccardo was in Melbourne, performing the lead in her latest play, *Sons o'Guns*, when Hood, who was based in Sydney, decided that he would fly out to surprise her. He departed Mascot airport on schedule, at 8:10 a.m. on Saturday, March 21st, 1931, on a plane called the Southern Cloud for the relatively quick and easy flight. He never arrived.

The weather that morning was inclement, with rain and squalls forecast. The Southern Cloud was carrying six passengers, including Hood, and two pilots. What exactly happened has never been established, but the plane failed to arrive in Melbourne. Riccardo went onstage that night after being told that her husband was on his way, reassured by the fact that it was not uncommon for a pilot to land somewhere *en route* to refuel and wait-out storms if they were bad enough. Ironically, her co-star was none other than Alfred Frith, a.k.a. "Butterworth the Warden" from Lugosi's *Dracula*. Despite reassurances, Riccardo knew in her heart something was very wrong…but the show must go on.

The plane had still not been found ten days later,

FAMOUS STAGE PLAY, "DRACULA," TO BE AT NILE THEATER MONDAY NIGHT

Harriet George and the famous Hungarian actor, Bela Lugosi, as they appear in "Dracula," which will play the Nile Monday night and for which seats are now being sold.

American newspaper item (from *The Bakersfield Californian* for July 15, 1929), when Lugosi was at the top of his game

and Riccardo had appeared every night without fail. To outsiders it appeared as though she didn't have a worry in the world, putting on a brave face and telling people that Hood would soon arrive to greet her. Privately she was falling apart with worry, though. She was halfway through the play on the 1st of April, 1932 when she had the following exchange:

Riccardo: I cannot find my Jimmy. You don't know where he is, do you?"
Frith: "I don't know where your Jimmy is. I hope you never find him."

After Frith delivered his lines, Riccardo let out an inhuman howl that shocked both cast and audience alike. She slipped to the floor and curled up, weeping, in front of the audience. By the time she was carried off-stage she was hysterical and unable to be consoled. She was cared for backstage by a doctor who happened to be in attendance in the audience then sent home to "rest".

"It is a scene," Frith later told reporters, "that is supposed to get a big laugh. I think it is the most tragic thing I have ever heard on the stage. I always feel that I will not be able to reply to Miss Riccardo. I know just what she is thinking when she speaks her lines." Riccardo consoled herself and finished the run after taking a few days off. The search was officially called off just under three weeks later. Riccardo, barely into her twenties, was now a widow, and without her husband's body to bury to boot.

After taking stock of her life, Riccardo left the country that had brought her so much joy—and just as much heartbreak—and returned to London. She began to appear on stage, finally realizing her dream. It didn't take her long to land work; she was appearing in plays by January, 1932 when she appeared in a minor part in a run of *The Improper Duchess*.

Despite positive reviews and steady work, as well as a name-change to Billie Riccardo, lead roles were hard to come by, and after a run of *Whistling in the Dark* wrapped up in early 1934, she slipped into obscurity.

The wreckage of the Southern Cloud was finally found in 1958 when a worker on the Snowy Mountains Hydro-Electric Scheme discovered the remains of the plane during a trek. The aircraft had gotten lost in thick cloud and blown off course, resulting in it slamming into the side of a densely-timbered mountain ridge called Deep Creek, just outside of Goulburn, New South Wales. Nobody could have survived. Once news broke of the plane being discovered, locals began to pick through the wreckage for souvenirs. The remains of the plane and its passengers were removed to Sydney, where they were examined. Pilot error was ruled out; the accident had been caused by the weather. A plaque now sits at a lookout where the Southern Cloud tragically came to rest.

There was a sad postscript to the story: In late 1960, Hood's bones, along with the others who perished in the crash, still remained at the Cooma police station, unclaimed. It wasn't until 1961 that Clyde Hood was finally given a Christian burial, paid for by the state of New South Wales. Despite widespread publicity and pleas for family members to claim the remains, Riccardo never came back for her beloved Clyde Hood.

Frank Royde, the second Van Helsing, went back to playing Orientals onstage until he wore the "gimmick" out. He thereafter returned to his native England and moved into movies, his best role coming as a clergyman in the epic David Niven adventure **AROUND THE WORLD IN EIGHTY DAYS** (1956, USA, Ds: Michael Anderson, John Farrow). He died in England in November 1962.

"They pay you well here, but they're wolves to work you."
--Nat Madison, 1931, talking about Hollywood

After stopping by briefly in New Zealand to announce the tour's cancellation, Nat Madison, whose turn as Renfield would prove to be his Australian swansong, sailed to Hollywood, where his father's connections had arranged a screen-test for him with Warner Brothers. His test was successful, he photographed well and his speaking voice was pleasant, both valued attributes in the early sound era where the careers of many once-big-name stars were ending due to problems with their voices or projection. Upon his arrival, he was warmly welcomed by the Hollywood Raj. "Charlie Chaplin gave me a marvelous party at his wonderful house on top of Beverly Hills," he wrote. "I knew him well in the early days. Noel Coward, Gloria Swanson, John MacCormack and Marion Davies were there." Once he had been accepted and gotten settled, he changed his name back to Noel and never looked back.

His first major movie was also the first "talkie" for Gloria Swanson, **QUEEN KELLY** (1928, USA, D: Erich von Stroheim). Madison went on to a successful career in film, appearing mainly as a character actor or gangster, if never in a starring role. However, his path did cross in a major way with both *the* Dracula, Bela Lugosi, and *the* Frankenstein's Monster, Boris Karloff...

In 1933, six actors met in Hollywood to discuss the concept of a union, or a guild, that would oversee all actors and provide them with some form of security while they were making movies. Coming away from that meeting, the six formed the Screen Actors Guild and began to approach others to gain support. Three months later, the original six were joined by eighteen others and the Guild elected its first President and other board members. Included was none other than Boris Karloff, who had endured hours under heavy makeup in the heat of summer while making **FRANKENSTEIN** (1931, USA, D: James Whale), often leaving for work at 4:00 a.m. and returning home at 11:00 a.m., all for only a basic wage. Others present were C. Aubrey Smith, Lyle Talbot, Ralph Morgan and Noel Madison. As Madison later wrote to Kenneth Thompson, "You ought to see conditions over here in studios. British Actors Equity has no authority whatsoever in films...nobody cares and nobody wants to do anything. No standard contract, no definite pay-day, no weather-permitting clause, no 12 hours rest period (except for Madison, because I wouldn't come back), no nothing. A few of those bastards in Hollywood who refuse to join the Guild ought to work over here for a while."

Madison would go on to serve as the SAG's Treasurer, and was handed the #5 membership card.

Vintage US stage production billing

"DRACULA" THRILLS WERBA AUDIENCE

"Ahs" Greet the Vampire Count's Wicked Work

January is hardly the season to see a show like "Dracula." The management of Werba's Brooklyn Theatre, where it entered a week's engagement last night, after a successful Broadway run, keeps the playhouse at a nice, comfortable temperature—for ordinary shows.

But, when Count Dracula, the vampire, stars his satanic machinations, you feel the chills running along your spine, and your hair lifts up until you begin to feel that the janitor might turn on more heat.

This is the best thriller of its kind in the past year. Played by a corking cast and blending the weird beliefs of an almost forgotten superstition with modern-day life, it is plausible enough to send you home determined to keep the lights on.

The story centers around a vampire, neither dead nor alive, but holding to earthly activity through preying on humans.

A beautiful blonde girl (Dorothy Peterson) is his victim. The story details the fight to save her life and soul, while his satanic majesty leers at you just around the corner. "Dracula" is something not to be missed.

Raymond Huntley plays Count Dracula, the vampire, and in his stage personality Mr. Huntley is truly a bad dream. Miss Peterson, as the beautiful victim of his devilishness, makes a perfect foil for him. Throughout the theatre last night there were "ohs" and "ahs" and half-suppressed screams of excitement when he got in his worst—and best—work.

He can almost convince you that, perhaps, there are vampires and were-wolfs, after all.   **J. J. H.**

NYC press review for the Raymond Huntley version of the play (from *The Standard Union* for January 29, 1929)

Karloff was handed the #18 card. Lugosi came in shortly after; he was member #33. While Lugosi might not have heard of Madison's involvement in *Dracula*, Madison would no doubt have known about Lugosi's connection to the character. It would be a romantic notion indeed to imagine Lugosi and Madison, Dracula and Renfield, sitting

down one evening at a meeting and discussing their respective stage experiences!

Madison was also part of the Hollywood Cricket Club, a group of expatriate Anglo actors who would come together and play cricket when it suited them, even playing a game against the visiting Australian team in 1932 (a team that included Sir Donald Bradman, arguably the best cricketer ever). Formed in 1932, the Hollywood Cricket Club was headed-up by Sir C. Aubrey Smith (himself a former captain of the English test team and a one-time opponent of the legendary W.G. Grace), as well as virtually every other English and Australian actor currently in Hollywood. On any given weekend, teams would consist of Boris Karloff, David Niven, Ronald Coleman, Errol Flynn, Basil Rathbone, Leslie Howard, Nigel Bruce (who played Dr. Watson on screen to Rathbone's Sherlock Holmes) and Laurence Olivier (who, legend has it, once had to borrow Karloff's boots in order to play).

Cheering the men on were the female members of the English community, including Karloff's onscreen bride of Frankenstein, Elsa Lanchester, David Niven's early Hollywood love interest, Merle Oberon, and sisters Joan Fontaine and Olivia de Havilland.

Madison never returned to Australia. He left film in 1943, returning to the stage that he loved so much both as an actor and director. He passed away on the 6th of January, 1975, in Florida.

Ellis Irving married Scottish-born actress Sophie Stewart in California. The pair had met during a tour of the play *Marigold*. He and Stewart moved to England, where he enjoyed a minor film career. He often visited Australia, always cheerful and ready to speak to anyone who approached him. He passed away in 1983 at the age of 81, lamenting to the end that he had never gotten the chance to play *Hamlet*.

Others who featured in the *Dracula* tale had mixed fates:

Jack Hooker and Dorothy Seward, the dancers who adapted "Dracula's Guest" onstage, found they were just another vaudeville act in London. They stuck it out, achieving some degree of success, and remained in England until 1931, when they returned to Australia via South Africa. They had made a modest fortune and continued to work in the theatre. Australian audiences had changed their tastes by the early 1930s, and vaudeville wasn't as lucrative as it once was. They were talented and tenacious, though, and continued to work well into the '30s, after which they quietly retired and went into teaching dance. They never staged *Dracula's Guest* again after that week back in November 1925.

Edwin Geach, the producer who staged *The Power of the Cross* (which became an adaptation of *Dracula*), moved into film, working with F.W. Thring as a producer, director and writer. He was a true pioneer of the Australian film industry, helping to found the Greater Union theatre chain and becoming its first managing director. He passed away in July, 1940, at the age of 73, leaving an estate in excess of £18,000—a small fortune at that time—to his sisters and sisters-in-law.

Alfred Frith, the Australian who had played Butterworth the Warden to Bela Lugosi's Dracula, would continue his work on the stage and eventually branch out into film and radio, too. His main starring role was opposite the western author Zane Grey in the American-Australian co-production **WHITE DEATH** (1936, D: Edwin G. Bowen). A mischievous man, he suffered from a number of maladies in his later years, including a serious heart complaint which saw him hospitalized more than once. He passed away in April 1941, at the age of 57, after suffering a heart attack at home which caused him to fall down a flight of stairs, resulting in a fractured skull on top of it. He died in hospital a few days later. His funeral had a large turnout, as many who had worked with him came to pay their respects. Not one obituary mentioned his marital problems…nor did they make mention of his fleeting role onstage in the classic *Dracula*, either.

Australian-born actor W.E. Holloway moved from the stage and into film, featuring in several movies. In 1936 he was cast in the title role of *Dracula* as it toured England, appearing with none other than Hamilton Deane as Van Helsing. By playing the titular role, Holloway thus became the first Australian-born actor to portray *Dracula* in a major production on the stage. Reviews for Holloway were positive, and fellow actor, Ivan Butler, recalled him later as, "…an older man, gaunt, with deep-set eyes. He was much more like the real Dracula. There was no sexual attraction in those days. Dracula was there for one thing, and one thing only—to take his evening drink." Holloway would work with Deane again when the latter adapted Mary Shelley's *Frankenstein* (1818) for the London stage. Deane cast him as the Monster.

That Dracula man . . .
Bela Lugosi goes into a horror pose as he arrives at Southampton yesterday.

Right, Top to Bottom: The ailing Hollywood horror star hams it up while promoting his 1951 British *Dracula* tour in a local newspaper, and two local newspaper ads for Lugosi's '51 UK tour (the bottom one is from Brighton's *The Herald* for April 28, 1951)

If he had returned to Australia in 1929, then it is highly possible that he would have been given the title role in the production. Tait and Tallis were both eager to bring Holloway back to Australia for a major production, and his years of experience, and age, would have made him a logical, and perfect, choice. What will always remain in doubt is if a presence, such as Holloway's, would have made any difference on the success, or failure, of the play. This no slight on Jarry, whose *Dracula* was praised by all who saw it, but Holloway would have brought a certain expectation with him. Holloway never did return to Australia, but his passing, at the age of 66 in London in 1952, was widely reported. Not one obituary in Australia mentioned his star turn on the London stage as the Count.

Sadly, none of the actors ever wrote memoirs that mentioned *Dracula*, nor, outside of tantalizing glimpses provided by Ashton Jarry over the years, none of them were apparently ever even asked about it. It would appear that, to those involved, they either did not realize the historic significance of the play, or perhaps they just didn't want to acknowledge the fact that it had not been the success that it was expected to be.

Postscript

It would take nearly 50 years after the first attempt till a full-scale Australian tour of *Dracula* would

José Lifante (who later appeared in Jorge "Jordi" Grau's bleak zombie flick **THE LIVING DEAD AT THE MANCHESTER MORGUE**) as you-know-who in a 1972 Spanish stage production of you-know-what

prove a roaring success. This time the play had some serious heavyweights behind it. Using the script by Deane and Balderston, Sir Robert Helpmann put together a stunningly effective production, using Edward Gorey's set and costume designs from the American stage production of the 1970s.

Cast as Dracula was the popular young and handsomely debonair actor John Waters. Where others overacted the character or threw on a quasi-European accent, à la Bela Lugosi, Waters played the part relatively straight, which, added to the play's use of contemporary dress, no doubt helped its overall appeal. The reviews were excellent, and the play proved to be incredibly popular. Thanks to the Hammer films and Christopher Lee's interpretation, the public was ready for a Dracula who wasn't over-the-top.

The play ran in Sydney from August 1978, until the end of the year. It then hit the road, playing in Adelaide for all of January 1979, before moving to Melbourne for a successful run lasting just under two months.

It had taken nearly 50 years, but, finally, *Dracula* was the hit in Australia that Tallis and Tait had always expected it to be.

Sources

Books

Skal, David J, *Hollywood Gothic: The Tangled Web of Dracula from Novel to Stage to Screen*. New York: W.W. Norton, 1990
Tait, Viola: *A Family of Brothers*. William Heinmann Australia Pty Ltd., 1971

Newspapers

Australia

New South Wales
Barrier Miner
Braidwood Dispatch
Cessnock Eagle and South Maitland Recorder
Daily Advertiser
Newcastle Morning Herald and Miners Advocate
Northern Star
Southern Record
Sunday Times
Sydney Morning Herald
The Armidale Chronicle
Truth

Queensland
Brisbane Courier
Evening Post
Figaro
Truth

South Australia
News
The Advertiser
The Mail
The Register
Tasmania
Illustrated Tasmanian Mail
The Examiner
The Mercury
The North Western Advocate
VICTORIA
Table Talk
The Age
The Argus
The Australasian

Western Australia
Daily News
Geraldton Guardian
Kalgoorlie Miner
Mirror
Sunday Times
The West Australian

England
Bath Chronicle
Citizen
Cycling
Derby Daily Telegraph
Evening News
Freeman's Journal and Daily Commercial Advertiser
Glasgow Herald
Leamington Spa Courier and Warwickshire Standard
Manchester Courier
Punch
Sunderland Daily Echo
The Era
The Evening Telegraph and Post
The Globe
The Nottingham Evening Post
The Sheffield Daily Telegraph

New Zealand
Auckland Star
Evening Post
New Zealand Herald

Other Sources

J.C. Williamson Ltd. Magazine, June 1929

Unpublished

NLA MS 5783
NAA: A1336, 17929
Probate of Leon Henry Jarry
SAG History. *http://www.sagaftra.org/history/sag*

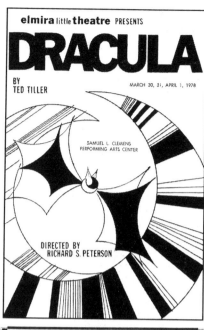

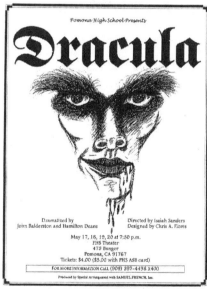

Top: Program for a 1978 stage version in Elmira, New York. **Above:** Ad for an American high school stage production from California, *circa* the 1980s (?)

THE AZTEC MUMMY – **Top:** Mexican lobby card for the first film in the trilogy. **Above Left:** The film's original Spanish title card. **Above:** Italian *2-fogli manifesto* poster (art by Saragna) for the same film. **Left:** A detail of Popoca's ugly mug from original poster artwork

¡VIVA LA MOMIA!

by Bill Adcock

Mexican cinema is something I think a lot of cult cinephiles overlook; they might be aware of El Santo's filmography, but overall I think much of the country's rich cinematic history, especially with genre films such as horror and sci-fi, is passed over. And that's a shame, because Mexico's produced some weird and wonderful gems. By way of example, I'll be looking at the Aztec Mummy *trilogy—a unique mélange of pop culture influences overlaid on top of Mexican cultural heritage, these films are perfect representatives of what Mexico was producing at this time.*

THE AZTEC MUMMY
(*La momia azteca*)
Mexico, 1957. D. Rafael Portillo

Dr. Eduardo Almada believes he can use hypnosis to regress a patient into a past life, waking them from hypnosis will full memory of who they were in the past. When he tries to present this hypothesis at a scientific conference, he's laughed out of the room. Determined to help him, his fiancée Flor offers to let him hypnotize her. When he does so, he learns that in a past life she was an Aztec maiden, Xóchitl, raised from birth to be sacrificed to the jaguar god Tezcatlipoca. When her virgin status is nearly compromised by her love for the warrior Popoca, she is sacrificed and he buried alive to guard her tomb, and with it, the map to find the "Aztec Treasure," inscribed on a breastplate worn by Xóchitl.

Dr. Almada realizes that if he finds the breastplate, he can prove his theory of past life regression (I feel like his plan's missing a few steps here – "I found this breastplate using recovered memories from my hypnotized girlfriend" doesn't seem any less laughable to me than his initial statement of "I think I can use hypnosis to make people remember past lives.") and restore his standing in the local scientific community, and immediately sets out with Flor, her father, and his cowardly assistant Pinacate to find the breastplate. Unfortunately,

Italian DVD set cover, which utilizes the original Italian poster art

one of the other scientists at the conference, Dr. Krupp, is secretly the masked criminal known as "the Bat"—and he intends to steal the breastplate and find the Aztec Treasure to finance his illegal

experiments. The Bat's thugs arrive at Dr. Almada's house at the same time as Popoca does…

One of the downsides of a film falling into the public domain, I think, is how rarely the effort gets put in to clean up and produce a really high-quality release. I have these three films in a boxed set put out by BCI/Eclipse, and the quality just isn't great. This film is very dark, at least in the copy I have, and during the last ten minutes or so it's almost impossible to tell exactly what's going on.

This film not only capitalizes on Universal's **THE MUMMY** (1932, USA) with its doomed romance involving a temple virgin, but also on the "past life" craze triggered by the 1952 case of Virginia Tighe, a Colorado housewife who, under hypnosis, recalled a former life as a 19th-Century Irishwoman named Bridey Murphy. Her story was sensationalized in two 1956 films, **THE SEARCH FOR BRIDEY MURPHY** and **I'VE LIVED BEFORE**. The AIP film **THE SHE-CREATURE** was likewise a capitalization on the Bridey Murphy craze, for what it's worth.

Popoca is no Imhotep, however, being essentially a big, dry zombie, capable of sneaking around but mostly just snarling like Karloff's Frankenstein's Monster and flailing his arms. Despite having the film named after him, the Aztec Mummy only has about five minutes of screentime.

THE CURSE OF THE AZTEC MUMMY

(*La maldición de la momia azteca*)
Mexico, 1957. D. Rafael Portillo

Yes, the sequel came out the same year as the original; yes, I know that's never a good sign. Bear with me here. I've seen this film referred to as the weakest in the franchise, and it tends to be the film people who watch this series see last due to the release history of these films in the USA, but while it has its weak links, it's also, in my opinion, the most tightly-focused of the three *Aztec Mummy* films.

Unmasked as the Bat at the end of the previous film, Dr. Krupp is arrested for his crimes, but when attempts at interrogating him at the police station go nowhere (it couldn't possibly be because Dr. Almada and his entire entourage, including his little brother Pepe, are in the room!), the chief of police arranges to have Krupp transferred to another facility. This, of course, sets up the perfect opportunity for Krupp's gang to stage a rescue. The rescue attempt is almost foiled when masked *luchador* superhero El Ángel shows up—yes, readers, this film adds a *lucha* hero element! El Ángel is no El Santo, however, and Krupp and his gang get away.

Dr. Almada & Co. team-up with the mysterious El Ángel to try and track Dr. Krupp down and bring him back to justice; Krupp, meanwhile, is still on the track of the Aztec Treasure, and to find it without having to fight the mummy of Popoca, he kidnaps Flor for re-hypnosis. If Dr. Krupp can force her to remember her past life as Xóchitl again, he can use her to find the treasure chamber. As he gloatingly explains, with the Aztec Treasure, he'll be able to finance experiments guaranteed to make him immortal!

Once again, the Aztec Mummy is relegated to a side-note in his own film, arriving only in the last ten minutes of this very short feature (runtime 63 minutes). It's kind of interesting the way that works: we as audiences tend to be conditioned to seeing the monster as the villain of a film; we anticipate the conflict in these movies to be between Dr. Almada (as the good guy) and the Aztec Mummy (as the bad guy), but it's absolutely not the case here. Instead, we have the very pulpy Dr. Krupp/The Bat as our villain, and most of each film's runtime is devoted to the moral struggle between his villainy and Dr. Almada's nobility, with the Aztec Mummy existing almost in a separate storyline all together. Popoca is a cursed creature, tasked for all eternity with guarding the resting place of the Aztec Treasure, and his actions never stray from fulfilling that role.

The character of El Ángel is kind of problematic here; I will not spoil his secret identity, but I will say he's a character who appeared in the last film, in which he was most emphatically *not* moonlighting as a masked *luchador* superhero. With **CURSE OF THE AZTEC MUMMY** beginning only a few hours at most after the end of **THE AZTEC MUMMY**, it's not as if we can even pretend that the events of the first film inspired him to take up the mask and cape—there was literally no time in-between! If the filmmakers were attempting to capitalize on the popularity of figures like El Santo, they did not go about it successfully; El Ángel is—to put it bluntly—incompetent, his attempts to thwart villainy only serving to make the villains more successful. Given his absence from the third film in the series, I'm guessing that Rafael Portillo and writer/producer Alfredo Salazar realized that El Ángel elicited jeers, not cheers, from audiences, and wisely wrote him out.

THE ROBOT VS. THE AZTEC MUMMY

(*La momia azteca contra el robot humano*)
Mexico, 1958. D. Rafael Portillo

The final film in the series is also the one most people have seen. It was featured in a 1989 episode of *Mystery Science Theater 3000*, and has had numerous dollar-bin DVD releases. Since two-thirds of this film's running time (yes, *really!*) is taken up by recapping the previous two films, I won't linger too long on synopsis here.

Suffice to say, Dr. Krupp, having abandoned his alter-ego of The Bat, has hit upon a new scheme to seize the Aztec Treasure. He has built a "human robot"—assembled from human cadavers and mechanical parts, brought to life by the application of radium—which he intends to sic on Popoca, destroying the Aztec Mummy and thus leaving himself free to claim the treasure for himself, which he will use to finance the construction of an army of human robots and conquer the world!

To find and destroy Popoca, however, he once more kidnaps Flor, knowing that her past life as the maiden Xóchitl has given her a psychic link to the Aztec Mummy. This brings Dr. Almada & Co. quick on Krupp's heels, eager to rescue Flor, destroy the Human Robot and stop Dr. Krupp once and for all.

Mexican poster for **THE CURSE OF THE AZTEC MUMMY** (art unsigned)

Mummy's Coming! Popoca can't stand people messing with his stuff—gangsters least of all!

The robot is one of the more genuinely-mechanical examples I've seen in film, comparing favorably to the great Torg in **SANTA CLAUS CONQUERS THE MARTIANS** (1964, USA, D: Nicholas Webster) and a few sturdy steps up from the boxy brute in **DEVIL GIRL FROM MARS** (1954, UK, D: David MacDonald). The "Republic Robot" from the old serials is one of the few that I can think of offhand that looks more like a human-shaped machine, instead of a man in a boxy costume. Unfortunately, while the robot looks good, the fight sequence between it and Popoca is stunning in its lack of energy; a vague, halfhearted shoving match is all we get, and only a minute or two of that before Almada's intervention decides the fight.

Overall, it's a bit disappointing that this is the film people know the *Aztec Mummy* franchise for; while none of the films are indelible classics to stun and amaze, I think they deserve a better legacy than K. Gordon Murray's cheap dub of this film.

On the other hand, this, even more than the other two films, is Dr. Krupp's movie. While the other two movies are driven in large part by his machinations, it's here we really spend a lot of time with him front and center, and I have to say that he's one of my favorite cinematic mad scientists, and that favor can be laid squarely at the feet of

actor Luis Aceves Castaneda, who played him in all three films (his *luchador* alter-ego, the Bat, was played by actual *luchador* El Murciélago ["The Bat" in English]). Castaneda's performance swings from suave and manipulative to near-feral fury, baring his teeth with his eyeballs nearly bugging out of his head. He's also impressively physical; unlike the many physically-frail mad scientists one often sees, Castaneda was a beefy guy, and whenever he stands over Flor there's a constant sense of him being able to just *flatten* her like a bug under his thumb if he doesn't get his way, which really worked for me.

The rest of the cast I find very bland, with no real energy to the performances or standout characters, but having a good villain really makes these movies. Without Krupp chewing on the scenery, I think these films would be a lot less enjoyable.

I mentioned at the beginning that I considered this series a good representation of Mexican cinema. What did I mean by that? The *lucha* element is obvious, but a big one is the way the film blends and blurs distinctions between science and supernatural.

There's a sequence in the first film where, having laughed Dr. Almada out of the room for daring to suggest the possibility of reincarnation, his colleagues then proceed to warn him—upon learning he intends to seek the Aztec Breastplate—about the dangers of stirring-up evil spirits and getting cursed by them. I found this a bit confusing at first, until I realized: they weren't lambasting his reincarnation idea because it was unscientific, they were lambasting it because it was un-*Catholic*. Mexico being a strongly Catholic country, and even more so in 1957 than today, concerns of demons and spiritual evil are strong, and Dr. Almada's suggestion regarding past lives goes against everything his colleagues have grown up hearing in church. While in this film their concerns are often couched in language referencing "mysteries of nature," really they're talking about God, the Devil and Catholic doctrine.

And it's not just Dr. Almada's colleagues, either; Almada makes reference to the "mysteries of nature" after his first encounter with Popoca, agreeing that there are some things Man should not meddle in, and the "evil spirit" animating the mummy is one of them.

It's weird to hear this kind of talk from scientists in films; while B-movies from the United States during this period frequently ended with coda along the lines of "He tampered in God's domain" or "There are some things Man was not meant to know," it's typically just that—a token throwaway line at the end of the film while the monster's carcass is burning in the background. Here it's a through-line carried from beginning to end; the audience isn't bludgeoned with it, but it's definitely noticeable, which I think makes these films a good introduction for more secular viewers like myself to the strong Catholic influence in Mexican genre cinema; an easing into the realization that these films are the product of a different culture and a different set of values than we might be used to, especially in the 21st Century.

I can't think of any other country where I've seen this sort of thing, where sober, serious men of science discuss evil spirits and curses as if they were proven, quantifiable things whose existence were common knowledge. I'm much more used to encountering films wherein science and the supernatural are presented as being in conflict. As Van Helsing so aptly put it, the vampire's greatest strength lies in that his existence is disbelieved. It's not just in the *Aztec Mummy* films either. Other Mexican horror films I've watched, such as **THE BLACK PIT OF DR. M** (*Misterios de ultratumba*, 1959, D: Fernando Méndez) and **THE BRAINIAC** (*El barón del terror*, 1962, D: Chano Urueta) display the same sort of matter-of-factness in their approach to science and the supernatural.

la Momia Azteca

Above: Mexican poster. **Top:** "Alejandro Waldinski"/Alex Wald art for a cardboard mini-standee of Popoca which was included as part of trash rockers Southern Culture On The Skids' *Santo Swings* 7" EP (Estrus Records, 1996)

171

I would be remiss if I did not talk about the infusion of *luchador* superheroics in the series, since *luchador* heroes tend to be the first thing most people who are aware of Mexican genre cinema think of, thanks to the popularity of El Santo and Blue Demon. As far as the *lucha* element goes, I think that CURSE OF THE AZTEC MUMMY is a poor introduction to *luchador* movies, given El Ángel's propensity towards failure, but in a pinch, hey, it's a movie where a man in tights and a mask is working with the police and nobody bats an eye at any of that. It might be a bit of an adjustment to think of these wrestlers as "superheroes," but that's exactly the sort of role they play: more Batman than Superman, and in some cases closer to pulp heroic figures like Doc Savage. For that matter, Dr. Krupp's alter-ego of The Bat is very much in keeping with pulp villains like Dr. Satan.

I think this shows where Mexico stood in the pop culture pecking order of the day; though made in 1957 and 1958, these movies show the influence of American pop culture from twenty years earlier; pulp magazines, Republic serials, and Universal horror films. Was it a matter of these things taking time to diffuse down to Mexico? Or was this a matter of tribute from Rafael Portillo and producer/screenwriter Alfredo Salazar to pop culture they'd consumed 20 years earlier? I can't say.

The Aztec Mummy archetype would pop up again periodically in later films: THE WRESTLING WOMEN VS. THE AZTEC MUMMY (*Las luchadoras contra la momia*, 1964, D: René Cardona, Sr.) features a mummified Aztec warrior named Temozoc and is sometimes included as a fourth film in this series; then there's the 1975 episode of *Kolchak: The Night Stalker* entitled "Legacy of Terror", and even as recently as 2007, one menaced the *luchador* community in MIL MASCARAS VS. THE AZTEC MUMMY (USA, Ds: "Andrew Quint"/Jeff Burr, Chip Gubera). Even the reanimated Toltec sorcerers of 1985's THE DARK POWER (USA, D: Phil Smoot) could be considered close cousins of the Aztec Mummy.

While Popoca and Temozoc appear as "natural" mummies—i.e., bodies desiccated by the conditions of their burial, preventing decay—thus making them very similar to the real-life Mummies of Guanajuato, the remains of cholera victims from 1833. Later Aztec Mummies are frequently depicted as having been prepared similarly to Egyptian mummies, which simply isn't correct. When the Aztecs did prepare mummies (as opposed to letting the dry air of Mexico do it for them), they were posed in a sitting position and bound in rope instead of being wrapped in

Mexican lobby card for **THE ROBOT VS. THE AZTEC MUMMY** (art unsigned)

bandages and laying flat in a sarcophagus, as the mummy in **MIL MASCARAS VS. THE AZTEC MUMMY** is shown to be.

Unfortunately, the Aztec Mummy does not seem to have caught on in film the way his Egyptian cousins have, most likely because of the huge media frenzy around the opening of Tutankhamen's tomb in 1922, right near the birth of cinema. I would love to see a renaissance of Mesoamerican horror, especially as we learn more and more about the fascinating civilizations of the Aztecs, the Maya, the Zapotecs, the Toltecs, Olmecs, and other cultures of Central and South America. Their folklore offers endless opportunities to breathe new life into classic monsters, from mummies to lycanthropes, vampires and more. We could be up to our lip labrets in werejaguars, demonic Camazotz bats, feathered serpents and Aztec Mummies… now, isn't *that* a cinematic world you'd rather live in?!

Above: US press ad-mat for a classic K. Gordon Murray Mexi-monster double-bill. **Left:** Hispanic US DVD cover for **THE WRESTLING WOMEN VS. THE AZTEC MUMMY**, with gorgeous grapplin' gals The Golden Rubí (Elizabeth Campbell) and her tag-partner Gloria Venus (Lorena Velázquez) placed prominently, for obvious reasons

MONSTERS!

AN ILLUSTRATED MOVIE HISTORY

MONSTER! A WORD, THE VERY MENTION OF WHICH, EVOKES OUR DEEPEST AND MOST PRIMAL OF FEARS. AS OLD AS TIME, THE CONCEPT OF THE MONSTER (A SUPER-HUMAN OR SUPER-NATURAL BEING THAT DWELLS WITHIN OUR COLLECTIVE CONSCIOUSNESS) IS AS OLD AS THE HUMAN RACE ITSELF.

A CONCEPT THAT GREW OUT OF PRIMITIVE RELIGIONS, AND THROUGH ART AND LITERATURE GAINED CULTURAL IMPORTANCE, WITH THE EMERGENCE OF THE MOVING IMAGE, THE CONSTRUCT OF THE MONSTER WAS TO TAKE ON A BY FAR GREATER SIGNIFICANCE. A NATURAL PROGRESSION OF THE CINEMATIC FORMULA, THE MONSTER MOVIE (AT LEAST AS WE UNDERSTAND IT TODAY) FIRST CAME TO FRUITION IN 1910.

A RATHER LOOSE ADAPTATION OF MARY SHELLEY'S FRANKENSTEIN (OR THE MODERN PROMETHEUS), IT WAS THE PIONEERING THOMAS EDISON THAT FIRST BROUGHT THE CREATURE FEATURE TO THEATRICAL AUDIENCES.

FEATURING CHARLES OGLE IN SOMEWHAT RUDIMENTARY (BUT NO LESS EFFECTIVE) MAKE-UP, EDISON'S WORK WAS TO REALISE THE TRUE POTENTIAL OF THE MONSTER MOVIE. A 16 MINUTE SHORT THAT FOCUSSED ON FRANKENSTEIN'S DIVIDED LOYALTIES BETWEEN HIS CREATION AND HIS BRIDE-TO-BE, DESPITE IT'S RATHER EXAGGERATED THEATRICS, THE FILM WAS TO FORWARD A RATHER UNIQUE TAKE ON SHELLEY'S ORIGINAL SOURCE-WORK.

PART ONE:
THE SILENT ERA

WORDS AND
PICTURES
BY ANDY ROSS

WITH THE MOTION PICTURE AN EXCITING NEW TREND, THE RAW APPEAL OF THE MONSTER MOVIE WAS READILY EMBRACED ON GERMANIC SOIL. HEAVILY INFLUENCED BY JEWISH FOLKLORE, DER GOLEM (1920) CAME TO TELL OF A RESURRECTED CLAY BEHOMETH'S UNREQUITED LOVE FOR A BEAUTIFUL WOMAN.

SIMILARLY EMBRACING THE ARTISTIC VOGUE OF EXPRESSIONISM, DAS CABINET DES DR. CALIGARI (1920) PROFFERED A SURREAL TAKE ON BOTH SONAMBULISM AND MIND CONTROL.

AN UNAUTHORISED RE-TELLING OF BRAM STOKER'S 1897 NOVEL DRACULA, IN THE WAKE OF LEGAL ACTION BROUGHT ABOUT BY THE AUTHOR'S WIDOW, NOSFERATU (1922) WAS TO FORCE ITS PRODUCERS, PRANA FILMS INTO BANKRUPTCY.

A FILM THAT EXISTS SOLELY THROUGH THE TENACTITY OF FILM HISTORIANS, THAT NOSFERATU CAN BE VIEWED IN ITS ENTIRETY STANDS AS A TESTAMENT TO THOSE WHO UNDERSTOOD ITS ARTISTIC IMPORTANCE.

DIRECTED BY F.W. MURNAU AND STARRING MAX SHRECK AS THE NEFARIOUS COUNT ORLOCK, GIVEN ITS SOMEWHAT CONTROVERSIAL NATURE, NOSFERATU HAS NEVER THE LESS STOOD THE TEST OF TIME TO BECOME ONE OF THE MOST LAUDED OF THE SILENT ERA MONSTER MOVIES.

A JOINT DANISH/SWEDISH PRODUCTION RELEASED IN 1922 HAXAN OR WITCHCRAFT THROUGH THE AGES WAS TO VENTURE INTO THE GRIZZLY REALMS OF MEDIEVAL SUPERSTITION.

A LABOR OF LOVE FROM WRITER/DIRECTOR BENJEMEN CHRISTENSON (WHO ALSO APPEARED AS THE DEVIL IN THE PRODUCTION), THROUGH IT'S VIBRANT STORY-TELLING, WONDERFUL CHARACTERIZATIONS AND INGENIOUS SPECIAL EFFECTS, THE FILM WAS TO PROFFER A PARTICULARLY CHILLING REMINDER OF OUR ANCESTOR'S BELIEFS IN DIABOLICAL WITCHCRAFT.

A FEATURE LENGTH ADAPTATION OF ROBERT LOUIS STEVENSON'S TIMELESS CLASSIC, DR JEKYLL AND MR HYDE (1920) WITNESSED THE WONDERFUL JOHN BARRYMORE IN THE FILM'S DUAL CENTRAL PERFORMANCE. LIKE SHELLEY'S FRANKENSTEIN , A JOURNEY INTO THE FOLLIES OF THE SCIENTIFIC MIND, WHEN JEKYLL SEEKS TO PHYSICALLY SEPERATE THE POLAR OPPOSITES OF HIS PERSONALITY, THE MONSTROUS MR HYDE IS BORN. A RELATIVELY FAITHFUL RE-TELLING OF THE STORY, DR JEKYLL AND MR HYDE PRE-EMPTED A PREFERENCE TOWARDS THE MORE ESTABLISHED ARCHETYPES OF HORROR LITERATURE.

FOUNDED IN 1912 BY CARL LAEMMLE, IT WAS THE CALIFORNIA BASED UNIVERSAL STUDIOS THAT NOT ONLY EMBRACED, BUT PERPETUATED THE CLASSIC MONSTER MOVIE.

BORN ON APRIL FOOL'S DAY 1883, AND UNDER THE TRUNCATED FORENAME OF 'LON', LEONIDAS FRANK CHANEY WAS TO RISE TO PROMINENCE AS UNIVERSAL'S TITULAR MASTER OF MENACE. BORN OF DEAF/MUTE PARENTS, AS A YOUNGSTER LON CHANEY HAD NOT ONLY LEARNED SIGN LANGUAGE, BUT HAD LIKEWISE MASTERED THE ART OF MIME. AN ACTOR WHO GENUINELY SUFFERED FOR HIS ART, THROUGH HIS MOST FAMOUS ROLES AS QUASIMODO IN THE HUNCHBACK OF NOTRE DAME (1923), AND AS ERIK IN THE PHANTOM OF THE OPERA (1925) LON CHANEY WAS TO SECURE LEGENDARY STATUS IN THE HORROR HALL OF FAME.

WITH THE ACTOR SCHEDULED TO PLAY STOKER'S COUNT IN THE FIRST OFFICIAL ADAPTATION OF UNIVERSAL'S DRACULA, CHANEY'S UNTIMELY DEATH FROM THROAT CANCER WAS TO PAVE THE WAY FOR AN ACTOR WHO, IN 1927 HAD APPEARED IN A BROADWAY RENDITON OF THE STORY.

WITH HIS THICK HUNGARIAN ACCENT, PIERCING GAZE, AND FLAMOYANT ON-SCREEN PERSONA, EVEN TO THIS DAY, HIS IS A NAME THAT REMAINS SYNONYMOUS WITH THE ROLE.

BELA LUGOSI.

177

The suitably lurid US one-sheet poster (art unsigned)

MY MONSTER MOVIE MARATHON DIARY
(Part 3)

Tackling the **Alligator** *films, plus other assorted goodies!*

A selection of reviews by Christos Mouroukis

Lunchtime for baby – baby alien that is! From the gloriously grotesque UK clas*sick* **INSEMINOID**

Greetings from Greece (where I live), and welcome to Pt. 3 of "My Monster Movie Marathon Diary"! Since, as per the title, this series of articles is presented in "diary" form, please allow me to give you a bit of context before we head on to the film reviews…

Just so you know, Greece is a small country in the Mediterranean area, with a population of around 11,000,000, currently in its sixth year of deep financial crisis and under the Memorandum of Understanding regime, which prevents the people from having any basic human rights. It is also the only country in the world in which capital controls have been enforced to all bank accounts, allowing only for a daily withdrawal of up to €60 (that's Euros) per account. There are plenty of conspiracy theories surrounding these facts, but I have one of my own: that this latest measure was taken as a means for panic-stricken upper class idiots to queue in front of ATMs, in order to meet, mate, and multiply their breed.

Right now in Greece there is a huge wave of refugees from Syria and elsewhere entering the country, looking for a better life in Europe, because war destroyed everything they had back home. Once they enter Greece, usually via boat, they have to face plenty of assholes who exploit them, and sell them bottles of water, bathroom use, and mobile phone battery charge at insane amounts of money. Luckily, they also come across kind people who volunteer to help them. The reason the second group does that is because they recognize that a refugee kid drowning in the middle of the ocean is no different to their own kid. However, Greece's parliament right now is home to the largest Nazi party in the world, and racism is rampant. The 450,000-some votes that this party assembled are mostly from people who all they know about the immigration situation is what they see on television. If all you know about a situation is what you saw on TV, then you don't know jack shit. The news on TV is these people's entertainment, and musical cues are offered along

Italian *2-fogli manifesto* poster for **INVASION OF THE BODY SNATCHERS** (art by Alessandro Biffignandi)

with dramatic performances from the hosts, all in the name of brainwashing.

Cinema, on the other hand, is a totally different beast. Even the major studio films are usually "by-the-numbers" only when it comes to their strict screenplays, and running times, for example, are just random. There is rarely a pattern about running times in feature films, which is the exact opposite of TV series and their time slots. Sure, many have turned running

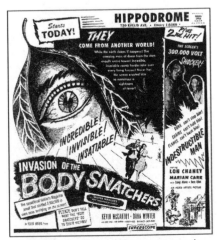

Contemporaneous US newspaper ad

times into a formula before, such as the 60-minute cheapies from the exploitation producers of the '30s, or the 70-minute Roger Corman films, or the 60-minute adult films that'd get screened in New York's 42nd Street theaters, or the 90-minute Fred Olen Ray pictures, but luckily, this is one aspect in which there is still great freedom in movie-making.

I used to avoid TV at all costs, but with the recent flood of quality genre material this has changed. The best thing I watched this month was the second season of *Agent Carter* (2015-present) which is highly recommended (although I'm dying to make an "Agent Farter" joke here). In another attempt of catching-up with good television, I sat down and watched **ICE AGE: THE GREAT EGG-SCAPADE** (2016, USA, D: Ricardo Curtis) only to discover that the so-called "TV special" was just a rehash of sequences from the previous theatrical features.

Small-screen fare aside, please read below my reviews of all monster features that I had the pleasure of acquiring recently. To be more precise—and honest—I had a pile of 50 SyFy discs stashed here in my place which I was planning to review for this column in due time, but a series of (fortunately happy) events in my life took the majority of my free time, and these had to go. I know you can't live without my commentary on silly CGI monster movies, but I had to sacrifice something. Not to mention that I was really suffering watching such flicks, and entertainment had to again become a priority, rather than self-torture. As a result, the remaining flicks that will make up the content of this column until its end will look more serious.

Tuesday, March 1, 2016

INVASION OF THE BODY SNATCHERS

USA, 1956. D: Don Siegel

Ad-lines: *"...there was nothing to hold onto – except each other." "They come from another world!"*

Dr. Hill (an uncredited Whit Bissell who went on to star in **THE TIME MACHINE** [1960, USA, D: George Pal]) is seeing a patient (Kevin McCarthy, who can also be seen in this magazine's favourite lycanthrope-fest **THE HOWLING** [1981, USA, D: Joe Dante]) recently admitted to the California hospital he is working at, and he says that he is a doctor from Santa Mira where, again as he says, terrible things have happened. He will narrate all these unbelievable things in an extended flashback which is actually the entire movie, and although some of the suspense is taken away due to the employment of this technique (for example, we know for sure, that the protagonist will survive, no matter what, hence despite what happens, no danger appears to be too big for him) the film never fails to excite. In other "don't go there" methods, Orson Welles was approached to participate in the introductory voice-over, but he passed.

The events go like this: Several people in Santa Mira believe that their loved ones have been replaced by other people with identical appearances. In psychiatry this is the quite rare Capgras delusion (about which you can read more over at: *https://en.wikipedia.org/wiki/Capgras_delusion*) and at first this is what the good doctor believes, that his townsfolk suffer some kind of mass paranoia (you can't blame him either, as this was somewhat prevalent in the mid-'50s when this was made), but one thing leads to another and he joins forces with his ex-girlfriend (TV-star Dana Wynter, who also appeared in the occasional feature such as **THE CRIMSON PIRATE** [1952, USA, D: Robert Siodmak]). This is a pioneering move on the screenplay's part, as the "exes getting back together and becoming heroes" didn't become popular until '90s Hollywood action films. Together they will discover that pods (the film features a huge cast of practical pods, making this the origin of the "pod-cast" term) that came from the sky have invaded their small town, and slowly ("cell for cell, atom for atom" as one already-infected character says) replace the human population with identical aliens, in what was the most horrific "identity theft" scenario of all film history up to that point. There are ways to beat the invasion (which sounds like a huge *The X Files* [1993-present] inspiration if you ask me), such as staying awake (**A NIGHTMARE ON ELM STREET** [1984, USA, D: Wes Craven], anyone?) and trying to leave town as soon as possible and ask for help from the authorities that have not yet been corrupted, but there will be obstacles. It certainly sounds like anti-communist propaganda, but today it is better viewed as an Id-commentary.

Based on Jack Finney's *Collier's* magazine serial (also published in novel form; it was called *The Body Snatchers*, and this is the title that the film would originally use, but plans were changed in order to avoid confusion with the Boris Karloff/Bela Lugosi vehicle **THE BODY SNATCHER** [1945, USA, D: Robert Wise]. The titles that were since then proposed, included *They Come from Another World, Better Off Dead, Sleep No More, Evil in the Night,* and *World in Danger*, but the one we came to know was ultimately chosen) and adapted into screenplay format by Daniel Mainwaring (who previously penned many a film *noir*, including **OUT OF THE PAST** [1947, USA, D: Jacques Tourneur], and this style is apparent especially to the actions of the lead couple

here) and an uncredited Richard Collins (mostly known for his TV work), this is clearly one of the most influential works of science fiction from the '50s and was deservedly selected for preservation by the Library of Congress' U.S. National Film Registry in 1994. This ultimate genre classic has also been famously remade as **INVASION OF THE BODY SNATCHERS** (1978, USA, D: Philip Kaufman) and **BODY SNATCHERS** (1993, USA, D: Abel Ferrara). Its most recent remake is the Nicole Kidman vehicle **THE INVASION** (2007, USA, Australia, Ds: Oliver Hirschbiegel, James McTeigue) which I will review in one of the near future instalments of this column.

It was originally planned as a $454,864-budget film that would be shot in 24 days, but it was soon cut down to $350,000 and could afford only 20 days of shooting. At the end of the day, the principal photography was finished in (depending on your source) 19 or 23 days; although it may be 19 days of shooting + breaks = 23 days (not counting some later, additional filming), and the footage was delivered on a $382,190 budget. It was worth every penny, as it grossed more than $3,000,000. The promotional campaign famously included papier-mâché pods displayed in theatre lobbies. I wish we had gimmicks like this today.

Much discussion ensued in regards to the film's fram-

Italian *locandina* for **INVASION OF THE BODYSNATCHERS** (art by Studio Favalli)

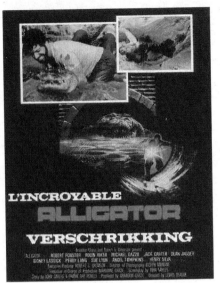

L'INCROYABLE

ALLIGATOR

VERSCHRIKKING

ALLIGATOR ROBERT FORSTER ROBIN RIKER MICHAEL GAZZO JACK CARTER DEAN JAGGER
SIDNEY LASSICK PERRY LANG SUE LYON ANGEL TOMPKINS HENRY SILVA

Belgian poster for **ALLIGATOR**

ing. It was originally set to be cinematographed using the Superscope aspect ratio; however it was shot in 1.85:1. Superscope was finally employed in post-production and resulted in a 2.00:1 aspect ratio. It is still very debatable on which version, format, and aspect ratio you should choose in order to see this properly (and as closely to director of photography Ellsworth Fredericks' intentions; his final credit as a cinematographer was **EYE OF THE CAT** [1969, USA, D: David Lowell Rich], which is a film that may be of interest to Wildside/Kronos readers.), but I trust that Tim and Steve will sort some home video release options at the end of this very issue!

Tuesday, March 15, 2016

ALLIGATOR

USA, 1980. D: Lewis Teague

Ad-lines: *"At first, no one believed. But now, no one will ever forget!" "Beneath Those Manholes, a Man-Eater is waiting..." "It lives 50 feet beneath the city. It's 36 feet long. It weighs 2,000 pounds...And it's about to break out!" "He's Up From the Sewers And Nobody's Safe..." "It's 36 feet long, weighs 2000 pounds, lives 50 feet below the city. Nobody knows it's down there except the people it eats."*

An average American family is visiting a zoo in which crocodiles are used as spectacle. Things go wrong and one of their trainers gets slaughtered before the audience's eyes—amid comments from

them on the blood being fake, etc. This is actually a slap-in-your-face kind of commentary on entertainment, and it's not the only thing this film has to say. Their young daughter Marisa (Leslie Brown) purchases a baby crocodile there...and to be honest with you, I was expecting her to get bored by it and flush it down the drain, in order for the film to comment on irresponsible youngsters owning pets as if they are toys, but instead the film goes into further liberal commentary by having the father throw the animal down the toilet as he says he had done the same thing previously with a hamster! The baby alligator finds his way to the Chicago sewer system[1], which is of course polluted, and it mutates the beast into the biggest (36 feet, as it is often said in the film) crocodile ever. How did he become that big? He was feeding on pet dog corpses that were disposed there by an underground industry that thrives on illegal experiments (backed by sleazy rich person Slade, played by Dean Jagger from **GAME OF DEATH** [1978, Hong Kong/USA, Ds: Robert Clouse, Bruce Lee]); in case you needed further aggressive commentary. Anyway, two people lost their lives in the Chicago sewers, and police officer David Madison (Robert Forster, many years before his career's revival with **JACKIE BROWN** [1997, USA, D: Quentin Tarantino]) is assigned to the case. Once the alligator eats his partner Kelly (TV-actor and director Perry Lang)—an important theme here, because as it is said, the protagonist had his previous partner killed in a shootout, too—he seeks assistance from the authority on reptiles, namely Marisa Kendall (now grown-up and played by TV-actress Robin Riker), and together they develop an attraction for each other; because being Robert Forster and kicking alligator butt is not enough; you also need to get the girl! But before reptile butt gets kicked, professional wild animal hunter Colonel Brock comes into the picture, and he is played by badass Henry Silva (just so you get a brief context of where his career was at this point, take into concern that three years later he went on to co-star in **CHAINED HEAT** [1983, USA/West Germany, D: Paul Nicholas]), who surprisingly is not allowed to steal the show, because this is Robert Forster time! And alligator time, because—guess what—the monster has just escaped the sewer and is now free in the city, killing kids in pools, and slaughtering

---

1 The location is debatable. Although Chicago is the most common theory that most reviewers give, if you pay a little bit of attention to detail, you will discover many references that point to Missouri. The story is quite universal, and its aesthetics are really of the "Anywhere Town, USA" variety, so this confusion should not bother you too much. The film was shot in Los Angeles. An earlier version of the film was set in Milwaukee, but that version's screenplay by Frank Ray Perilli was scrapped, and although I haven't read it, I suspect it was for the best, because it has been said that it concerned a beer factory polluting the sewer system...

wealthy people in posh yard parties! Just the way we like our monster movies: anti-authoritarian and unsafe to all!

This is essentially a cop procedure film with a huge monster thrown in, but it is gory enough (it was rated R) to be loved by the average '80s horror movie fan. It may not be as realistic as, say **CRITTERS** (1986, USA/UK, D: Stephen Herek) but it still a piece of cinema about things we don't know, or we mostly didn't knew about back then. What's more, the well-calculated screenplay (it was written by John Sayles of **PIRANHA** [1978, USA/Netherlands, D: Joe Dante] fame, based on his own and Frank Ray Perilli's story—see "Greek VHS Mayhem Part 4: Charles Band" in *Weng's Chop* #7, p.91[2]) makes this an enjoyable experience. Produced by Brandon Chase and Mark L. Rosen (**THE SWORD AND THE SORCERER** [1982, USA, D: Albert Pyun]) on a mere budget of $1,750,000, the film's harsh and welcome commentary along with its self-awareness bordering on parody, worked in its favour with audiences (although it didn't click with all critics) and grossed more than $6,450,000. It was directed by Lewis Teague, whose **CUJO** (1983, USA) will be reviewed in a future *Weng's Chop* "Greek VHS Mayhem" instalment.

---

2   *Weng's Chop* is the genre film bible, and you should be reading its gospels.

ALLIGATOR II: THE MUTATION

USA, 1991. D: Jon Hess

Ad-lines: *"It erupted from the bowels of the city in a lethal frenzy." "It crashed out of the sewers... now there's hell to pay!" "The balance of nature has been tipped... To terror"*

Set in Regent Park City, this film is again about a giant alligator terrorizing citizens, but although it is never made clear, I believe it is not the baby alligator that was left behind in the first film's ending and left the door open for a sequel. Vincent "Vinnie" Brown (Steve Railsback, whose **THE STUNT MAN** [1980, USA, D: Richard Rush] will be reviewed in a future "Greek VHS Mayhem" instalment) is the evil businessman here, who in the name of profit will not take precautions in regards to the threat. It's now up to tough police officer David Hodges (Joseph Bologna, who in recent times did voice work in **ICE AGE: THE MELTDOWN** [2006, USA, D: Carlos Saldanha]) to take action, and he has to do so whilst maintaining a healthy relationship with his reptile expert scientist wife (Dee Wallace, who was doing a lot

Got Gator? Polish poster *[left]* for **ALLIGATOR** (art by Saudok [?]), and *[right]* French poster for **ALLIGATOR II: THE MUTATION**

a **FRIGHTENING** movie with a sense of **FUN**!

Alligator

"EYE-POPPING SCARES AND A SNAPPY SENSE OF HUMOUR"
TIME MAGAZINE

"FULL OF WIT AND LIVELINESS...A TREAT"
L.A WEEKLY

ROBERT FORSTER · ROBIN RIKER · DEAN JAGGER · SUE LYON · HENRY SILVA
Story by JOHN SAYLES & FRANK RAY PERILLI · Produced by BRANDON CHASE · Directed by LEWIS TEAGUE

UK quad poster (art unsigned)

of TV work at this stage in her career) and kicking bad habits such as smoking and parking his car in places he shouldn't. Just so this film is not about middle-aged people, there is also younger cop Rich Harmon (Woody Brown, who is mostly known for his TV work, but could be caught in the occasional feature, such as **THE ACCUSED** [1988, Canada/USA, D: Jonathan Kaplan]) who also has a romantic relationship evolving with Sheri Anderson (Holly Gagnier, also mostly known for her TV work, but could be caught in the occasional feature, such as **GIRLS JUST WANT TO HAVE FUN** [1985, USA, D: Alan Metter]). When the shit hits the fan(s), crocodile hunter Hawk Hawkins (Richard Lynch, who kids today mostly know from Rob Zombie's **HALLOWEEN** [2007, USA]) along with his brother (Kane Hodder; just so you get a brief context on his career at this stage, you have to think that a couple of years later he returned to his favorite part in **JASON GOES TO HELL: THE FINAL FRIDAY**

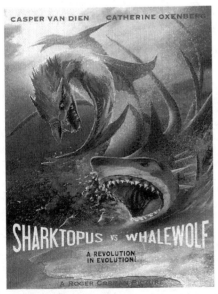

CASPER VAN DIEN   CATHERINE OXENBERG

SHARKTOPUS VS WHALEWOLF

A REVOLUTION IN EVOLUTION!

A ROGER CORMAN PICTURE

[1993, USA, D: Adam Marcus]) join the party, but surprisingly they don't get to steal the show.

This is essentially a PG-13 rehash of the first film, and being a straight-to-video one, you should take this as a warning. It was produced (on a $3,000,000 budget) by Cary Glieberman (who was an associate producer in my favorite Sam Raimi film, **CRIMEWAVE** [1985, USA]) and Brandon Chase, the latter of which was originally set to direct, until Jon Hess (**WATCHERS** [1988, Canada]) was brought onboard, working from a screenplay by Curt Allen (**BLOODSTONE** [1988, USA/India, D: Dwight H. Little]).

Wednesday, March 23, 2016

SHARKTOPUS VS. WHALEWOLF

USA, 2015. D: Kevin O'Neill

Set in the Dominican Republic, this film is about the gang of witch doctor Francois Tiny (Tony Almont from **NOCHE DE CIRCO** [2013, Dominican Republic, D: Alan Nadal Piantini]) that is interested in obtaining the heart of Sharktopus (it is not very clear why this mutant fish is at these sores or why the criminals want it dead) and to achieve that, they hire drunk boat owner and Captain Ray Brady (Casper Van Dien, who looks to be very far from his glory days in films such as Tim Burton's **SLEEPY HOLLOW** [1999, USA/Germany]) along with his assistant Pablo (Jorge Eduardo De Los Santos). In the meantime Dr. Elsa Reinhardt (TV-actress Catherine Oxenberg, who can also be caught in the occasional feature such as **THE LAIR OF THE WHITE WORM** [1988, UK, D: Ken Russell])—in what is a clear nod to Dyanne Thorne and her iconic titular role in **ILSA: SHE WOLF OF THE SS** (1975, Canada, D: Don Edmonds)—and her corny (even for SyFy standards) sidekick nurse Betty (Jennifer Wenger, who was also in the same year's **ALL THROUGH THE HOUSE** [2015, USA, D: Todd Nunes]) are using has-been baseball player Felix Rosa (Mario Arturo Hernández, who was also in the franchise's previous film, albeit in a different part) for an experiment which turns him (in *Frankenstein* fashion) into a creature that resembles a combination of a werewolf and a whale, essentially a whalewolf. What's more, the evil scientist is teaching it some tricks, because, it needs to be a good pet... It is inevitable that the two creatures will fight each other, and will even kill a few humans on their way to the showdown's location which is—*ahem*—a baseball stadium!

An interesting observation I made when I was watching this film was how concerned it was about technology, and how this has become part of our lives, essentially going to the extent of dictating the way we live. We almost have a heart attack if our mobile phone runs out of battery. We always need to be connected to social media, and an online cloud that we don't know who has access to. I know for example, that when I wake up, or when I return home from work, the first thing I do is check my emails, as if my life depended on it. We also don't mind helping secret services keeping a file on us, by constantly recording our lives and keeping them updated on social media. Why don't we all quit and go live in the forest and become hippies again?

I reviewed the **SHARKTOPUS** (2010, USA, D: Declan O'Brien) Blu-ray and the **SHARKTO-PUS VS. PTERACUDA** (2014, USA, D: Kevin O'Neill) DVD in Greek, and I was waiting for a while for **SHARKTOPUS VS WHALEWOLF** to be released in some kind of disc, but to no avail; since its July 2015 television broadcasting it has received no physical media release, and I don't see this changing anytime soon (or ever). As it is so often the case with these TV flicks, a further, fourth film was announced on the credits, but to be honest, I doubt that even this will materialize. Produced by Roger Corman (I'm more interested in seeing his upcoming **DEATH RACE 2050** [2016, USA, D: G.J. Echternkamp]), this will probably be remembered for a humorous cameo by rock legend Iggy Pop (of all people).

If this pic is from **SHARKTOPUS VS. WHALEWOLF**, this can only be the latter

Friday, March 25, 2016

INSEMINOID
(a.k.a. **HORROR PLANET**)

UK, 1981. D: Norman J. Warren

Ad-lines: *"A Crawling Terror from the Depths of Doom…"* *"Somewhere in the Depth of Space… A Horrific Nightmare is About to Become a Reality."* *"Beyond Time and Somewhere In Space Is… Horror Planet"* *"The horror-birth spawned in space!"* *"Conceived in violence, carried in terror, born to devastate and brutalize a universe!"* *"A far from human birth"*

Okay, just so you get a bit of context, let me brief you by telling you that Sci-Fi films were the thing to do in the early '80s if you were a genre filmmaker, and the film under review had been compared one time too many (and not favourably) with **ALIEN** (1979, USA/UK, D: Ridley Scott). It also has to be said that, although we still live in a sexist world, we have evolved a little bit and rape is not socially accepted in civilized countries. However, in the late '70s and

Slack-Jawed: Whatever the hell that thing behind him is (we're assuming it must be the Sharktopus), Casper Van Dien sure seems in a hurry to get away from it

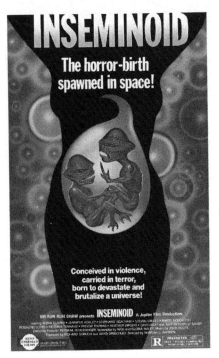

INSEMINOID

The horror-birth spawned in space!

Conceived in violence,
carried in terror,
born to devastate and
brutalize a universe!

SIR RUN RUN SHAW presents **INSEMINOID** A Jupiter Film Production

[R]

who can also be seen in the occasional feature, such as the Marlon Brando vehicle **THE NIGHT-COMERS** [1971, UK, D: Michael Winner]). Seemingly the scientists have not learned their lesson, or they simply will sacrifice everything in the name of progress—including their lives—and a further adventure is arranged, this time the result being the dismemberment of Mitch (Trevor Thomas from **SHEENA** [1984, UK/USA, D: John Guillermin]) and the rape of Sandy (Judy Geeson who was recently in Rob Zombie's **THE LORDS OF SALEM** [2012, UK/Canada/USA]) by a monstrous creature (fans of manga imagery will most definitely enjoy). The poor girl survived the attack and is now under treatment from doctors Sharon (TV-actress Heather Wright, who also had a small part in the now much-celebrated **PSYCHOMANIA** [1973, UK, D: Don Sharp]) and Karl (Barrie Houghton, who did his debut in the Mia Farrow vehicle **BLIND TERROR** [1971, UK, D: Richard Fleischer]), who discover that the victim is two months pregnant already! Shortly, she is transformed into a menacing alien creature herself, and goes on a killing rampage and her first victims in this hide-and-seek game in space are Barbra (Victoria Tennant from **FLOWERS IN THE ATTIC** [1987, USA, D: Jeffrey Bloom]) and Dean. How will it be stopped?

Nick Maley and Gloria Maley's screenplay (originally entitled *Doomseeds*, but changed to the title we all know, in order to avoid confusion with **DEMON SEED** [1977, USA, D: Donald Cammell]) was originally written as a vehicle for the duo in order to showcase several special effects (the real-life couple went on to work in **STAR WARS: EPISODE V - THE EMPIRE STRIKES BACK** [1980, USA, D: Irvin Kershner]), ended up as being mostly criticized for this particular aspect, which was poorly performed during production. It offers one of the most confusing, weird, and interesting themes for analysis of '80s genre cinema. First of all it concerns a rape. The film's promotion, and indeed word-of-mouth by people who have seen it, always seem to revolve around the infamous beast/woman rape scene which, other than being depicted shamelessly in real time in front of your very eyes, Peter Boyle's (**1408** [2007, USA, D: Mikael Håfström]) editing takes us back to that scene again and again, several times until the end. The rape victim then understandably goes under treatment, but when her pregnancy is confirmed, commentary follows in regards to her inability to conceive due to the medical measures taken before the trip and to all females on board. She is also believed to be mentally challenged, not because she had to face the nightmare of rape, but because nobody believes her that the rapist was a monster, which is an aspect that has been analysed to death. She conceived

early '80s, every other film appeared to have a rape scene in it (not to mention the porn films that had them), further confirming the rape culture that was rampant back then. It was inevitable for exploitation filmmakers to mix the two (as they often do, as crossover entries were usually very popular with moviegoers) and turn a cocktail that would offer rape in space! My favourite of these films (yes, I have one) is **GALAXY OF TERROR** (1981, USA, D: Bruce D. Clark) which's producer Roger Corman autographed my copy of it. However, the classic film of this subgenre is this one here.

Astronaut scientists on an excavation project discover an unknown language (site photographer Dean—played by Dominic Jephcott who was previously in Delbert Mann's TV movie **ALL QUIET ON THE WESTERN FRONT** [1979, USA/UK]—is documenting the findings that ruin his life) and along with a series of other events including crystals with energy fields, find them believing that there was indeed an intelligent ancient civilization on these shores. Something appears to be lurking in the caves, and soon afterwards Gail (Rosalind Lloyd, who was previously in my favourite action-fest **THE WILD GEESE** [1978, UK/Switzerland, D: Andrew V. McLaglen]) commits suicide and Ricky (David Baxt, who went on to **BATMAN** [1989, USA/UK, D: Tim Burton]) is killed by Kate (TV-actress Stephanie Beacham,

a baby—an alien one at that—while she technically couldn't…by a monster rapist! Theorizing further, much thought should also be given that she, whilst becoming some kind of "the other" has now become menacing and murderous, because she is about to become an over-protective mother; all this would be quite chaotic, if it wasn't so blatantly misogynist.

Thinking that the screenplay was just a work that Warren (perhaps best remembered for his **SATAN'S SLAVE** [1976, UK]) commissioned because he had the money in place but no story to film, it is amazing how he ended up reportedly impressing Roger Corman. Actually, the most impressive thing about this film is its opening credits, and these were provided by Oxford Scientific Films. Its first half is outstandingly boring, and John Scott's (he recently composed **THE WICKER TREE** [2011, UK, D: Robin Hardy]) soundtrack is much too reminiscent of **BUIO OMEGA** (1979, Italy, D: Joe D'Amato)'s score by Goblin.

This may be a £1 million production[3] (that was filmed exclusively in interiors) but it was shot on 35mm by John Metcalfe (just the next year, he

---

3 Technically the producers were Richard Gordon (who had backed the superior **HORROR HOSPITAL** [1973, UK, D: Antony Balch]) and David Speechley (**OUTER TOUCH** [1979, UK, D: Norman J. Warren]), but legendary Hong Kong producers Shaw Brothers were also involved, and one of them is credited as the film's presenter, making many a source referring this as a UK/Hong Kong co-production.

shot another gruesome space epic, namely **XTRO** [1982, UK/USA, D: Harry Bromley Davenport]) and the correct aspect ratio to see this is 2.35:1. It received an X rating in the U.K. (its country of origin) and a relatively wide theatrical release, whilst in the U.S.A. it received an R rating. Times have changed even for the ever-conservative BBFC (British Board of Film Classification) and an uncut DVD of the film can be purchased now at DVD stores with a harmless 15 rating. Some circles thought that this was part of the infamous Video Nasties list, probably because Vipco released a copy with cuts, but this is not the case and Vipco has a reputation for releasing incomplete copies.

But why did all this hustle, word of mouth, criticism, analysis, and whatnot, not change a thing? Simply because this ended up being a "special interest" piece by Norman Warren. Unfortunately, the system, at least when it comes to themes and subjects, is changing only from the inside. Had this being a Quentin Tarantino film, everyone would still boast of how ground-breaking and taboo-destroying it was. As it is, not too many care…

Below: Japanese VHS jacket. (This is the very super-widescreen copy which Dennis Capicik gave me back in about 1999 or so! ~SF)

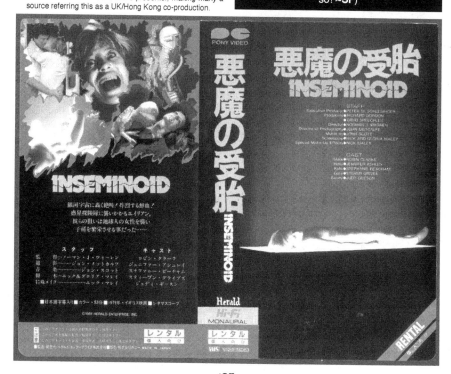

MONSTER!
BACK ISSUES

Fantastic Films of the Decades, Volume 2: The 1930s

by Wayne Kinsey

(@ *www.peverilpublishing.co.uk*)

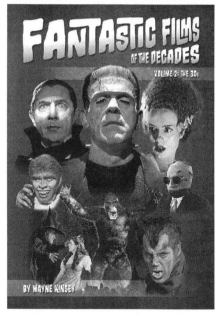

The 1930s. The decade that gave us the definitive monsters: Lugosi's Dracula, Karloff's Frankenstein Monster and The Mummy, March's Jekyll & Hyde—icons that shine as bright today as they did back then. There were also other very memorable moments, such as when Rathbone's Sherlock Holmes battled Dr. Moriarty and also protected the Baskervilles from their hell-hound; when King Kong fell in love with his blonde captive; where a witch and a teenage girl fought over a pair of ruby slippers and men dressed in winged monkey suits. All made at a time when there was no CGI. It was an age of film like no other—where boundaries were pushed, an actor's career could be made and broken by the studio system, some of the most controversial films were made and banned[1] in what some consider to be Hollywood's Golden Age. More importantly than all that, it was the decade that shaped the future of the fantastic film.

Much has been written about this era, often called "The Golden Age of Horror", and therefore it has been predominately this genre that has been continually dissected. It is also this particular era of film that especially interests me, so when a new book on the subject comes along, my ears prick up (so to speak) and I take interest.

Wayne Kinsey, following on from his *Fantastic Films of the Decades Volume 1: The Silents* (Peveril Publishing), has recently released his second volume in the *FFotD* series, *The 1930s*. Kinsey is an authority on Hammer Films, having published several books on the subject: *Hammer Films: The Bray Studio Years* (Reynolds & Hearn), *Hammer Films: The Elstree Studio Years*, *Hammer Films: A Life In Pictures*, and *Hammer Films: The Unsung Heroes* (all Tomahawk Press) and through his own Peveril Publishing house has published *Hammer Films: On Location* (sold out), *The Peter Cushing Scrapbook*, *Hammer's Film Legacy* (sold

out), as well as *The Hammer Dracula Scrapbook*, which is forthcoming. Peveril Publishing has also brought out *Running Scared* by Phil Campbell and Brian Reynolds.

Kinsey is a man who well knows his subject and who loves putting out books that not only entertain, but inform as well. As he states in his introduction to *FFotD V2*: "After years of writing magazines and books about Hammer Films, it was a refreshing change to dip into the silent film era with *Fantastic Films of the Decades, Volume 1*. It's an ambitious and challenging series, pledging me to watch and chronicle as many fantasy films as I can find each decade and presenting them as sumptuous pictorial coffee table books [...] to emulate the magic of Alan Frank and Dennis Gifford in the '70s, when it all began for me. That's why I'll be ending the series with the '70s, covering the 'classic era' of the fantasy film..." In other words, what he plans to do is release a series of books that will give the reader a volume-to-volume, year-by-year encyclopaedia of fantastical films, which should by all accounts put previous books in the shade. This is no insult to, say, Phil Hardy's *Encyclopaedia* series (i.e., Horror, Sci-Fi, The Western and Gangster Movies) or Workman & Howarth's ambitious *Tome of Terror* series, as Kinsey is doing something utterly different.

---

1   Horror films were banned in many parts of the world, including the UK and Australia.

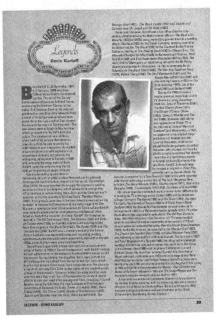

are all given informative, well-researched pieces; as are directors Robert Florey, Edgar G. Ulmer, Lew Landers, James Whale, Rowland V. Lee, Stuart Walker and Lambert Hillyer. There are also separate pieces on the special effects men John P. Fulton and Kenneth Strickfaden. Not only that, but Kinsey gives nine series links to certain titles: *Fu Manchu*, Universal's *Dracula, Frankenstein, Mummy* and *Invisible Man* films, Zombie films, Universal films, Karloff and Lugosi films, Werewolf films and Rathbone Holmes Films. These are informative pieces that can lead the reader on to new films in that particular area. Each year begins with a month-by-month breakdown of important events, births, Film notes and Academy Awards notes. The amount of films covered each year is as follows: 1930 = 8, 1931 = 9, 1932 = 22, 1933 = 13, 1934 = 10, 1935 20, 1936 = 14, 1937 = 4, 1938 = 4 and 1939 = 14 and the diversity of material covered goes as far as *Flash Gordon* and *Buck Rogers*, through to A CHRISTMAS CAROL and THE WIZARD OF OZ, as well as the usual suspects. This is all good and brilliant, but what really makes this book stand out from the crowd is the use of full-color throughout the book. Posters, lobby cards, publicity shots, and some rarities too—all presented in sumptuous color— are plentiful throughout, without detracting from the information an iota. In fact, they go hand-in-hand together, and if Kinsey were to cover every single film from this era in this way, then he would need to make this decade alone a three-, if not four-volume work in itself. It is a beautiful book, made into a real work of art by Steve Kirkham (at his Tree Frog Communications), and his craftsmanship in graphic design is top-notch, as always. On the strength of a PDF review copy that was kindly sent to me, I have since obtained a hard copy for my film book collection and future research.

Please note: This book is strictly a limited edition run of only 500 copies, and is solely available direct from the publisher, not any other outlet.

On the strength of this volume, I have also ordered *FFotD V1, The Silents*, and am looking forward to further volumes. To say that I am excited is an understatement! ~ **Matthew E Banks** © 2016

To describe a book as a thing of beauty could be seen as being too over-the-top, too dramatic, but that is what this book is, and I shall try to explain why. Firstly, let's look at the cover. Over a blue background we have Karloff's Frankenstein Monster dominating, whilst surrounding him we have Lugosi's Count Mora, March's Hyde and the Wicked Witch of the West threatening Dorothy. Lanchester's Bride of Frankenstein, Rains' Invisible Man, Hull's Werewolf of London, and King Kong make up the rest of the assemblage. It's not over-the-top, it is elegant, tasteful and beautifully drawn. Then, over the next 250-odd pages, Kinsey takes us on a journey like no other. In his introduction he points out the one major difference that this volume has over his previous one, in that he has introduced a skull rating awards system for each film: five skulls = timeless classic, four skulls = great stuff, three skulls = not bad, two skulls = nothing special and one skull = oh dear! This gives the reader an opportunity to either agree or disagree with his opinions. Secondly, as the volume is not as text-heavy as other volumes, nor is every single film covered (only 118 of the '30s finest genre films are covered in detail), Kinsey is allowed the elbow room to do what no other book has done before, and that is to have mini-bios of the leading actors, directors and filmmakers of that era: Lugosi, Karloff, Edward Van Sloan, Dwight Frye, Colin Clive, Peter Lorre, Lionel Atwill, Fay Wray, Charles Laughton, Elsa Lanchester, Sir Cedric Hardwicke, Ernest Thesiger, Claude Rains, Tod Slaughter, George Zucco and Basil Rathbone

Night of the Fire-Beast

Story & Script: Jonathan Clode
Story & Art: Christopher Martinez
Insane Comics, 2015
(@ *www.insanecomics.com*)

Issue #1

Producing *giant* monster narratives presents a series of challenges that are often ignored until the heat of actual production. Sure, giant monsters are fun to draw—drawing them in battle is even more fun—but there won't be much conversation among the monsters, so having a compelling human component is necessary, and balancing the ratio between monster element and human element becomes the real job. Gareth Edwards was taken to task by many a giant monster-lover for his big-screen take on Toho's **GODZILLA** (2014, USA). The largest criticism raised by fans was that there was not "enough monsters", but, seriously watching a giant monster brawl of any kind gets boring pretty quickly. Good monster stories of any kind (e.g., **CAT PEOPLE** [1942, USA, D: Jacques Tourneur), **ATTACK OF THE MUSHROOM PEOPLE** (マタンゴ / *Matango*, 1963, Japan, D: Ishirō Honda], **JAWS** [1975, USA, D: Steven Spielberg], **ALIEN** [1979, UK/USA, D: Ridley Scott]) keep you wanting more by giving you quick tasters, glimpses of the unimaginable, flanked by human characters we can actually relate to.

This is one thing the creators of *Night of the Fire-Beast* get right; the giant monsters don't even show up until page 12. We're introduced to the crew of the "Fair Spanish Lady" on the high seas in 1948 (the captain gives us a flashback sequence of his WWI experience; this page is drawn by Neil McClements) and quickly the ship and crew find themselves engulfed in a freakish lightning storm which not only displaces the "Fair Spanish Lady" by hundreds of miles, but conjures up an island just off the ship's bow. Despite the impossibility of the situation, this doesn't deter our crew from venturing onto the mysterious island, where they discover all is not as it seems. Our first monster erupts from the ground and, in a neat bit of storytelling in which the crew members realize it has been attracted by their flaming torch, the second, and "main monster"—our Fire-Beast—is introduced through the disposal of said torch.

At this moment, the ubiquitous monster brawl begins, but creators Clode and Martinez have something more interesting in mind; the dynamic double-page spread of our battling monsters breaks traditional adventure narrative by seemingly transporting the reader to a movie soundstage where the monsters are clearly now suit-actors, with the Fire-Beast's tail suspended by a wire. The monsters square-off, with the narrative switching into three different points of view: that of the monsters fighting each other, our human cast fleeing the fisticuffs, and the suit-actors throwing each other through the air, visible wires and all. The "Fire-Beast" defeats his foe, and our crew safely return to their ship.

I should mention now that on the inside cover of *Night of the Fire-Beast*, the comic is introduced as a retelling of a lost, 1959 film of the same name by low-budget producer Randall Williamson. All of this—the film, Mr. Williamson, etc.—is complete fiction. This is merely an introductory device that preps the reader for the comic and, while maybe unnecessary, I think it's kind of a clever touch. I liked this variation on "fourth-wall-breaking"—the sudden shift from straight-ahead monster/ adventure story to moving the action to a film soundstage—but I wanted more commitment to this shift. Clode and Martinez could have taken a few extra pages introducing us to Randal Williamson and his bare-bones production stage, showing us all the trappings of a film set, (etc.), then shift us back to the familiar comic story again.

Thrills, chills, and spills in this *kaijū*-packed comic adaptation of the 1959 monster movie **NIGHT OF THE FIRE-BEAST!**

At the conclusion of the book, they even go to the trouble of listing the cast of the "film." The cover further informs us of the movie tie-in by displaying a generic, two-legged monster silhouette encasing a simple, stick-figure suit actor.

Technically, the comic is fairly solid. Clode keeps the script very spare, but it accomplishes what it has to do. Most comics are produced by several people, usually a writer who handles plot and script chores and an artist who lays-out the story, breaking it down into panels and then penciling and sometimes inking his or her own work, which is

then lettered. The writer, Clode, displays maturity by deftly supplying the necessary dialogue to the characters and nothing else; no awkward, verbose, explanatory bubbles to clutter the page. His script leaves the artist room to move.

The overall storytelling is good, with a thoughtful mix of medium- and long-shots and not many close-ups; latter a pet-peeve of mine. The close-up is best used in film when a character is talking, in conversation with others, or to themselves and in "film-time" this lasts seconds, but a comic, obviously, is static. That face is just *sitting there* along with a word-balloon. With each panel the artist has to do more; I think there are few things more important in comic-narrative than establishing your characters in whatever space they occupy and doing it over and over again, constantly showing the reader their movements in space and reestablishing the space among the characters, and Christopher Martinez does this well. His art isn't flashy, or beautiful to behold, but there is a good, kinetic, dynamic energy to it.

There are a couple of unclear panels and pages. For instance, p.8, which introduces the mysterious island, is hard to read. The ship gets lost in all the black ink at the bottom of the splash-page. Clarity and placement of all your forms in a panel is a lifelong learning experience. The only other obvious nitpick is the use and placement of sound effects; almost all of which get lost in the art. They seem like too much of an afterthought, and, well, comics *are* silent, and giant-monster comics need all the impact they can get, so those "sounds" should be *leaping* off the page! Again, the effects and word balloons should not overpower or cover-up the art. This is a discipline in and of itself. I'd look at the work of Artie Simek, Joe Rosen, John Costanza and Tom Orzechowski to get schooled on lettering and sound effects. ~ **Ian Coleman**

INTERVIEW WITH NIGHT OF THE FIRE-BEAST'S
J ALAN DOUGLAS
A MOST SCURVY MONSTER!

In 1959, a monster movie sailed through cinemas so quickly that you probably didn't even notice it. That picture was **NIGHT OF THE FIRE-BEAST**, *and while its quality outmatched its box office receipts, most traces of its existence have since been erased from modern movie history. That is until one eagle-eyed* Monster! *reader from across the pond discovered an obscure interview with the movie's star, J. Alan Douglas. Reprinted here for the first time, it originally appeared in the weekly Welsh newspaper,* The Glamorgan Gazette *in June 1963.* [Well, whaddaya know. Talk about a small world! I used to live in Swansea, South Wales, which is a town in West Glamorgan ☺ – SF.]

****
Interview conducted by Gazette *Arts Correspondent Clive Ranger*
****

J. Alan Douglas will be appearing as Prospero in William Shakespeare's The Tempest *at Porthcawl Pavilion from the 12ᵗʰ-18ᵗʰ June.*

While the rest of the nation loses itself in Beatlemania, the small coastal town of Porthcawl is preparing to host a touring production of Shakespeare's *The Tempest*. Starring as Prospero is veteran English actor J. Alan Douglas. We sat down just after a dress rehearsal to discuss his career on both stage and screen.

You've been acting since you left school, but what might our readers recognise you from?

Theatregoers may recall my lengthy runs in *Waiting for Godot* and *An Inspector Calls* in the mid-'Fifties. Most recently I've done some television roles in *Armchair Theatre* and *Danger*

Man. I've also done a few small films, but I must confess they've not been the best experiences.

I wanted to ask you about one of those films, the American picture NIGHT OF THE FIRE-BEAST.

Oh, good grief, you've heard of that?

What was it like working for a Hollywood studio, and how does it compare to traditional theatre?

I honestly couldn't tell you! My experience of working on that blasted film was a disaster. There was no studio to speak of. Just an egocentric producer who fancied himself as all things to all men! There was barely a script, no budget that I could see, and the crew—what little there was—had to work under the most appalling conditions. With *The Tempest*, or any classic piece of theatre, we have a good understanding of what we're trying to achieve. We have a strong text, competent direction, and the benefit of working as a company. Everyone knows their job.

And that wasn't the case on the FIRE-BEAST film?

Not at all. We were asked to do the impossible on a daily basis. Now, I know acting can be a challenge, it's what I adore about it, but running away from giant creatures that you can't even see; what kind of way to make a film is that?! The director swore that would be the future of filmmaking. Well, I think we all know how *that* will turn out!

A number of modern features seem to be veering toward more fantastical, over-the-top stories. What are your thoughts on those types of films?

Well, I must say it's not really for me. I think that it's all well and good to try these things, but they won't last. I was offered an audition for a new BBC drama about a doctor who travels in time, or some such nonsense. Needless to say I turned it down in favour of Prospero. Now that's a *real* part!

So it's safe to say you don't see much of a future in these kind of stories?

Not at all. Whether it's that "Doctor" programme, this new James Bond character everybody seems to love, or great big monsters fighting it out for no good reason; if you think people will still be interested in such drivel fifty years from now, then you've got another thing coming!

And lastly, what would be your advice for a budding actor?

Stick with the classics and make sure your work has some substance. It's a very competitive industry and one must take a job where one can find it, but if you have any choice then try to avoid the fanciful rubbish that litters our screens. And if you ever get a call from a chap called Randall Williamson, put the ruddy phone down immediately!

FUN FACTOID:

NIGHT OF THE FIRE-BEAST is a 1959 giant monster film written and directed by low budget movie producer Randall Williamson.

The idea for the film was born not out of creative endeavor, but rather from Williamson's desire to cash in on the popular wave of science fiction and giant monster films of the 1950s. His "idea" was to craft extremely low budget knock offs of more popular films, thus providing him with a ready-made audience.

To this end he refused to hire writers or even a director, claiming that "Anybody can do this crap!"

J. Alan Douglas, circa 2015

MONSTER MAGAZINES THAT TIME FORGOT:

by John Harrison

The success of Warren Publishing's *Famous Monsters of Filmland* magazine, along with the whole monster movie craze of the 1960s which it helped instigate, inspired a lot of rival publishers to jump on the bandwagon and try to make a few bucks while the fad was still hot.

I recall picking up a copy of Bob Michelluci's *The Collector's Guide to Monster Magazine* (ABC Press, USA, 1977) from Space Age Books in Melbourne when it was first published in 1978, and being amazed at the number of different titles it covered which I had never heard of. Growing up in the Australia of the late 'Seventies, the Golden Age of monster magazines had already passed me by, and even during the height of their popularity many foreign monster magazines did not make it to the newsstands over here (it took until the early 'Seventies even for *Famous Monsters* to be allowed into the country!). While some of these rival magazines gave *FM* a run for their 50 cents (*Castle of Frankenstein* being an obvious one, Ron Haydock's and Paul Blaisdell's *Fantastic Monsters of the Films* being another), most of them were quickly put together and just as quickly forgotten about once their run of a handful of issues was over and the publisher had moved on to another subject or teen craze to briefly exploit.

A monster magazine that always fascinated me whenever I glanced through Michelluci's guide was one called *Shriek!*, which ran for only four issues spread out between1965 and 1967. The pulpish, painted covers which three of the issues contained appealed to my artistic sensibilities, especially since it was not obvious exactly what movie each painting was meant to represent (if any).[1] The font used for the magazine's title on the covers was also memorable, reminiscent of the graphic design used on horror comics from the pre-

Issue #1 (1965)

code era; looking like a combination of blood and veins (or perhaps dripping wax), and punctuated by an exclamation mark. A chance trawling through eBay a decade or so ago uncovered a listing for all four issues at a very reasonable "Buy It Now" price, which I jumped on and eagerly awaited their arrival to see if *Shriek!* managed to stand out from a very large pack.

Edited by the creatively named Frank N. Stein, *Shriek!* seems to have been a transatlantic publication, with the editorial office (dubbed "The House of Horror") based in London but the printing done in New York (all advertising for products sold within its pages also feature a New York postal address). The indicia claims that the magazine was produced by the mysterious London staff on behalf of Acme News Co. Inc., a magazine distributor that at the time was publishing other youth-oriented titles such as *Beatles 'Round the World*. Under the

---

1 Although for the debut issue—which is the only one I possess—the cover artist did obviously utilize reference materials from **THE BLACK SCORPION** for his artwork ~**SF**

Issue #2

decades and concentrating on more modern genre fare. This issue also devotes pages to some non-horror, though certainly horrific, films, including ten pages on Hammer's World War II POW film **THE SECRET OF BLOOD ISLAND** (1964, UK, D: Quentin Lawrence) and another major article on the Japanese samurai classic **HARAKIRI** (切腹 / *Seppuku*, 1962, Japan, D: Masaki Kobayashi). Perhaps the most memorable—and memorably un-PC—article to be found in *Shriek!*'s first issue is one titled "Horror Hags", which looks at some of the memorably twisted turns put in by the more mature ladies, such as Bette Davis in **WHATEVER HAPPENED TO BABY JANE?** (1962, USA, D: Robert Aldrich), Joan Crawford in William Castle's **STRAIT-JACKET** (1964, USA, D: William Castle), and Tallulah Bankhead in **DIE! DIE! MY DARLING!** (1965, UK, D: Silvio Narizzano).

Issue number 2, dated October 1965 and featuring a B&W cover photo from **THE HOUSE AT THE END OF THE WORLD** (1965, UK, D: Daniel Haller; which was eventually released as **DIE, MONSTER, DIE!**) surrounded by a bold red jagged frame, continues the British-heavy content with articles on the Amicus anthology **DR. TERROR'S HOUSE OF HORROR** (1965, D: Freddie Francis), **THE SKULL** (1965, D: Freddie Francis; based on *The Skull of the Marquis de Sade* by Robert Bloch) and screenwriter Lyn Fairhurst talking about her work on Lance Comfort's witchcraft/vampire meld **DEVILS OF DARKNESS** (1965).

alternate name of Health Knowledge, Inc., Acme had already dabbled in the field of genre publishing with digest magazines like *Magazine of Horror* and *Startling Mystery Stories*, which specialized in reprinting stories from the old pulp magazines. The debut issue of *Shriek!*, cover-dated May 1965, certainly contains an eclectic mix of coverage, eschewing the classic horror films of previous

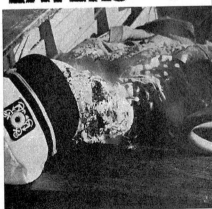

A double-page spread (pp.4+5) from *Shriek!* #1

My favorite pieces in this issue, though, would have to be the coverage of Lindsay Shonteff's killer ventriloquist's doll classic **DEVIL DOLL** (1964, UK), and the article on Mario Bava's gothic horror **THE WHIP AND THE BODY** (*La frusta e il corpo*, a.k.a. **NIGHT IS THE PHANTOM**, 1963, Italy/France). Elsewhere in this sophomore issue are interviews with Boris Karloff and Vincent Price (the conclusion of an interview started in the first issue) and an article on the growing trend of violence in cinema, focusing on four films to illustrate their point to varying degrees of success: Franklin J. Schaffner's **THE WAR LORD** (1965, USA), **LORD JIM** (1965, UK/USA, D: Richard Brooks), William Castle's **I SAW WHAT YOU DID** (1965, USA), and Hammer's adaptation of H. Rider Haggard's fantasy/adventure novel **SHE** (1965, UK, D: Robert Day).

The penultimate issue of *Shriek!* (#3) appeared in the summer of 1966, and it's certainly a must-have for any fan of Hammer, containing as it does a multitude of articles devoted to the studio and its films, including an interview with Christopher Lee and coverage of **DRACULA – PRINCE OF DARKNESS** (1966, D: Terence Fisher), **THE REPTILE** and **THE PLAGUE OF THE ZOMBIES** (both 1966, D: John Gilling) and **RASPUTIN, THE MAD MONK** (1966, D: Don Sharp). More UK-centric coverage in this issue looks at Don Sharp's **THE FACE OF FU-MANCHU** (1965) and Amicus' **THE PSYCHOPATH** (1966, D: Freddie Francis), while the English borders are briefly broken by a two-page article on the Japanese historical horror drama **ONIBABA** (鬼婆, 1964, Japan, D: Kaneto Shindō).

The fourth and final issue of *Shriek!* is dated Winter 1967 and features my favorite cover from the magazine's brief run, depicting some type of zombie stumbling through a graveyard, beams of moonlight shining through gaping bullet holes in its chest as bats flap their way through the dark brown sky in the background. Pure pre-code comic book horror! The interior of this issue is also a great mix and includes articles on **THE PROJECTED MAN** (1966, UK, D: Ian Curteis [see p. 12]), the Japanese *kaijū* **FRANKENSTEIN CONQUERS THE WORLD** (フランケンシュタイン対地底怪獣バラゴン / *Furankenshutain Tai Chitei Kaijū Baragon* ,1965, Japan, D: Ishirō Honda), the great 3D horror film **THE MASK** (a.k.a. **EYES OF HELL**, 1961, Canada, D: Julian Roffman), **THE BRIDES OF FU MANCHU** (1966, UK/West Germany, D: Don Sharp), **THE DEADLY BEES** (1966, UK, D: Freddie Francis), **13** (a.k.a. **EYE OF THE DEVIL**, 1966, UK, D: J. Lee Thompson), as well as the Peter Cushing *Dr. Who* adventure **DALEKS' INVASION EARTH,**

Top: *Issue #3.* **Above:** *Issue #4*

2150 A.D. (1966, UK, D: Gordon Flemyng). Monster comedies from both sides of the Atlantic also get a look in with coverage of **MUNSTER, GO HOME** (1966, USA, D: Earl Bellamy) and **CARRY ON SCREAMING!** (1966, UK, D: Gerald Thomas).

In the editorial for the final issue, entitled "It's No Scream!" the mysterious Frank N. Stein seems to be predicting the magazine's imminent demise, lamenting the somewhat premature demise of the serious horror film and placing the blame on

everything from James Bond, monster spoofs and "the return to the old sentimental formula after **THE SOUND OF MUSIC**".

Apart from the interviews, the text to the articles contained in *Shriek!* consisted mostly of press material or plot synopses (sometimes including the shock or twist endings), but where the content of the magazine really excelled was in its use of stills, which were often printed large-size and even over the occasional two-page spread. Also, like most monster mags from the period, *Shriek!* offered up a selection of mail-order goodies in order to supplement its income. Full page ads within its pages peddled the usual range of Topstone masks, rubber bats and spiders, 8mm monster home movies and "Mani-Yack" transfers, all obtainable from a New York-based company simply known as Globe.

Tracking the listed price guide values for *Shriek!*, the original Michelluci guide gave a price between $2.50 and $5.00, while his 1988 updated volume saw the values upgraded to $30.00 - $50.00. Michael W. Pierce's *Monsters Among Us: Monster Magazine & Fanzine Collector's Guide*, published in 1995, had *Shriek!* valued at $25.00 per issue for

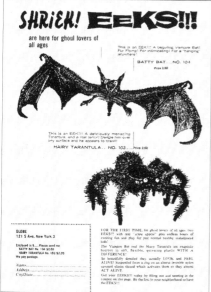

Pages Of Horror! Samples of the gloriously ghoulish stuff *[opposite page and above]* you could have bought if you wanted; and *[above right]* a full-page (p.8) image from the **DIE, MONSTER, DIE!** coverage in *Shriek!* #2 (October, 1965) *[All* Shriek! *images copyright ©1965 Acme News Co., Inc.]*

copies in Very Fine/Near Mint condition, however the discovery of a large batch of uncirculated copies several years ago saw nice copies start circulating online and at collectors' fairs for much more reasonable prices, with issues usually able to be bought for around the $10 mark or less. *Shriek!* is well worth grabbing if you ever come across a set... the Monster Kid in you will not be disappointed!

O MORTO DO PÂNTANO

EUGÊNIO COLONNESE

AN OBSCURE BRANCH OF THE HEAP'S FAMILY TREE: O MORTO DO PÂNTONO

AH!...AH!...AH!

By John Goodrich

(with translation assistance from David Ribeiro)

I am a long-time fan of a character almost unique to comics, Hillman Periodicals' The Heap and its derivatives. I'm aware that The Heap itself was inspired by Theodore Sturgeon's classic 1940 short story "It". The swamp man back from the dead hasn't taken off in any other medium, but it's thriving in the comics. The Heap has inspired a multitude of literary progeny, from DC Comics' *Swamp Thing* and Marvel's *Man-Thing* to at least four reinventions of The Heap itself. That's an impressive legacy for a character created in 1943, and whose publisher stopped making comics in 1953.

I had the good fortune to stumble on a lesser-known literary descendant of The Heap. As far as I know, *O Morto do Pântono* ("The Dead Man from the Swamp") has never been formally translated into English. It is a Brazilian comic, the creation of Eugênio Colonnese[1], a multitalented and prolific artist who wrote and illustrated movie posters, World War Two comics, created several superheroes, and was partially responsible for the widespread use of comics in Brazilian education to engage and motivate students. His most famous creation, however, is Mirza, *mulher* vampire (Mirza, the Vampire Woman). Mirza should be familiar to anyone who knows Warren Publishing's *Vampirella*; aristocratic, voluptuous and scantily-

clad. It should be said, however, that while *Vampirella*'s first issue came out in September 1969, Mirza arrived in 1967.

As a backup to the *Mirza* series, Colonnese created *O Morto do Pântono*. This swamp creature, which I'll refer to as O Morto ("The Dead Man") has enough similarities to strongly imply that it was indeed inspired by The Heap. Although I cannot make any direct connection, it is a human-derived-but-deceased creature of the swamp. In the same way that The Heap's later stories were structured, O Morto is a vessel of narrative justice via retribution, although O Morto's methods aren't quite as varied as The Heap's are. It seems to have inhuman strength despite the spindly nature of its limbs and short, hunched torso. Like The Heap and all swamp creatures that followed it, O Morto is immune to bullets.

At the same time, the character has enough dissimilarities to give O Morto his own distinctive flavor. Unlike most swamp monsters descended from The Heap, and again ahead of later muck-men like Swamp Thing and Sludge, O Morto can reason, and even talk. Although its skin is heavily-textured, where that of regular people is undecorated, it retains a more human shape than either The Heap or Man-Thing, even having a halo of hair with a balding pattern. In another departure,

1   *https://pt.wikipedia.org/wiki/Eug%C3%AAnio_Colonnese*

O Morto never wanders far from his swamp. The Heap's stories were set in locations across the globe; Africa, China, the Middle East, America and Europe. O Morto remains right where he is and waits for the evildoers to come to him. And come they do! Blackmailers, marijuana smokers, and other bad men. Uniquely among the muck-monsters of comics, O Morto always carries an enormous single-bit axe.

As the name implies, O Morto regards himself as a dead person. His immunity to bullets seems to back this up. It isn't until 1985, nearly two decades after O Morto's first appearance, that his origin is even hinted at. In "Bodies Without Heads Do Not Speak", a legend is recounted that O Morto was once a judge who was dragged to the wetlands and killed with an axe. His subsequent resurrection is left as a mystery, but this explains some of the moral yet harsh nature of his justice, and his territoriality. Despite this new understanding of the character's background, he solves his problems the same way he always has: with an axe-blow to the head.

Problem-Solving, *O Morto* Style:
"Murderers! Wretches! You deserve to live
only in my world! I shall bring them!"

Unlike Dr. Ted Sallis, who became the Man-Thing, Dr. Alec Holland who became the Swamp Thing, or Baron von Immelmann, O Morto does not seem to be highly educated. Judges of this period in Brazil were not required to have a law background, merely to pass a test on the local laws. He's a bit more down to earth than the previous lives of other of The Heap's literary descendants. In this way, O Morto seems to presage such slasher fare such as Jason Voorhees. But where Jason varied his implements and tended to merely start with immoral youths then move on to their friends, O Morto just goes after the bad people. With a huge axe. He occasionally meets people who are not reprehensible, such as Sílvia in "Little Sílvia", as well as Bernardo in "Bad Smell". He does not kill indiscriminately. Only the bad.

Another interesting quirk that sets O Morto apart from other swamp monsters is its tendency to speak directly to the reader, likely reflecting the hosts of EC's 'Fifties anthologies, The Vault-Keeper, The Crypt-Keeper, and The Old Witch. O Morto does double-duty, however, serving as both character and narrator. In the earlier stories, he has a splash image taking up the majority of the page, usually delivering a ghoulish or misanthropic message. In "The Gnats", he doesn't actually appear in the story, serving instead as an outside observer of human wickedness and cruelty.

O Morto definitely has a personality. He is misanthropic, several times referring to humanity as "muck" or "slime", and is happy when the mulch of humanity returns to the muck of the swamp. And he is more than willing to refer to the reader in such terms. But, at the end of "Damn Herbs", he lets us know that this is not the only side to him:

"A coisa melhor do mundo e o lodo. Lodo e o podridão como estes dois! Ervas malditas, Mosquitos, pernilongos, oh! Que sinfonia harmoniosa! Tudo isso enche sde satisfação minha sensibilidade de poeta, bem no fundo de minha alma! Ah Ah Ah! Embora eu não tenha 'fundo' E muito menos alma!" ("The best thing in the world and the mud. Slime and rot, like these two! *[people he's just killed]* Damn herbs, mosquitoes, gnats, oh! That symphony! All this fulfills my poet's sensitivity, deep in my soul! Ah-ah-ah! Although I do not have 'background', and much less soul!")

With ten, or possibly eleven, stories published between 1967 and 1968, Morto went dormant in the 'Seventies, with the exception of a single story published in *O Vampiro* in 1974. But like Swamp Thing and Man-Thing, O Morto do Pântono was revived in the early 'Eighties, when eight new stories were written for the Brazilian comics *Spektro* ("Specter"), *Calafrio* ("Chill"), and *Mestres do Terror* ("Masters of Terror"). One final story, "The Night of the Kidnappers", was created, for the *Mirza, A Vampira*, collection from Opera Graphica in 2002, with a script by Franco de Rosa. The final story of Morto, and the one in which Mirza and O Morto finally meet.

What makes these black-and-white stories stand out so much is the life—if you'll pardon me—and energy that Eugênio Colonnese imparts to his creation. The swamp is lit like a *noir* film, dark and white, with no grey tones. Although I suspect this is a necessity of the printing process originally used more than anything, Colonnese's art makes fantastic use of the medium. The line work is reminiscent of both Bernie Wrightson and Steve Bissette: fine and frenetic in places, at other times using broad gestures to suggest more than is actually present on the page. Colonnese has a fine eye for the grotesque, and constantly creates memorable images.

I could only get my hands on the 2005 release, *O Morto do Pântono*, which contains seven of the twenty stories, and I'm a bit sad that I have been unable to locate any more of the stories. But pursuing this would involve a search for 40-year-old comics in a country I'm more than 2,700 miles away from, and in a language I don't understand. Additionally, there seems to be a contradiction in the introduction: three of the stories, "Hellish Herb", "The Gnats" and "The Red Jalopy" all bear the byline of Luis Meri, but the history section claims they were written by Luis Quevedo. For all I know, Mali is a pseudonym for Quevedo, or vice-versa, but it's not something I have been able find any information on. I would send queries to the publisher, but Opera Graphica ceased operations in 2009.

It has been suggested by Amazon reviewer Lawrance Bernabo in his review of *Swamp Thing: Dark Genesis*

"They say love, without a touch of madness, is not true love. But this can only be answered by the lovely vultures and beautiful mosquitoes ... those who live commit follies! Don't you think?"

that Swamp Thing was inspired by O Morto do Pantono, but it seems very unlikely. Though Morto was created in 1967, I can't find any evidence that it was ever translated into English. Further, I have not been able to find any reference to Len Wein or Bernie Wrightson (the same for Roy Thomas, Gerry Conway, and Gray Morrow, creators of Man-Thing, which famously and contentiously debuted months before Swamp-Thing did) mentioning O Morto when they recount the origins of their own muck-monster. And given what an exhaustive job Jon Cooke did interviewing those creators for the monumental and extremely thorough *Swamp Men* book from Twomorrows Publishing, I find it very unlikely that they wouldn't have mentioned it.

I was extraordinarily pleased to come across *O Morto do Pântono*, because I love all the permutations of Hillman's *The Heap*. O Morto is another very entertaining, unique offshoot from the Heap's fecund trunk. There's a charm to the stories, and Colonnese's art is stunning. Hopefully—and perhaps this article will help—the character will get more of the exposure that it deserves. I would love to read the rest of O Morto's stories.

****

O Morto Stories

O Morto appeared in 20 different stories, spread out over 35 years. Only seven appeared in the eponymous collection which was published in 2005. I won't include a list of the illustrations that appear in various magazines, although Opera Graphica's editors note a number them for their complete history of O Morto. All stories were illustrated by Colonnese. Starred stories appear in the Opera Graphica collection.

* *"Sou: O Morto do Pântano"* ("I Am the Dead Man of the Swamp"), in *Mirza, Mulher Vampiro* #1, 1967. Script by Luis Quevedo.

"Orquídea Vermelha... Cor do Sangue" ("Red Orchid... the Color of Blood"), in *Mirza, Mulher Vampiro* #2 1967. Script by Luis Quevedo.

"Prisão Macabra" ("Macabre Prison"), in *Mirza, Mulher Vampiro* #4, 1967. Script by Luis Quevedo.

"Capturem... O Morto do Pântano" ("Capture... The Dead Man of the Swamp"), in *Mirza, Mulher Vampiro* #5, 1967. Script by Luis Quevedo.

* *"Erva Maldita!"* ("Hellish Herb!"), in *Mirza, Mulher Vampiro* #6, 1967. Script by Luis Quevedo.

* *"Os Pernilogos!"* ("The Gnats"), in *Mirza, Mulher Vampiro* #7, 1967. Script by Luis Quevedo.

* *"O Calhambeque Vermelho"* ("The Red Jalopy"), in *Mirza, Mulher Vampiro* #8, 1967. Script by Luis Quevedo.

"Sem Titulo" ("Untitled"), in *Mirza, Mulher Vampiro* #9, 1967. Script by Luis Quevedo.

"Um Amigo!" ("A Friend!"), in *Mirza, Mulher Vampiro* #10, 1967. Script by Luis Quevedo.

"O Peso do Ouro" ("The Weight of the Gold"), in *O Vampiro* # 13, 1974 (possibly a reprint from *Mirza, Mulher Vampiro* #11, but the editors at Opera Graphica weren't able to lay hands on a copy). Script by Eugênio Colonnese.

"De Volta ao Mundo do Terror!" ("Back to the World of Terror"), in *Spektro* #23, 1981. Script by Basilio Almeida.

"Sem Titulo" ("Untitled"), in *Mestres do Terror* #1, 1982. Script by Décio Miranda Júnior.

"O Crime Perfeito" ("The Perfect Crime"), in *Mestres do Terror* #2, 1982. Script by Eugênio Colonnese.

* *"A Pequena Silvia"* ("Little Sílvia"), in *Mestres do Terror* #7, 1982. Script by Osvalo Talo.

"Fuga Para o Amor we a Morte!" ("Escape to Love and Death!"), in *Mestres do Terror* #8, 1982. Script by Octacilio D'Assunção.

"Noite de Luar... no Pântano!" ("Night Moonlight... in the Swamp!"), in *Mestres do Terror* #9, 1982. Script by Osvalo Talo.

"Uma História de Amor!" ("A Love Story!"), in *Mestres do Terror* #18, 1983. Script by Osvalo Talo.

* *"Corpos Sem Cabeças Não Falam..."* ("Bodies Without Heads Don't Speak..."), in *Mestres do Terror* #29, 1985. Script by Osvalo Talo.

* *"Mau Cheiro"* ("Bad Smell"), in *Mestres do Terror* #36, 1986. Script by Osvalo Talo and Reinaldo do Oliveira.

"A Noite dos Seqüestradores" ("Night of the Kidnappers"), in *Mirza, A Vampira*, 2002. Script by Franco de Rosa.

MONSTER! #28/29 MOVIE CHECKLIST

MONSTER! Public Service posting: Title availability of films reviewed or mentioned in this issue of MONSTER!
Information dug up and presented by Steve Fenton and Tim Paxton.

The Fine Print: Unless otherwise noted, all Blu-rays and DVDs listed in this section are in the NTSC Region A/Region 1 format and widescreen, as well as coming complete with English dialogue (i.e., were either originally shot in that language, or else dubbed/subbed into it). If there are any deviations from the norm, such as full-frame format, discs from different regions or foreign-language dialogue (etc.), it shall be duly noted under the headings of the individual entries below. We also include whatever related—and sometimes even totally unrelated!—ephemera/trivia which takes our fancy, and will hopefully take yours too.

ALLIGATOR (1980) *[p.182]* – Roadshow Home Video's Aussie/Kiwi VHS/Beta ad-lines: *"It's 36 Feet Long, Weighs 2000 Pounds. It Lives 50 Feet Below the City. Nobody Knows It's There. Except the People it Eats."* Lionsgate's tagline: *"Beneath Those Manholes, A Man-Eater Is Waiting..."* Packaged behind cover art depicting a CG-rendered 'gator that looks so typical of the kinds of "giant-crocodilian-on-a-rampage" stuff pumped-out on DVD by The Asylum and the likes in recent years, this classic of its kind—in fact, it's one of the *first* of its particular now-well-tapped subgenre—was released on domestic DVD by Lionsgate in 2007. Under the same English title and boasting the same artwork, it was also released on Brazilian DVD, with both English and Portuguese audio options. As **LA BESTIA BAJO EL ASFALTO** (*"The Beast Beneath the Streets"*), it was more recently issued on Region B European (= Spain and Portugal) Blu-ray by Satán Media, at a 1.85:1 aspect ratio, with Spanish/Portuguese language options, but with the film's optional original English audio track also included. Paired-up with its sequel **ALLIGATOR II: THE MUTATION** (see next entry), Anchor Bay UK have put it out on PAL Region 2 Blu in a "Double Disc Presentation", with some—if not a lot of—special features. The first film is also available on All-Region DVD from South Korea (label unknown), in English, with Korean soft-subs; said release is apparently legit, and not a bootleg. Quality-wise it supposedly compares quite favorably with the now-OOP domestic North American disc version... downside is that it appears to be available only in fullscreen rather than widescreen, as per its original frame proportions. Under its Anglo title given here, the film was formerly available on Beta/VHS in Norway from Mayco A.S., in English, with Norwegian subs.

ALLIGATOR II: THE MUTATION (1991) *[p.183]* – New Line's VHS ad-line: *"The balance of nature has been tipped... to terror."* This belated sequel to the above was reissued on VHS by New Line Home Video in 1998. Spain's Satán Media

Korean All-Region DVD, with English audio

(as with **ALLIGATOR** [see previous entry]) released **A2:TM** on Region B Blu, in Spanish, but with optional Anglo audio track, under the title **LA BESTIA BAJO EL ASFALTO 2: LA MUTACIÓN** (*"The Beast Beneath the Streets 2: The Mutation"*). It's also out on Region 2 German DVD as **ALLIGATOR II: DIE MUTATION** (@ 1.77:1), with both English or German audio options; other details unknown. It's out on R2 DVD in France, too (as **ALLIGATOR II - LA MUTATION**), but—being French!—it doesn't include any English-language option (tagline: *"L'ultime prédateur"*).

ÁREA MALDITA (1979) *[p.39]* – We couldn't find diddly squat online about this, at least so far as actual legit video releases are concerned, but, as

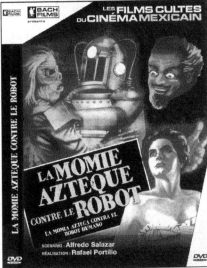

Mexi-Mummy Mayhem! Apprehensive Films / Midnight Matinee's 2013 All-Region DVD *[top]*, and the French DVD cover for **THE ROBOT VS. THE AZTEC MUMMY** *[above]*

THE AZTEC MUMMY series (1957/1964) *[pp.167-172]* – Obtaining copies of this trilogy of humble mexi-*momia* movies is hit-and-miss at best, as—having now fallen into the public domain ("PD")—copies are available of varying degrees of quality via all sorts of sources, both "legit" and more grey market in origin. The third and final entry (**THE ROBOT VS. THE AZTEC MUMMY**) seems to be the title which is most readily available, at least in English-dubbed form. There now follows a random sampling of some of the various versions extant... **THE AZTEC MUMMY** *[p.167]*: The Mexican retail site Mercado Libre (@ *mercadolibre.com.mx*) has this the first *AM* entry on offer, although they misleadingly advertise it as starring "El Santo" (*not!*) and are asking 100 smackers (i.e., in Mexican bucks) for it. It doesn't appear to be on YouTube in English, but there is a Spanish-language copy of it up on YT at the link "1957 LA MOMIA AZTECA" (@ *https://www.youtube. com/watch?v=56uwi1qZL1s*). Formerly (*circa* 1980s/1990s) available as an English-dubbed Beta/VHS release from Sinister Cinema, **THE CURSE OF THE AZTEC MUMMY** *[p.168]* is currently viewable in an English dub on YouTube at the link entitled "Curse of the Aztec Mummy (1957 - Horror) Full Movie" (@ *https://www. youtube.com/watch?v=q6a1_GQrABI*). It's also on the same site in its original Spanish-language version, at "1957 LA MALDICION DE LA MOMIA AZTECA" (@ *https://www.youtube.com/ results?search_query=La+Momia+Azteca*). As for series' most famous title, **THE ROBOT VS. THE AZTEC MUMMY** *[p.169]*, I (SF) originally acquired this back in the late '80s c/o Admit One Video of Toronto's clamshell VHS edition (it was the only one of the three *AM* films they released). It was also put out in the dreaded, penny-pinching LP ("long-play") mode on American VHS by Good Times Home Video in 1986. In 2013, Apprehensive Films/Midnight Matinee released **TRVTAM** in an All-Region DVD edition that came with some pretty cool cover artwork that was evidently (?) put together from imagery pinched/cut'n'pasted from Mexican comics. Probably the film's earliest ever domestic DVD was in 2000, as part of the *el cheapo* series of Mexi-monster movies (K. Gordon Murray *gringo* dub-jobs all) put out by NYC's fly-by-night outfit Beverly Wilshire Filmworks/ Telefilms International. For those who feel so inclined, *Mystery Science Theater 3000* have released a royally-fucked-with version on DVD; so if you're a fan of *MST3K*, you know what you're letting yourself in for, and may indeed even prefer their "modified" edition to the untampered-with original (to each their own, as they say, but give us the unadulterated original any day!). **TRVTAM**

of this writing, an Italian (?) bootleg website called Rare Films (@ *www.rarefilms.altervista.org*) were offering it for sale on DVD-R, presumably struck from an old videotape source (?). Other than that, we can't help you, I'm afraid, although there are a few clips pertaining to **ÁM** on YouTube, where nothing ever really dies.

is up on YT in English at the link "The Robot vs. the Aztec Mummy (1958) [Adventure] [Horror] [Science Fiction]" (@ *https://www.youtube.com/watch?v=iNQWSJ570rg*); it's also on YT in its original Mexican version as "La Momia Azteca vs El Robot Humano" (@ *https://www.youtube.com/watch?v=pOGtRHFh324*). And while you're there, why not check out the 1971 masked wrestling monster movie "Santo En La Venganza De La Momia" (@ *https://www.youtube.com/watch?v=Hdm-TotfLkY*) too... only be warned, as, despite featuring a way-cool AM-style mummy, it has a real lame-ola "Scooby-Doo" ending! Presented by Luigi Cozzi, all three original *AM* flicks (under their Italo import titles) have been packaged together as a boxed set on PAL Region 2 DVD from Italy, albeit coming only with Italian or Spanish audio options. The trilogy's semi-official '64 fourth outing **THE WRESTLING WOMEN VS. THE AZTEC MUMMY** *[p.172]* was formerly (1980s) available from the US' Rhino Video, both in a "straight" version plus as a pointless, needlessly camped-up so-called "special edition" that was retitled **ROCK'N ROLL WRESTLING WOMEN VS. THE AZTEC MUMMY**, and boasted awful added "r 'n 'r" tunes by Johnny "Sleazemania" Legend (about the best thing about it was its cover-blurbs: *"Wrestling Wild Women! Flesh-Crazed Fighting Females! Maniacal Mummies! And Bat-Beasts from the Beyond!"*). Oh yes, and last but definitely by no means least, the late-breaking gringo *lucha libre* movie "homage" **MIL MASCARAS VS. THE AZTEC MUMMY** (2007, USA, Ds: "Andrew Quint"/Jeff Burr, Chip Gubera) is available on domestic DVD from Osmium Entertainment, hyped on Amazon as *"The greatest lucha film of all time starring Mil Mascaras with the son of El Santo, Blue Demon Jr, and many other legendary luchadores in an epic battle against a resurrected Aztec mummy hellbent on world domination."*

THE BLOOD BEAST TERROR (1967) *[p.25]* – Formerly (back in 1986) released on domestic US videocassette by Monterey Home Video, in "big box" Beta/VHS editions (which were only "G"-rated, which shows how tame the material is). Within the same period (*circa* 1988 or so), **TBBT** also circulated for a time on Canadian cable TV (for instance, the now-long-defunct "First Choice/SuperChannel" station). I (SF) once taped a copy of the film from one of those airings, and a dark, murky and unattractive print it was, too; and not only that, but full-frame and pan-and-scan besides. Yes indeed, Redemption's much more recent (2012) Region B/2 digital disc release—issued on both Blu-ray and DVD—in an 88-minute "Remastered Edition" presents

BLOOD BEAST in a vastly superior format that makes it an entirely new viewing experience; it is generally considered a marked improvement over Image Entertainment's year 2000 (as part of their "Euroshock Collection") domestic DVD edition ("Redemption Remaster Makes Image DVD Look Pathetic!" screams one customer review on Amazon. Although the Screenbound label of the UK have more recently released it on Region B Blu and Region 1 DVD as part of their "The Best of British Collection" (both versions are orderable on Classic Films Direct [@ *www.classicfilmsdirect.com*]), thus far Redemption's definitely seems to be the one to beat, quality-wise! The same edition,

Top: Mexican DVD cover for **THE AZTEC MUMMY**. **Above:** Derann Films' late '60s British 8mm (200 ft.) film box for **THE BLOOD BEAST TERROR**

from Kino Lorber International is also up for grabs to stream VOD on Amazon as an SD-only rental or purchase (@ $2.99 for the former option or $9.99 for the latter). Somebody called Egami is also streaming **TBBT** at the same site, albeit in a shorter (80m) version; but whaddaya want for *free*?! (It's viewable gratis to those with a Prime Membership). Earlier in the new millennium, under the Spanish retitle **EL DESEO Y LA BESTIA** (*"Desire and the Beast"*), Filmax Home Video/Hollywood *[sic!]* Classics of Spain released it on Region 2 Spanish-language DVD, albeit with its original English dialogue track. In the '80s, it was released on Japanese VHS/Beta cassettes by Toshiba Video, possibly in English, with native subs. Under its Anglo title given here, the film was also released on Betamax/VHS videocassettes in Sweden by Video For Pleasure, in its original English dialogue, with Swedish hard-subs. The film was much later put out on British Region 2 DVD by Simply Media in 2005, as part of their "Masters of Horror" series.

BLOOD OF THE VAMPIRES (1964) *[p.131]* – Tagline: *"A Cult of Undead Creatures Seek Fresh, Warm, Human Blood!"* This was released on DVD in 2010, in a special edition which contains some deleted sequences, a promotional short for *House of Terror*, the original theatrical trailer, and a commentary track by exploitation producer Sam Sherman (which sadly doesn't reveal a whole lot of info about the production of the film itself, but talks more about the history of Hemisphere Pictures, which Sherman was at one point handling the publicity campaigns for). It's up for viewing on YouTube under both its more famous alternate Anglo title **THE BLOOD DRINKERS** and its original Tagalog title **KULAY DUGO ANG GABI**. Other Recommended Viewing: **MACHETE MAIDENS UNLEASHED** (2010) is an excellent Australian documentary from filmmaker Mark Hartley, which explores the history, production, influence and legacy of the exploitation films produced during the 1960s-'80s. Apart from all of the great clips and trailer snippets that are included in **MACHETE MAIDENS UNLEASHED**, some of the people interviewed throughout the documentary include Roger Corman, Joe Dante, Eddie Romero, Cirio H. Santiago, Jack Hill, Pam Grier and more. Highly recommended for fans of the genre! Hartley preceded **MACHETE MAIDENS UNLEASHED** with the excellent **NOT QUITE HOLLYWOOD** (2010, Australia), which covered Australian exploitation cinema of the 1970s and '80s; he followed it up with **ELECTRIC BOOGALOO**, a look at producers Menahem Golan and Yoram Globus and their notorious Cannon Films empire of the 1980s. ~ **John Harrison**

THE COLOR OUT OF SPACE (2010) *[p.8]* – As of 2012, this interesting HPL adaptation has been available to stream VOD as an Amazon Instant Video, in SD quality format only (for $2.99 to rent or $7.99 to buy). It was made available on domestic North American DVD in 2012 from BrinkVision.

COUNTESS DRACULA (1971) *[p.139]* – Synapse Films issued this on Region A/1 Blu-ray/DVD in 2014 (@ a 1.66:1 aspect ratio), well-kitted-out with extras (including the special featurette *Immortal Countess: The Cinematic Life of Ingrid Pitt*, plus an on-camera interview with the late actress, as well as audio commentary featuring Pitt, director Peter Sasdy and writers Jeremy Paul and Jonathan Sothcott). MGM Home Entertainment had previously released it on both DVD (2003) and VHS tape domestically, including as a Double Feature in their "Midinite Movies" series, paired-up with another "Hammer Glamor" vamp outing, **THE VAMPIRE LOVERS** (1970, UK, D: Roy Ward Baker). **CD** was once (1986) available in that latter format (and on Betamax cassette, too) from the UK's Video Collection International company. In 2002, Carlton Visual Entertainment put it out on PAL Region 2 DVD in Britain. As **GREVINNE DRACULA**, it was released on Norwegian Beta/VHS tape in the 1980s by Rank Film Distributors, in English, with Norse subtitles.

CULT OF THE COBRA (1955) *[p.32]* – While there is literally *nothing whatsoever* in the least bit "science-fictional" about **COTC**, it was nonetheless included as one of the 10 titles in Universal Studios Home Entertainment's essential "The Classic Sci-Fi Ultimate Collection" Region 1 DVD box set, released in 2008 (both Volumes 1 & 2—six discs in total—came packaged together as a single unit in two separate clamshell boxes (with 3 discs apiece), all contained in a clear, snug-fitting plastic slipcase. Bold, colorful graphics make the package that much nicer!). The other 9 Universal-International science fiction/monster flicks comped with the present title are Jack Arnold's **THE INCREDIBLE SHRINKING MAN** and John Sherwood's **THE MONOLITH MONSTERS** (both 1957), as well as Edward Dein's non-SF'er **THE LEECH WOMAN** ([1960] all three starring Grant Williams [see *Weng's Chop* #6.5 for a review of that lattermost title]); along with Arnold's **TARANTULA** (1955) and **MONSTER ON THE CAMPUS** (1958), Nathan Hertz Juran's **THE DEADLY MANTIS** (1957), Virgil W. Vogel's **THE MOLE PEOPLE** (1956) and **THE LAND UNKNOWN** (1957); and, last but definitely not least, Ernest B. Schoedsack's prototypical "shrunken humans" thriller **DR.**

CYCLOPS (1940), a film which was originally produced for Paramount Pictures, but (as with Erle C. Kenton's utterly fabulous **ISLAND OF LOST SOULS** [1932]) its rights subsequently became the property of Universal, hence that former title's inclusion with all these other U-I properties listed here. Although some of the films compiled in said set are lesser than others, it nonetheless amounts to a true must-have collection indeed for fans of '50s fantasy cinema in general and of the Universal universe in particular. Uni have also issued their "The Classic Sci-Fi Ultimate Collection" broken up into two separate 3-disc volumes, splitting the above-listed 10 titles into 5 per each set. All films are individually presented at whatever their original theatrical aspect ratio was (ranging from plain ol' fullscreen to various degrees of widescreen [i.e., 1.33:1, 1.78:1, 1.85:1 and 2.35:1]). As of this writing, copies of both those sets and the above-cited 10-film deluxe version were up for sale on Amazon and eBay. Prices vary sharply, so shop wisely. Better to get the entire 10-pack for cheaper than buying both 5-packs separately and paying more! (Well, *duuuhhhh!* ☺) As with all those other titles cited in this entry, **MM** was formerly (*circa* the early/mid-'90s) put out on VHS/Beta tape by MCA/Universal Home Video, although those releases—which were state-of-the-art at the time, with pristine transfer prints and pretty sharp picture quality—unfortunately presented everything in the full-frame format. *[*NB. The bulk of this entry was reprinted from THE MONOLITH MONSTERS' entry in* Monster! *#14 [p.100] – SF]*

CTHULHU MANSION (1990) *[p.16]* – Released on domestic Beta/VHS by Republic Pictures Home Video in 1991.

DAGON (2001) *[p.5]* – Originally put out on domestic DVD by Lions Gate/Avalanche Home Entertainment in 2001 (bearing the inevitable cover-blurb *"From the Creators of RE-ANIMATOR"*), that edition was a nice widescreen presentation (@ 1.78:1) which even came with a few extras, including production commentary tracks with Stuart Gordon, Dennis Paoli and Ezra Godden. This same LG edition is currently available as an Amazon insta-vid in SD mode only. Metrodome Distribution/Filmax issued it on British Region 2 DVD in 2002. The film was released on German (Region B) Blu-ray by 3L Film in October 2012, and that edition came with an English-language audio option (?), as well as containing a number of German-subtitled English special features. In 2003, it came out widescreen on Region 2 disc in the Netherlands from A-Film/Filmax Entertainment, in English but with Dutch subs. As **DAGON – LA MUTAZIONE DEL MALE** (*"Dagon – Mutation*

Top: Republic's 1991 US VHS box. **Above:** German Blu-ray

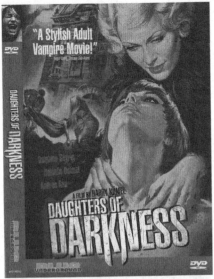

Top: Blue Underground's 2008 domestic DVD edition. **Above:** 1986 Italian VHS cover for **THE DEVIL'S WEDDING NIGHT**

from the Sea"), the film was made available on Region B/2 Blu-ray/DVD in Italy from Eagle Pictures/Edizioni Master, in English with Italian audio or subtitles options. On Region B Blu in Spain (its country of origin) from Filmax Home Video, it is known as **DAGON – LA SECTA DEL MAR** (*"Dagon – Sect from the Sea"*); once again, in English, with native audio/subs options. There's also a Russian BR of it available, which presumably

(?) also comes with an English audio track. Hence, there are many ways for those who want to see this to do so! On a related note, according to the IMDb, an Australian production entitled **DAGON** (D: Damien Lay) is due out this year sometime. Also, one Michael Chase directed a mere 2-minute-long short called *Dagon* in 2010 (it doesn't appear to be on YouTube, though).

DARK INTRUDER (1965) *[p.56]* – Back in the day (circa the 1990s), **DI** used to be available in all sorts of cruddy bootleg videotape versions. We've heard an unsubstantiated rumor that MGM (?) have offered this much-sought-after and long-elusive gem for sale on VOD DVD (?). Under the somewhat generic title **LA CRÉATURE DES TÉNÈBRES** ("Creature of Darkness")— which was also the French release title for the more "authentic" HPL-based movie **THE UNNAMABLE II** (see *Monster!* #26 [p.27])—**DI** has evidently been issued on PAL Region 2 DVD in France, but we'll be buggered if we could turn up the name of the company, though. That said, it may have merely been some fan-made, French-titled/subbed modification of a more official Anglo release, because the (Cinemageddon) copy we saw is really nice; in fact, the screen captures used to illustrate Steve B's article were snapped from it. Incidentally, **LA CRÉATURE DES TÉNÈBRES** was apparently also a Québecoise video title for **THE DARK** (1979, USA, Ds: John "Bud" Cardos, Tobe Hooper). As of this writing, there was a tolerably watchable copy of the present film—albeit only 56-minute rather than the full 59 minutes—copy on Dailymotion, at the link "Dark Intruder [1966][Unsold Pilot]" (@ *http://www. dailymotion.com/video/xssxms_dark-intruder-1966-unsold-pilot_shortfilms*). *[*NB. This entry is reprinted from last issue – SF]*

DAUGHTERS OF DARKNESS (1971) *[p.140]* – Released on domestic DVD by Blue Underground in 2008, loaded with extras.

THE DEVIL'S WEDDING NIGHT (1973) *[p.144]* – US sell-through specialists Alpha Video issued it full-frame as the top half of a "Satanic Double Feature" which also included **THE WITCHES MOUNTAIN** (*El monte de las brujas*, 1972, Spain, D: Raúl Artigot). In 2008, Sinister Cinema released TDWN singly on DVD under the same title; of which, a customer review on Amazon complains of its "terrible transfer to DVD. This film looks like a sixth generation VHS tape recording". The same version is also streamable VOD as an Amazon insta-vid. In 2006, it was released in a full-screen version as part of "Elvira's Movie Macabre" series from Shout! Factory, both as a single release and doubled-up with **LEGACY OF BLOOD** (1978, USA, D: Andy Milligan). **TDWN** was available on domestic videocassette way back when from VCI Home Video. Under its original Italo title **IL PLENILUNIO DELLE VERGINI** (*"Full Moon of the Virgins"*), it was released on Italian DVD in a *"Versione Integrale"* ("Uncut Edition") by Nocturno Video. It was put out on Italo VHS cassette in 1986 by Magnum 3B.

DRACULA, PRISONER OF FRANKENSTEIN (1971) *[p.49]* – Australian newspaper ad-line: *"The Erotic Screamer That Makes Vampires Turn In Their Graves!"* (it was double-billed on some dates in Australia with **TOMBS OF THE BLIND DEAD** [*La noche del terror ciego*, 1971, D: Amando de Ossorio). As their "Jess Franco Double Bill Volume 1", Britain's Tartan Video jointly packaged this film with a retitled print of **THE EROTIC RITES OF FRANKENSTEIN** (see separate entry below) earlier in the 2000s. Back in the 'Eighties, this was one of the more notoriously much-maligned Franco flicks on domestic home video, not just because of its contents—which many budding JF buffs didn't "get"—but even more-so because of its horrendous presentation on videocassette. Although it came in one of those celebrated (if with utterly misleading artwork!) "big boxes" c/o Wizard/Gorgon Video (who issued it on N. American Beta/VHS way back in 1985), it was deceptively retitled **THE SCREAMING DEAD**, plus the transfer print included on the tape was full-frame (and then some!), plus horribly panned-and-scanned. Amusingly enough, to give you some indication of just how badly this originally ultra-widescreen movie was cropped on '80s video, actor Howard Vernon's name got informally truncated at both ends to the catchy "WARD VERN" (!) instead. The claustrophobia of the master's exceedingly tight framing caused Franco's infamous "zoom-thrusts" with the camera to make things that much more incomprehensible to the viewer! Entitled **VAMPIR KILL**, this film was issued on German videocassette back in the '80s by United Video; whose strange cover art incorporated an artist's impression of the mutated-mugged monsterman from the British eco-horror **DOOMWATCH** (1972, D: Peter Sasdy). **DPOF** was released on Japanese VHS/Beta tape in 1987 by Sony Video Software/ Mount Light/Exc!t!ng *[sic]*.

DRACULA'S DAUGHTER (1972) *[p.52]* – As **DAUGHTER OF DRACULA** (its more commonly given Anglo title), it was issued on domestic DVD by Sinister Cinema in 2009, and again in the same format under the same title by Desert Island Films in 2014. It's also streamable VOD on Amazon via CreateSpace under that same title, in SD only ($1.99 to rent, $7.99 to buy).

THE EROTIC RITES OF FRANKENSTEIN (1973) *[p.53]* – Available on domestic Blu-ray from Redemption. It was issued on German DVD in 2004 (in an 82-minute print presented in 2.35:1 anamorphic widescreen) by X-Rated Cultvideo under the elongate title **EINE JUNGFRAU IN DEN KRALLEN VON FRANKENSTEIN: DR. FRANKENSTEINS TODES** ("A Virgin in

Fang-tastic Franco! X-Rated Cult's 2004 German DVD edition *[top]* and the US Blu-ray cover *[above]* of **THE EROTIC RITES OF FRANKENSTEIN**

They have awakened...
and they are the sound of terror!

the Screaming Dead

WIZARD VIDEO

Wizard Video's 1985 "big box" US VHS art for **DRACULA, PRISONER OF FRANKENSTEIN**

the Clutches of Frankenstein: Dr. Frankenstein's Death"). This edition includes three audio options (English, German and Spanish), also including a number of special features (totaling some 35m in all), including a then "all-new" (as of '04) interview with director Jess Franco. As part of their "Grindhouse" series, the UK's Tartan Video retitled the film **THE CURSE OF FRANKENSTEIN** and doubled it up with **DRACULA, PRISONER OF FRANKENSTEIN** (see separate entry above). During the '80s, it was out on British cassette from Go Video (*"Brutal! Exciting"*).

FRANKENSTEIN (1973) *[p.126]* – Both co-written and produced by TV horror great Dan Curtis, this 3½-hour miniseries (D: Glenn Jordan) originally initially aired in January '73 as a pair of consecutive episodes of the teleseries *The Wide World of Mystery* (1973-76, USA). It was released on DVD by Dark Sky Films in 2007 (@ a 1.33:1 aspect ratio, as per its original TV airing). Back in the '80s (1985, to be exact), it was released on Beta/VHS tape as part of the Thriller Video series, hosted by the boobacious, loquacious Elvira, Mistress of the Dark. It was subsequently (1994) released on videocassette by MPI Home Video.

FRANKENSTEIN: THE TRUE STORY (1973) *[p.126]* – In 2006, **F:TTS** was made available on domestic DVD (i.e., full-frame @ a 1.33:1 aspect ratio, as per its original TV airing) from Universal Studios Home Entertainment, in a 183-minute edition.

HOUSE (1986) *[p.23]* – This easy-to-find movie has been released on innumerable different video labels in many formats over the decades since its first-run theatrical release. In 2011, Image Entertainment put it out on domestic DVD (albeit fullscreen [?]) as part of their "Midnight Madness Series". Anchor Bay Entertainment also issued it on both DVD and VHS early into the new millennium (2001). Previous to that, it was out on Japanese VHS from Toshiba Video, possibly with its original Anglo audio track and Japanese subtitles (?). Its other international releases are legion.

IMMORAL TALES (1974) *[p.144]* – Released on domestic DVD by Anchor Bay Entertainment (in 2000), in Australia by Umbrella Entertainment (in 2009), and in the UK by Arrow Film & Video (in 2015).

IN THE MOUTH OF MADNESS (1994) *[p.36]* – Tagline: *"Lived Any Good Books Lately?"* Complete with artwork that makes it resemble a battered paperback book, this was put out on

US DVD

domestic Blu-ray by Arcane. Via Warner Bros., it can be streamed VOD on Amazon UK (@ *www. amazon.co.uk*) in High Definition (£3.49 for rental, £13.99 to purchase [not that's in pounds sterling, not dollars]). It is also extant as what is evidently a legit South Korean All-Region DVD release (@ its full 2.35:1 aspect ratio), in English with optional Korean subtitles. Earlier in the 2000s, Roadshow Entertainment released it (full-frame, at 1.33:1) on DVD in both Australia and New Zealand. In the '90s, it was released on British PAL Beta/VHS by Entertainment In Video (ad-line: *"Reality Isn't What It Used To Be"*). Under the present Anglo title, it came out on Beta/VHS cassette in the Netherlands (in 1995) from Polygram Video, in English, with Dutch subs.

INSEMINOID (1981) *[p.185]* – US theatrical ad-line: *"Conceived in violence, carried in terror, born to devastate and brutalize a universe!"* Elite Entertainment's disc taglines: *"Somewhere in the Depth of Space... A Horrific Nightmare is About to Become a Reality."* Elite first issued it full-length on domestic DVD (widescreen) in 1999. Elite subsequently rereleased it as part of their 2004 boxed set *The British Horror Collection* ("4 Bloody Good Tales of Terror From Famed Producer Richard Gordon"), which also included **CURSE OF THE VOODOO** (a.k.a. **VOODOO BLOOD DEATH**, 1965, D: Lindsay Shonteff), **TOWER OF EVIL** (a.k.a. **HORROR ON SNAPE ISLAND**, 1972, D: Jim O'Connolly) and **HORROR HOSPITAL**

(a.k.a. **COMPUTER KILLERS**, 1973, D: Antony Balch); evidently, all of the titles included in this set came in their original widescreen theatrical aspect ratios. Under the title **INSEMINOID: UN TEMPO DEL FUTURO**, the film is available on PAL Region 2 DVD, complete with both English and Italian audio options. During the early' 80s, **INSEMINOID** was released on "X"-rated British Beta/VHS cassette by Brent Walker Video/VideoSpace Ltd. (tagline: *"He is the last remaining alien... she is its only means of perpetuating his race"*). It later became placed on the UK's "Video Nasties" list and was unavailable there in its uncut form for a number of years. The UK's VIPCO vid label subsequently reissued it (as a *"Cult Classic Monster Bonker – The Sci-Fi Bunk-Up of All Time!!"*) on PAL Beta/VHS, albeit not in completely uncut form (only the incomplete version which had previously been approved for theatrical release by the British Board of Film Censors [BBFC] was included in this tape edition; approximately 3½ to 4 minutes shorter than the full 93-minute print). It was released in the same tape formats in the Netherlands in 1983 by Spectrum/Polygram Video, in English but with Dutch subtitles. One of the best sources for this title back in the pre-digital disc '80s was Pony Canyon Video/Herald Enterprise, Inc.'s 1985 Japanese Betamax/VHS cassette release, which not only came uncut (93m) and super-widescreen (at its full 2.35:1 aspect ratio), but also included the original English audio track, albeit with Japanese hard-subs (natch!). At the time of its initial theatrical release, a tie-in

novelization penned by Larry Miller was published by New English Library (NEL) which featured the cover-blurb *"A Far From Human Birth."*

INVASION OF THE BODY SNATCHERS (1956) *[p.180]* – Released on domestic Blu-ray/DVD by Olive Films in 2012, which is about the version to beat to date.

THE LEGEND OF BLOOD CASTLE (1973) *[p.143]* – Sinister Cinema put it out on VHS in 1999, and Mya Communication released it on domestic disc in 2009. It was put out on Region 2 DVD in Spain by Divisa Home Video in 2011, presumably without (?) any English language option.

NIGHT OF THE FIRE-BEAST (1959) *[p.191]* – While this little-known film—a minor if nonetheless key missing slice of monster movie history—has long been considered lost (at least since its last known regional theatrical screening at some backwoods Kentucky drive-in *circa* 1963), various surviving excerpts/snippets of footage have surfaced from time to time over the decades, including a battered-to-ratshit 30-second teaser trailer—evidently for a TV showing, although it was apparently never televised, possibly due to its reputed excessive violence, including a rather graphic beheading via monster jaws—which showed up on an obscure mid-1980s Betamax (and VHS?) trailer compilation entitled *Forgotten Fright Flick Previews, Vol. 2* (label unknown). In the little-known one-off Italian fanzine *Paura Profondo* (*circa* Summer 1992), I remember seeing the present title incorrectly listed as an alternate one for **GIGANTIS, THE FIRE MONSTER**, the Anglo dub of the first *Gojira* sequel that got released stateside; however, like many other "facts" in that shoddily-researched zine, they got it worng *[sic!]*. Also, someone I chatted with briefly on Facebook from Down Under whose name now eludes me but who claims to know both our Aussie correspondents Daniel Best and John Harrison (a.k.a. "The Wizards of Oz") real well, told me that **NOTFB** was given an ultra-obscure Australian release in two parts on Super 8mm home movie reels (a pair of 200-footers; approximately 18 minutes total runtime), under the titles *The Flaming Creature Strikes!* and *Battling the Fire Beast*. Once again, the name of the company that released these is unknown at this time, but we shall be sure to report any additional news when (and more importantly, *if*) it becomes available. ~ **Les Moore ;-)**

NYARLATHOTEP (2001) *[p.3]* – Video sources for this are unknown at the present time, but it's viewable on YouTube at the link entitled "H.P. Lovecraft's Nyarlathotep (2001)" (@ *https://www.youtube.com/watch?v=jWijkeEzCb8*).

Dutch VHS

THE PROJECTED MAN (1966) *[p.12]* – UK tagline: *"A Million Volts of Death in Each Hand."* It's available on PAL Regions 2 (from Second Sight Films) & 4 DVD. According to the Black Hole blog (@ *blackholereviews.blogspot.ca*), "[It's] On DVD in the UK (but edge-cropped to 16:9 – only the UK VHS has the full 2.35 widescreen Techniscope image)". Under the title **LASER X: OPERAZIONE UOMO** (its original theatrical release title in Italy), the film was released on Italian PAL Region 2 DVD (encoded for Europe and Japan) from Sinister Film/Cecchi Gori HV (CG Entertainment), as #34 in their "Sci-Fi d'Essai" line, a series which also includes many other Italo versions of classic Anglo (as in Limey and Yank) SF titles and creature features of the '30s, '40s, '50s and '60s. While Sinister's edition of **TPM** does come in its original English dialogue with an Italian-language option (i.e., either dubbed or subbed), the downside is that it is a substantially-shortened (possibly vintage TV?) print, which runs only 62 minutes—full-length US release prints run a quarter-hour longer at 77m, while the original British edition even lengthier at 86m—and it's in B&W (*"bianco e nero"*) on top of it (it was originally shot in Technicolor). But apparently it is presented in 1.85: 1 anamorphic widescreen though, which would at least preserve the original's Techniscope aspect ratio. For those that want them, copies of this Sinister disc can be ordered online via such sources as the Italian retail website DVD-Store (@ *http://www.dvd-store.it/DVD/DVD-Video/ID-35302/a.aspx*) and also at DVD.It (@ *http://film-dvd.dvd.it/dvd-fanta*scienza/laser-x-operazione-uomo-dvd/dettaglio/id-3237934/). From what we saw at those two sites, prices generally range from around €10 to €12 (note that's in euros). What is apparently a bootleg DVD-R was up for sale on iOffer (www.ioffer.com), but you pays your money and you takes your chances on that one, cuz judging by the packaging we saw, it looks awful shifty. On a note of trivia, in 1980 the Topps company issued a set of picture cards under the heading Creature Feature; one of which included a shot of **TPM**'s Haliday in his mucked-up post-projection state, with an attached gag caption which read, "This acne is getting out of hand!" (*Hahaha! Oh, stop! STOP!*) That joke's probably *waaaaaaayyyy* funnier than any made during *MS3TK*'s piss-take on **TPM**, though. (That version is included as part of Shout! Factory's 4-film *MST3K* set entitled "**XXX**", their 30th volume of tomfuckery. Therein they also have a go at **THE BLACK SCORPION** [1957], which is an even better reason to shun that set like the proverbial plague!) There was a pretty decent widescreen copy of the unfucked-with version on YouTube last year sometime, but it since seems to have been taken down.

THE PROMISE KEEPER (2006) *[p.41]* – Tagline: *"Some Promises Should Never Be Broken."* Released on domestic DVD by York Home Video, but copies are real hard to track down, that's how obscure it is. If you just key in the movie title, tons of other unrelated links pop up on Amazon, so it's a real bitch to find; therefore we're including its specific URL addy (*http://www. amazon.com/Promise-Keeper-Kevin-Michaels-Anderson/dp/B000QGDIGQ/ref=sr_1_10?ie=U TF8&qid=1464718507&sr=8-10&keywords=t he+promise+keeper+dvd*). < If you can actually be bothered to type *that* lot in, you MUST really wanna see it bad!

SHARKTOPUS VS. WHALEWOLF (2015) *[p.184]* – Evidently unavailable on disc as of this writing, but it did air on SyFy close to a year ago, so you'd think it'd be on DVD somewhere by now...

TERROR OF FRANKENSTEIN (1977) *[p.127]* – Available on domestic DVD from Fox Lorber (i.e., full-frame @ a 1.33:1 aspect ratio, as per its original TV airing). It was formerly released on Beta/VHS in 1985 by Super Video, the home vid wing of its original distributor, Independent-International (I-I) Pictures.

THE TWILIGHT PEOPLE (1972) *[p.132]* – Ad-line: *"Animal Desires... Human Lust."* VCI Entertainment released **THE TWILIGHT PEOPLE** on DVD in 2006 in a nice remastered print, and with the original trailer. It was available on Beta/VHS cassette back in the day from a number of different domestic companies, including VCI's 1980s precursor, VCI Home Video.

Über-obscure Super 8mm home movie of **NIGHT OF THE FIRE-BEAST**, last seen for sale on eBay for the unheard-of price of $500

52758909R00133

Made in the USA
Lexington, KY
09 June 2016